20 Practice Sets

Indian Railways (RRB)

Assistant Loco Pilot

Exam 2018 Stage I

- **Corporate Office :** 45, 2nd Floor, Maharishi Dayanand Marg, Corner Market, Malviya Nagar, New Delhi-110017
  Tel. : 011-49842349 / 49842350

Typeset by Disha DTP Team

Printed at Repro Knowledgecast Limited, Thane

For further information about the books from DISHA,
Log on to **www.dishapublication.com** or email to **info@dishapublication.com**

CONTENT

RRB ALP Syllabus 2018 & Exam Pattern

RRB ALP Syllabus 2018 for first stage computer based test consist of Mathematics, General Science and General Intelligence & Reasoning sections for 75 marks and It will be held for the duration of 1 hour. A total of 75 multiple choice based questions to be given and each question equally carries 1 mark. Candidates need to qualify the exam by securing cut off marks to be decided by the respective railway recruitment board.

RRB ALP Syllabus 2018 for First Stage CBT

S.No.	Section	Qns	Marks	Time
1	Mathematics			
2	General Intelligence and Reasoning			
3	General Science	75	75	60 Min
4	General awareness on current affairs			

The First Stage Computer Bases Test is objective in nature and the score of first stage exam shall be used only for short listing of candidates for second stage exam as per their merit. Candidates who are shortlisted for Second Stage CBT availing the reservation benefits of a community shall continue to be considered only against that community for all subsequent stages of recruitment process.

RRB ALP Syllabus 2018 for Second Stage CBT

Paper	Sections	Qs	Marks	Duration
-	Total	175	175	150 Minutes
Part A	1. Mathematics 2. General Intelligence and Reasoning 3.Basic Science and Engineering 4.General Awareness on Current Affairs	100	100	90 Minutes
Part B	Technical Trade	75	75	60 Minutes

Stage 2 of Computer Based online test to be conducted for selected candidates in stage 1 only. RRB ALP Syllabus for stage 2 CBT consist of 175 questions for 175 marks with time duration of 2 hours 30 minutes. For each wrong answer 1/3rd marks will be deducted from final score.

1. Which of the following states of India has the longest coastline?
   (a) Kerala
   (b) Gujarat
   (c) Tamil Nadu
   (d) Andhra Pradesh

2. Where was the capital of Ranjit Singh, the king of Punjab, located?
   (a) Peshawar
   (b) Amritsar
   (c) Lahore
   (d) Rawalpindi

3. The fundamental duties are enshrined in which Article of the Indian Constitution?
   (a) Article 51 A
   (b) Article 50 A
   (c) Article 50 B
   (d) Article 51 B

4. The mineral structure of diamond is
   (a) Zinc
   (b) Nickel
   (c) Nitrogen
   (d) Carbon

5. Which part of the body is affected by Jaundice?
   (a) Small intestine
   (b) Liver
   (c) Stomach
   (d) Pancreas

6. Which country of the world has the largest number of post offices?
   (a) France
   (b) China
   (c) India
   (d) Japan

7. Uttar pradesh tops in the production of -in India.
   (a) sugar cane
   (b) rice
   (c) barley
   (d) wheat

8. The safe temperature to keep eatables fresh in refrigerator is
   (a) 4°C
   (b) 0°C
   (c) 18°C
   (d) 10°C

9. The instrument used to measure the blood pressure of human body is–
   (a) Barometer
   (b) Altimeter
   (c) Sphygmomano meter
   (d) Tachometer

10. Automatic wrist watches get energy from–
    (a) twist in spring
    (b) liquid crystal
    (c) kinetic energy
    (d) movement of our hands

11. When a television is switched on
    (a) We listen the sound first and then see the picture
    (b) We see the picture first and then listen sound
    (c) It depends on the TV manufacturing company
    (d) We get audio and visual at the same time

12. Goitre in human body is caused due to deficiency of–
    (a) Iodine
    (b) Phosphorus
    (c) Nitrogen
    (d) Calcium

13. Who sent Huensant as ambassador in the court of Harsha?
    (a) Fu Chen-Chu
    (b) Tai Sung
    (c) Tung Cuan
    (d) None of these

14. Who wrote Akbarnama?
    (a) Faizi
    (b) Abdul Rahim Khankhana
    (c) Abul Fazal
    (d) Abdul Kadir Badayun

15. Which metal is generally used to make electro magnets?
    (a) Copper
    (b) Nickel
    (c) Iron
    (d) Cobalt

16. Artificial silk is called–
    (a) Rayon
    (b) Dacron
    (c) Fibre glass
    (d) Nylon

17. Dynamo converts–
    (a) electrical energy into mechanical energy
    (b) High voltage into low voltage
    (c) Low voltage into high voltage
    (d) Mechanical energy into electrical energy

18. The instrument used to measure the electric current is
    (a) Barometer
    (b) Altimeter
    (c) Ammeter
    (d) Anemometer

19. The best conductor of electricity is
    (a) Aluminium
    (b) Copper
    (c) Iron
    (d) Silver

20. Urea supplies– to the plants.
    (a) Calcium
    (b) Phosphorus
    (c) Potassium
    (d) Nitrogen

21. Mica is used in–
    (a) Furnace
    (b) Electric industry
    (c) Steel Industry
    (d) Glass Manufacturing

22. Which of the following is a physical change?
    (a) Burning of cooking gas
    (b) Fermentation of milk
    (c) Digestion of food
    (d) Dissolution of sugar in water

23. The chemical compound used in photography is
    (a) Aluminium Hydroxide
    (b) Silver Bromide
    (c) Potassium Nitrate
    (d) Sodium Chloride

24. What causes cholera?
    (a) Bacteria
    (b) Virus
    (c) Fungus
    (d) Algae

25. An apparatus for viewing objects lying above the eye level of the observer and whose direct vision is obstructed is known as–
   (a) Photometer   (b) Periscope
   (c) Planimeter   (d) Spectrometer

26. Which atom has only one electron?
   (a) Potassium   (b) Nitrogen
   (c) Oxygen   (d) Hydrogen

27. What the electrode that is connected to the negative pole of the battery is called?
   (a) Cathode   (b) Electroplate
   (c) Ion   (d) Anode

28. The organic acid present in vinegar is–
   (a) butanoic acid   (b) propanoic acid
   (c) methanoic acid   (d) ethanoic acid

29. Which of the following is an example of fossil fuel?
   (a) Coke   (b) Natural gas
   (c) Coal gas   (d) Producer gas

30. Water gas consists of
   (a) a mixture of carbon monoxide and hydrogen
   (b) water vapour and coal dust
   (c) a mixture of carbon monoxide and nitrogen
   (d) water vapour and methane

31. A body strike the floor vertically with a velocity u and rebounds at the same speed. The change of speed would be–
   (a) 3u   (b) Zero
   (c) u   (d) 2u

32. Which of the following is different from others?
   (a) Speed   (b) Time
   (c) Density   (d) Force

33. Momentum has the same unit as that of–
   (a) torque   (b) couple
   (c) impulse   (d) moment of momentum

34. What is the momentum of a man of mass 75 kg when he walks with a uniform velocity of 2m/s?
   (a) 50 kg m/s   (b) 75 kg m/s
   (c) 100 kg m/s   (d) 150 kg/s

35. At the centre of the earth, the value of g becomes-
   (a) infinity   (b) unity
   (c) zero   (d) None of these

36. Two unequal masses possess the same momentum, then the kinetic energy of the heavier mass is ....the kinetic energy of the lighter mass.
   (a) smaller than   (b) greater than
   (c) same as   (d) none of these

37. 15 Bulbs of 60 W each, run for 6 hours daily and a fridge of 300 W runs for 5 hours daily. Find the forthrightly bill at the rate of 30 paise per unit.
   (a) ₹31.05   (b) ₹45.55
   (c) ₹62.10   (d) ₹75.10

38. Sheaths are used in cables to–
   (a) Provide proper insulation
   (b) Provide mechanical strength
   (c) Prevent ingress of moisture
   (d) None of these

39. For the stable operation of interconnected system, the passive element that can be used as interconnecting element is
   (a) Reactor   (b) Resistor
   (c) Capacitor   (d) Resistor and Capacitor

40. The insulation resistance of a cable of length 10 km is $1\,M\Omega$, its resistance for 50 km length will be–
   (a) $M\Omega$ (b) $5\,M\Omega$
   (c) $0.2\,M\Omega$ (d) $10\,M\Omega$

41. The rate of change of momentum is directly proportional to–
   (a) Force   (b) Inertia
   (c) Moment   (d) None of these

42. If four 80 μF capacitors are connected in parallel, the net capacitance is–
   (a) $20\,\mu F$ (b) $80\,\mu F$
   (c) $160\,\mu F$ (d) $320\,\mu F$

43. The transformer used to decrease the magnitude of the alternating voltage is a–
   (a) step-up transformer   (b) step-down transformer
   (c) step-in transformer   (d) step-out transformer

44. When two bodies are rubbed against each other
   (a) They acquire equal and similar charges
   (b) They acquire equal and opposite charges
   (c) They acquire unequal and similar charges
   (d) They acquire unequal and opposite charges

45. Lightning is caused in the sky due to the flow of charge between–
   (a) two oppositely charged clouds
   (b) two similarly charged clouds
   (c) one neutral and one charged cloud
   (d) None of the these

46. Which of these converts sunlight directly into electrical energy?
   (a) Solar cooker   (b) Solar cell
   (c) Solar furnace   (d) Solar water heater

47. Electric charge can flow through–
   (a) insulators
   (b) conductors
   (c) both insulators and conductors
   (d) neither conductors nor insulators

48. The electric current which changes its direction after fixed intervals of time is called–
   (a) induced current
   (b) direct current
   (c) alternating current
   (d) None of these

49. A device used to stabilise the voltage supplied by electric supply station is a–
   (a) dynamo   (b) transformer
   (c) ammeter   (d) generator

50. Silver is a
   (a) magnetic substance
   (b) good conductor of electricity
   (c) bad conductor of electricity
   (d) none of these

51. An instrument used to observe heavenly bodies is the–
    (a) telescope (b) camera
    (c) microscope (d) periscope
52. The maximum percentage in the atmosphere is of
    (a) Oxygen (b) Nitrogen
    (c) Carbon dioxide (d) Helium
53. What is the function of Ozone layer?
    (a) Prevents harmful infra-red rays of the sun from reaching the earth
    (b) Prevents radiation escaping the earth, hence keeping it warm
    (c) It is essential for rainfall
    (d) It filters harmful ultra-violet rays of the sun
54. In the International system of measurement, the 'Kelvin' is the unit of–
    (a) mass (b) temperature
    (c) electric current (d) air
55. The Sanchi Stupa was constructed by–
    (a) Chandragupta (b) Ashoka
    (c) Kunal (d) Harshavardhan
56. The first atomic power plant was started in India at–
    (a) Narora (b) Tarapur
    (c) Rawat bhata (d) None of these
57. To conserve the eatables we use–
    (a) Benzoic acid (b) Sodium chloride
    (c) Sodium carbonate (d) None of these
58. The least polluting fuel is–
    (a) Hydrogen (b) Diesel
    (c) Kerosene (d) Coal
59. Malaria spreads by–
    (a) Culex mosquito
    (b) Anopheles mosquito
    (c) Water borne mosquito
    (d) None of these
60. Heart disease is caused by increase in–
    (a) Glucose (b) Cholesterol
    (c) Heparin (d) Haemoglobin
61. Which vitamin helps in clotting of blood?
    (a) Vitamin B (b) Vitamin B_2
    (c) Vitamin K (d) Vitamin D
62. The chief source of energy is–
    (a) Vitamin (b) Minerals
    (c) Carbohydrate (d) Water
63. The chief centre of learning during lord Buddha era was-
    (a) Nalanda (b) Delhi
    (c) Varanasi (d) Bodh Gaya
64. Mustard is grown in–
    (a) Kharif season (b) Rabi season
    (c) Jayad season (d) Whole year
65. In case the posts of President and Vice-President lie vacant, who officiates as the President?
    (a) Speaker of the Lok Sabha
    (b) Chief Justice of India
    (c) Attorney General of India
    (d) Chairman of Rajya Sabha
66. Magnetic needle directs to–
    (a) East (b) Sky
    (c) North (d) West
67. Lord Buddha got emancipation (Mahapari nirvana) at–
    (a) Kushinagar (b) Lumbini
    (c) Bodh Gaya (d) Kapilvastu
68. The colours on a colour code resistor are green, white, orange and silver. Find the value of resistor.
    (a) $5.9 \times 10^3 \pm 10\%$ (b) $59 \times 10^3 \pm 10\%$
    (c) $590 \times 10^3 \pm 10\%$ (d) $5900 \times 10^2 \pm 10\%$
69. The eddy current loss is directly proportional to
    (a) Area of metal (b) Volume of metal
    (c) Length of metal (d) Weight of metal
70. Direction of dynamically induced e.m.f is given by-
    (a) Lenz's law
    (b) Flemings right hand rule
    (c) Flemings left hand rule
    (d) Cork screw rule
71. The Rowlatt Act, 1919 empowered the British Government to:
    (a) extend the period of imprisonment for Indians
    (b) close down any industrial unit at its discretion
    (c) release all the political prisoners by 1921
    (d) detain a person for any duration without trial
72. The latitude of a place situated on the equator is:
    (a) $0°$ (b) $23\dfrac{1}{2}°$
    (c) $33\dfrac{1}{2}°$ (d) $66\dfrac{1}{2}°$
73. The purpose of inclusion of Directive Principles in the Constitution is to establish:
    (a) A Social democracy
    (b) Gandhian democracy
    (c) Social and economic democracy
    (d) Political democracy
74. A fisherman is stranded in a lake because the motor of his motor-boat has failed. What should he do to reach the shore?
    (a) He should start walking in his boat towards the shore
    (b) He should start throwing the fish he has collected away from the shore
    (c) He should lie flat on his boat
    (d) He should start throwing the fish he has collected towards the shore
75. The elements in the portland cement is/are –
    (a) Silica, Alumina and Magnesia
    (b) Lime, Silica and Magnesia
    (c) Lime, Silica and Iron oxide
    (d) Lime, Silica and Alumina
76. The Indian Constitution came into force on –
    (a) January 21, 1950 (b) January 23, 1950
    (c) January 26, 1950 (d) January 30, 1950

77. Insulin activates in
   (a) Pancreas   (b) Parathyroid
   (c) Liver   (d) Pituitary

78. The whole structure of the world is regulated by –
   (a) Magnetic force   (b) Gravitational force
   (c) Electric force   (d) None of these

79. In India State Legislature includes-
   (a) Legislative Assembly & Legislative Council
   (b) Legislative Assembly & Council of Ministers
   (c) Governor, Legislative Assembly & Legislative Council
   (d) Only Legislative Assembly

80. Which country is on the top in Gold production?
   (a) China   (b) South Africa
   (c) Brazil   (d) Argentina

81. Who wrote "Causes of the Indian Mutiny"?
   (a) Sayyid Ahmad Khan   (b) D.H.Buchanan
   (c) R.P.Dutt   (d) Chittaranjan Das

82. Ranji Trophy and Aga Khan Cup are associated with:
   (a) Cricket and Volleyball
   (b) Badminton and Hockey
   (c) Cricket and Football
   (d) Cricket and Hockey

83. Where is the headquarters of the International Red Cross Committee?
   (a) Prague   (b) Geneva
   (c) Moscow   (d) Berlin

84. Which Article in the Indian Constitution empowers the President to dissolve the Lok Sabha?
   (a) Article 82   (b) Article 84
   (c) Article 85   (d) Article 90

85. Which among the following countries has made 'euthanasia' legally valid?
   (a) Newzealand   (b) Denmark
   (c) Australia   (d) Netherlands

Directions (86-88): Find the missing in the following series.

86. 6, 10, 27, 52, 153, ?
   (a) 308   (b) 305
   (c) 304   (d) 306

87. 12, 15, 30, 37.5, 75, ?
   (a) $93\frac{1}{2}$ (b) $93\frac{3}{5}$
   (c) $93\frac{3}{4}$ (d) $93\frac{5}{4}$

88. 88, 56, 19, ?
   (a) 8   (b) 7
   (c) 10   (d) –8

Directions (89-91): In the following number series, one of the numbers does not fit into the series. Find the wrong number.

89. 7, 9, 16, 27, 47, 77, 119
   (a) 9   (b) 16
   (c) 77   (d) 27

90. 4, 5, 12, 39, 160, 804, 4836
   (a) 12   (b) 804
   (c) 39   (d) 4836

91. 844, 420, 208, 102, 47, 22.5, 9.25
   (a) 420   (b) 208
   (c) 47   (d) 22.5

92. In a certain code "DEVIL" is written as ABSEFI. How is "OTHER" written in that code?
   (a) LRECO   (b) LQEBO
   (c) LWEBU   (d) RWKHU

93. In a certain code language "637" means sea is black. "547" means colour is beautiful and "35" means black colour. Which digit in the language means beautiful?
   (a) 6   (b) 4
   (c) 5   (d) 3

Directions (94-98): Read the following information to answer the given questions:

(i) A, B, C, D, E and F are six family members.
(ii) There is one doctor, one lawyer, one pilot, one student and one housewife.
(iii) There are two married couples in the family
(iv) F who is a lawyer is father of A.
(v) B is a pilot and mother of C
(vi) D is grandmother of C and is a housewife.
(vii) E is father of F and is a doctor
(viii) C is brother of A

94. How many female members are there in the family?
   (a) 3   (b) 2
   (c) 3 or 4   (d) None of these

95. How is A related to D?
   (a) Granddaughter
   (b) Grandson
   (c) Son
   (d) Either granddaughter or grandson

96. Which of the following statements is definitely true?
   (a) A is engineer
   (b) F is the father of the pilot
   (c) D is the mother of the Pilot
   (d) F is the father of the engineer

97. Who is student?
   (a) Either C or A   (b) B's son
   (c) A   (d) C

98. Which of the following is one of the pair of married couples?
   (a) FB   (b) FA
   (c) CF   (d) FD

Directions (99-100): Find the wrong one.

99. (a) River   (b) Pond
   (c) Well   (d) Tank

100. (a) North   (b) Right
   (c) East   (d) South

101. The basis for measuring thermodynamic property of temperature is given by–
   (a) zeroth law of thermodynamics
   (b) first law of thermodynamics
   (c) second law of thermodynamics
   (d) third law of thermodynamics

102. One watt is equal to–
    (a)　1 Nm/s　　　　　(b)　1 N/mt
    (c)　1 Nm/t　　　　　(d)　1 k Nm/mt
103. Work done is zero for the following process–
    (a)　constant volume　(b)　free expansion
    (c)　throttling　　　　(d)　all of the above
104. One calorie in kgm is equal to
    (a)　0.427　　　　　(b)　4.27
    (c)　42.7　　　　　(d)　427
105. On volume basis, air contains following parts of Oxygen
    (a)　21　　　　　　(b)　23
    (c)　25　　　　　　(d)　77
106. Universal gas constant is defined as equal to product of the molecular weight of the gas and
    (a)　specific heat at constant pressure
    (b)　specific heat at constant volume
    (c)　ratio of two specific heat
    (d) gas constant
107. Strictly speaking all engineering processes are–
    (a)　quasi-static
    (b)　thermodynamically in equilibrium
    (c)　irreversible
    (d)　reversible
108. In a free expansion process
    (a)　work done is zero
    (b)　heat transfer is zero
    (c)　both (a) and (b)
    (d)　work done is zero but heat increases
109. Which of the following process is irreversible process
    (a)　isothermal　　　(b)　adiabatic
    (c)　throttling　　　　(d)　all of the above

110. Minimum work in compressor is possible when the value of adiabatic index n is equal to–
    (a)　0.75　　　　　(b)　1
    (c)　1.27　　　　　(d)　1.35
111. In DC motor the direction of induced emf is opposite to main bars as per–
    (a)　fleming's left hand rule
    (b)　lenz's law
    (c)　fleming's right hand rule
    (d)　faradays' law
112. The condition for max power developed by the motor–
    (a)　$E_b = v/2$
    (b)　Cost losses = variable losses
    (c)　Both (a) and (d)
    (d)　$I^2 aRa$ = mechanical loss
113. The Ta/Ia graph of a DC series motor is a–
    (a)　parabola from no load to over load
    (b)　straight line through out
    (c)　parabola up to full load and a time at over load
    (d)　parabola through out
114. 220V shunt motor develops torque of 54 nM at armature current of 10A. The torque produced when the armature current is 20A is–
    (a)　54 NM　　　　　(b)　81 N.M
    (c)　108 N.M　　　　(d)　27 N.M
115. Which type of DC generator is used in welding machines–
    (a)　series generator
    (b)　shunt generator
    (c)　cumulatively compound
    (d)　differential compound

ANSWER KEY

1	(b)	11	(a)	21	(b)	31	(d)	41	(a)	51	(a)	61	(c)	71	(d)	81	(b)	91	(c)	101	(a)	111	(b)
2	(c)	12	(a)	22	(d)	32	(b)	42	(d)	52	(b)	62	(c)	72	(b)	82	(d)	92	(b)	102	(a)	112	(a)
3	(a)	13	(b)	23	(b)	33	(c)	43	(b)	53	(d)	63	(a)	73	(c)	83	(d)	93	(b)	103	(d)	113	(c)
4	(d)	14	(c)	24	(a)	34	(d)	44	(b)	54	(b)	64	(b)	74	(c)	84	(b)	94	(d)	104	(a)	114	(c)
5	(b)	15	(c)	25	(b)	35	(c)	45	(a)	55	(b)	65	(b)	75	(c)	85	(d)	95	(d)	105	(a)	115	(d)
6	(c)	16	(a)	26	(d)	36	(a)	46	(b)	56	(b)	66	(c)	76	(c)	86	(c)	96	(c)	106	(d)		
7	(d)	17	(d)	27	(a)	37	(a)	47	(b)	57	(a)	67	(a)	77	(a)	87	(c)	97	(a)	107	(c)		
8	(a)	18	(c)	28	(b)	38	(a)	48	(c)	58	(a)	68	(b)	78	(b)	88	(d)	98	(a)	108	(c)		
9	(c)	19	(d)	29	(a)	39	(c)	49	(b)	59	(b)	69	(b)	79	(c)	89	(b)	99	(a)	109	(c)		
10	(a)	20	(d)	30	(a)	40	(b)	50	(b)	60	(b)	70	(b)	80	(b)	90	(b)	100	(b)	110	(b)		

HINTS AND SOLUTIONS

86. (c) The pattern is as follower as:
$6 \times 2 - 2 = 10$
$10 \times 3 - 3 = 27$
$27 \times 2 - 2 = 52$
$52 \times 3 - 3 = 153$
$153 \times 2 - 2 = 304$
So, The missing number is $= 304$.

87. (c) The pattern is as follow as:
$12 \times 1.25 = 15$
$15 \times 2 = 30$
$30 \times 1.25 = 37.5$
$37.5 \times 2 = 75$

$75 \times 1.25 = 93.75 = 93\dfrac{4}{5}$

So, The missing number is $= 93\dfrac{4}{5}$.

88. (d) The pattern is as follow as :

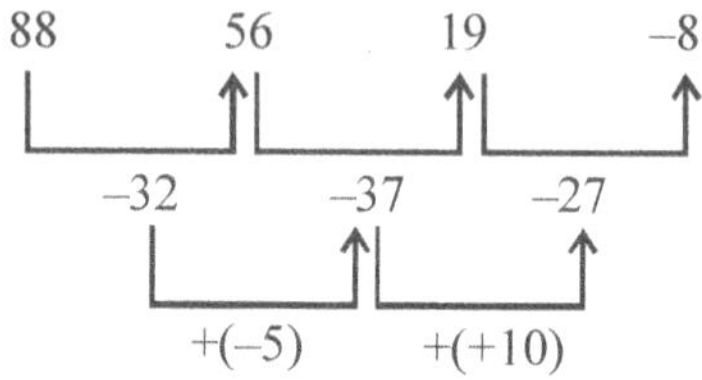

So, The missing number is $= -8$

89. (b) The pattern is as follow as :

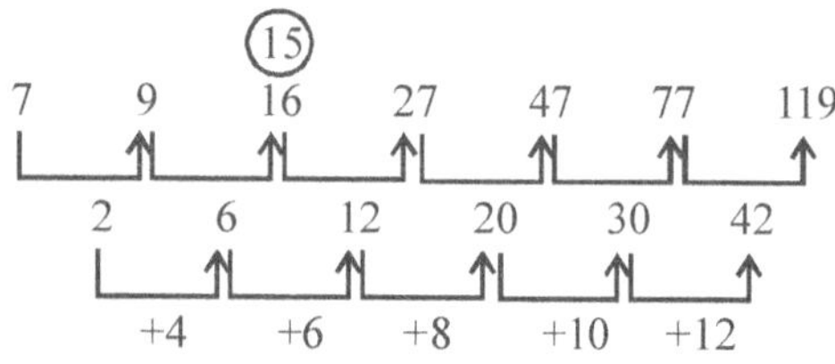

So, The wrong number is $= 16$

90. (b) The pattern is as follow as:
$4 \times 1 + 1 = 5$
$5 \times 2 + 2 = 12$

$12 \times 3 + 3 = 39$
$39 \times 4 + 4 = 160$
$160 \times 5 + 5 = 805 \neq 804$
$805 \times 6 + 6 = 4836$
So, The wrong number is $= 804$

91. (c) The pattern is as follow as:

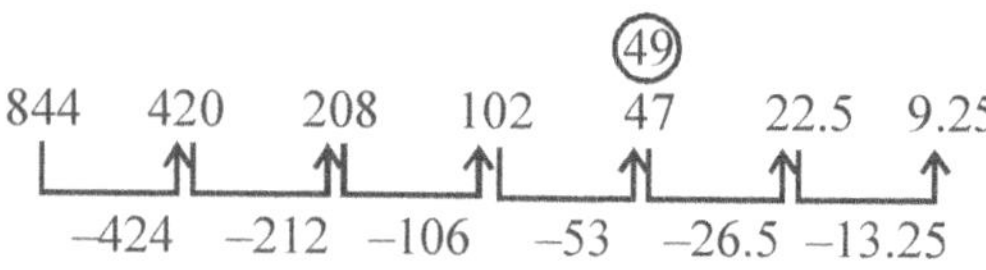

So, The wrong number is $= 47$

92. (b)

93. (b) According to question,

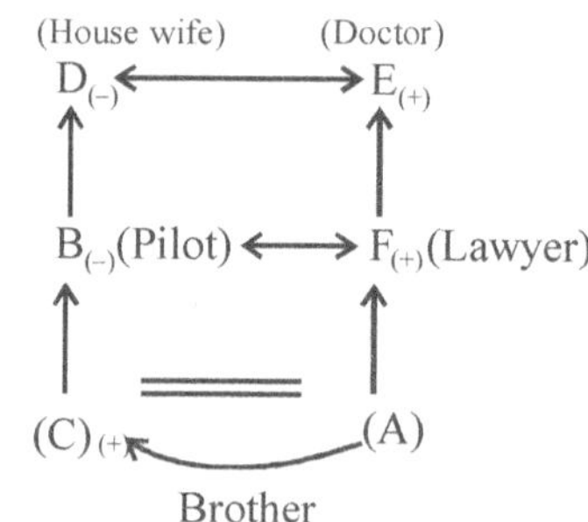

$\therefore 4 \to$ Beautiful.

Solutions (94-98)

94. (d)
95. (d)
96. (c)
97. (a)
98. (a)
99. (a) Except River, All others have not flow.
100. (b) Except Right, All others are direction.

1. The Islam was established in:
   (a) 7th A.D.   (b) 5th A.D.
   (c) 3rd B.C.   (d) 5th B.C.

2. The Olympic Games 2012 will be held in:
   (a) Moscow   (b) Paris
   (c) New York   (d) London

3. The main factor of air pollution is:
   (a) Lead   (b) Copper
   (c) Zinc   (d) Gold

4. The bauxite ore is found in:
   (a) Musabani   (b) Karnapura
   (c) Koderma   (d) Palamu

5. The first fertilizer plant in India was established in:
   (a) Trombay   (b) Nangal
   (c) Alwaye   (d) Sindri

6. Which of the following had strong navy?
   (a) Bahmani   (b) Chalukya
   (c) Chola   (d) Rashtrakuta

7. The last king of Maurya Dynasty was:
   (a) Brihdarth   (b) Kunal
   (c) Samprati   (d) Salishuk

8. How will the image formed by a convex lens be affected if the central part of the lens is covered by black paper?
   (a) Remaining part of the lens will form no image
   (b) The central position of the image is absent
   (c) There will be no effect
   (d) The full image will be formed with lessened brightness

9. The force between two parallel wires conducting current is used to define
   (a) Ampere   (b) Coulomb
   (c) Volt   (d) Newton

10. A body is thrown vertically upward and it reaches 10m high. Find the velocity with which the body was thrown? (g = 9.8 m/s)
    (a) 10 m/sec.   (b) 18 m/sec.
    (c) 14 m/sec.   (d) 7 m/sec.

11. The buoyancy depends on the:
    (a) Depth of the fluid   (b) Density of the fluid
    (c) Volume of the fluid   (d) Weight of the fluid

12. Pankaj Advani is associated with:
    (a) Snooker   (b) Golf
    (c) Shooting   (d) Archery

13. Which city in the world is known as the forbidden city?
    (a) Aberdeen   (b) Jerusalem
    (c) Mecca   (d) Lhasa

14. Rajeev Gandhi Khel Ratna Award carries a sum of:
    (a) ₹ 3 lakhs   (b) ₹ 5 lakhs
    (c) ₹ 1 lakh   (d) ₹ 7 lakhs

15. Who is known as 'Nightingale of India'?
    (a) Asha Bhonsle   (b) Begum Akhtar
    (c) Sarojini Naidu   (d) Vijaylaxmi Pandit

16. Which one of the following is not included in the UNESCO's list of world heritage site?
    (a) Kaziranga National Park
    (b) Qutab Minar
    (c) Champaner Pavagarh
    (d) None of these

17. Which of the following is not an electric resistant?
    (a) Lead   (b) Ebonite
    (c) Charcoal   (d) Lac

18. Which of the following is a complementary colour?
    (a) Blue   (b) Yellow
    (c) Magenta   (d) Yellow and Magenta

19. The velocity of sound increases in air by .... for every degree Celsius increase of temperature.
    (a) 60 m/sec.   (b) 0.61 m/sec
    (c) 60 ft/sec.   (d) 0.61 km/sec.

20. Henry is a unit of:
    (a) Capacity   (b) Magnetic field
    (c) Inductance   (d) Frequency

21. The velocity of rotation of earth is:
    (a) 28 km/min   (b) 30 km/min
    (c) 25 km/min   (d) 39.5 km/min

22. The chemical name of vitamin A is:
    (a) Retinol   (b) Jhiamin
    (c) Biotic   (d) Riboflavin

23. A 130 m long train crosses a bridge in 30 seconds at 45 kmph. The length of the bridge is
    (a) 200 m   (b) 245 m
    (c) 225 m   (d) 250 m

24. By selling an article at some price a person gains 10%. If the article is sold at twice of the price, the gain per cent will be:
    (a) 20%   (b) 60%
    (c) 100%   (d) 120%

25. Atoms are electrically charged as:
    (a) Positive   (b) Negative
    (c) Bi-positive   (d) Neutral

26. Ionic bond exists in:
    (a) KCl   (b) H_2O
    (c) NH_3 (d) Cl_3

27. Which force is required to increase the momentum of an object to 40 kg m/s in 5 seconds?
    (a) 2 N   (b) 4 N
    (c) 8 N   (d) 10 N
28. The river that does not form delta is:
    (a) Mahanadi   (b) Tapti
    (c) Krishna   (d) Cauvery
29. The ratio of the radius and height of a cone is 5 : 12, respectively. Its volume is 314 cm^3.
    Find its slant height.
    (a) 13 cm   (b) 14 cm
    (c) 17 cm   (d) 26 cm
30. A man buys 50 pencils for ₹ 100 and sells 45 pencils for ₹ 90. Find his gain or loss %.
    (a) 20%   (b) 35%
    (c) 25%   (d) No gain, No loss
31. When a ray of light passes from an optically denser medium to a rarer medium, it:
    (a) Remains undeviated
    (b) Bends towards normal
    (c) Bends away from normal
    (d) None of these
32. Who is the author of "Anand-math"?
    (a) Rabindranath Tagore
    (b) Bankim Chandra Chattopadhyaya
    (c) Sarojini Naidu
    (d) Jyotiba Phule
33. Thimpu is the capital of:
    (a) Nepal   (b) Bhutan
    (c) Thailand   (d) Myanmar
34. The time period of a seconds pendulum is:
    (a) 1 second   (b) 4 seconds
    (c) 3 seconds   (d) 2 seconds
35. The nuclear fuel in the sun is:
    (a) Helium   (b) Uranium
    (c) Hydrogen   (d) Oxygen
36. The second's hand of a watch is 2 cm long. The velocity of its tip is:
    (a) 0.21 cm/sec.   (b) 2.1 cm/sec.
    (c) 21 cm/sec.   (d) None of these
37. In diesel engine, ignition is caused by:
    (a) Spark   (b) Automatic starter
    (c) Compression   (d) Friction
38. The mass-energy equivalence, relationship $E = mc^2$ was propounded by:
    (a) Max Plank   (b) Einstein
    (c) Newton   (d) Hertz
39. The filament of bulb is made of:
    (a) Tungsten   (b) Iron
    (c) Nichrome   (d) Carbon
40. Anti-knocking can be lessened by:
    (a) Iso Octane   (b) N Heptane
    (c) TEL   (d) Benzene
41. Who was the first winner of Dada Saheb Phalke Award?
    (a) B. N. Sarkar   (b) Prithvi Raj Kapoor
    (c) Devika Rani   (d) Kanan Devi

42. How many members are nominated by the President in the Rajya Sabha?
    (a) 12   (b) 15
    (c) 10   (d) 20
43. Who was the founder of Brahmo Samaj?
    (a) Raja Rammohan Roy (b) Aurobindo Ghosh
    (c) Vivekanand   (d) Dyanand Saraswati
44. The Parliamentary System in India has been taken from:
    (a) America   (b) Britain
    (c) Australia   (d) Ireland
45. The electric supply in India was first started in:
    (a) Kolkata   (b) Chennai
    (c) Mumbai   (d) Darjeeling
46. Bhatnagar Prize is given in the field of:
    (a) Peace
    (b) Music and dance
    (c) Science and technology
    (d) Fine arts
47. Who discovered the solar system?
    (a) Copernicus   (b) Kepler
    (c) Aryabhatta   (d) Newton
48. The Nobel Prize in Economics was started in:
    (a) 1901   (b) 1936
    (c) 1957   (d) 1967
49. In India, the second largest language is:
    (a) Bengali   (b) Urdu
    (c) Telugu   (d) Marathi
50. The first Asian Games were held in:
    (a) Manila   (b) Tokyo
    (c) Jakarta   (d) New Delhi
51. The iron produced in blast furnace is:
    (a) Pig iron   (b) Wrought iron
    (c) Stainless steel (d) Steel
52. Fermentation is a 40% solution of:
    (a) Methanol   (b) Methenal
    (c) Methanoic acid   (d) None of these
53. Which of the following is not an ore of aluminium?
    (a) Cryolite   (b) Feldspar
    (c) Bauxite   (d) Azurite
54. Rhombic monoclinic and plastic sulphur are:
    (a) Isomers   (b) Isotopes
    (c) Allotropes   (d) Hydrides of sulphur
55. The alkaline hydrolysis of oils or fats gives soap and:
    (a) Glycerol   (b) Ethenol
    (c) Glycol   (d) Ethanoic acid
56. The sight of a delicious food usually makes month watery. It is a:
    (a) Hormonal response (b) Neural response
    (c) Optic response   (d) Olfactory response
57. Nitrogen fixing bacteria are normally found in:
    (a) Parasitic plants   (b) Epiphytic plants
    (c) Leguminous plants (d) Aquatic plants
58. Powdery mildew of wheat is caused by:
    (a) Bacteria   (b) Virus
    (c) Fungi   (d) Protozoans
59. Septic sore throat is caused by:
    (a) Protozoans   (b) Virus
    (c) Fungi   (d) Bacteria

60. A person of blood group AB can give blood , to:
    (a) 'A' and 'B' (b) Only 'AB'
    (c) 'A', 'B' and 'O' (d) All of these

61. In which of the following oxidation shows a positive oxidation state?
    (a) CO (b) N_2O
    (c) NO (d) F_2O

62. Which of the following is used in photography?
    (a) Silver Bromide (b) Sodium Bromide
    (c) Potassium Chloride (d) Sodium Sulphate

63. Which of the following is used in accumulator cell?
    (a) Copper (b) Iron
    (c) Lead (d) Zinc

64. Choose the wrong statement:
    (a) Single magnetic poles can exist
    (b) Magnetic poles are always of equal strength
    (c) Like poles repel each other
    (d) None of these

65. Laws of electrolysis are given by:
    (a) Faraday (b) Maxwell
    (c) Lenz (d) Bohr

66. Flemings left hand rule is used to find out:
    (a) Direction of magnetic field due to flow of current
    (b) Direction of induced current due to effect of magnetic field
    (c) Direction of motion of a current carrying conductor in magnetic field
    (d) None of these

67. The pH of a neutral solution at 25°C is:
    (a) 0 (b) 1.0
    (c) 7.0 (d) 1.4

68. The raw material used for the manufacture of Portland cement is:
    (a) Limestone and clay
    (b) Alumina, clay and gypsum
    (c) Gypsum and limestone
    (d) Gypsum and clay

69. $CaOCl_2$ is the chemical formula for a compound commonly known as:
    (a) Soda Ash
    (b) Lime
    (c) Bleaching Powder
    (d) Plaster of Paris

70. The glass used for making laboratory apparatus is:
    (a) Pyrex glass (b) Hard glass
    (c) Soft glass (d) Safety glass

71. Cell activities are controlled by:
    (a) Chloroplast (b) Nitochondria
    (c) Cytoplasm (d) Nucleus

72. Which of the following helps eye to adjust the focal length of the eye lens?
    (a) Cornea (b) Conjunctiva
    (c) Ciliary body (d) Iris

73. When pollen of a flower is transferred to the stigma of the same plant, pollination type is referred to as:
    (a) Autogamy (b) Allogamy
    (c) Xenogamy (d) Geitonogamy

74. Respiration is a:
    (a) Catabolic process (b) Anabolic process
    (c) Both (a) and (b) (d) None of these

75. The structural and functional unit of kidneys are:
    (a) Neurons (b) Nephrons
    (c) Medula (d) None of these

76. Which of the following enzymes is generally not present in adult human?
    (a) Renin (b) Pepsin
    (c) Trypsin (d) Amylopsin

77. The part of the plant which is responsible for carrying water and solutes from roots to various parts of plants is:
    (a) Phloem (b) Xylem
    (c) Duodenum (d) Sclercids

78. Widal test' is used for susceptibility of:
    (a) Malaria (b) Typhoid
    (c) Cholera (d) Yellow fever

79. Exchange of gases in plants takes place through:
    (a) Stomata (b) Lenticels
    (c) Cuticle (d) All of these

80. 'Lieutenant' in army is equivalent to following rank in navy:
    (a) Lieutenant
    (b) Sub Lieutenant
    (c) Lieutenant Commander
    (d) None of these

81. What is Hubble?
    (a) Warship (b) Star
    (c) Telescope (d) Missile

82. Which acid is normally found in lemon and grape fruits?
    (a) Citric acid (b) Tartaric acid
    (c) Ascorbic acid (d) Lactic acid

83. At which temperature Fahrenheit and Celsius show same reading?
    (a) −40° (b) 0°
    (c) −574.25° (d) 273°

84. Limestone is metamorphosed to form:
    (a) Graphite (b) Quartz
    (c) Granite (d) Marble

85. Rift valley is formed by:
    (a) Earthquake (b) Folding
    (c) Faulting (d) All of these

86. If a piece of ice at 0°C is mixed with water at 0°C, then:
    (a) Whole ice melts
    (b) Some ice melts
    (c) No ice melts
    (d) Temperature decreases

87. Mettur Dam is built on the river:
    (a) Krishna (b) Cauvery
    (c) Narmada (d) Mahanadi

88. Mahendra Giri peak is situated in the:
    (a) Eastern Ghats (b) Western Ghats
    (c) Shiwaliks (d) Vindhyachal

89. In what time a sum will double itself at 20% per annum rate of interest?
    (a) 2 years (b) 3 years
    (c) 4 years (d) 5 years

90. The famous Dilwara Temple is situated in:
   (a) Madhya Pradesh   (b) Maharashtra
   (c) Gujarat   (d) Rajasthan

91. Pneumonia affects:
   (a) Lungs   (b) Tongue
   (c) Liver   (d) Kidney

92. A man, a woman and a boy can together complete a piece of work in 3 days. If a man alone can do it in 6 days and a boy alone in 18 days, how long will a woman alone take to complete the work?
   (a) 9 days   (b) 21 days
   (c) 24 days   (d) 27 days

93. A does half as much work as B in one-sixth of the time. If together they take 10 days to complete a work, how much time shall B alone take to do it?
   (a) 70 days   (b) 30 days
   (c) 40 days   (d) 50 days

94. Two pipes can fill a tank with water in 15 and 12 hours respectively and a third pipe can empty it in 4 hours. If the pipes be opened in order, at 8, 9 and 11 a.m. respectively, the tank will be emptied at:
   (a) 11 : 40 a.m.   (b) 12 : 40 p.m.
   (c) 1 : 40 p.m.   (d) 2 : 40 p.m.

95. The percentage of loss when an article is sold at ₹ 50 is the same as that of the profit when it is sold at ₹ 70. The above-mentioned percentage of profit or loss on the article is:
   (a) 10%   (b) $16\dfrac{2}{3}\%$
   (c) 20%   (d) $22\dfrac{2}{3}\%$

96. A radio is sold for ₹ 990 at a profit of 10%. What would have been the actual profit or loss on it, had it been sold . for ₹ 890?
   (a) ₹ 10 loss   (b) ₹ 10 profit
   (c) ₹ 90 loss   (d) ₹ 90 profit

97. If an article is sold at a gain of 5% instead of being sold at a loss of 5% one gets ₹ 5 more. What is the cost price of the article?
   (a) ₹ 100   (b) ₹ 105
   (c) ₹ 50   (d) ₹ 110

98. Ravi buys some toffees at 2 for a rupees and sells them at 5 for a rupee. His loss per cent is:
   (a) 120   (c) 90
   (b) 30   (d) 60

99. Raghavan purchased a scooter at $\dfrac{13}{15}$ of its selling price and sold it at 12% more than its selling price. His gain is:
   (a) 20%   (b) 30%
   (c) $38\dfrac{3}{30}\%$ (d) $29\dfrac{3}{13}\%$

100. A person sold two pipes at ₹ 12 each. His profit on one was 20% and his loss on the other was 20%. On the whole, he:
   (a) Neither loss nor gained
   (b) Gained ₹ 1
   (c) Lost ₹ 1
   (d) Gained ₹ 2

101. A car travelling with $\dfrac{5}{7}$ of its usual speed covers 42 km in 1 hr 40 min 48 sec. What is the usual speed of the car?
   (a) $17\dfrac{6}{7}$ km/hr   (b) 35 km/hr
   (c) 25 km/hr   (d) 30 km/hr

102. A and B run a kilometre and A wins by 25 sec. A and C run a kilometre and 'A wins by 275 m. When B and C run the same distance, B wins by 30 sec. The time taken by A to run a kilometre is:
   (a) 2 min 25 sec   (b) 2 min 50 sec
   (c) 3 min 20 sec   (d) 3 min 30 sec

103. A train passes a man standing on a platform in 8 seconds and also crosses the platform which is 264 metres long in 20 seconds. The length (in metres) of the train is:
   (a) 188   (b) 176
   (c) 175   (d) 96

104. A boat goes 8 km in one hour along the stream and 2 km in one hour against the stream. The speed (in km/hr) of the stream is:
   (a) 2   (b) 3
   (c) 4   (d) 5

105. Walking at three-fourth of his usual speed, a man covers a certain distance in 2 hours more than the time he takes to cover the distance at his usual speed. The time taken by him to cover the same distance with his usual speed is:
   (a) 4.5 hr.   (b) 5.5 hr.
   (c) 6 hr.   (d) 5 hr.

106. In a certain code SHIFT is written as 37$%5 and RATE is written as #★59. How is FIRST written in that code?
   (a) %$★37   (b) %$#57
   (c) ★$#35   (d) None of these

107. In a certain code COMPUTE is written as FSVONND. How is DISTURB written in that code?
   (a) CSVSTHE   (b) CQVSTHE
   (c) CQVTSHE   (d) CSVTSHE

108. Pointing to a photograph Vinod said 'She is the daughter of my wife's mother's only daughter'. How is Vinod related to the girl in the photograph?
   (a) Cousin   (b) Uncle
   (c) Father   (d) Cannot be determined

109. How many such pairs of letters are there in the word FUNCTIONAL, each of which has as many letters between them in the word as they have in the English alphabet?
   (a) NIL   (b) One
   (c) Two   (d) More than three

110. If Sun means Moon, Moon means Sky, Sky means Cloud, Cloud means Rain and Rain means Sun, then where do the Birds fly?
    - (a) Sky
    - (b) Moon
    - (c) Sun
    - (d) Cloud

111. The centre of gravity of a plane lamina will not be at its geometrical centre if it is a
    - (a) circle
    - (b) equilateral triangle
    - (c) rectangle
    - (d) right angled triangle

112. Which of the following is not an extensive property ?
    - (a) Entropy
    - (b) Enthalpy
    - (c) Internal energy
    - (d) Density

113. For ordinary telegraphy, bandwidth is sufficient of
    - (a) 150 Hz only
    - (b) 120 Hz only
    - (c) 75 Hz only
    - (d) 50 Hz only

114. Facsimile is on of the original
    - (a) arts
    - (b) engineering arts
    - (c) electrical engineering arts
    - (d) both (b) and (c)

115. Baudot Distributor is a most important part of Baudot system and each Baudot station is provided with its own
    - (a) codes
    - (b) distributors
    - (c) both (a) and (b)
    - (d) none of these

116. Baudot Governor is used with weight-driven
    - (a) distributors
    - (b) ring
    - (c) segment
    - (d) none of these

117. Which one of the following does not form a part of the fuel supply system for a diesel engine?
    - (a) Air cleaner
    - (b) filter
    - (c) injector
    - (d) spray nozzles

118. The number of exhaust manifolds in a V-8 engine:
    - (a) two
    - (b) one
    - (c) four
    - (d) eight

119. The ratio of difussion constant for electrons D_e to the mobility for electrons m_e is
    - (a) independent of T
    - (b) inversely proportional to T
    - (c) proportional to T^2
    - (d) proportional to T

120. Muemonic symbols are used
    - (a) to denote address
    - (b) to employ hamming code
    - (c) to denote errors
    - (d) to assist human memory

ANSWER KEY

1	(a)	21	(a)	41	(c)	61	(d)	81	(c)	101	(b)
2	(d)	22	(a)	42	(a)	62	(a)	82	(a)	102	(a)
3	(a)	23	(c)	43	(a)	63	(c)	83	(a)	103	(b)
4	(d)	24	(d)	44	(b)	64	(a)	84	(d)	104	(b)
5	(d)	25	(d)	45	(d)	65	(a)	85	(c)	105	(c)
6	(c)	26	(a)	46	(c)	66	(c)	86	(c)	106	(d)
7	(a)	27	(c)	47	(a)	67	(c)	87	(b)	107	(b)
8	(d)	28	(b)	48	(d)	68	(b)	88	(a)	108	(c)
9	(a)	29	(a)	49	(c)	69	(c)	89	(d)	109	(d)
10	(c)	30	(c)	50	(d)	70	(a)	90	(d)	110	(d)
11	(b)	31	(c)	51	(a)	71	(d)	91	(a)	111	(b)
12	(a)	32	(b)	52	(b)	72	(c)	92	(a)	112	(b)
13	(d)	33	(b)	53	(d)	73	(a)	93	(c)	113	(d)
14	(b)	34	(d)	54	(c)	74	(a)	94	(d)	114	(b)
15	(c)	35	(c)	55	(a)	75	(b)	95	(b)	115	(d)
16	(d)	36	(a)	56	(d)	76	(a)	96	(a)	116	(d)
17	(a)	37	(c)	57	(c)	77	(b)	97	(c)	117	(b)
18	(d)	38	(b)	58	(c)	78	(b)	98	(d)	118	(a)
19	(b)	39	(a)	59	(b)	79	(d)	99	(d)	119	(a)
20	(c)	40	(a)	60	(b)	80	(b)	100	(c)	120	(d)

HINTS AND SOLUTIONS

10. (c) Here $u = \sqrt{2gh} = \sqrt{2 \times 9.8 \times 10} = \sqrt{196} = 14$ m/sec.

23. (b) Speed $= 45$ kmph $= 45 \times \dfrac{5}{18} = 12.5$ m/s

Let, length of the bridge $= x$ m; then $\dfrac{130 + x}{12.5} = 30$

$\Rightarrow \quad 130 + x = 375$

$\therefore \quad x = 375 - 130 = 245$ m.

24. (d) Let, C.P. ₹ $= 100$; then

S.P. with gain 10% $=$ ₹ 110

But when S.P. $= 2 \times$ ₹ 110 $=$ ₹ 220

Gain $= 220 - 100 =$ ₹ 120

$\therefore \quad$ Gain % $= \dfrac{120 \times 100}{100} = 120\%$

29. (a) Let radius and height of a cone are $5x$ and $12x$ cm

respectively; then $\dfrac{1}{3} \times \pi \times (5x)^2 \times 12x = 314$

$\Rightarrow \quad 3.14 \times 25x^2 \times 4x = 314$

$\Rightarrow \quad x^3 = \dfrac{314}{314} = 1$

$\therefore \quad x = 1$

Since, radius and height will be 5 cm and 12cm. Now, slant height,

$l = \sqrt{h^2 + r^2} = \sqrt{(12)^2 + (5)^2} = \sqrt{169} = 13$ cm

30. (d) C.P. of 50 pencils $=$ ₹ 100

$\therefore \quad$ C.P. of 45 pencils $= \dfrac{100}{50} \times 45 =$ ₹ 90

$=$ S.P. of 45 pencils

$\therefore \quad$ No gain, No loss

89. (d) Let, principal be ₹ x then amount will be $2x$; then

S.I. $= 2x - x =$ ₹ x

Time $= \dfrac{x \times 100}{x \times 20} = 5$ years.

92. (a) Work of (1 man + 1 women + 1 boy) for 1 day $= \dfrac{1}{3}$

$\therefore \quad$ Work of 1 man for 1 day $= \dfrac{1}{6}$

and work of 1 boy for 1 day $= \dfrac{1}{18}$

$\therefore \quad$ Work of 1 women for 1 day $= \dfrac{1}{3} - \dfrac{1}{6} - \dfrac{1}{18} = \dfrac{1}{9}$

Hence woman alone will complete the work in 9 days.

93. (c) Let the time taken by B alone to complete the work be x days.

$\therefore \quad$ Time taken by A to complete

$\dfrac{1}{2}$ work $= \dfrac{x}{6}$ days

$\therefore$ Work of A for 1 day $= \dfrac{1}{2} \times \dfrac{6}{x} = \dfrac{3}{x}$

and Work of B for 1 day $= \dfrac{1}{x}$

$\Rightarrow \quad \dfrac{3}{x} + \dfrac{1}{x} = \dfrac{1}{10}$

$\Rightarrow \quad \dfrac{4}{x} = \dfrac{1}{10}$

$x = 40$ days

94.   (d)   Let the tank will be emptied at x a.m.

Tank filled by first pipe $= \dfrac{1}{15} \times (x - 8)$

Tank filled by second pipe $= \dfrac{1}{12} \times (x - 9)$

and tank emptied by third pipe $= \dfrac{1}{4} \times (x - 11)$

$\therefore \quad \dfrac{x-8}{15} + \dfrac{x-9}{12} = \dfrac{x-11}{4}$

$\Rightarrow \quad \dfrac{4x - 32 + 5x - 45}{60} = \dfrac{x-11}{4}$

$\Rightarrow \quad 9x - 77 = 15x - 165$

$\Rightarrow \quad 6x = 88$

$\therefore \quad x = \dfrac{88}{6} = 14\dfrac{2}{3}$

i.e. $2 : 40$ p.m.

95.   (b)   Let percentage of profit or loss on the article be x

$\therefore \quad \dfrac{50 \times 100}{100 - x} = \dfrac{70 \times 100}{100 + x}$

$\Rightarrow \quad 5000\,(100 + x) = 7000\,(100 - x)$

$\Rightarrow \quad 500 + 5x = 700 - 7x$

$\Rightarrow \quad 12x = 200$

$\therefore \quad x = \dfrac{200}{12} = 16\dfrac{2}{3}\%$

96.   (a) $\because$ C.P. of radio $= \dfrac{990 \times 100}{(100 + 10)} = ₹\,900$

$\therefore$ Actual loss $= 900 - 890 = ₹\,10$

97.   (c)   C.P. of the article $= ₹\,\dfrac{c \times 100}{(a+b)}$

(Here $a = 5,\, b = 5$ and $c = 5$)

$= \dfrac{5 \times 100}{(5+5)} = ₹\,50$

98.   (d)   C.P. of 1 toffee $= ₹\,\dfrac{1}{2}$

and S.P. of 1 toffee $= ₹\,\dfrac{1}{5}$

$\therefore$ Reqd. loss % $= \dfrac{\left(\dfrac{1}{2} - \dfrac{1}{5}\right) \times 100}{\dfrac{1}{2}}$

$= \dfrac{3}{10} \times 100 \times 2 = 60\%$

99.   (d)   Let S.P. of the Scooter be $₹\,x$

$\therefore$ C.P. of the Scooter $= ₹\,\dfrac{13x}{15}$

and S.P. of the Scooter $= ₹\,\dfrac{112 \times x}{100}$

$\therefore$ Gain % $= \left(\dfrac{12x}{100} - \dfrac{13x}{15}\right) \times \dfrac{100 \times 5}{13x}\%$

$= \dfrac{336x - 260x}{300} \times \dfrac{1500}{13x}\% = 29\dfrac{3}{13}\%$

100.   (c) $\because$ C. P. of first pipe $= \dfrac{12 \times 100}{(100 + 20)} = ₹\,10$

$\Rightarrow$ C.P. of second pipe $= \dfrac{12 \times 100}{(100 - 20)} = ₹\,15$

$\Rightarrow$ C.P. of both the pipes $= 10 + 15 = ₹\,25$

$\Rightarrow$ S.P. of both the pipes $= 12 + 12 = ₹.24$

$\therefore$ Loss on the whole $= 25 - 24 = ₹\,1$

101.   (b)   Usual speed of the car $= \dfrac{42}{\dfrac{42}{25}} \times \dfrac{7}{5}$

$= \dfrac{42 \times 7 \times 25}{42 \times 5} = 35\,\text{km/hr}$

103.   (b)   Let the length of train be x meters

$\because \quad \dfrac{x}{8} = \dfrac{x + 264}{20}$

$\Rightarrow 20x = 8x + 2112$

$\Rightarrow 12x = 2112$

$\therefore x = \dfrac{2112}{12} = 176$ meters

104.   (b)   Speed of the stream $= \dfrac{8 - 2}{2} = 3\,$ km/hr

105.   (c)   Let the usual speed be x km/hr and time taken by usual speed by y hour

$\because \; x \times y = \dfrac{3}{4} x (y + 2)$

$\Rightarrow 4xy = 3xy + 6x$

$\Rightarrow xy = 6x$

$\therefore y = 6$ hours

106. (d) As, $S\,H\,I\,F\,T \rightarrow 3\,7\,\$\,\%\,5$
and $R\,A\,T\,E \rightarrow \#\,*\,5\,9$
Similarly
$\quad F\,I\,R\,S\,T \rightarrow \%\,\$\,\#\,3\,5$

107. (b) As

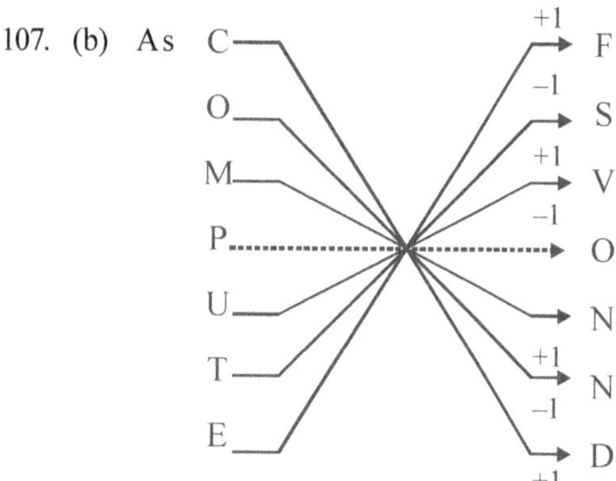

Similarly,

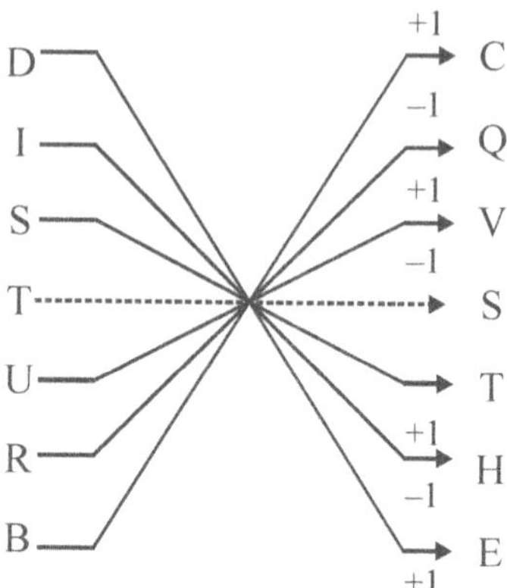

108. (c) The only daughter of Vinod's wife's mother is the wife of Vinod and the daughter of Vinod's wife is daughter of Vinod. Hence Vinod is the father of the girl in the photograph.

109. (d) $F\ U\ N\ C\ T\ I\ O\ N\ A\ L$

Hence, required pairs are: $F-C, O-N, N-L, O-L$

110. (d) Hence, sky means cloud, Hence the Birds fly in the cloud.

1   PRACTICE SET

INSTRUCTIONS

1. This practice set consists of 75 questions will be of objective type with multiple choices.

2. Practice set have MCQs from Mathematics, General Intelligence & Reasoning, General Science and General Awareness on Current Affairs.

3. Duration of practice set is 60 minutes.

Time : 60 Min.   **Max. Marks : 75**

DIRECTIONS (Qs. 1-2): *Choose the odd word/letters number/number pair from the given alternatives.*

1.   (a) Sirius   (b) Proximacentauri
    (c) Deimos   (d) Alpha centauri

2.   (a) PON   (b) SRQ
    (c) XYZ   (d) VUT

DIRECTIONS (Qs. 3): *A series is given with one term missing. Choose the correct alternative from the given ones that will complete the series.*

3.   30, 60, 360, 3600, ?
    (a) 48500   (b) 50500
    (c) 50400   (d) 40800

4.   Five boys A, B, C, D and E are standing in a line. A is taller than E but shorter than D. B is shorter than E and C is the tallest. Who is in the middle?
    (a) A   (b) C
    (c) D   (d) E

5.   In a certain code language, "RIVER" is written as "12351" and "RED" is written as "156". How is "DRIVER" written in that code language?
    (a) 612311   (b) 612531
    (c) 621351   (d) 612351

6.   In the following question, select the missing number from the given series.

49	169	484
81	144	625
16	25	?

    (a) 37   (b) 47
    (c) 48   (d) 25

7.   If "+" means "minus", "×" means "divided by", "÷" means "plus" and "−" means "multiplied by", then
$126 \times 14 + 7 - 3 \div 2 = ?$
    (a) −10   (b) −12
    (c) −17   (d) −41

8.   In the following question, which one set of letters when sequentially placed at the gaps in the given letter series shall complete it?
d _ ba_c_a_cb_
    (a) cdbda   (b) cdbad
    (c) bdacd   (d) abdca

9.   Neeraj is facing north, then he turns 45 degree right and goes 25 m, then turns in south – east direction to move 25 m and from there 25 m to east. In which direction/place is he from his original place?
    (a) North   (b) East
    (c) West   (d) South

10.   Introducing a boy Ankit said, "He is the son of daughter of my grandfather's son". How is that boy related to Ankit?
    (a) Cousin   (b) Brother
    (c) Father – in – law   (d) Nephew

11.   What is the LCM (least common multiple) of 57 and 93?
    (a) 1767   (b) 1567
    (c) 1576   (d) 1919

12.   Marked price of an item is Rs 500. On purchase of 2 items discount is 8%, on purchase of 3 items discount is 16%. Radha buys 5 items, what is the effective discount?
    (a) 20.4 percent   (b) 23.25 percent
    (c) 12.8 percent   (d) 35 percent

13.   The mean of marks secured by 60 students in division A of class X is 64, 40 students of division B is 60 and that of 60 students of division C is 58. Find the mean of marks of the students of three divisions of Class X.
    (a) 60.05   (b) 59.35
    (c) 62.15   (d) 60.75

14.   The price of an article is cut by 33%, to restore to its original value, the new price must be increased by
    (a) 33 percent   (b) 49.25 percent
    (c) 24.81 percent   (d) 41.25 percent

15.   The total surface area of a hemisphere is 166.32 sq cm, find its radius?
    (a) 4.2 cm   (b) 8.4 cm
    (c) 1.4 cm   (d) 2.1 cm

16. The line passing through $(-2, 5)$ and $(6, b)$ is perpendicular to the line $20x + 5y = 3$. Find b?
    (a) -7 (b) 4
    (c) 7 (d) -4

17. If $3x - 8(2 - x) = -19$, then the value of x is
    (a) $-3/11$ (b) $-33/11$
    (c) $-3/5$ (d) $-33/5$

18. If $2x - 3(2x - 2) > x - 1 < 2 + 2x$, then x can take which of the following values?
    (a) 2 (b) -2
    (c) 4 (d) -4

19. B-1, D-2, F-4, H-8, J-16, ___ .
    (a) K-64   (b) L-32
    (c) M-32   (d) L-64

20. If A = 1, B = 2 and N = 14, then BEADING = ?
    (a) 2154 (14) 97
    (b) 2514 (14) 79
    (c) 25149 (14) 7
    (d) 2154(14)79

DIRECTIONS (Qs. 21) : *In question, which one set of letters when sequentially placed at the gaps in the given letter series shall complete it ?*

21. a _ n _ b _ _ n c b _ _ n c b
    (a) b c a b a b   (b) b a c b a b
    (c) a b c b c b   (d) a b b c c a

22. Introducing a girl, Ram said to his son-in-law. "Her brother is the only son of my brother-in-law." Who is the girl of Ram?
    (a) Sister-in-law   (b) Niece
    (c) Daughter   (d) Sister

23. The ussnit's digit in the product $7^{35} \times 3^{71} \times 11^{55}$ is :
    (a) 1   (b) 3
    (c) 7   (d) 9

24. When the price of a radio was reduced by 20%, its sale increased by 80%. What was the net effect on the sale?
    (a) 44% increase   (b) 44% decrease
    (c) 66% increase   (d) 75% increase

25. The batting average of 40 innings of a cricket player is 50 runs. His highest score exceeds his lowest score by 172 runs. If these two innings are excluded, the average of the remaining 38 innings is 48. His highest score was :
    (a) 172   (b) 173
    (c) 174   (d) 176

26. Bromine is-
    (a) colourless gas insoluble in water
    (b) A highly inflammable gas
    (c) A Black solid.
    (d) A red liquid.

27. The metal used in storage batteries-
    (a) Iron   (b) Copper
    (c) Lead   (d) Zinc

28. Water has maximum density at-
    (a) $-4°C$ (b) $0°C$
    (c) $4°C$ (d) $100°C$

29. The colour of Emerald is-
    (a) Violet   (b) Yellow
    (c) Deep Green   (d) Prussian Blue

30. Permanent hardness of water, due to sulphates of the metal, can be destroyed by the use of
    (a) Nitrates   (b) Zeolites
    (c) Sulphonates   (d) None of these

31. Rust is-
    (a) A mixture of Fe_2O_3 and $Fe(OH)_2$
    (b) A mixture of FeO and $Fe(OH)_2$
    (c) FeO only
    (d) A mixture of Fe_2O_3, $3H_2O$ and FeO

32. Which of the following characters is not shown by hydrogen-
    (a) It burns in air to form water
    (b) It supports combustion
    (c) It combines with almost all metals forming hydrides
    (d) It readily combines with fluorine and chlorine

33. Which of the following elements is obtained from sea weeds ?
    (a) Argon   (b) Sulphur
    (c) Vanadium   (d) Iodine

34. The metallic constituents of hard water are
    (a) Magnesium, Calcium and tin
    (b) Iron, tin and calcium
    (c) Calcium, magnesium and iron
    (d) Magnesium, tin and iron

35. Who suggested that the most of the mass of atom is located in nucleus ?
    (a) Bohr   (b) Thomson
    (c) Rutherford   (d) Avogadro

36. Meson particles are found in-
    (a) R-rays   (b) X-rays
    (c) Laser beam   (d) Cosmic rays

37. An atom of an element with mass number 23 and atomic number 11 will have-
    (a) 11 neutrons, 12 protons and 11 electrons
    (b) 11 protons, 12 neutrons and 11 electrons
    (c) 11 protons, 12 electrons and 11 neutrons
    (d) 23 protons and 11 electrons

38. Which of the following is a protein ?
    (a) Wool   (b) Starch
    (c) Natural rubber   (d) Cellulose

39. Optical fibres are mainly used in-
    (a) Communication
    (b) Weaving
    (c) Musical Instruments
    (d) Food Industry

40. The first synthetic fibre made by man was-
    (a) Rayon   (b) Nylon
    (c) Polyester   (d) Terycott

41. Polythene is industrially prepared by the polymerization of
    (a) Methane   (b) Styrene
    (c) Acetylene   (d) Ethylene

42. A mixture of water and alcohol can be separated by
    (a) Filtration   (b) Evaporation
    (c) Distillation   (d) Decantation

43. One micron is equal to-
    (a) 1/10th of mm   (b) 1/100th of mm
    (c) 1/1000th of mm   (d) 1/10000th of mm

44. Equal volumes of different gases at any definite temperature and pressure have-
    (a) Equal weights   (b) equal masses
    (c) equal density   (d) equal no. of molecules

45. Milk is an example of
    (a) suspension   (b) true solution
    (c) emulsion   (d) gel

46. Which of the following modes of expressing concentration is independent of temperature-
    (a) Molarity   (b) Molality
    (c) Normality   (d) Formality
47. Which of the following substances undergoes chemical change on heating ?
    (a) Sodium chloride   (b) Silica
    (c) Lead nitrate   (d) Platinum wire
48. Cooking oil can be converted into vegetable ghee by the process of
    (a) oxidation   (b) hydrogenation
    (c) distillation   (d) crystalisation
49. The contact process is involved in the manufacture of-
    (a) nitric acid   (b) Sulphuric acid
    (c) Ammonia   (d) Caustic soda
50. Antidiuretic hormone (ADH)-
    (a) inhibits the secretion of growth hormone by the pituitary
    (b) inhibits the rate of heart beat
    (c) causes the muscular walls of the arterioles to contract that simulates the reabsorption of water from the kidney tubules.
    (d) causes an increase in the blood pressure
51. Which of the following is used as lubricant ?
    (a) Graphite   (b) Silica
    (c) Diamond   (d) Iron Oxide
52. The purest form of iron is
    (a) Steel   (b) Pig iron
    (c) Cast iron   (d) Wrought iron
53. The percentage of carbon is the least in-
    (a) Grey cast iron   (b) Wrought iron
    (c) White cast iron   (d) Steel
54. An element that does not occur in nature but can be produced artificially is
    (a) Thorium   (b) Radium
    (c) Plutonium   (d) Uranium
55. The inert gas which is substituted for nitrogen in the air, used by deep sea drivers for breathing is-
    (a) Helium   (b) Argon
    (c) Krypton   (d) Xenon
56. Old-written material, which cannot be read easily can be read by
    (a) Cosmic Rays   (b) Ultraviolet rays
    (c) Infra Red rays   (d) None of these
57. In an atomic nucleus, neutrons and protons are held together by
    (a) Gravitational forces
    (b) Magnetic forces
    (c) Exchange forces
    (d) Coulombic forces
58. The type of glass used in making prisms and lenses is-
    (a) Soft glass   (b) Pyrex glass
    (c) Jena glass   (d) Flint glass
59. Carbon tetrachloride fire extinguisher should not be used in closed room because it produces poisonous glass called-
    (a) Carbon Monoxide   (b) Phosphine
    (c) Phosgene   (d) None of these
60. Which of the following is commonly called a polyamide ?
    (a) Rayon   (b) Orion
    (c) Terylene   (d) Nylon
61. Who is referred as the Father of Indian Economic Planning?
    (a) Jawaharlal Nehru (b) Sardar Vallabhai Patel
    (c) Visveswaraiyah   (d) Radha Kant
62. The Article associated with Compulsory Education is
    (a) Article 20   (b) Article 20A
    (c) Article 21   (d) Article 21A
63. The Khangchendzonga National Park is in
    (a) Manipur   (b) Meghalaya
    (c) Sikkhim   (d) Uttarakhand
64. Koniology is ths study of
    (a) Muscle Movements
    (b) Dust in relation to its effect on health
    (c) Form and Structure
    (d) Chemicals Living at molecular level
65. The World Tourism Day is observed on
    (a) September 23   (b) September 25
    (c) September 27   (d) September 29
66. When is Border Security Force Formed?
    (a) 1952   (b) 1962
    (c) 1970   (d) 1965
67. Which classical dance is famous in Assam?
    (a) Manipuri   (b) Sattriya
    (c) Kathak   (d) Kuchipudi
68. What is the head quarters of North Central railway Zone?
    (a) Delhi   (b) Mumbai
    (c) Allahabad   (d) Jaipur
69. The Highest Civilian Award in India
    (a) Padma Bushan   (b) Padma Shri
    (c) Padma Vibhushan   (d) Bharat ratna
70. Pyridoxine is
    (a) Vitamin B2   (b) Vitamin B1
    (c) Vitamin B6   (d) Vitamin B12
71. The Vikram Sarabhai Space Centre is located in which state?
    (a) Karnataka   (b) Andhra Pradesh
    (c) Kerala   (d) Tamil Nadu
72. The National Housing Bank (NHB) was established as a wholly owned subsidiary of RBI under which act?
    (a) Reserve Bank of India Act, 1934
    (b) National Housing Bank Act, 1987
    (c) Banking Regulation Act, 1949
    (d) Companies Act, 1956
73. Which country will host the 21st Commonwealth Games?
    (a) Kuala Lumpur, Malaysia
    (b) Birmingham, England
    (c) Glasgow, Scotland
    (d) Gold Coast, Australia
74. As per the Economic Survey 2017-18, the GDP growth of India is pegged at _______ percent for the fiscal ending March 31, 2017
    (a) 7.2 Percent   (b) 6.50 Percent
    (c) 7 Percent   (d) 6.75 Percent
75. Who has been elected as the President of Finland?
    (a) Sauli Niinisto
    (b) Stefan Lofven
    (c) Valentina Matviyenko
    (d) Erna Solberg

RESPONSE SHEET

1. ⓐⓑⓒⓓ	2. ⓐⓑⓒⓓ	3. ⓐⓑⓒⓓ	4. ⓐⓑⓒⓓ	5. ⓐⓑⓒⓓ
6. ⓐⓑⓒⓓ	7. ⓐⓑⓒⓓ	8. ⓐⓑⓒⓓ	9. ⓐⓑⓒⓓ	10. ⓐⓑⓒⓓ
11. ⓐⓑⓒⓓ	12. ⓐⓑⓒⓓ	13. ⓐⓑⓒⓓ	14. ⓐⓑⓒⓓ	15. ⓐⓑⓒⓓ
16. ⓐⓑⓒⓓ	17. ⓐⓑⓒⓓ	18. ⓐⓑⓒⓓ	19. ⓐⓑⓒⓓ	20. ⓐⓑⓒⓓ
21. ⓐⓑⓒⓓ	22. ⓐⓑⓒⓓ	23. ⓐⓑⓒⓓ	24. ⓐⓑⓒⓓ	25. ⓐⓑⓒⓓ
26. ⓐⓑⓒⓓ	27. ⓐⓑⓒⓓ	28. ⓐⓑⓒⓓ	29. ⓐⓑⓒⓓ	30. ⓐⓑⓒⓓ
31. ⓐⓑⓒⓓ	32. ⓐⓑⓒⓓ	33. ⓐⓑⓒⓓ	34. ⓐⓑⓒⓓ	35. ⓐⓑⓒⓓ
36. ⓐⓑⓒⓓ	37. ⓐⓑⓒⓓ	38. ⓐⓑⓒⓓ	39. ⓐⓑⓒⓓ	40. ⓐⓑⓒⓓ
41. ⓐⓑⓒⓓ	42. ⓐⓑⓒⓓ	43. ⓐⓑⓒⓓ	44. ⓐⓑⓒⓓ	45. ⓐⓑⓒⓓ
46. ⓐⓑⓒⓓ	47. ⓐⓑⓒⓓ	48. ⓐⓑⓒⓓ	49. ⓐⓑⓒⓓ	50. ⓐⓑⓒⓓ
51. ⓐⓑⓒⓓ	52. ⓐⓑⓒⓓ	53. ⓐⓑⓒⓓ	54. ⓐⓑⓒⓓ	55. ⓐⓑⓒⓓ
56. ⓐⓑⓒⓓ	57. ⓐⓑⓒⓓ	58. ⓐⓑⓒⓓ	59. ⓐⓑⓒⓓ	60. ⓐⓑⓒⓓ
61. ⓐⓑⓒⓓ	62. ⓐⓑⓒⓓ	63. ⓐⓑⓒⓓ	64. ⓐⓑⓒⓓ	65. ⓐⓑⓒⓓ
66. ⓐⓑⓒⓓ	67. ⓐⓑⓒⓓ	68. ⓐⓑⓒⓓ	69. ⓐⓑⓒⓓ	70. ⓐⓑⓒⓓ
71. ⓐⓑⓒⓓ	72. ⓐⓑⓒⓓ	73. ⓐⓑⓒⓓ	74. ⓐⓑⓒⓓ	75. ⓐⓑⓒⓓ

HINTS & SOLUTIONS

1. (c) Except Deimos (It is a satellite), All others are Star systems.

2. (c) Except, XYZ, All others are opposite alphabetical sequence.

3. (c) 30   60   360   3600 $\boxed{50400}$

   $\times 2$ $\times 6$ $\times 10$ $\times 14$

   $+4$ $+4$ $+4$

4. (a) $C > D > A > E > B$
   So, A is in the middle.

5. (d) As,

   R   I   V   E   R   R   E   D
   ↓   ↓   ↓   ↓   ↓   ↓   ↓   ↓
   1   2   3   5   1   1   5   6

   Similarly,

   D   R   I   V   E   R
   ↓   ↓   ↓   ↓   ↓   ↓
   6   1   2   3   5   1

6. (b) $\sqrt{49} = 7$ $\sqrt{169} = 13$ $\sqrt{484} = 22$

   $\sqrt{81} = \dfrac{+9}{16}$ $\sqrt{144} = \dfrac{+12}{25}$ $\sqrt{625} = \dfrac{+25}{47}$

   So, Answer is 47.

7. (a) If,

$+ = -$	$\times = \div$
$\div = +$	$- = \times$

   then,
   $126 \div 14 - 7 \times 3 + 2 = -10$

8. (a) d$\underline{c}$ba / dc$\underline{b}$a / d$\underline{c}$ba
   So, answer is cdbda.

9. (b)

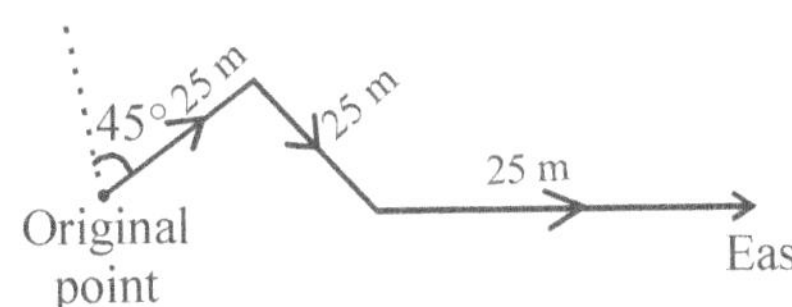

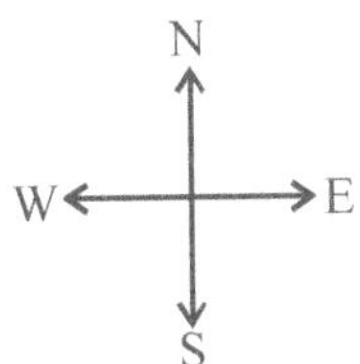

   So, answer is East direction.

10. (d) Nephew.

11. (a) LCM of 57 and 93,

   $$\begin{array}{c|cc} 3 & 57, & 93 \\ \hline & 19, & 31 \end{array}$$

   $\Rightarrow$ $3 \times 19 \times 31 = 1767$.
   So, Required answer is 1767.

12. (c) Marked price of each item = 500
   No. of items = 5
   $\therefore$ Total marked price = $500 \times 5 = 2500$

   Total discount $= 2 \times 500 \times \dfrac{8}{100} + 3 \times 500 \times \dfrac{16}{100} = 320$

   $\therefore$ Effective discount $= \dfrac{320}{2500} \times 100$

   $= 12.8\%$

13. (d) Mean of marks of the students

   $$= \frac{(60 \times 64 + 40 \times 60 + 60 \times 58)}{160}$$

   $$= \frac{9720}{160} = 60.75$$

14. (b) Let the price of the article = ₹ 100
   New Price = $100 - 33 = 67$
   Therefore the new price must be increased by

   $$\frac{(100 - 67) \times 100}{67} = \frac{3300}{67} = 49.25\%$$

15. (a) Here,
   Total surface area of hemisphere = 166.32 sq cm.
   r = ?

   $\because$ $3\pi r^2 = 166.32$

   $3 \times \dfrac{22}{7} \times r^2 = 166.32$

   $\therefore$ $r^2 = \dfrac{166.32 \times 7}{3 \times 22} = 17.64$

   $\therefore$ r = 4.2 cm.

16. (c) Here,
   $20x + 5y = 3$
   $\Rightarrow$ $5y = -20x + 3$

   $\therefore$ $y = -4x + \dfrac{3}{5}$

   Slope of $20x + 5y = 3$ þ -4

We know, product of slopes $= -1$ for perpendicular lines

Hence, the slope of the line which passes through $(-2, 5)$

and $(6, b) = \dfrac{b-5}{6-(-2)}$

Now,

$$\dfrac{b-5}{6+2} = \dfrac{1}{4}$$

$\Rightarrow \quad b - 5 = 2$

$\therefore \quad b = 5 + 2 = 7$

17. (a) $3x - 8(2 - x) = -19$

$3x - 16 + 8x = -19$

$11x = -3$

$\therefore \quad x = \dfrac{-3}{11}$

18. (b) Here,

$2x - 3(2x - 2) > x - 1 < 2 + 2x$

$2x - 6x + 6 > x - 1$

$\Rightarrow \quad 2x - 6x - x > -7$

$\Rightarrow \quad -5x > -7$

$x < 7/5$ ...(i)

$(x - 1) < (2 + 2x)$

$x - 1 < 2 + 2x$

$-3 < x$ ...(ii)

From (i) and (ii),

$x = -2$.

19. (b) The pattern of the series is as follows:

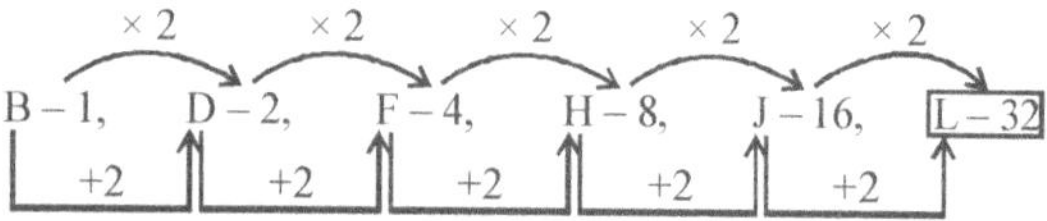

20. (c) It is based on position of English alphabet.

B E A D I N G
↓ ↓ ↓ ↓ ↓ ↓ ↓
2 5 1 4 9 (14) 7

21. (a) **a b n c b / a b n c b / a b n c b**

22. (b)

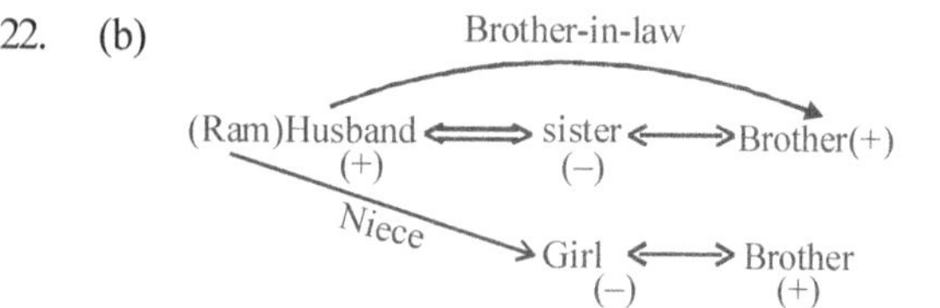

Hence, girl is the niece of Ram.

23. (a) Unit's digit in $(7^4) = 1$. Therefore, unit's digit in $(7^4)^8$

i.e. 7^{32} will be 1. Hence, unit's digit in

$(7)^{35} = 1 \times 7 \times 7 \times 7 = 3$

Again, unit's digit in $(3)^4 = 1$

Therefore, unit's digit in the expansion of

$(3^4)^{17} = (3)^{68} = 1$

$\Rightarrow$ Unit's digit in the expansion of

$(3^{71}) = 1 \times 3 \times 3 \times 3 = 7$

and unit's digit in the expanison of $(11^{35}) = 1$

Hence, unit's digit in the expansion of

$7^{35} \times 3^{71} \times 11^{55} = 3 \times 7 \times 1 = 1$

24. (a) Let the original price be x and sale be of y units.

Then, the revenue collected initially $= x \times y$

Now, new price $= 0.8x$, new sale $= 1.8y$

Then, new revenue collected $= 1.44xy$

% increase in revenue $= \dfrac{0.44xy}{xy} \times 100 = 44\%$

Shortcut Method

Net effect $= -20 + 80 + \dfrac{(-20 \times 80)}{100}$

$= 60 - 16 = 44\%$

25. (c) Total score of 40 innings $= 40 \times 50 = 2000$

Total score of 38 innings $= 38 \times 48 = 1824$

Let the highest score be x and the lowest score be y.

Sum of the highest and the lowest score

$= x + y = 2000 - 1824$

$\Rightarrow \quad x + y = 176$ ...(i)

and by question, $x - y = 172$ ...(ii)

Solving (i) and (ii), we get $x = 174$

26.	(d)	27.	(c)	28.	(c)	29.	(c)	30.	(b)
31.	(d)	32.	(b)	33.	(d)	34.	(c)	35.	(c)
36.	(d)	37.	(b)	38.	(c)	39.	(a)	40.	(b)
41.	(d)	42.	(c)	43.	(c)	44.	(d)	45.	(c)
46.	(b)	47.	(c)	48.	(b)	49.	(b)	50.	(c)
51.	(a)	52.	(d)	53.	(d)	54.	(c)	55.	(a)
56.	(c)	57.	(c)	58.	(d)	59.	(d)	60.	(d)
61.	(c)	62.	(d)	63.	(c)	64.	(b)	65.	(c)
66.	(d)	67.	(b)	68.	(c)	69.	(d)	70.	(c)
71.	(c)	72.	(b)	73.	(d)	74.	(d)	75.	(a)

2 — PRACTICE SET

Time : 60 Min. **Max. Marks : 75**

DIRECTIONS (Qs. 1-2): *Find the odd word/letters/ number pair from the given alternatives.*

1. (a) GLOVES (b) SWEATER
   (c) SHAWL (d) UMBRELLA
2. (a) PORTRAIT (b) DRAW
   (c) PAINT (d) SKETCH

DIRECTIONS (Qs. 3): *A series is given, with one/two term missing. Choose the correct alternatives from the given ones that will complete the series.*

3. 6, 2, 9, 4, 12 , –, –
   (a) 6, 15 (b) 4, 13
   (c) 8, 24 (d) 13, 15
4. In a line, Naresh is 17th from the left & 22nd from the right. How many students are there in the line ?
   (a) 40 (b) 38
   (c) 39 (d) 37
5. Some equations have been solved on the basis of certain system. Find the correct answer for the unsolved equations on that basis ?
   If $72 \times 19 = 23$, $13 \times 48 = 35$ and $16 \times 43 = 18$ then $39 \times 22 = ?$
   (a) 27 (b) 51
   (c) 31 (d) 21
6. Which one set of letters when sequentially placed at the gaps in the given letter series shall complete it ?
   ab_cba_bcc_aabccb_ _ bccba
   (a) abbac (b) cccab
   (c) cabaa (d) abcab
7. If LISTEN is coded as 593417 then SILENT is code as :
   (a) 591734 (b) 391754
   (c) 591743 (d) 395174
8. Find out the set of numbers amongst the four sets of numbers given in the alternative which is most like the set given in the question. (12, 24, 144)

   (a) (15, 45, 90) (b) (10, 25, 100)
   (c) (14, 28, 112) (d) (13, 26, 169)
9. In a class of 45, Neha's rank is 15th from first, what is her rank from the last ?
   (a) 30 (b) 32
   (c) 33 (d) 31
10. If $+$ means $\div$, $\div$ means $\times$, and $\times$ means $+$, then following will be :
    $64 + 8 \times 32 \div 4$
    (a) 128 (b) 160
    (c) 136 (d) 144
11. Find the wrong number in the given series ?
    15, 28, 30, 39, 48
    (a) 28 (b) 15
    (c) 30 (d) 39
12. The average of 13 results is 70. The average of first seven is 65 and that of the last seven is 75, the seventh result is :
    (a) 70 (b) 70.5
    (c) 68 (d) 67
13. A contractor was engaged to construct a road in 16 days. After working for 12 days with 20 labours it was found that only 5/8th of the road had been constructed. To complete the work in stipulated time the number of extra labours required is :
    (a) 12 (b) 10
    (c) 18 (d) 16
14. The length of two parallel sides of a trapezium are 15 cm and 20 cm. If its area is 175 sq. cm, then its height is :
    (a) 10 cm (b) 15 cm
    (c) 25 cm (d) 20 cm
15. A train 150 m long passes a km stone in 30 seconds and another train of the same length travelling in opposite direction in 10 seconds. The speed of the second train is :
    (a) 125 km/hr (b) 25 km/hr
    (c) 90 km/hr (d) 75 km/hr

16. If water is freezed to become ice, its volume is increased by 10%, then if the ice is melted to water again, its volume will be decreased by :

(a) 8% (b) $9\dfrac{1}{2}\%$

(c) 9% (d) $9\dfrac{1}{11}\%$

17. A number of boys raised ₹ 12,544 for a famine fund, each boy has given as many rupees as there were boys. The number of boys was:

(a) 122 (b) 132
(c) 112 (d) 102

18. The current ages of Sonali and Monali are in the ratio 5 : 3. Five years from now, their ages will be in the ratio 10 : 7. Then, Monali's current age is:

(a) 9 years (b) 15 years
(c) 3 years (d) 5 years

19. In $\triangle ABC$, $AB = BC = K$, $AC = \sqrt{2}\,K$, then $\triangle ABC$ is a :

(a) Isosceles triangle (b) Right angled triangle
(c) Equilateral triangle (d) Right isosceles triangle

20. If $(2a - 1)^2 + (4b - 3)^2 + (4c + 5)^2 = 0$ then the value of

$$\dfrac{a^3 + b^3 + c^3 - 3abc}{a^2 + b^2 + c^2} \text{ is:}$$

(a) $1\dfrac{3}{8}$ (b) $3\dfrac{3}{8}$

(c) $2\dfrac{3}{8}$ (d) 0

DIRECTIONS (Qs.21-22): *Study the information given below and answer the questions following it:*

Mohan is son of Arun's father's sister. Prakash is son of Reva, who is mother of Vikash and grandmother of Arun. Pranab is father of Neela and grandfather of Mohan. Reva is wife of Pranab.

21. How is Mohan related to Reva?
(a) Grandson (b) Son
(c) Nephew (d) Data inadaequate

22. How is Vikash's wife related to Neela?
(a) Sister (b) Niece
(c) Sister-in-law (d) Data inadaequate

23. In a certain code language BEAM is written as 5 % * K and COME is written as $ 7 K %. How is BOMB written in that code?
(a) 5 % K 5 (b) 5 7 K 5
(c) $ 7 K $ (d) 5$%5

24. In a certain code language NATIONALISM is written as OINTANMSAIL. How is DEPARTMENTS written in that code?
(a) RADEPTSTMNE (b) RADPETSTMNE
(c) RADPESTMTNE (d) RADPETSTNME

DIRECTIONS (Qs.25): *In a certain code language meanings of some words are as follows:*

(i) *'pit na sa'* mean 'you are welcome'.
(ii) *'na ho pa la'* means 'they are very good'.
(iii) *'ka da la'* means 'who is good'?
(iv) *'od ho pit la'* means 'they welcome good people'.

25. Which of the following means 'people' in that code language?
(a) *ho* (b) *pit*
(c) *la* (d) *od*

26. Chromosomes are made up of
(a) DNA (b) Protein
(c) DNA and Protein (d) RNA

27. While the computer executes a program, the program is held in
(a) RAM (b) ROM
(c) Hard Disk (d) Floppy Disk

28. The danger signals are red while the eye is more sensitive to yellow because
(a) absorption in red is less than yellow and hence red is visible from a distance
(b) scattering in yellow light is less than red
(c) the wavelength of red light is more than yellow light
(d) none of the above reasons

29. Hemophilia is –
(a) caused by bacteria (b) caused by virus
(c) caused by pollutants (d) a hereditary defect

30. In human body, vitamin A is stored in the –
(a) liver (b) skin
(c) lung (d) kidney

31. Ondometer is a –
(a) Measuring instrument for distance covered by motor wheels
(b) Measuring instrument for frequency of electromagnetic waves
(c) Device for measuring sound intensity
(d) Measuring instrument for electric power

32. Which acid is used in rubber, textile, leather and electroplating industries ?
(a) Ethanoic acid (b) Methanoic acid
(c) Malanic acid (d) Butairic acid

33. To protect yourself from computer hacker intrusions you should install a______.
(a) Firewell (b) Mailer
(c) Macro (d) Script

34. For a person having hypermetropia, the near point is ……..
(a) Greater than 20 cm (b) Lesser than 25cm
(c) Greater than 25cm (d) Lesser than 30cm

35. Cryogenic is a science deals with
(a) High Temperatures (b) Low Pressure
(c) High Pressure (d) Low Temperature

36. Wood Spirit is which of the following ?
    (a) Ethyl Alcohol   (b) Propanol
    (c) Methyl Alcohol   (d) Butanol
37. Which of the following is chief source of Napthalene ?
    (a) Moth balls   (b) Mothflakes
    (c) Tar Camphor   (d) Coal tar
38. Study of crop production is ………………
    (a) Entology   (b) Ecology
    (c) Botany   (d) Agronomy
39. Bos Taurus is a scientific name of ………………..
    (a) Buffalo   (b) Horse
    (c) Cow   (d) Cat
40. …………….. includes all prokaryotic organism likes bacteria, cynobacterioa and archiobacteria
    (a) Animalia   (b) Protista
    (c) Monera   (d) Planatae
41. Which one of the following is not a computer language?
    (a) Cobol   (b) Visual Basic
    (c) HTML   (d) Netscape
42. Which one of the following is not a constituent of biogas?
    (a) Methane   (b) Carbon dioxide
    (c) Hydrogen   (d) Nitrogen dioxide
43. Bar is a unit of which one of the following?
    (a) Force   (b) Energy
    (c) Pressure   (d) Frequency
44. Which of the following metals are present in haemoglobin and chlorophyll, respectively?
    (a) Fe and Mg   (b) Fe and Zn
    (c) Mg and Zn   (d) Zn and Mg
45. A mother of blood group O has a group O child. What could be the blood group of father of the child?
    (a) Only O   (b) A or B or O
    (c) A or B   (d) Only AB
46. Which one of the following causes the chikungunia disease?
    (a) Bacteria   (b) Helminthic worm
    (c) Protozoan   (d) Virus
47. Which one of the following vitamins helps in clotting of blood?
    (a) Vitamin-A   (b) Vitamin-B_6
    (c) Vitamin-D   (d) Vitamin-K
48. What is the purpose of adding baking soda to dough?
    (a) To generate moisture
    (b) To give a good flavour
    (c) To give good colour
    (d) To generate carbon dioxide
49. Which one of the following glands in the human body stores iodine?
    (a) Parathyroid   (b) Thyroid
    (c) Pituitary   (d) Adrenal
50. Junk e-mail is also called ………………
    (a) Crap   (b) Spoof
    (c) Sniffer script   (d) Spam
51. A program designed to destroy data on your computer which can travel to 'infect' other computers is called a ………
    (a) Disease   (b) Torpedo
    (c) Hurricane   (d) Virus
52. Which one of the following glands produces the growth hormone (somatotrophin)?
    (a) Adrenal   (b) Pancreas
    (c) Pituitary   (d) Thyroid
53. Carbon dioxide is called a greenhouse gas because
    (a) its concentration remains always higher than other gases
    (b) it is used in photosynthesis
    (c) it absorbs infrared radiation .
    (d) it emits visible radiation
54. Laser is a device to produce
    (a) a beam of white light
    (b) coherent light
    (c) microwaves
    (d) X-rays
55. In the human body, Cowper's glands form a part of which one of the following system?
    (a) Digestive system
    (b) Endocrine system
    (c) Reproductive system
    (d) Nervous system
56. Mist is a result of which one of the following
    (a) Condensation   (b) Evaporation
    (c) Sublimation   (d) Saturation
57. Fat can be separated from milk in a cream separation because of
    (a) cohesive force   (b) gravitational force
    (c) centrifugal force   (d) centripetal force
58. Malaria in the human body is caused by which one of the following organisms?
    (a) Bacteria   (b) Virus
    (c) Mosquito   (d) Protozoan
59. The focal length of convex lens is
    (a) the same for all colours
    (b) shorter for blue light than for red
    (c) shorter for red light than for blue
    (d) maximum for yellow light
60. The headquaters of which one of the following organizations is not in Geneva?
    (a) Food and Agricultural Organisation
    (b) World Meteorological Organisation
    (c) World Health Organisation
    (d) World Trade Organisation
61. Which Amendment Act is referred as mini constitution?
    (a) 7th Constitutional Amendment Act, 1956
    (b) 24th Constitutional Amendment Act, 1971
    (c) 42nd Constitutional Amendment Act, 1976
    (d) 44th Consitutional Amendment Act, 1978

62. Inflation is caused by
    (a) decrease in production
    (b) increase in money supply and decrease in production
    (c) increase in money supply
    (d) increase in production

63. Arihant is a
    (a) Multi barrel rocket launcher
    (b) Airborne Early Warning and Control System
    (c) Unmarmed Combat Aerial Vehicle
    (d) Nuclear-powered ballistic missile submarine

64. The city of Prayag was named Allahabad - the city of Allah by
    (a) Aurangzeb   (b) Akbar
    (c) Shahjahan   (d) Bahadur Shah Zafar

65. Which Article of the Indian Constitution guarantees rights to arrested persons ?
    (a) Article 22   (b) Article 35
    (c) Article 20   (d) Article 42

66. .... is an active factor of production
    (a) Product   (b) Labour
    (c) Wages   (d) Price

67. Who was the last guru of the Sikhs ?
    (a) Guru Granth Sahib
    (b) Guru Gobind Singh
    (c) Guru Angad
    (d) Guru Amar Das

68. Tattvabodhini Sabha was founded by ……........ In 1839
    (a) Swami Vivekanand
    (b) Keshav Chandra Sen
    (c) Dabendranath Tagore
    (d) Swami Sahajanamd

69. After the revolt of 1857, British pursued the policy of ......
    (a) Divide and Policies
    (b) Rules and Regulation
    (c) Divide and Rule
    (d) Unity and Poliy

70. .... is the Kuchipudi dancer
    (a) Anupama Mohan   (b) Bimbavati Devi
    (c) Arush Mudgal   (d) Swapnasundari

71. The treaty of Mangalore was signed between
    (a) the English East India Company and Haidar Ali
    (b) the English East India Company and Tipu Sultan
    (c) Haidar Ali and the Zamorin of Calicut
    (d) the French East India Company and Tipu Sultan

72. World's largest Charkha (spinning wheels) that was unveiled at Terminal 3 of the Indira Gandhi International Airport (IGI), New Delhi is made of the teak wood of which country?
    (a) Burma   (b) Sri Lanka
    (c) Nepal   (d) Ukraine

73. In which of the following cities are located 3 zonal headquarters of Indian Railways?
    (a) Guwahati   (b) Mumbai
    (c) New Delhi   (d) Kolkata

74. Who of the following is known for having designed the first railway timetables?
    (a) George Bradman
    (b) George Bernard Shaw
    (c) George Bradshaw
    (d) George Brummel

75. Which HRD Ministry - appointed committee is drafting new National Education Policy (NEP)?
    (a) Ram Shanker Kureel committee
    (b) K Kasturisangan committee
    (c) V G S Rathore committee
    (d) KJ Alphonse committee

RESPONSE SHEET

1. Ⓐ Ⓑ Ⓒ Ⓓ	2. Ⓐ Ⓑ Ⓒ Ⓓ	3. Ⓐ Ⓑ Ⓒ Ⓓ	4. Ⓐ Ⓑ Ⓒ Ⓓ	5. Ⓐ Ⓑ Ⓒ Ⓓ
6. Ⓐ Ⓑ Ⓒ Ⓓ	7. Ⓐ Ⓑ Ⓒ Ⓓ	8. Ⓐ Ⓑ Ⓒ Ⓓ	9. Ⓐ Ⓑ Ⓒ Ⓓ	10. Ⓐ Ⓑ Ⓒ Ⓓ
11. Ⓐ Ⓑ Ⓒ Ⓓ	12. Ⓐ Ⓑ Ⓒ Ⓓ	13. Ⓐ Ⓑ Ⓒ Ⓓ	14. Ⓐ Ⓑ Ⓒ Ⓓ	15. Ⓐ Ⓑ Ⓒ Ⓓ
16. Ⓐ Ⓑ Ⓒ Ⓓ	17. Ⓐ Ⓑ Ⓒ Ⓓ	18. Ⓐ Ⓑ Ⓒ Ⓓ	19. Ⓐ Ⓑ Ⓒ Ⓓ	20. Ⓐ Ⓑ Ⓒ Ⓓ
21. Ⓐ Ⓑ Ⓒ Ⓓ	22. Ⓐ Ⓑ Ⓒ Ⓓ	23. Ⓐ Ⓑ Ⓒ Ⓓ	24. Ⓐ Ⓑ Ⓒ Ⓓ	25. Ⓐ Ⓑ Ⓒ Ⓓ
26. Ⓐ Ⓑ Ⓒ Ⓓ	27. Ⓐ Ⓑ Ⓒ Ⓓ	28. Ⓐ Ⓑ Ⓒ Ⓓ	29. Ⓐ Ⓑ Ⓒ Ⓓ	30. Ⓐ Ⓑ Ⓒ Ⓓ
31. Ⓐ Ⓑ Ⓒ Ⓓ	32. Ⓐ Ⓑ Ⓒ Ⓓ	33. Ⓐ Ⓑ Ⓒ Ⓓ	34. Ⓐ Ⓑ Ⓒ Ⓓ	35. Ⓐ Ⓑ Ⓒ Ⓓ
36. Ⓐ Ⓑ Ⓒ Ⓓ	37. Ⓐ Ⓑ Ⓒ Ⓓ	38. Ⓐ Ⓑ Ⓒ Ⓓ	39. Ⓐ Ⓑ Ⓒ Ⓓ	40. Ⓐ Ⓑ Ⓒ Ⓓ
41. Ⓐ Ⓑ Ⓒ Ⓓ	42. Ⓐ Ⓑ Ⓒ Ⓓ	43. Ⓐ Ⓑ Ⓒ Ⓓ	44. Ⓐ Ⓑ Ⓒ Ⓓ	45. Ⓐ Ⓑ Ⓒ Ⓓ
46. Ⓐ Ⓑ Ⓒ Ⓓ	47. Ⓐ Ⓑ Ⓒ Ⓓ	48. Ⓐ Ⓑ Ⓒ Ⓓ	49. Ⓐ Ⓑ Ⓒ Ⓓ	50. Ⓐ Ⓑ Ⓒ Ⓓ
51. Ⓐ Ⓑ Ⓒ Ⓓ	52. Ⓐ Ⓑ Ⓒ Ⓓ	53. Ⓐ Ⓑ Ⓒ Ⓓ	54. Ⓐ Ⓑ Ⓒ Ⓓ	55. Ⓐ Ⓑ Ⓒ Ⓓ
56. Ⓐ Ⓑ Ⓒ Ⓓ	57. Ⓐ Ⓑ Ⓒ Ⓓ	58. Ⓐ Ⓑ Ⓒ Ⓓ	59. Ⓐ Ⓑ Ⓒ Ⓓ	60. Ⓐ Ⓑ Ⓒ Ⓓ
61. Ⓐ Ⓑ Ⓒ Ⓓ	62. Ⓐ Ⓑ Ⓒ Ⓓ	63. Ⓐ Ⓑ Ⓒ Ⓓ	64. Ⓐ Ⓑ Ⓒ Ⓓ	65. Ⓐ Ⓑ Ⓒ Ⓓ
66. Ⓐ Ⓑ Ⓒ Ⓓ	67. Ⓐ Ⓑ Ⓒ Ⓓ	68. Ⓐ Ⓑ Ⓒ Ⓓ	69. Ⓐ Ⓑ Ⓒ Ⓓ	70. Ⓐ Ⓑ Ⓒ Ⓓ
71. Ⓐ Ⓑ Ⓒ Ⓓ	72. Ⓐ Ⓑ Ⓒ Ⓓ	73. Ⓐ Ⓑ Ⓒ Ⓓ	74. Ⓐ Ⓑ Ⓒ Ⓓ	75. Ⓐ Ⓑ Ⓒ Ⓓ

HINTS & SOLUTIONS

1. (d) Gloves, Sweater, shawl are worn in winter season while umbrella is used in rainy season.

2. (a) We used to draw, sketch or paint a portrait.

3. (a)

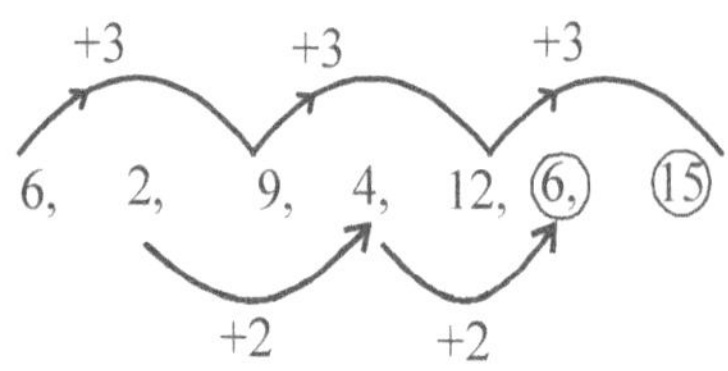

So, missing terms in the series are 6, 15.

4. (b) Naresh is 17th from left and 22nd from the right.
So, total number of students in the line $= 17 + 22 - 1 = 38$

5. (c) $72 \times 19 = 23 \Rightarrow (7 \times 2 + 1 \times 9 = 23)$
$13 \times 48 = 35 \Rightarrow (1 \times 3 + 4 \times 8 = 35)$
$16 \times 43 = 18 \Rightarrow (1 \times 6 + 4 \times 3 = 18)$
So, $39 \times 22 = ? \Rightarrow (3 \times 9 + 2 \times 2 = 31)$

6. (c) The series is
a b c c b a a b c c b a a b c c b a a b c c b a
So, missing set of letters is c a b a a.

7. (d)   L I S T E N
$\downarrow \downarrow \downarrow \downarrow \downarrow \downarrow$
5 9 3 4 1 7

So, code for word SILENT is 395174.

8. (d) $12 \xrightarrow{\times 2} 24, 12 \xrightarrow{\times 12} 144$

$13 \xrightarrow{\times 2} 26, 13 \xrightarrow{\times 13} 169$

So, (13, 26, 169) follows the same pattern.

9. (d) Total number of students in the class $= 45$.
Neha's rank from first $= 15^{th}$
So number of students from the last $= 45 - (1 + 14) = 30$
So, Neha's rank from the last is 31st.

10. (c) Writing the expression with actual sign
$64 \div 8 + 32 \times 4 = 8 + 128 = 136$

11. (c)

12. (a) Sum of 13 results $= 13 \times 70 = 910$
Sum of 7 results $= 7 \times 65 = 455$
Sum of last 7 results $= 7 \times 75 = 525$
So, 7th result $(455 + 525) - 910 = 70$

13. (d)

Days	No.of Labourers	Work done
12	20	5/8
4	?	$1 - \dfrac{5}{8} = \dfrac{3}{8}$

$M_1 D_1 \cdot W_2 = M_2 D_2 W_1$

$20 \times 12 \times \dfrac{3}{8} = M_2 \times 4 \times \dfrac{5}{8} \Rightarrow M_2 = \dfrac{20 \times 12 \times 3 \times 8}{4 \times 5 \times 8} = 36$

Hence, $36 - 20 = 16$ more men needed to complete the remaining work in 4 days.

14. (a) Area of trapezium

$= \dfrac{\text{Sum of length of parallel sides}}{2} \times \text{Height (H)}$

$175 = \dfrac{15 + 20}{2} \times H$

$H = \dfrac{175 \times 2}{35} = 10 \text{cm}.$

15. (c) Speed of first train $= \dfrac{150}{30} = 5 \text{m/sec}$

Let the speed of second train be x m/sec
Relative speed $= (5 + x)$ m /sec

$\therefore \dfrac{300}{5 + x} = 10$

$50 + 10x = 300$

$x = \dfrac{300 - 50}{10} = 25 \text{m/sec}$

$= 25 \times \dfrac{18}{5} = 90 \text{km/h}$

16. (d) Let initial volume $= 100$

Volume after increase $= 100 \times \dfrac{110}{100} = 110$

So, decrease $= \dfrac{110 - 100}{110} \times 100$

$= \dfrac{10}{110} \times 100 = 9\dfrac{1}{11} \%$

17. (c) Contribution of each boy $=$ Number of boys
Total contribution raised $= ₹\ 12544$

So, number of boys $= \sqrt{12544} = 112$

18. (a) Ratio of present ages of Sonali and Monali $= 5 : 3$
After 5 years ratio of ages of both girls $= 10:7$
Let actual present ages are 5x and 3x years.

$= \dfrac{5x + 5}{3x + 5} = \dfrac{10}{7}$

$= 35x + 35 = 30x + 50$

$5x = 15$

$x = 3$

So, Monali age $= 3 \times 3 = 9$ years

19. (d) In $\triangle ABC$

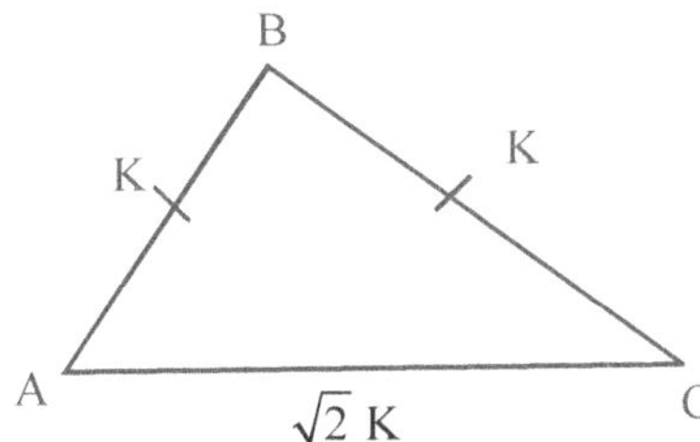

$AC = \sqrt{2}K$

$AC^2 = 2K^2$

$AC^2 = AB^2 + BC^2$

So $\triangle ABC$ is right angled triangle

So, in $\triangle ABC$

$$\frac{AB}{AC} = \frac{K}{\sqrt{2}K} = \frac{1}{\sqrt{2}}$$

So $\cos\theta = \dfrac{1}{\sqrt{2}}$

$\theta = 45°$

So, ABC, $\angle B = 90°$; $\angle C = 45°$; $\angle A = 45°$

So, ABC is right isoscles triangle.

20. (d) $(2a-1)^2 + (4b-3)^2 + (4c+5)^2 = 0$

$= 2a - 1 = 0;$ $4b - 3 = 0;$ $4c + 5 = 0$

$a = \dfrac{1}{2};$ $b = \dfrac{3}{4};$ $c = \dfrac{-5}{4}$

$a^3 + b^3 + c^3 - 3abc = (a + b + c)(a^2 + b^2 + c^2 - ab - bc - ca)$

But $a + b + c = 0$

So, $a^3 + b^3 + c^3 - 3abc = 0$

So, $\dfrac{a^3 + b^3 + c^3 - 3abc}{a^2 + b^2 + c^2} = 0$

(21-22) :

Pranab $\Leftrightarrow$ Reva

(+)   (−)

↓   ↓   ↓

Neela Prakash Vikash

(−)   (+)

↓

Mohan   Arun

(+)

21. (a)   22. (d)

23. (b) Here, $B \Rightarrow 5, E \Rightarrow \%, A \Rightarrow *,$

$M \Rightarrow K, C \Rightarrow \$, O \Rightarrow 7$

Therefore, BOMB $\Rightarrow$ 57K5

24. (b) Divide the word into two groups of five letters each. The first five letters are in group I and the last five letters are in group II. Now, for its coding the middle letters remain unchanged. While the letters in each group change their position as $1 \to 3, 2 \to 5, 3 \to 4,$ $4 \to 2$ and $5 \to 1.$

25. (d) *pit na sa* $\Rightarrow$ you are welcome   ...(i)

na ho pa la $\Rightarrow$ they are very good   ...(ii)

ka da la $\Rightarrow$ who is good   ...(iii)

od ho pit la $\Rightarrow$ they welcome good people   ...(iv)

Code for

(a) 'good' is *la* [from (ii) and (iv)].

(b) 'they' is *ho* [from (ii), (iv) and (III)].

(c) 'welcome' is *pit* [from (i) and (iv)].

(d) 'people' is *od* [by elimination in (iv)].

(e) 'are' is *na* [from (i) and (ii)].

(f) 'very' is *pa* [by elimination in (ii)].

26. (c)   27. (a)

28. (c) This is because the scattering in red light is less than that of yellow colour. The longest visible wavelength is red and the shortest is violet. The wavelength of red light is more than yellow light.

29. (d) Hemophilia is a **hereditary defect.**

30. (a) In human body, vitamin A is stored in the **liver.**

31. (b) Ondometer is a **measuring instrument for frequency of electromagnetic waves.**

32. (b) **Methanoic acid** is a colorless, pungent smelling liquid with a boiling point 373.5 K. Due to the presence of aldehyde-like hydrogen, it is powerful reducing agent.It reduces Tollen's reagent and Fehling's solution.

It is used in **rubber, textile, dyeing, leather** and **electroplating industries.**

33. (a)

34. (c) Hypermetropia Myopia is corrected by spectacles having concave lens.Near point of aperson suffering from hypermetropia is more than 25cm.

35. (d) Cryogenics is the study of the production and behaviour of materials at very low temperatures.

36. (c) Wood spirit is a poisonous colorless liquid used as a solvent and fuel; ingestion may cause blindness or death. Called also methyl or wood alcohol.

37. (d) Naphthalene is an organic compound with formula C 10H 8. It is the simplest polycyclic. Naphthalene is the most abundant single component of coal tar.

38. (d) Agronomy is the science and technology of producing and using plants for food, fuel, fiber, and land reclamation

39. (c) Cows are raised in many different countries around the world, mainly for the cowsnatural resources such as milk, meat

40. (c) Monera Kingdom- All the organisms of this kingdom are prokaryotes

41. (d) Netscape is an Internet browser that was popular during the early 1990's.

42. (d) Nitrogen dioxide (NO_2) is not a component of biogas.

43. (c) 1 Bar = 10^5 Pa. Both bar and Pa are the unit of pressure.

44. (a) Fe and Mg metals are present in haemoglobin and chlorophyll respectively.

45. (b) The blood group of father of the child could be A or B or O.

46. (d) Chikungunia is caused by chikenguniya virus which is an insect borne virus of genus *Alphavirus*. Symptoms show high fever, maculopapular rash, headache, etc.

47. (d) Vitamin-K adds in blood clotting. Vitamin-K acts as an essential cofactor for factor-II, VII, IX, X and also for proteins Z, C and S.

48. (d) Baking soda has sodium bicarbonate as the chief constituent. It decomposes on heating giving carbon dioxide. This causes dough, cakes, biscuits etc. to expand and become light.

49. (b) Thyroid gland in human body contains iodine. Deficiency of iodine creates goitre disease. Which is observed by the enlargement of larynx.

50. (d) 51. (d)

52. (c) Somatotrophin is produced by the anterior pituitary. It is a peptide hormone that induces growth, cell reproduction and regeneration.

53. (c) Greenhouse gases catch the sun's radiation on its way back into space and reflect some of that warmth back to Earth, increasing temperatures. Carbon dioxide is known as greenhouse gas because of their ability to trap and reflect the sun's radiation back to Earth.

54. (b) A laser is a device that emits coherent light through a process called stimulated emission.

55. (c) Cowper's gland is related to reproductive system. Cowper's gland is the ulbourethal gland found in human males. They are found in pair and secrete viscous secretion called pre ejaculate that helps in coitus.

56. (a) Mist is a thin fog resulting from condensation in the air near to the earth's surface.

57. (c) Centrifugal force separates fat from milk.

58. (d) Malaria is a mosquito borne disease of humans and other animals caused by Plasmodium protozoan. Severe disease is largely caused by Plasmodium falciparum whereas mild forms are due to *P vivax*, *P oval* and *P malariae*.

59. (b) The focal length of a convex lens is shorter for blue light than for red.

60. (a) 61. (c) 62. (b)

63. (d) Arihant is a Nuclear powered ballistic missile submarine.

64. (b) Emperor Akbar named Prayag as Allahabad - City of God- also called Allahabad in 1575 AD. The city of Allahabad is situated at the confluence of three rivers - Ganga, Yamuna and the invisible Saraswati. Every 12th year when the waters are felt to be especially purifying, Allahabad holds a much greater festival called Kumbh Mela. Built by Emperor Akbar in 1583 AD, the Allahbad fort stands on the banks of the river Yamuna near the confluence site i.e SANGAM.

65. (a) Article 22 proceeds to guarantee certain fundamental rights to every arrested person.

66. (b) Some of the important factors of production are: (i) Land (ii) Labour (iii) Capital (iv) Enterprnuer. Land is a passive factor whereas labour is an active factor of production

67. (b) Guru Gobind Singh was The Tenth Nanak or the last of the Sikhpreachers to live.

68. (c) The Tattwabodhinl Sabha ("Truth Propagating/ Searching Society") was a group started in Calcutta on 6 October 1839 as a splinter group of the Brahmo Samaj, reformers of Hinduism and Indian Society. The founding member was Debendranath Tagore

69. (c) After the revolt, the British pursued the policy of divide and rule, towards the general populace.

70. (a) Anupama Mohan is one of the best-known disciples of Kuchipudi.

71. (b) 72. (a) 73. (d) 74. (c) 75. (b)

3   PRACTICE SET

Time : 60 Min.　　　　　　　　　　　　**Max. Marks : 75**

---

1. In following series find 20th number
   $9, 5, 1, -3, -7, -11.....$
   - (a) −64
   - (b) −75
   - (c) −70
   - (d) −67

2. Which one set of letters when sequentially placed at the gaps in the given letter series shall complete it?
   _bbm_amb_m_a_bbm
   - (a) ambbm
   - (b) mabam
   - (c) abmab
   - (d) mbabm

3. If '−' stands for addition, '+' for multiplication, '÷' for subtraction and '×' for division, which one of the following equations is correct?
   - (a) $5 + 2 - 12 \times 6 \div 2 = 10$
   - (b) $5 \div 2 + 12 \times 6 - 2 = 4$
   - (c) $5 - 2 + 12 \times 6 \div 2 = 27$
   - (d) $5 + 2 - 12 \div 6 \times 2 = 13$

4. If FADE is coded as 3854 then how can GAGE be coded?
   - (a) 2834
   - (b) 2824
   - (c) 2814
   - (d) 1824

5. If SUNDAY= 18, MONSOON=21, YEAR=12, then THURSDAY=?
   - (a) 26
   - (b) 42
   - (c) 28
   - (d) 24

DIRECTIONS : *In question numbers 6 to 7, find the odd word/ letters/number pairs from the given alternatives.*

6.
   - (a) Tea : Beverages
   - (b) Legumes : Nodules
   - (c) Beans : Pulses
   - (d) Rice : Cereals

7.
   - (a) Knock
   - (b) Wrong
   - (c) Psychology
   - (d) Fast

DIRECTION : *In question numbers 8, a series is given, with one term missing. Choose the correct alternative from the given ones that will complete the series.*

8. $4, 11, 17, 22, \ ? \ , 29, 31, 32$
   - (a) 26
   - (b) 27
   - (c) 23
   - (d) 24

DIRECTIONS : *In question numbers 9, select the missing number from the given responses.*

9. 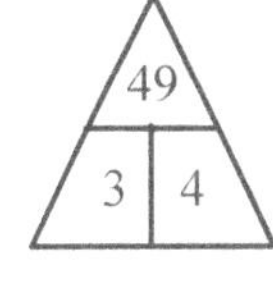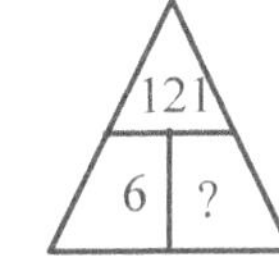

   - (a) 20
   - (b) 5
   - (c) 4
   - (d) 21

10. The average of 12 numbers is 15 and the average of the first two is 14. What is the average of the rest ?
    - (a) $15\dfrac{1}{5}$
    - (b) 14
    - (c) $14\dfrac{1}{5}$
    - (d) 15

11. The volume of a right circular cone which is obtained from a wooden cube of edge 4.2 dm wasting minimum among of wood is :
    - (a) 194.04 cu.dm
    - (b) 19.404 cu.dm
    - (c) 1940.4 cu.dm
    - (d) 19404 cu.dm

12. A number x is divisible by 7. When this number is divided by 8, 12 and 16, it leaves a remainder 3 in each case. The least value of x is :
    - (a) 149
    - (b) 150
    - (c) 147
    - (d) 148

13. A candidate who gets 20% marks in an examination, fails by 30 marks. But if he gets 32% marks, he gets 42 marks more than the minimum pass marks. Find the pass percentage of marks.
    - (a) 20%
    - (b) 25%
    - (c) 12%
    - (d) 52%

14. If Rahim deposited the same amount of ₹ x in a bank at the beginning of successive 3 years and the bank pays simple interest of 5% per annum, then the amount at his credit at the end of 3rd year will be :

(a) ₹ $\dfrac{1261}{400}$ x

(b) ₹ $\dfrac{21}{20}$ x

(c) ₹ $\dfrac{26481}{8000}$ x

(d) ₹ $\dfrac{861}{400}$ x

15. A merchant has 1000 kg sugar, part of which he sells at 8% profit and the rest at 18% profit. He gains 14% on he whole. The quantity sold at 8% profit is :

(a) 600 kg

(b) 640 kg

(c) 400 kg

(d) 560 kg

16. If $\dfrac{a}{b} + \dfrac{b}{a} = 2$, then the value of $a - b$ is :

(a) 2

(b) −1

(c) 0

(d) 1

17. The average expenditure of a man for the first five months is ₹ 1200 and for the next seven months is ₹ 1300. If he saves ₹ 2900 in that year, his monthly average income is :

(a) ₹ 1600

(b) ₹ 1700

(c) ₹ 1400

(d) ₹ 1500

DIRECTIONS *In question numbers 18 to 19, Study the following information and answer the questions given below.*

(a) '$A \div B$' means 'B is father of A'

(b) '$A \times B$' means 'A is sister of B'.

(c) $A + B$' means 'A is brother of B'.

(d) '$A - B$' means 'B is mother of A'.

18. Which of the following means R is nephew of T?

(a) $R + N - Q \times T$

(b) $R - Q \times N \times T$

(c) $R - N \times T$

(d) $T + M \div R$

19. Which of the following is/are redundant to answer the above question?

(a) (ii) only

(b) (i) only

(c) (i) and (iv) only

(d) Either (i) and (iii) or (ii) and (iv)

20. Pointing to a lady in the photograph, Shaloo said, "Her son's father is the son-in-law of my mother". How is Shaloo related to the lady?

(a) Aunt

(b) Sister

(b) Cousin

(d) Mother

21. In a certain code language OUTCOME is written as OQWWEQOE. How is REFRACT written in that code?

(a) RTGITCET

(b) RTGTICET

(c) RTGITECT

(c) RTGICTET

22. In a certain code language BORN is written as APQON and LACK is written as KBBLK. How will the word GRID be written in that code language?

(a) FQHCD

(b) FSHED

(c) HSJED

(d) FSHCD

23. In a certain code language STREAMLING is written as CGTVUHOJMN. How will the word PERIODICAL be written in that language?

(a) PJSFQMNBJE

(b) QKTGRMBDJE

(c) QKTGRMCEKF

(d) PJSFQMBDJE

24. In the following number series a **wrong** number is given. Find out the **wrong** number.

3 10 35 172 885 5346 37471

(a) 10

(b) 5346

(c) 885

(d) 35

25. What is the next number in this sequence ?

1, 3, 8, 19, 42, 89, ?

(a) 108

(b) 184

(c) 167

(d) 97

26. Many Fungi belonging to the genera Microporum Trichophyton and Epidermophyton are responsible for –

(a) Filarial

(b) Cancer

(c) Ringworms

(d) AIDS

27. Which organ of Human body is affected by Alzheimer disease ?

(a) Brain

(b) Bone Marrow

(c) Lung

(d) Intestine

28. What is the chemical name of vitamin E ?

(a) Calciferol

(b) Tocopherol

(c) Riboflavin

(d) Phylloquinone

29. 'Freon' used as refrigerants is chemically known as

(a) chlorinated hydrocarbon

(b) fluorinated hydrocarbon

(c) chlorofluoro hydrocarbon

(d) fluorinated aromatic compound

30. The humidity of air measured in percentage is called

(a) absolute humidity

(b) specific humidity

(c) relative humidity

(d) all of these

31. Bluetooth technology allows

(a) wireless communications between equipments

(b) signal transmission on mobile phones only

(c) landline to mobile phone communication

(d) satellite television communication

32. As which one of the following, does carbon occur in its purest form in nature?

(a) Carbon black

(b) Graphite

(c) Diamond

(d) Coal

33. Which one of the following diseases is caused by virus?

(a) Tuberculosis

(b) Typhoid

(c) Influenza

(d) Diphtheria

34. Movement of cell against concentration gradient is called
    - (a) osmosis
    - (b) active transport
    - (c) diffusion
    - (d) passive transport
35. Prokaryotic cells lack
    - (a) nucleolus
    - (b) nuclear membrane
    - (c) membrane bound by organelles
    - (d) All of these
36. Plants that grow in saline water are called
    - (a) halophytes
    - (b) hydrophytes
    - (c) mesophytes
    - (d) thallophytes
37. Which of the following is not an algae?
    - (a) Blue Algae
    - (b) Green Algae
    - (c) Red Algae
    - (d) Brown Algae
38. What is erythroblastosis fetalis?
    - (a) It is Haemolytic disease of the fetus and newborn.
    - (b) It is a type of Leukemia in the new born.
    - (c) It happens typically when father is Rh^-ve and mother is Rh^+ve.
    - (d) It is seen only in human beings.
39. 'Red Ink' is prepared from –
    - (a) Phenol
    - (b) Aniline
    - (c) Congo red
    - (d) Eosin
40. Which one is not micro nutrient?
    - (a) Iron (b)
    - Zinc
    - (c) Sulphur
    - (d) Manganese
41. An air bubble inside water behave as an:
    - (a) bifocal lens /
    - (b) convergent lens /
    - (c) divergent lens /
    - (d) cylindrical lens
42. ICAO stands for
    - (a) International Civil Aviation Organization
    - (b) Indian Corporation of Agriculture Organization
    - (c) Institute of Company of Accounts Organization
    - (d) None of the above
43. Which among the following blood protein regulates the amount of water in plasma?
    - (a) Globulin
    - (b) Albumin
    - (c) Fibrin
    - (d) Fibulin
44. Viruses are made up of
    - (a) Protein and lipids
    - (b) Nucleic and protein
    - (c) Lipids and carbohydrate
    - (d) Carbohydrate and Nucleic acid
45. Light year is the unit of
    - (a) Frequency
    - (b) Distance
    - (c) Energy
    - (d) Time
46. Which of the following physical quantities has no dimension?
    - (a) Force
    - (b) Momentum
    - (c) Impulse
    - (d) Angle
47. The working principle of a washing machine is :
    - (a) centrifugation
    - (b) dialysis
    - (c) reverse osmosis
    - (d) diffusion
48. Acid rain is caused by the pollution of environment by
    - (a) carbon dioxide and nitrogen
    - (b) carbon monoxide and carbon dioxide
    - (c) ozone and carbon dioxide
    - (d) nitrous oxide and sulphur dioxide
49. The wine is prepared by the process of
    - (a) fermentation
    - (b) catalysation
    - (c) conjugation
    - (d) displacement
50. Which one of the following hormones contains iodine?
    - (a) Thyroxine
    - (b) Testosterone
    - (c) Insulin
    - (d) Adrenaline
51. The major component of honey is
    - (a) glucose
    - (b) sucrose
    - (c) maltose
    - (d) fructose
52. In eye donation, which one of the following parts of donor's eye is utilized?
    - (a) Iris
    - (b) Lens
    - (c) Cornea
    - (d) Retina
53. Octopus is
    - (a) an arthropod
    - (b) an echinoderm
    - (c) a hemichordate
    - (d) a mollusc
54. Which one of the following is used to remove Astigmatism for a human eye?
    - (a) Concave lens
    - (b) Convex lens
    - (c) Cylindrical lens
    - (d) Prismatic lens
55. Which one of the following is a mixed fertilizer?
    - (a) Urea
    - (b) CAN
    - (c) Ammonium sulphate
    - (d) NPK
56. The most reactive among the halogens is
    - (a) Fluorine
    - (b) Chlorine
    - (c) Bromine
    - (d) Iodine
57. Which one of the following is a modified stem?
    - (a) Carrot
    - (b) Sweet potato
    - (c) Coconut
    - (d) Potato
58. 'Athlete's Foot' is a disease caused by
    - (a) Bacteria
    - (b) Fungus
    - (c) Protozoan
    - (d) Nematode

59. Which one of the following is present in chlorophyll which gives a green colour to plant leaves?
    (a) Calcium
    (b) Magnesium
    (c) Iron
    (d) Manganese
60. In human beings, the opening of the stomach into the small intestine is called
    (a) caecum
    (b) ileum
    (c) oeaophagus
    (d) pylorus
61. When had Muslim league passed the resolution "Divide and Quit" movement ?
    (a) 1945
    (b) 1943
    (c) 1944
    (d) None of these
62. 88th amendement of the Indian Constitution is related to –
    (a) The demarcation of new boundaries between states
    (b) The Constitution of the National Judicial Commission
    (c) Empowering the Centre to levy and appropriate Service tax
    (d) Readjustment of electroal constituencies on the basis of the population census 2001
63. The joint sitting of both Houses of Indian Parliament is held in connection with –
    (a) Constitutional amendment bill
    (b) Ordinary bill
    (c) Money bill
    (d) Election of the Vice – President of India
64. According to the Constitution of India, the Right to Property is a –
    (a) Fundamental Right
    (b) Directive Principle
    (c) Legal Right
    (d) Social Right
65. Babar declared himself as an emperor first at –
    (a) Samarqand
    (b) Farghana
    (c) Kabul
    (d) Panipat
66. Who is the author of "The Unseen Indira Gandhi"?
    (a) K.P. Mathur
    (b) Bilal Siddique
    (c) Anurag Mathur
    (d) N.R. Narayana Murthy
67. Which of the following is the largest zone in terms of route kilometers?
    (a) Western Railways
    (b) Eastern Railways
    (c) Northern Railways
    (d) Southern Railways
68. Which of the following is the largest marshalling yard in India (also the longest in Asia)?
    (a) Mughalsarai
    (b) Mathura
    (c) Itarasi
    (d) Guntakal
69. Who among the following had founded the Theosophical Society in the United States of America?
    (a) Swami Dayanand Saraswati
    (b) Madam Blavatsky
    (c) Madam Cama
    (d) Lala Hardayal
70. In which of the following years was the first Railway line between Bombay and Thane laid?
    (a) 1853   (b) 1854
    (c) 1856   (d) 1858
71. Which one of the following was the original name of Tansen, the famous musician in the court of Akbar?
    (a) Mahananda Pande (b) Lal Kalwant
    (c) Baz Bahadur   (d) Ramtanu Pande
72. Who drafted the Constitution of Muslim League, 'The Green Book'?
    (a) Rahamat Ali
    (b) Muhammad Iqbal
    (c) Muhammad Ali Jinnah
    (d) Maulana Muhammad Ali Jauhar
73. The 'Arthasastra' is a treatise on which one of the following?
    (a) Economics
    (b) Environment
    (c) Political Philosophy
    (d) Religion in Administration
74. In the Union Budget 2018, the Union government has announced to build a tunnel through the Sela Pass. The Sela pass in located in which state?
    (a) Sikkim
    (b) Arunachal Pradesh
    (c) Manipur
    (d) Himachal Pradesh
75. Which country is the partner country at the 33nd Surajkund International Craft Mela 2018?
    (a) Uzbekistan
    (b) Turkmenistan
    (c) Kyrgyzstan
    (d) Oman

RESPONSE SHEET

1. ⓐⓑⓒⓓ	2. ⓐⓑⓒⓓ	3. ⓐⓑⓒⓓ	4. ⓐⓑⓒⓓ	5. ⓐⓑⓒⓓ
6. ⓐⓑⓒⓓ	7. ⓐⓑⓒⓓ	8. ⓐⓑⓒⓓ	9. ⓐⓑⓒⓓ	10. ⓐⓑⓒⓓ
11. ⓐⓑⓒⓓ	12. ⓐⓑⓒⓓ	13. ⓐⓑⓒⓓ	14. ⓐⓑⓒⓓ	15. ⓐⓑⓒⓓ
16. ⓐⓑⓒⓓ	17. ⓐⓑⓒⓓ	18. ⓐⓑⓒⓓ	19. ⓐⓑⓒⓓ	20. ⓐⓑⓒⓓ
21. ⓐⓑⓒⓓ	22. ⓐⓑⓒⓓ	23. ⓐⓑⓒⓓ	24. ⓐⓑⓒⓓ	25. ⓐⓑⓒⓓ
26. ⓐⓑⓒⓓ	27. ⓐⓑⓒⓓ	28. ⓐⓑⓒⓓ	29. ⓐⓑⓒⓓ	30. ⓐⓑⓒⓓ
31. ⓐⓑⓒⓓ	32. ⓐⓑⓒⓓ	33. ⓐⓑⓒⓓ	34. ⓐⓑⓒⓓ	35. ⓐⓑⓒⓓ
36. ⓐⓑⓒⓓ	37. ⓐⓑⓒⓓ	38. ⓐⓑⓒⓓ	39. ⓐⓑⓒⓓ	40. ⓐⓑⓒⓓ
41. ⓐⓑⓒⓓ	42. ⓐⓑⓒⓓ	43. ⓐⓑⓒⓓ	44. ⓐⓑⓒⓓ	45. ⓐⓑⓒⓓ
46. ⓐⓑⓒⓓ	47. ⓐⓑⓒⓓ	48. ⓐⓑⓒⓓ	49. ⓐⓑⓒⓓ	50. ⓐⓑⓒⓓ
51. ⓐⓑⓒⓓ	52. ⓐⓑⓒⓓ	53. ⓐⓑⓒⓓ	54. ⓐⓑⓒⓓ	55. ⓐⓑⓒⓓ
56. ⓐⓑⓒⓓ	57. ⓐⓑⓒⓓ	58. ⓐⓑⓒⓓ	59. ⓐⓑⓒⓓ	60. ⓐⓑⓒⓓ
61. ⓐⓑⓒⓓ	62. ⓐⓑⓒⓓ	63. ⓐⓑⓒⓓ	64. ⓐⓑⓒⓓ	65. ⓐⓑⓒⓓ
66. ⓐⓑⓒⓓ	67. ⓐⓑⓒⓓ	68. ⓐⓑⓒⓓ	69. ⓐⓑⓒⓓ	70. ⓐⓑⓒⓓ
71. ⓐⓑⓒⓓ	72. ⓐⓑⓒⓓ	73. ⓐⓑⓒⓓ	74. ⓐⓑⓒⓓ	75. ⓐⓑⓒⓓ

HINTS & SOLUTIONS

1. (d) First term (a) of A.P. = 9
   Common difference (d) = –4
   So, 20th term $T_{20} = a + (20 - 1)(d)$
   $= 9 + (20 - 1)(-4)$
   $= 9 - 76$
   $= -67$

2. (b) The series is m̲bbm̲aa̲mb̲b̲m̲aa̲m̲bbm
   So, missing set of letters is mabam

3. (a) $5 + 2 - 12 \times 6 \div 2 = 10$
   Can be written in original signs as
   $5 \times 2 + 12 \div 6 - 2 = 10 + 2 - 2 = 10$

4. (b)   F   A   D   E
          ↓   ↓   ↓   ↓
          3   8   5   4

          G   A   G   E
   So,   ↓   ↓   ↓   ↓
          2   8   2   4

5. (d) SUNDAY
   No. of letters × 3 = 6 × 3 = 18
   MONSOON
   No. of letters × 3 = 7 × 3 = 21
   YEAR
   No. of letters × 3 = 4 × 3 = 12
   So THURSDAY
   No. of letters × 3 = 8 × 3 = 24

6. (b) Tea is a type of beverage, rice is type of cereal and beans is a type of pulse but nodule is source of nitrogen for legume plant.

7. (d) In all other except (d) first letter is silent.

8. (a) $4 \xrightarrow{+7} 11 \xrightarrow{+6} 17 \xrightarrow{+5} 22$
   $22 \xrightarrow{+4} 26$
   $32 \xleftarrow{+1} 31 \xleftarrow{+2} 29 \xleftarrow{+3} 26$

9. (b) $225 = (15)^2 \Rightarrow (8 + 7)^2$
   $49 = (7)^2 \Rightarrow (3 + 4)^2$
   $121 = (11)^2 \Rightarrow (6 + 5)^2$
   So missing number is 5.

10. (a) Average of rest two
   $= \dfrac{15 \times 12 - 14 \times 2}{10}$
   $= \dfrac{180 - 28}{10} = 15.2 = 15\dfrac{1}{5}$

11. (b) Volume of right circular cone $= \dfrac{1}{3}\pi r^2 h$

   Cone radius $= \dfrac{4.2}{2} = 2.1$ dm
   Cone height = 4.2 dm

   So volume of cone $= \dfrac{1}{3} \times \dfrac{22}{7} \times (2.1)^2 \times (4.2)$
   $= 19.404$ dm³.

12. (c) The least number which leaves a remainder 3 when divided by 8, 12 and 16 is (LCM of 8, 12, 16) k + 3.
   LCM of 8, 12, 16 is 48
   So least number is 48 k + 3
   48 k + 3 is divisible by 7 only when k = 3
   So, 48 k + 3 = 48 (3) + 3 = 147
   So, correct answer is 147.

13. (b) Let total marks on examination = x.

   So, minimum passing marks $= \dfrac{20}{100}x + 30$

   $\dfrac{20}{100}x + 30 = \dfrac{32}{100}x - 42$
   After solving, x = 600.
   ∴ Minimum passing marks
   $= 600 \times \dfrac{20}{100} + 30 = 150$

   ∴ Pass percentage marks $\dfrac{150}{600} \times 100 = 25\%$

14. (c) Amount deposited in first year = ₹ x
   Amount deposited in second year = ₹ x
   Amount deposited in third year = ₹ x
   Principle = ₹ 3x (₹ x for 3 year, ₹ x for 2 years and ₹ x for 1 year)

   Simple interest on ₹ x for 6 years $= x \times \dfrac{5}{100} \times 6 = 0.3x$

   So, amount at the end of 3rd year = 3x + 0.3x = 3.3x

   So, correct answer is (c) $= ₹ \dfrac{26481}{8000}x$

15. (c) By rule of alligation

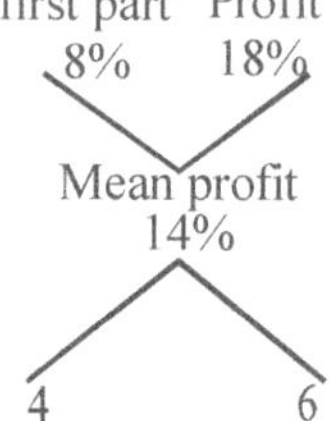

So ratio of Ist and 2nd part $= 4 : 6 = 2 : 3$

Quantity of Ist kind $= \dfrac{2}{5} \times 1000 = 400 \, kg$

16. (c) $\dfrac{a}{b} + \dfrac{b}{a} = 2$

$\Rightarrow \dfrac{a^2 + b^2}{ab} = 2$

$\Rightarrow \dfrac{(a-b)^2 + 2ab}{ab} = 2$

$(a-b)^2 = 2ab - 2ab$

$(a-b)^2 = 0$

$a - b = 0$

17. (d) Total expenditure for first 5 months $= 5 \times 1200$
$= ₹ 6000$

Total expenditure for next 7 months $= 7 \times 1300$
$= ₹ 9100$

Total saving $= ₹ 2900$
So, total yearly income $= 6000 + 9100 + 2900$
$= ₹ 18000$

Monthly average income $= \dfrac{18000}{12} = ₹ 1500$

18. (a) If R is nephew of T then the required equation must depict R as a male. Reject (b) and (c) because in these equations the symbol '—' denotes the sex of Q and N respectively. The sex of R remains unknown. Reject (d) because these equations depict R older then T. Now, check (a)

$Q_{(-)} \!—\! T$
$\qquad |$
$R_{(+)} \!—\! N$

Obviously, R is the nephew of T.

19. (b) $R + N - Q \times T$ is the required equation to answer the previous question. Here the used symbols are '+', '–' and '×'. Therefore, redundant part of the symbols given in the direction is statement (i).

20. (b) Lady's son's father is lady's husband. So, the lady's husband is the son-in-law of Shaloo's mother i.e., the lady is the daughter of Shaloo's mother. Thus, Shaloo is the lady's sister.

21. (a) The first letter is coded as two letters: the first remains unchanged and the second two letters forward as in English alphabet. The second, fourth, fifth and sixth letters are coded as two letters forward while the third letter is coded as three letters forward as in English alphabet. The last letter remains unchanged.

22. (b)

B	O	R	N	
−1	+1	−1	+1	
A	P	Q	O	N
L	A	C	K	

−1	+1	−1	+1	
K	B	B	L	K

Similarly,

G	R	I	D	
−1	+1	−1	+1	
F	S	H	E	D

23. (b) Split the word STREAMLING into two groups consisting of equal letters. You get STREA and MLING. Now, reverse both the groups. You get AERTS and GNILM. Now, write each letter of first group two places forward. You get CGTVU. Write each letter of second group one place forward. You get HOJMN. Now, join both the groups without changing the order of letters. You get CGTVUHOJMN.

Similarly, PERIODICAL is coded as

PERIODICAL $\rightarrow$ OIREPLACID $\rightarrow$ QKTGRMBDJE

24. (d) Series is $\times 2 + 2^2, \times 3 + 3^2, \times 4 + 4^2, ...$

25. (b) Each of the numbers is doubled and 1, 2, 3, 4, 5, 6 is added in turn, so $89 \times 2 + 6 = 184$.

26. (c)

27. (a) Alzheimer's disease affects the brain. The disease causes degeneration of brain tissues and nerve cells.

28. (b) Chemical namee of Vitamin E is Tocopherols.

29. (c) Chlorofluoro carbon (CF_2Cl_2) is also known as freon. It is used as refrigerants in refrigerators and air conditions. It is also used as propellant in aerosols and foams.

30. (c) The amount of water vapour in the air at any given time is usually less than that required to saturate the air. The relative humidity is the percent of saturation humidity, generally calculated in relation to saturated vapour density.

$$Relative\ Humidity = \dfrac{actual\ vapor\ density}{saturation\ vapor\ density} \times 100\%$$

31. (a) Bluetooth technology allows wireless communications between equipments.

32. (c) Diamond occurs in its purest form of carbon black in nature.

33. (c) Influenza is caused by virus and all other three diseases are bacterial, Influenza, generally called flu, is an infectious disease caused by RNA viruses of family Orthomyxoviridae.

34. (b) 35. (d) 36. (a)

37. (a) Blue-green algae or Cyanobacteria are microscopic cells that grow naturally in Australian fresh and salt waters. They are a type of bacteria, but in some ways act like plants by using sunlight to manufacture carbohydrates from carbon dioxide and water, a process known as photosynthesis. In doing so, they release oxygen. They grow in dams, rivers, creeks, reservoirs, lakes and even hot springs.

38. (a)

39. (d) Eosin is a dye used to prepare red ink.

40. (c)

41. (c) The air bubble will behave as a diverging lens due to its bulging curvature.

42. (a) 43. (b) 44. (b) 45. (b) 46. (d)

47. (a) Washing machine works on the principle of centrifugation. Centrifugation is a process that involves the use of the centrifugal force for the separation of mixtures with a centrifuge, used in industry and in laboratory settings. More-dense components of the mixture migrate away from the axis of the centrifuge, while less-dense components of the mixture migrate towards the axis.

48. (a) Fuel value can be expressed in terms of calorific value of fuel. The calorific value of a fuel is the amount of heat produced by burning 1 kg of fuel. Hydrogen has the highest calorific value of (141,790 KJ/kg) thus have highest fuel value. Calorific value of charcoal, natural gas and gasoline are (29,600; 43,000; 47,300 kJ/kg) respectively. Natural gas majorly consists of methane.

49. (a)

50. (a) Thyroxine hormone and tri-iodothyronine hormone are secreted by thyroid follicular cells of thyroid gland. The major component of thyroxine hormone is iodine. Deficiency of iodine causes goitre in human.

51. (d) The major component of honey is fructose.
Composition of honey in (percentage)

Fructose	– 38.2	Sucrose	– 1.5
Glucose	– 31	Minerals	– 0.5
Water	– 17.1		
Maltose	– 7.2		
Carbohydrate	– 4.2		

52. (c) Generally blindness is caused by the dryness and hardness of cornea. Cornea is a clear layer which helps passing of light. It is an outer layer and can be transfer from one person to another.

53. (d) Octopus is an animal of class-Cephalopoda and phylum Mollusca. The shell is absent. It is found at bottom of the sea. It kills its prey with poisonous saliva. It can change its colour.

54. (c) In Astigmatism, eye cannot see objects in two orthogonal directions clearly simultaneously. This abnormality is removed by using cylindrical lens.

55. (d) Fertilizers are those compounds which provide essential primary nutrients (nitrogen, phosphorus and potassium) required for healthy growth of plants and crops. Nitrogeneous fertilizer provide nitrogen, phosphatic fertilizer provide phosphorus whereas potassh fertilizer provide potassium to soil.
NPK fertilizers are mixed fertilizers. They provide all three essential nutrients (nitrogen, phosphorus and potassium). NPK fertilizers contains nitrogen, phosphorus and potassium in different proportion depending upon the requirement of soil.

56. (a) Fluorine is the most reactive among all halogens. However the reactivity deceases from F_2 to I_2 (from top to bottom of group) may be attributed to
(1)   Low dissociation enthalpies
(2)   High electron affinities

57. (d) Potato tuber bears buds in small pits known as eyes. Buds develops to branches. Some of the branches become green, erect & leafy stems that grow horizontally under ground.

58. (b) Athlete's Foot disease is caused by parasitic fungus of genus Trichophyton. Scaling, flaking and itching of affected areas are the symptoms of this disease. This disease transmitted in moist areas where people walk bare foot.

59. (b) Chlorophyll is a tetrapyrole ring system that chelate the magnesium ion. The tetrapyrole ring system that chelates this magnesium shows a conjugated double bond. This bond provide the light absorption feature to chlorophyll and gives it green colour.

60. (d) The stomach is divided into two parts fundic and pyloric region. The pyloric region opens into small intestine through pyloric valve of pylorus.

61. (b) The communal question had become a baffling one as the Muslim League tightened its demand for Pakistan. Against the congress demand of "quit India", the Muslim League's new slogan was "Divide and quit". On March 21, 1943, Muslim League observed as Pakistan Day.

62. (c) 63. (b)

64. (c) The Indian Constitution does not recognize the property right as a fundamental right. In the year 1977, the 44th amendment eliminated the right to acquire, hold and dispose of property as a fundamental right. However, in another part of the Constitution, Article 300 (a) was inserted to affirm that no person shall be deprived of his property by the authority of law.

65. (d) Babur declared himself as the emperor at Panipat.

66. (a) The book "The Unseen Indira Gandhi" has been authored by Dr. KP Mathur, who was the personal physician of the former Prime Minister Indira Gandhi for nearly 20 years till her assassination in 1984. The foreword of the book was written by her granddaughter Priyanka Gandhi Vadra. The book provides some interesting peeps into the responses of Mrs. Gandhi's to challenges both personal and political.

67. (c) 68. (a)

69. (b) The Theosophical Society was formed by Helena Petrovna Blavatsky, Henry Steel Olcott, William Quan Judge and others in November 1875 in New York. The aim of the society was to promote spiritual principles and search for truth known as Theosophy.

70. (a) The country's first railway, built by the Great Indian Peninsula Railway (GIPR), opened in 1853 between Bombay and Thane.

71. (d) Tansen, who was one of the nine jewels or navaratnas in the court of Emperor Akbar, was born in a Hindu family at Behat near Gwalior in the Madhya Pradesh state. Father of Tansen was Makarand Pande, who named him Ramtanu Pandey.

72. (c) Muhammad Ali Jinnah drafted the constitution of Muslim league 'The green Book'.

73. (c) The Arthasastra is a treatise on Political philosophy. The book, written in Sanskrit, discusses theories and principles of governing a state. The meaning of Arthashastrais 'Science of Polity'. It is written by Kautilya.

74. (b) 75. (c)

4   PRACTICE SET

INSTRUCTIONS

1. This practice set consists of 75 questions will be of objective type with multiple choices.

2. Practice set have MCQs from Mathematics, General Intelligence & Reasoning, General Science and General Awareness on Current Affairs.

3. Duration of practice set is 60 minutes.

Time : 60 Min.   **Max. Marks : 75**

DIRECTIONS : *In Question Nos. 1 to 2, find the odd word/number letters/number pair from the given alternatives.*

1. (a) Chameleon   (b) Crocodile
   (c) Alligator   (d) Locust
2. (a) Polaris   (b) Nike
   (c) Crux   (d) Phoenix
3. Find the wrong number in the series :
   30, 27, 36, 45, 72
   (a) 30   (b) 27
   (c) 36   (d) 72

DIRECTIONS : *In Question Nos. 4, a series is given, with one term missing. Choose the correct alternative from the given ones that will complete the series.*

4. 3, 15, 4, 16, 5, 17, 6, **?**, 7
   (a) 12   (b) 13
   (c) 15   (d) 18
5. Which one set of letters when sequentially placed at the gaps in the given letter series shall complete it ?
   _ cb _ ca _ bacb _ ca _ bac _ d .
   (a) baddddb   (b) bbbddd
   (c) addddb   (d) addbbb
6. If PALE is coded as 2134, EARTH is coded as 41590, how is PEARL coded as ?
   (a) 29530   (b) 24153
   (c) 25413   (d) 25430
7. If the word PRINCIPAL is written as LAPICNIRP, how ADOLESCENCE can be written in that code ?
   (a) ECNCESELODA   (b) ECNECSLEODA
   (c) ECNSCEELODA   (d) ECNECSELODA
8. The H.C.F. and L.C.M. of two numbers are 44 and 264 respectively. If the first number is divided by 2, the quotient is 44. The other number is
   (a) 147   (b) 528
   (c) 132   (d) 264

9. A teacher wants to arrange his students in an equal number of rows and columns. If there are 1369 students, the number of students in the last row are
   (a) 37   (b) 33
   (c) 63   (d) 47
10. The marked price of a saree is ₹ 200. After allowing a discount of 20% on the marked price, the shopkeeper makes a profit of ₹ 16. Find the gain percent.
    (a) $11\frac{1}{9}\%$ (b) $9\frac{1}{11}\%$
    (c) 11%   (d) 8%
11. The marked price of an item is twice the cost price. For a gain of 15%, the discount should be
    (a) 7.5%   (b) 20.5%   (c) 32.5%   (d) 42.5%
12. If the sum of the dimensions of a rectangular parallelepiped is 24 cm and the length of the diagonal is 15 cm, then the total surface area of it is
    (a) 420 cm^2 (b) 275 cm^2
    (c) 351 cm^2 (d) 378 cm^2
13. A total profit of ₹ 3,600 is to be distributed amongst A, B and C such that A : B = 5 : 4 and B : C = 8 : 9. The share of C in the profit is
    (a) ₹ 1,200   (b) ₹ 1,500
    (c) ₹ 1,650   (d) ₹ 1,700
14. The average salary of all the workers in a workshop is ₹ 8,000. The average salary of 7 technicians is ₹ 12,000 and the average salary of the rest is ₹ 6,000. The total number of workers in the workshop is
    (a) 20   (b) 21
    (c) 22   (d) 23
15. 3 years ago the average age of a family of 5 members was 17 years. A baby having been born, the average age of the family is the same today. The present age of the baby is
    (a) 1 year   (b) 1½ years
    (c) 2 years   (d) 3 years

16. The area of a square park is 25 sq. km. The time taken to complete a round of the field once, at a speed of 3 km/hour is
    (a) 4 hours 60 minutes   (b) 4 hours 50 minutes
    (c) 6 hours 40 minutes   (d) 5 hours 40 minutes

17. Deepak said to Nitin, "That boy playing with the football is the younger of the two brothers of the daughter of my father's wife." How is the boy playing football related to Deepak?
    (a) Son   (b) Brother
    (c) Causin   (d) Nephew

18. A is the mother of B. C is the father of B and C has 3 children. On the basis of this information, find out which of the following relations is correct :
    (a) C has three daughters.
    (b) C has three sons.
    (c) B is the son.
    (d) None of these.

19. M is to the East of D, F is to the South of D and K is to the West of F. M is in which direction with respect to K?
    (a) South-West   (b) North-West
    (c) North-East   (d) South-East

20. Find the missing number in the given question.

8	9	10
5	4	3
28	?	16
12	25	14

    (a) 28   (b) 11
    (c) 32   (d) 18

21. If 'green' is called `white', `white' is called `yellow , 'yellow' is called `red', `red' is called `orange', then which of the following represents the colour of sunflower?
    (a) red   (b) yellow
    (c) brown   (d) indigo

22. In a certain code language GEOPHYSICS is written as IOPDHZRJBT. How is ALTIMETER written in that code'?
    (a) NHULBFSDQT   (b) NIUKBFSDQT
    (c) NHUKCFSDQT   (d) None of these

23. In a certain code 'FEAR' is written as ' + × ÷ * ' and 'READ' is written as '* × ÷ $ '. How is 'FADE' written in that code?
    (a) + ÷ $ ×   (b) × ÷ + $
    (c) $ ÷ + *   (d) ÷ $ + ×

24. Fifteen children are standing in a row facing north. Ravi is to the immediate left of Prabha and is eighth from the left end. Arjun is second from the right end. Which of the following statements is not true?
    (a) Prabha is 7th from right end.
    (b) There are four children between Prabha and Arjun.
    (c) There are five children between Ravi and Arjun.
    (d) Arjun is 13th from the left end.

25. In a class some students play cricket only, some other students play football only and remaining $\frac{1}{6}$th students play both cricket and football. Which of the following statements is **definitely true?**

    (a) Two-thirds of the students play cricket.
    (b) Three-fourths of the students play football only.
    (c) One-thirds of the students play football only.
    (d) None of these

26. In context of Mauryan period 'Gudhapurushas' referred to –
    (a) Detectives
    (b) Blacksmith
    (c) Army commander
    (d) Chariot rider

27. Which among the following parts of a plant is involved in gaseous exchange?
    (a) Stomata
    (b) Lenticels
    (c) Vacuoles
    (d) Stomata & Lenticels

28. Graphite is used in nuclear reactors for –
    (a) reducing the speed of fast neutrons
    (b) cooling the reactor
    (c) absorbing neutrons
    (d) None of the above

29. Which of the following book is centred on "Environment"?
    (a) The Late, Great Planet Earth
    (b) Silent Spring
    (c) Here I stand
    (d) And then One Day

30. If an insect that feeds on feces sits on the food you are going to eat, you are most likely to be infected by which disease?
    (a) Tuberculosis
    (b) Cholera
    (c) Typhoid
    (d) Hepatitis B

31. Which of the following is not an antibiotics?
    (a) Penicilin   (b) Ampicilin
    (c) Streptomycin   (d) Aspirin

32. Mitosis is a type of cell division in which –
    (a) The chromosomes maintain their original number.
    (b) The chromosome number is reduced to half.
    (c) The Chromosome number is doubled.
    (d) The chromosome number is reduced to one fourth.

33. Ginger is an example of –
    (a) Modified Node
    (b) Modified Root
    (c) Modified Stem
    (d) Tap Root

34. Before X-ray examination (coloured X-ray) of the stomach, patients are given suitable salt of barium because.
    (a) barium is a good absorber of X-rays and helps stomach to appear clearly
    (b) barium salts are white in colour and this helps stomach to appear clearly
    (c) barium allows X-rays to pass through the stomach
    (d) barium salts are easily available

35. If the length of a simple pendulum is halved then its period of oscillation is –
    (a) doubled
    (b) halved
    (c) increased by a factor $\sqrt{2}$
    (d) decreased by a factor $\sqrt{2}$

36. Scientists has genetically modified photosynthesis process to increase crop yield by
    (a) 11 Percent   (b) 12 Percent
    (c) 15 Percent   (d) 17 Percent

37. A satellite in vacuum -
    (a) is kept in orbit by remote control
    (b) is kept in orbit by retro-rocket
    (c) derives energy from gravitational field
    (d) does not require any energy for orbiting

38. The nuclear force is -
    (a) Short range repulsive force
    (b) Short range attractive force
    (c) Long range repulsive force
    (d) Long range attractive force

39. The required DC voltage for arc welding is -
    (a) 6 to 9 V   (b) 50 to 60 V
    (c) 200 to 250 V   (d) 90 to 100 V

40. For a body floating in water, the apparent weight is equal to -
    (a) Actual weight of the body
    (b) Zero
    (c) Weight of the body minus weight of the liquid
    (d) Weight of the body plus upward thrust

41. An amplifier is said to suffer from distortion when its output is
    (a) low
    (b) different from input
    (c) noisy
    (d) larger than its input

42. Sound in TV is modulating -
    (a) AM   (b) FM
    (c) PCM   (d) PM

43. The threshold frequency is the frequency below which -
    (a) photo current is constant
    (b) photo current increases with voltage
    (c) photo current decreases with voltage
    (d) photo electric emission is not possible

44. The damage of the human body due to radiation (χ-rays or γ-rays etc,) is measured in -
    (a) Rads   (b) Rems
    (c) Roentgen   (d) Curie

45. The mass number of a nucleus is
    (a) always less than its atomic number
    (b) the sum of the number of protons and neutrons present in the nucleus
    (c) always more than the atomic weight
    (d) a fraction

46. The nucleus of an atom consists of
    (a) electrons and neutrons
    (b) electrons and protons
    (c) protons and neutrons
    (d) All of the above

47. What is the full form of 'http' ?
    (a) Hypo Test Transfer Protocol
    (b) Hyper Text Transfer Protocol
    (c) Hyper Test Transfer Proxy
    (d) None of these

48. LAN stands for ....
    (a) Local Access Network
    (b) Local Area Network
    (c) Logical access network
    (d) Logical Area Network

49. What will happen if a transformer is connected to D.C. voltage?
    (a) It will induce more voltage
    (b) Its reactance will increase
    (c) The primary will burn out and no emf will be induced in the secondary
    (d) None of these

50. The unit of noise pollution (level) is -
    (a) decibel   (b) decimal
    (c) ppm   (d) None of these

51. Transition ions absorb light in -
    (a) visible region   (b) infrared region
    (c) ultraviolet region (d) microwave region

52. According to kinetic theory gases, at the temperature absolute zero, the gas molecules -
    (a) Start movement
    (b) Become massless
    (c) Start emitting light
    (d) Stop movement

53. Electric fuse wire is made of alloys because alloys -
    (a) Have low melting point
    (b) Have high melting point
    (c) Are economical
    (d) Do not get heated easily

54. Which two colours can be mixed to make green?
    (a) Yellow and Balck   (b) Yellow and Blue
    (c) Orange and Violet (d) Purple and Yellow

55. The freezing point of fresh water is -
    (a) 0°C   (b) 4°C
    (c) 3°C   (d) 5°C

56. Flywheel is an important part of a steam engine because it -
    (a) gives strength to the engine
    (b) accelerates the speed of the engine
    (c) helps the engine in keeping the speed uniform
    (d) decreases the moment of inertia

57. Study of Fossils is known as?
    (a) Paleantology   (b) Petrology
    (c) Seismology   (d) None of the above

58. Supersonic plane fly with the speed
    (a) less than the speed of sound
    (b) of sound
    (c) greater than the speed of sound
    (d) of light

59. Rainbow is due to
    (a) absorption of sunlight in minute water droplets
    (b) diffusion of sunlight through water droplets
    (c) ionisation of water deposits
    (d) refraction and reflection of sunlight by water droplets
60. Stars which appear single to the naked eye but are double when seen through a telescope are
    (a) novas & supernovas (b) binaries
    (c) asteroids   (d) quasars
61. The Four Varnas are described in which Mandal of Rigveda?
    (a) First Mandal   (b) Third Mandal
    (c) Tenth Mandal   (d) Ninth Mandal
62. The Chief of State Election Commission is appointed by –
    (a) The President
    (b) The Governor
    (c) The committee of elected members of State Legislative Assembly
    (d) Election Commission of India
63. Any session of State Legislature is prorogated by –
    (a) Presiding officer of the house
    (b) The Chief Minister of the State
    (c) The Governor
    (d) None of the above
64. The right to 'equality before the law' contained in Article 14 of the Constitution of India is available to —
    (a) natural persons only
    (b) legal persons only
    (c) citizens of India
    (d) all persons whether natural or legal
65. Name the Viceroy who was killed in Andaman & Nicobar Island?
    (a) Lord Mayo   (b) Lord Elgin
    (c) Lord Hastings   (d) Lord Dalhousie
66. When did India become a member of the International Monetary Fund?
    (a) 1952   (b) 1950
    (c) 1947   (d) 1945
67. "Hopman cup" is related to which sports?
    (a) Football   (b) Lawn Tennis
    (c) Badminton   (d) Cricket
68. The famous national song 'Vande Mataram' was written by
    (a) Bankim Chandra Chatterji
    (b) Rabindrantha Tagore
    (c) Kamala Das
    (d) Sarojini Naidu
69. The first telegraph line between Calcutta and Agra was opened in
    (a) 1852   (b) 1853
    (c) 1854   (d) 1855
70. Which of the following is not evident at Mohenjodaro?
    (a) Pasupati seal
    (b) Great granary and great bath
    (c) Multi-pillared assembly hall
    (d) Evidence of double burials
71. When did Delhi first become capital of a kingdom?
    (a) At the time of Tomar dynasty
    (b) Tughlaq dynasty
    (c) Lodhi dynasty
    (d) None of these
72. First underground railway (Metro Railway) started in which year?
    (a) 1982   (b) 1989
    (c) 1984   (d) 1992
73. Shatabdi Express train introduced in
    (a) 1984   (b) 1988
    (c) 1990   (d) 1985
74. Who has been honoured with the 2018 Sahitya Akademi Bhasa Samman Award?
    (a) Thakazhi Sivasankara Pillai
    (b) Rahul Sankarnarayan
    (c) Shesh Anand Madhukar
    (d) Visvanatha Satyanarayana
75. Mary Kom has won gold in which weight category at the 2018 India Open boxing Tournament?
    (a) 64kg category
    (b) 60 kg category
    (c) 54 kg category
    (d) 48 kg category

RESPONSE SHEET

1. (a)(b)(c)(d)	2. (a)(b)(c)(d)	3. (a)(b)(c)(d)	4. (a)(b)(c)(d)	5. (a)(b)(c)(d)
6. (a)(b)(c)(d)	7. (a)(b)(c)(d)	8. (a)(b)(c)(d)	9. (a)(b)(c)(d)	10. (a)(b)(c)(d)
11. (a)(b)(c)(d)	12. (a)(b)(c)(d)	13. (a)(b)(c)(d)	14. (a)(b)(c)(d)	15. (a)(b)(c)(d)
16. (a)(b)(c)(d)	17. (a)(b)(c)(d)	18. (a)(b)(c)(d)	19. (a)(b)(c)(d)	20. (a)(b)(c)(d)
21. (a)(b)(c)(d)	22. (a)(b)(c)(d)	23. (a)(b)(c)(d)	24. (a)(b)(c)(d)	25. (a)(b)(c)(d)
26. (a)(b)(c)(d)	27. (a)(b)(c)(d)	28. (a)(b)(c)(d)	29. (a)(b)(c)(d)	30. (a)(b)(c)(d)
31. (a)(b)(c)(d)	32. (a)(b)(c)(d)	33. (a)(b)(c)(d)	34. (a)(b)(c)(d)	35. (a)(b)(c)(d)
36. (a)(b)(c)(d)	37. (a)(b)(c)(d)	38. (a)(b)(c)(d)	39. (a)(b)(c)(d)	40. (a)(b)(c)(d)
41. (a)(b)(c)(d)	42. (a)(b)(c)(d)	43. (a)(b)(c)(d)	44. (a)(b)(c)(d)	45. (a)(b)(c)(d)
46. (a)(b)(c)(d)	47. (a)(b)(c)(d)	48. (a)(b)(c)(d)	49. (a)(b)(c)(d)	50. (a)(b)(c)(d)
51. (a)(b)(c)(d)	52. (a)(b)(c)(d)	53. (a)(b)(c)(d)	54. (a)(b)(c)(d)	55. (a)(b)(c)(d)
56. (a)(b)(c)(d)	57. (a)(b)(c)(d)	58. (a)(b)(c)(d)	59. (a)(b)(c)(d)	60. (a)(b)(c)(d)
61. (a)(b)(c)(d)	62. (a)(b)(c)(d)	63. (a)(b)(c)(d)	64. (a)(b)(c)(d)	65. (a)(b)(c)(d)
66. (a)(b)(c)(d)	67. (a)(b)(c)(d)	68. (a)(b)(c)(d)	69. (a)(b)(c)(d)	70. (a)(b)(c)(d)
71. (a)(b)(c)(d)	72. (a)(b)(c)(d)	73. (a)(b)(c)(d)	74. (a)(b)(c)(d)	75. (a)(b)(c)(d)

HINTS & SOLUTIONS

1. (d) Except (d) all others are reptiles.
   While locust is a large insect.

2. (b) Except (b) all others mean the central point.

3. (a) $3 + 0 = 3$
   $2 + 7 = 9$
   $3 + 6 = 9$
   $4 + 5 = 9$
   $7 + 2 = 9$

4. (d) There are two series:

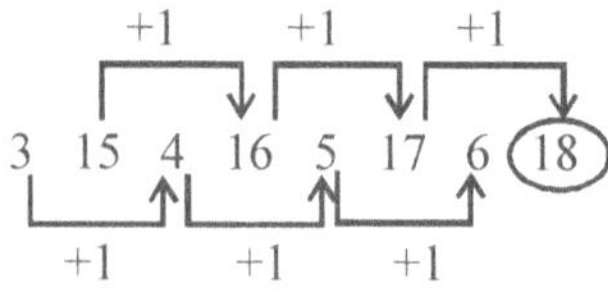

5. (c) $\underline{a}\,c\,b\,\underline{d}/$
   $c\,a\,\underline{d}\,b/$
   $a\,c\,b\,\underline{d}/$
   $c\,a\,\underline{d}\,b/$
   $a\,c\,\underline{b}\,d$

6. (b) P A L E R T H
   ↓ ↓ ↓ ↓ ↓ ↓ ↓
   2 1 3 4 5 9 0
   The code for PEARL is 24153

7. (d) Reversing the order $\dfrac{\text{P R I N C I P A L}}{\text{L A P I C N I R P}}\longrightarrow$

   Similarly

   Reversing the order $\dfrac{\text{A D O L E S C E N C E}}{\text{E C N E C S E L O D A}}\longrightarrow$

8. (c) First number $= 2 \times 44 = 88$

   Other number $= \dfrac{44 \times 264}{88} = 132$

9. (a) If they are equal number of rows and columns then,
   $\sqrt{1369} = 37$

10. (a) Selling price = Marked price – Discount
    $= 200 - 20\% \text{ of } 200 = 160$
    Cost Price $= 160 - 16 = 144$

    Gain% $= \dfrac{16}{144} \times 100 = \dfrac{100}{9}\% = 11\dfrac{1}{9}\%$

11. (d) Marked Price, M $= 2C$, where C is cost price for 15%

    gain, S.P. $= C + \dfrac{15}{100}C = 1.15C$

    Let discount be x%

    $2C - \dfrac{x}{100} \times 2C = 1.15C \Rightarrow x = 42.5\%$

12. (c) Let length, breadth and height of parallelopiped be l, b and h respectively.
    $l + b + h = 24$ cm

    $\sqrt{l^2 + b^2 + h^2} = 15\text{cm} \Rightarrow l^2 + b^2 + h^2 = 225$ cm^2
    $(l + b + h)^2 - 2(lb + hb + lh) = 225$
    $(24)^2 - 225 = 2(lb + bh + hl)$
    $351 = 2\,(lb + bh + hl)$
    Total surface area is 351 cm^2.

13. (a) A : B = 5 : 4, B : C = 8 : 9
    A : B : C = $5 \times 8 : 4 \times 8 : 4 \times 9 = 40 : 32 : 36$
    A : B : C = 10 : 8 : 9

    Share of C in the profit = $\dfrac{9}{10 + 8 + 9} \times 3600 = ₹\,1{,}200$

14. (b) Let total number of workers be n
    total salary of all workers = 8000 n
    total salary of 7 technicians = $7 \times 12000 = 84{,}000$
    total salary of remaining workers = $(n - 7) \times 6000$
    $84000 + (n - 7) \times 6000 = 8000\,n$
    $84 + 6n - 42 = 8n$
    $42 = 2n$
    $n = 21$

15. (c) Let total age of family be S years
    3 years ago, total age = $S - 3 \times 5 = S - 15$

    $\dfrac{S - 15}{5} = 17$

    $S = 17 \times 5 + 15 = 100$
    Let present age of baby be x years

    $\dfrac{S + x}{6} = 17$

    $100 + x = 17 \times 6$
    $x = 102 - 100 = 2$ years

16. (c) Side of square park = $\sqrt{25}$ km = 5 km
    Perimeter of park = $4 \times 5 = 20$ km

    Time taken = $\dfrac{20\text{km}}{3\text{ km}/\text{h}} = 6$ hours 40 minutes

17. (b) Father's wife — Mother; Mother's daughter — Sister; Sister's younger brother — His brother. So, the boy is Deepak's brother.

18. (d) A — Mother — C — Father — B
    ∵ C has three children but we can't say that he has three daughters or three sons.
    So, options (a) and (b) are incorrect.
    Also, we don't know that B is a boy or girl.
    So, option (c) is also incorrect.

19. (c)

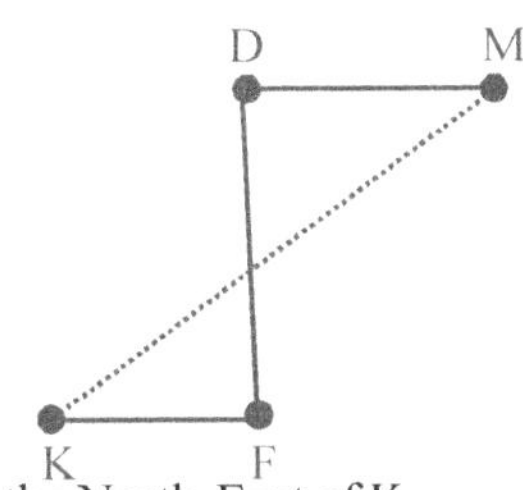

   M is to the North-East of K.

20. (b) $8 \times 5 - 12 = 28$
   $9 \times 4 - 25 = 11$
   $10 \times 3 - 14 = 16$

21. (a) The colour of sunflower is yellow and yellow is called 'red'. Hence sunflower is red.

22. (d) Divide the word into two halves. Now, reverse the order of the letters of the first half and replace odd positioned letters with one letter forward and even positioned letter with one letter backward as in English alphabet.

   For the second half letters, the odd-positioned letters are coded as one letter forward and even-positioned letters are coded as one letter backward' as in English alphabet.

23. (a) It is clear that $F \to +, A \to \div, D \to \$$ and $E \to \times$

   $\therefore$ FADE $\to + \div \$ \times$

24. (d) 8th   9th   14th
   Ravi   Prabha   Arjun

25. (d) We can't find the proportion of those students out of the total students who play only cricket. Similarly, we can't find the proportion of those students out of the total students who play only football. But 5/6th of the total strength play either cricket only or football only.

26.	(a)	27.	(d)	28.	(a)	29.	(b)	30.	(c)
31.	(d)	32.	(c)	33.	(c)	34.	(a)	35.	(d)
36.	(c)	37.	(d)	38.	(b)	39.	(c)	40.	(c)
41.	(c)	42.	(a)	43.	(d)	44.	(a)	45.	(b)
46.	(c)	47.	(b)	48.	(b)	49.	(c)	50.	(a)
51.	(a)	52.	(d)	53.	(a)	54.	(b)	55.	(a)
56.	(c)	57.	(a)	58.	(c)	59.	(d)	60.	(b)

61. (c) The four classes were mentioned in Purush Sukta in 10th mandal of Rigveda.

62. (b) According to the Article 243 K (1), the chief of the State Election Commission is appointed by the Governor.

63. (c) Any session of the state legislation is prorogated by the Governor.

64. (d) The right to equality before the law contained in article 14 of the Constitution of India is available to all persons whether natural or legal.

65. (a) Mayo came in India in 1869. He founded Mayo College in Ajmer. He was killed by an Afghan in 1872.

66. (d) India joined the IMF on December 27, 1945, as one of the IMF's original members. India accepted the obligations of Article VIII of the IMF Articles of Agreement on current account convertibility on August 20, 1994.

67.	(b)	68.	(a)	69.	(b)	70.	(d)	71.	(a)
72.	(c)	73.	(b)	74.	(c)	75.	(d)		

5   PRACTICE SET

Time : 60 Min.   **Max. Marks : 75**

DIRECTIONS (Qs. 1-2): *Find the odd words /letters / number pair from the given alternatives. .*

1. (a) Poet   (b) Publisher
   (c) Author   (d) Novelist

2. (a) Hexagon : Angle   (b) Square : Line
   (c) Circle : Arc   (d) Line : Dot

3. Which one set of letters when sequentially placed at the gaps in the given letter series shall complete it ?
   a – a – abad — ba —
   (a) abba   (b) bbab
   (c) abab   (d) baab

4. In the following letter series, how many times does 'P' occur in such a way that after 'P', N' O should occur?
   A P N Q P N O S P T O Z P N O Y M P N O
   (a) 2   (b) 5
   (c) 4   (d) 3

5. Find the missing number. 2, 8, 18, 32, 50, ?
   (a) 70   (b) 68
   (c) 64   (d) 72

6. C is the mother of A and B. If D is the husband of B, what is C to D ?
   (a) Mother-in-law   (b) Sister
   (c) Mother   (d) Aunt

7. If A = 1, ACE = 9, then ART = ?
   (a) 29   (b) 38
   (c) 10   (d) 39

8. If PARK is coded as 5394, SHIRT is coded as 17698 and PANDIT is coded as 532068, how would you code NISHAR in that code language?
   (a) 201739   (b) 261739
   (c) 266734   (d) 231954

9. If the 5th date of a month is Tuesday, what date will be 3 days after the 3rd Friday in the month?
   (a) 17   (b) 22
   (c) 19   (d) 18

10. Seema's younger brother Sohan is older than Seeta. Sweta is younger than Deepti but elder than Seema. Who is the eldest ?
    (a) Seeta   (b) Deepti
    (c) Seema   (d) Sweta

11. If 'SYNDICATE' is written as 'SYTENDCAI then how can 'PSYCHOTIC' be written ?
    (a) PSICYOCTH   (b) PSICYCOTH
    (c) PSYICTCOH   (d) PSYCOHTCI

DIRECTION (Q. 12): *Select the missing number from the given responses.*

12.
5	25	5
7	49	7
6	?	6

    (a) 38   (b) 40
    (c) 36   (d) 35

13. A cyclist goes 30 km to North and then turning East he goes 40 km. Again he turns to his right and goes 20 km. After this, he turns to his right and goes 40 km. How far is he from his starting point ?
    (a) 25 km   (b) 40 km
    (c) 6 km   (d) 10 km

14. If '+' denotes ÷, '–' denotes ×, '×' denotes – and '÷' denotes +, then
    $35 + 7 – 5 ÷ 5 × 6 = ?$
    (a) 20   (b) 14
    (c) 36   (d) 24

15. 3 daily wage workers A, B and C are distributed ₹ 178 in such a way that A gets ₹ 4 less than C, B gets ₹ 15 more than A and C gets ₹ 11 less than B. What is the ratio of their shares ?
    (a) 53 : 68 : 57   (b) 57 : 53 : 68
    (c) 50 : 51 : 52   (d) 53 : 56 : 68

16. Five boys A, B, C, D and E are standing in a row. D is on the right of E. B is on the left of E, but on the right of A. D is on the left of C, who is standing on the extreme right. Who is standing in the middle ?
    (a) D
    (b) E
    (b) B
    (d) C

17. What is the height of a cylinder that has the same volume and radius as a sphere of diameter 12 cm?
    (a) 8 cm
    (b) 7 cm
    (c) 10 cm
    (d) 9 cm

18. Let $a = \sqrt{6} - \sqrt{5}, b = \sqrt{5} - 2, c = 2 - \sqrt{3}$.
    Then point out the correct alternative among the four alternatives given below.
    (a) $a < b < c$
    (b) $b < a < c$
    (c) $a < c < b$
    (d) $b < c < a$;

19. The volume of air in a room is 204 m^3 . The height of the room is 6 m. What is the floor area of the room?
    (a) 34 m^2
    (b) 32 m^2
    (c) 46 m^2
    (d) 44 m^2

20. The average of 30 numbers is 40 and that of other 40 numbers is 30. The average of all the numbers is
    (a) 34.5
    (b) $34\dfrac{2}{7}$
    (c) 35
    (d) 34

21. The length and breadth of a rectangle are doubled. Percentage increase in area is
    (a) 400%
    (b) 150%
    (c) 200%
    (d) 300%

22. In the annual examination Mahuya got 10% less marks than Supriyo in Mathematics. Mahuya got 81 marks. The marks of Supriyo are
    (a) 89
    (b) 90
    (c) 87
    (d) 88

23. A invests ₹ 64,000 in a business. After few months B joined him with ₹ 48,000. At the end of year, the total profit was divided between them in the ratio 2 : 1. After how many months did B join ?
    (a) 7
    (b) 8
    (c) 4
    (d) 6

24. A got 30% concession on the label price of an article sold for ₹ 8,750 with 25% profit on the price he bought. The label price was
    (a) 10,000
    (b) 13,000
    (c) 16,000
    (d) 12,000

25. In the following number series a wrong number is given. Find out the wrong number.
    318   158   76   38   18   8 3
    (a) 38
    (b) 18
    (c) 158
    (d) 76

26. Radio telescopes are better than optical telescopes because
    (a) they can detect faint galaxies which no optical telescope can
    (b) they can work even in cloudy conditions
    (c) they can work during the day and night
    (d) All of the above

27. Light Emitting Diodes (LED) is used in fancy electronic devices such as toys emit
    (a) X-rays
    (b) ultraviolet light
    (c) visible light
    (d) radio waves

28. Out of the following pairs, which one does not have identical dimension?
    (a) Moment of inertia and moment of a force
    (b) Work and Torque
    (c) Angular momentum and Planck's constant
    (d) Impulse and Momentum

29. Mercury is commonly used as a thermometric fluid rather than water because
    (a) specific heat of mercury is less than water
    (b) specific heat of mercury is more than water
    (c) mercury has greater visibility than water
    (d) density of mercury is more than the water

30. Optical fibre works on the
    (a) principle of refraction
    (b) total internal reflection
    (c) Scattering
    (d) Interference

31. What is silverfish?
    (a) A silvery freshwater fish
    (b) Leaf of silver oak
    (c) A small silvery wingles insect
    (d) An American fox with a silvery fur

32. Which of the following is correct?
    (a) Osteology is the study of bones
    (b) Philately is the study of coins
    (c) Limnology is the study of oceans
    (d) Ethology is the study of human races.

33. Which of the following is not correct?
    (a) Ammeter measures the strength of electric current.
    (b) Lactometer measures the relative density of milk.
    (c) Rain gauge measures rain fall.
    (d) Hygrometer measures sound under water.

34. Which of the following is the unit of distance in navigation?
    (a) Knot
    (b) Nautical mile
    (c) Bar
    (d) Angstrom

35. The study of phenomena at very low temperatures is called
    (a) heat transfer
    (b) morphology
    (c) crystallography
    (d) cryogenics

36. The branch of medical science which is concerned with the study of disease as it affects a community of people is called
    (a) epidemiology
    (b) oncology
    (c) paleontogy
    (d) pathology

37. Superconductivity is a material property associated with
    (a) cooling a substance without a phase change
    (b) frictionless liquid flow
    (c) a loss of thermal resistance
    (d) a loss of electrical resistance

38. If a metal can be drawn into wires relatively easily it is called
    (a) malleable
    (b) ductile
    (c) extractive
    (d) tactile

39. Cystitis is the infection of which of the following?
    (a) liver   (b) urinary bladder
    (c) pancreas   (d) lung
40. Which of the following is primarily composed of calcium carbonate?
    (a) Fish scales   (b) Shark teeth
    (c) Oyster Shells   (d) Whale bones
41. Water flows through a horizontal pipe at a constant volumetric rate. At a location where the cross sectional area decreases, the velocity of the fluid
    (a) increases   (b) decreases
    (c) stays the same   (d) none of the above
42. Yeast, used in making bread is a
    (a) fungus   (b) plant
    (c) bacteria   (d) seed
43. A cyclone is an engineering device that is used to
    (a) transport materials
    (b) segregate particles
    (c) control switching devices
    (d) model fractals
44. A gas used as a disinfectant in drinking water is
    (a) Hydrogen   (b) Oxygen
    (c) Fluorine   (d) Chlorine
45. Which is the longest bone in the human body?
    (a) Fibula   (b) Radius
    (c) Stapes   (d) Femur
46. When a particle and an antiparticle come in contact with each other, they
    (a) repell each other
    (b) annihilate each other
    (c) go undisturbed
    (d) spin about a common axis
47. How do most insects respire?
    (a) Through skin   (b) Through gills
    (c) By tracheal system (d) By lungs
48. Name the robot who created a new record by solving the famous rubik's cube puzzle.
    (a) Sub1   (b) Icuber
    (c) Tilted Twister   (d) RuBot2
49. Radiocarbon is produced in the atmosphere as a result of
    (a) collision between fast neutrons and nitrogen nuclei present in the atmosphere
    (b) action of ultraviolet light from the sun on atmospheric oxygen
    (c) action of solar radiations particularly cosmic rays on carbon dioxide present in the atmosphere
    (d) lightning discharge in atmosphere
50. It is easier to roll a stone up a sloping road than to lift it vertical upwards because
    (a) work done in rolling is more than in lifting
    (b) work done in lifting the stone is equal to rolling it
    (c) work done in both is same but the rate of doing work is less in rolling
    (d) work done in rolling a stone is less than in lifting it

51. The absorption of ink by blotting paper involves
    (a) viscosity of ink
    (b) capillary action phenomenon
    (c) diffusion of ink through the blotting
    (d) siphon action
52. Siphon will fail to work if
    (a) the densities of the liquid in the two vessels are equal
    (b) the level of the liquid in the two vessels are at the same height
    (c) both its limbs are of unequal length
    (d) the temperature of the liquids in the two vessels are the same
53. Large transformers, when used for some time, become very hot and are cooled by circulating oil. The heating of the transformer is due to
    (a) the heating effect of current alone
    (b) hysteresis loss alone
    (c) both the heating effect of current and hysteresis loss
    (d) intense sunlight at noon
54. Nuclear sizes are expressed in a unit named
    (a) Fermi   (b) angstrom
    (c) Newton   (d) tesla
55. Light year is a unit of
    (a) Time   (b) distance
    (c) Light   (d) intensity of light
56. Mirage is due to
    (a) unequal heating of different parts of the atmosphere
    (b) magnetic disturbances in the atmosphere
    (c) depletion of ozone layer in the atmosphere
    (d) equal heating of different parts of the atmosphere
57. Light from the Sun reaches us in nearly
    (a) 2 minutes   (b) 4 minutes
    (c) 8 minutes   (d) 16 minutes
58. Stars appears to move from east to west because
    (a) all stars move from east to west
    (b) the earth rotates from west to east
    (c) the earth rotates from east to west
    (d) the background of the stars moves from west to east
59. Ashtapradhan was a council of ministers:
    (a) in the Gupta administration
    (b) in the Chola administration
    (c) in the Vijayanagar administration
    (d) in the Maratha administration
60. Which one among the following newspapers was published first?
    (a) The Madras Mail
    (b) The Indian Social Reformer
    (c) The Bengal Gazette
    (d) The Times of India
61. Jiatrang Movement started in
    (a) Nagaland   (b) Tripura
    (c) Manipur   (d) Mizoram

62. How many types of writs can be issued by the supreme court?
    (a) 2   (b) 3
    (c) 5   (d) 6
63. The Indian Economy is characterised by
    (a) pre-dominance of agriculture
    (b) low per capita income
    (c) Massive unemployment
    (d) All of the above
64. The Green Revolution in India has contributed to
    (a) inter-regional inequality
    (b) inter-class inequality
    (c) inter-crop inequality
    (d) all of the above
65. Which of the dance forms enlisted in UNESCO?
    (a) Mudiyeltu   (b) Bidesia
    (c) Maach   (d) Yakshagan
66. With which game is 'Bully' associated ?
    (a) Cricket   (b) Football
    (c) Golf   (d) Hockey
67. A platform surrounded by rail lines from all the four sides, is called
    (a) dock platform
    (b) passenger platform
    (c) island platform
    (d) goods platform
68. Indian Railways Nationalised in which year ?
    (a) 1952   (b) 1950
    (c) 1951   (d) 1954
69. In which year Research, Design and Standard organization was established?
    (a) 1953   (b) 1957
    (c) 1956   (d) 1967
70. Railway Staff College is situated at
    (a) Mumbai   (b) Secundrabad
    (c) Ahmedabad   (d) Vadodara
71. The Republic Day parade, held every year, is organized by which of the following ministries?
    (a) Union Home Ministry
    (b) Union Ministry of Defence
    (c) Union Ministry of Finance
    (d) Union Ministry of Information and Broadcasting
72. How many members are nominated by the governor in the Legislative Council of the State?
    (a) 1/3rd of the total membership
    (b) 1/6th of the total membership
    (c) 1/12th of the total membership
    (d) 12 members
73. Pandit Jawaharlal Nehru drafted the resolution on Fundamental Rights an Economic Programme at which session of Indian National Congress?
    (a) Lahore Session   (b) Bombay Session
    (c) Calcutta Session (d) Karachi Session
74. What is the theme of the 48th annual meeting of the World Economic Forum (WEF-2018)?
    (a) Mastering the Fourth Industrial Revolution
    (b) Responsive and Responsible Leadership
    (c) Creating a shared future in a fractured world
    (d) Together create a United World
75. Which country to host the 6th edition of ICC Women's World Twenty 20 2018?
    (a) Australia   (b) England
    (c) New Zealand   (d) West Indies

RESPONSE SHEET

1. ⓐⓑⓒⓓ	2. ⓐⓑⓒⓓ	3. ⓐⓑⓒⓓ	4. ⓐⓑⓒⓓ	5. ⓐⓑⓒⓓ
6. ⓐⓑⓒⓓ	7. ⓐⓑⓒⓓ	8. ⓐⓑⓒⓓ	9. ⓐⓑⓒⓓ	10. ⓐⓑⓒⓓ
11. ⓐⓑⓒⓓ	12. ⓐⓑⓒⓓ	13. ⓐⓑⓒⓓ	14. ⓐⓑⓒⓓ	15. ⓐⓑⓒⓓ
16. ⓐⓑⓒⓓ	17. ⓐⓑⓒⓓ	18. ⓐⓑⓒⓓ	19. ⓐⓑⓒⓓ	20. ⓐⓑⓒⓓ
21. ⓐⓑⓒⓓ	22. ⓐⓑⓒⓓ	23. ⓐⓑⓒⓓ	24. ⓐⓑⓒⓓ	25. ⓐⓑⓒⓓ
26. ⓐⓑⓒⓓ	27. ⓐⓑⓒⓓ	28. ⓐⓑⓒⓓ	29. ⓐⓑⓒⓓ	30. ⓐⓑⓒⓓ
31. ⓐⓑⓒⓓ	32. ⓐⓑⓒⓓ	33. ⓐⓑⓒⓓ	34. ⓐⓑⓒⓓ	35. ⓐⓑⓒⓓ
36. ⓐⓑⓒⓓ	37. ⓐⓑⓒⓓ	38. ⓐⓑⓒⓓ	39. ⓐⓑⓒⓓ	40. ⓐⓑⓒⓓ
41. ⓐⓑⓒⓓ	42. ⓐⓑⓒⓓ	43. ⓐⓑⓒⓓ	44. ⓐⓑⓒⓓ	45. ⓐⓑⓒⓓ
46. ⓐⓑⓒⓓ	47. ⓐⓑⓒⓓ	48. ⓐⓑⓒⓓ	49. ⓐⓑⓒⓓ	50. ⓐⓑⓒⓓ
51. ⓐⓑⓒⓓ	52. ⓐⓑⓒⓓ	53. ⓐⓑⓒⓓ	54. ⓐⓑⓒⓓ	55. ⓐⓑⓒⓓ
56. ⓐⓑⓒⓓ	57. ⓐⓑⓒⓓ	58. ⓐⓑⓒⓓ	59. ⓐⓑⓒⓓ	60. ⓐⓑⓒⓓ
61. ⓐⓑⓒⓓ	62. ⓐⓑⓒⓓ	63. ⓐⓑⓒⓓ	64. ⓐⓑⓒⓓ	65. ⓐⓑⓒⓓ
66. ⓐⓑⓒⓓ	67. ⓐⓑⓒⓓ	68. ⓐⓑⓒⓓ	69. ⓐⓑⓒⓓ	70. ⓐⓑⓒⓓ
71. ⓐⓑⓒⓓ	72. ⓐⓑⓒⓓ	73. ⓐⓑⓒⓓ	74. ⓐⓑⓒⓓ	75. ⓐⓑⓒⓓ

HINTS & SOLUTIONS

1. (b) Except (b) others are creators.
2. (a) Hexagon is not made from angle.
3. (b) abababababab
4. (d) A P N Q |PNO| S P T O Z |PNO| Y M |PNO|

5. (d) 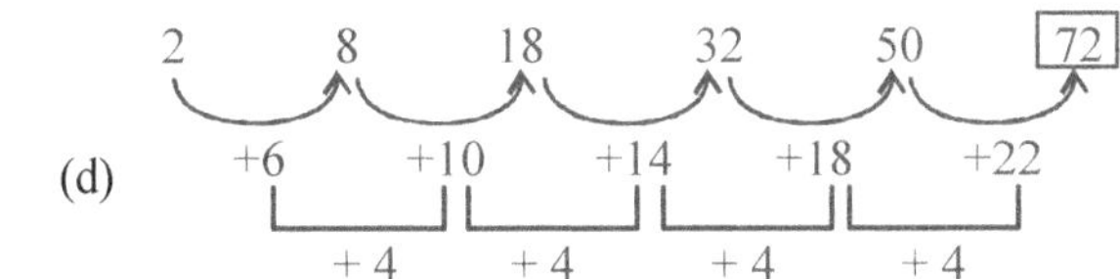

6. (a) 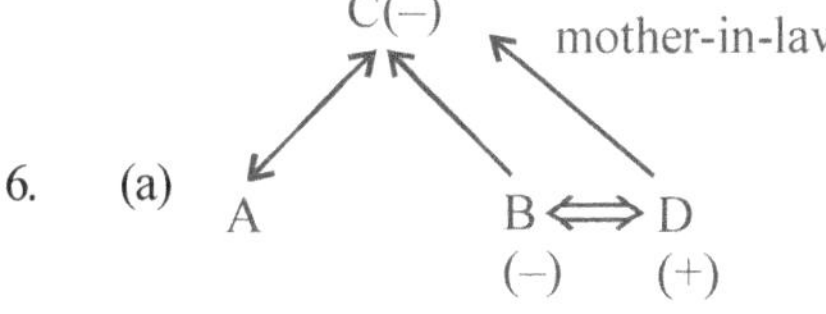

7. (d) $A = 1$, $A + C + E = 1 + 3 + 5 = 9$
   $A + R + T = 1 + 18 + 20 = 39$

8. (b) Letters have been coded as-

P	A	R	K	S	H	I	T	N	D
↓	↓	↓	↓	↓	↓	↓	↓	↓	↓
5	3	9	4	1	7	6	8	2	0

   Similarly

N	I	S	H	A	R
↓	↓	↓	↓	↓	↓
2	6	1	7	3	9

9. (d) 5th date of a month is Tuesday
   Friday will be on $= 5 + 3$
   $= 8^{th}$ of a month
   1st Friday is on 1st of a month
   2nd Friday is on 8th of a month
   3rd Friday will be on 15th of a month
   3 days after $15^{th} = 15 + 3 = 18$

10. (b) Seema > Sohan > Seeta ...(i)
    Deepti > Sweta > Seema ...(ii)
    Combining (i) and (ii) we get
    Deepti > Sweta > Seema > Sohan Seeta

11. (b)

1	2	3	4	5	6	7	8	9
S	Y	N	D	I	C	A	T	E

    Coded as

S	Y	T	E	N	D	C	A	I
1	2	8	9	3	4	6	7	5

    Similarly

1	2	3	4	5	6	7	8	9
P	S	Y	C	H	O	T	I	C

    Coded as

P	S	I	C	Y	C	O	T	H
1	2	8	9	3	4	6	7	5

12. (c) The second column number is the product of first and third column
    $25 = 5 \times 5$
    $49 = 7 \times 7$
    $36 = 6 \times 6$

13. (d) 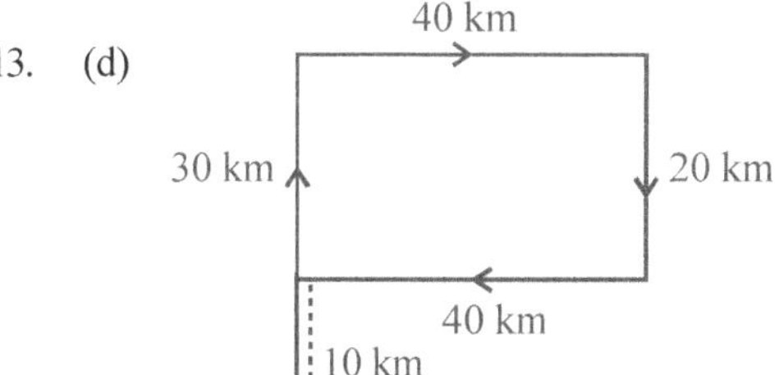

14. (d) $35 \div 7 \times 5 + 5 - 6$
    $= 5 \times 5 + 5 - 6$
    $25 + 5 - 6$
    $30 - 6 = 24$

15. (a) $A = C - 4$ ....(1)
    $B = A + 15$ ....(2)
    $C = B - 15$ ....(3)
    From (1) and (3)
    $A = B - 11 - 4$
    $A = B - 15$
    $A : B : C$
    $B - 15 : B : B - 11$
    $B - 15 + B + B - 11 = 178$
    $3B = 178 + 26 = 204 \Rightarrow B = 68$
    $A = 53$, $C = 57$

16. (b) A   B   Ⓔ   D   C

17. (a) Volume of cylinder = volume of sphere (Given)

    $$\pi r^2 h = \frac{4}{3}\pi r^3$$

    $$h = \frac{4}{3}r$$

    $$h = \frac{4}{3} \times 6\,cm = 8\ cm$$

18. (a) $\sqrt{6} = 2.44, \sqrt{5} = 2.23, \sqrt{3} = 1.73$

    $a = \sqrt{6} - \sqrt{5} = 0.21$

    $b = \sqrt{5} - 2 = 0.23$

    $c = 2 - \sqrt{3} = 0.27$

19. (a) Volume of air in room $= 204\ m^3$
    Area of floor × height of room $= 204\ m^3$
    Area of floor $\times 6 = 204\ m^3$

    $\therefore$ Area of floor $= \dfrac{204}{6} = 34\ m^2$

20. (b) Sum of 30 numbers $= 30 \times 40 = 1200$
    Sum of 40 numbers $= 40 \times 30 = 1200$

$$\text{Average of 70 numbers} = \frac{1200+1200}{70} = \frac{2400}{70} = 34\frac{2}{7}$$

21. (d) $A = \ell b$

$A' = (2\ell)(2b) = 4\ell b = 4A$

$$\% \text{ Change} = \frac{4A-A}{A} \times 100 = 300\%$$

22. (b) Marks of Supriyo = x marks

Accoding to question

Mahuya marks = Supriyo marks – 10% of Supriyo marks

$$81 = x - 10\% \text{ of } x \Rightarrow x\left(1 - \frac{10}{100}\right)$$

$$81 = \frac{9}{10}x \Rightarrow \frac{810}{9} = x$$

$\therefore x = 90$ marks

23. (c) Suppose, B Joined after x month

Then B's money was invested for $(12 - x)$ months

$\therefore$ According to question

$$\frac{64000 \times 12}{48000 \times (12-x)} = \frac{2}{1}$$

$$\frac{16}{12-x} = \frac{2}{1} \Rightarrow 16 = 24 - 2x$$

$2x = 24 - 16 = x = 4$

Hence, B joined after 4 months

24. (a) Let the labelled price be ₹ x

$$\text{Now, C.P} = \frac{100}{(100 + \text{profit }\%)} \times S.P$$

$$\text{C.P} = \frac{100}{(100+25)} \times 8750 = ₹ 7000$$

Now, $(1 - 30\% \text{ concession})$ label price = C.P

$$\left(1 - \frac{30}{100}\right)x = 7000$$

$$\frac{70}{100}x = 7000$$

$$x = \frac{7000 \times 100}{70}$$

$x = ₹ 10, 000$

25. (d) The series is $\div 2 - 1$ in each term.

26. (d)	27. (c)	28.(a)	29. (c)	30. (b)
31. (c)	32. (a)	33.(d)	34. (b)	35. (d)
36. (a)	37. (c)	38.(b)	39. (b)	40. (c)
41. (a)	42. (a)	43.(b)	44. (d)	

45. (d) The head of the femur articulates with the acetabulum in the pelvic bone forming the hip joint, while the distal part of the femur articulates with the tibia and patella forming the knee joint. By most measures the femur is the strongest bone in the body. The femur is also the longest bone in the body.

46. (b)	47. (c)	48. (a)	49. (a)	50.(d)
51. (b)	52. (b)	53. (c)	54. (a)	55.(b)
56. (a)	57. (c)	58. (b)		

59. (d) It was constituted by Shivaji in Maratha administration.

60. (c) Bengal Gazette was published by James Augustus Hikkey in 1780.

61. (c) Jatindra Nath Das (27 October 1904 - 13 September 1929), also known as Jatin Das, was an Indian freedom fighter and revolutionary. He died in Lahore jail after a continuous hunger strike for 63 days demanding equality for Indian prisoners and undertrials.

62. (c) There are 5 types of writs can be issued by the Supreme Court

63. (d) The Indian Economy is characterised by predominance of agriculture, low per capita income and massive unemployment.

64. (d) The Green Revolution in India has contributed to inter-regional, inter-class and inter-crop inequality.

65. (a)	66. (d)	67.(c)	68. (b)	69.(b)
70. (d)	71. (b)	72.(b)	73. (d)	74.(c)
75. (d)				

6   PRACTICE SET

Time : 60 Min.   **Max. Marks : 75**

DIRECTIONS (Qs. 1- 2) : *Select the one which is different from the other three responses.*

1.   (a) steering wheel   (b) engine
      (c) car   (d) tyre
2.   (a) uranus   (b) pluto
      (c) jupiter   (d) sun

DIRECTIONS (Qs. 3 -10) : *A series is given, with one number/ letter missing. Choose the correct alternative from the given ones that will complete the series.*

3.   3, 11, 38, 102, ______ , 443
      (a) 227   (b) 237
      (c) 247   (d) 217

4.   Which one of the letters when sequentially placed at the gaps in the given letter series shall complete it?
   m _ _ l m _ l _ m m _ l
      (a) mllml   (b) mlmll
      (c) llmlm   (d) mmlml

5.   Pointing towards a woman in a photograph Vijay said, "She is the daughter of the father of sister of my brother". How is the lady in the photograph related to Vijay?
      (a) Wife   (b) Mother
      (c) Sister   (d) Daughter

6.   Rajiv is the brother of Arun. Sonia is the sister of Sunil. Arun is the son of Sonia. How is Rajiv related to Sunil?
      (a) son
      (b) brother
      (c) father
      (d) nephew

7.   Which number is wrong in the series?
   5, 11, 23, 47, 96
      (a) 47   (b) 23
      (c) 96   (d) 11

8.   Among 5 boys, Vasant is taller than Manohar, but not as tall as Raju. Jayant is taller than Dutta but shorter than Manohar. Who is the tallest in the group?
      (a) Manohar   (b) Vasant
      (c) Jayant   (d) Raju

9.   If PALE is written as RCNG, how can LEAP be written in that code?
      (a) NGCR   (b) RCGN
      (c) CRNG   (d) NCRG

10.   If 'POST' is coded as 'KLHG', how is 'NURS' coded as?
      (a) MGJH   (b) MGJH
      (c) MFIH   (d) MFIG

DIRECTIONS (Qs. 11 -12) : *Select the missing number/letter from the given responses.*

11.

R	Q	L
S	P	M
T	?	N

   (a) O   (b) R
   (c) W   (d) V

12.

7	6	15
10	?	12
35	12	90

   (a) 9   (b) 4
   (c) 25   (d) 11

13. If '+' means '÷' ; '÷' means '–' ; '–' means '×' ; '×' means '+', then

$8 + 2 \div 3 - 4 \times 6 = ?$

(a) –12   (b) –2

(c) –10   (d) –15

14. Raghu starts from his house in his car and travels 8 km towards the North, then 6 km towards East then 10 m towards his right, 4 km towards his left, 10 km towards North and finally 4 km towards his right. In which Directions is he now with reference to the starting point?

(a) South   (b) North East

(c) South East   (d) North

15. Four students ABCD are sitting one each of the four corners of a square all facing the centre of the square. The student E sitting at the centre is facing only C and the student A is sitting facing the back of E. If D is sitting on the right of E, where B will be sitting to E?

(a) B is sitting on the left of E

(b) B is to the back of E

(c) A is facing B and E

(d) B is on the right of E

16. The length and breadth of a square are increased by 30% and 20% respectively. The area of the rectangle so formed exceeds the area of the square by:

(a) 46%   (b) 66%

(c) 42%   (d) 56%

17. A can do a piece of work in 20 days which B can do in 12 days. B worked at it for 9 days. A can finish the remaining work in :

(a) 5 days   (b) 7 days

(c) 11 days   (d) 3 days

18. A batsman in his 12th innings makes a score of 63 runs and there by increases his average scores by 2. What is his average after the 12th innings?

(a) 13   (b) 41

(c) 49   (d) 87

19. A man sold two articles at ₹375 each. On one, he gains 25% and on the other, he loses 25%. The gain or loss% on the whole transaction is :

(a) 6%   (b) $4\dfrac{1}{6}\%$

(c) ₹50   (d) $6\dfrac{1}{4}\%$

20. A team played 40 games in a season and won in 24 of them. What percent of games played did the team win ?

(a) 70%   (b) 40%

(c) 60%   (d) 35%

21. A bought an article, paying 5% less than the original price. A sold it with 20% profit on the price he had paid. What percent of profit did A earn on the original price ?

(a) 10   (b) 13

(c) 14   (d) $\dfrac{17}{2}$

22. The profit percent of a bookseller if he sells book at marked price after enjoying a commission of 25% on marked price will be:

(a) 30%   (b) 25%

(c) 20%   (d) $33\dfrac{1}{3}\%$

23. In a school, the ratio of boys to girls is 4 : 3 and the ratio of girls to teachers is 8 : 1. The ratio of student to teachers is :

(s) 56 : 3   (b) 55 : 1

(c) 49 : 3   (d) 56 : 1

24. If $\triangle ABC$ is an isosceles triangle with $\angle C = 90°$ and AC = 5 cm, then AB is :

(a) 5 cm   (b) 10 cm

(c) $5\sqrt{2}$ cm   (d) 2.5 cm

25. If the difference of two numbers is 3 and the difference of their squares is 39; then the larger number is :

(a) 9   (b) 12

(c) 13   (d) 8

26. Which of the following is the best conductor of Electricity?

(a) Ordinary water   (b) Sea water

(c) Boiled water   (d) Distilled water

27. Balloons are filled with-

(a) Helium   (b) Oxygen

(c) Nitrogen   (d) Argon

28. The charcoal used to decolourise raw sugar is-

(a) Animal charcoal

(b) Sugar charcoal

(c) Cocoanut charcoal

(d) Wood charcoal

29. Washing soda is the common name of-

(a) Calcium Carbonate   (b) Calcium Bi-Carbonate

(c) Sodium Carbonate   (d) Sodium Bi-Carbonate

30. The filament of electric bulb is made of-

(a) Iron   (b) Nichrome

(c) Tungsten   (d) Graphite

31. Which of the following is not a neutral oxide ?

(a) Carbon Monoxide   (b) Sulphur Dioxide

(c) Water   (d) Nitric Oxide

32. Potassium Permanganate is used for purifying drinking water, because-
    (a) It dissolves the impurities of water
    (b) It is a sterilizing agent
    (c) It is an oxidising agent
    (d) It is a reducing agent.

33. The presence of which of the following salts in water causes corrosion in steam boilers ?
    (a) Sodium Chloride   (b) Magnesium Chloride
    (c) Calcium bicarbonate   (d) Potassium bicarbonate

34. Water is a good solvent of ionic salts because-
    (a) It has no colour
    (b) It has a boiling point
    (c) It has a high dipole moment
    (d) It has a high specific heat

35. Nuclear fission is caused by the impact of-
    (a) Proton   (b) Electron
    (c) Neutron   (d) (a) and (b)

36. In an atomic explosion enormous energy is released which is due to the-
    (a) Conversions of neutrons into protons
    (b) Conversion of chemical energy into nuclear energy
    (c) Conversion of mechanical energy into nuclear energy
    (d) Conversion of mass into energy

37. Which of the following is used as a coolant in nuclear reactors?
    (a) Heavy water   (b) Cadmium
    (c) Liquid sodium   (d) Graphite

38. In vulcanization, natural rubber is heated with-
    (a) Carbon   (b) Sulphur
    (c) Silicon   (d) Phosphorus

39. Which type of fire extinguisher is used for petroleum fire?
    (a) Foam type   (b) Soda acid type
    (c) Powder type   (d) None of these

40. Which is/ are the important raw materials in cement industry?
    (a) Limestone   (b) Gypsum and Clay
    (c) Clay   (d) Limestone and Clay

41. In which following processes light energy is converted into chemical energy ?
    (a) Respiration
    (b) Fermentation
    (c) Photosynthesis
    (d) Photorespiration

42. Cooking oil can be converted into vegetables ghee by the process of-
    (a) Oxidation
    (b) Hydrogenation
    (c) Distillation
    (d) Crystallisation

43. Photosynthesis is-
    (a) An exothermic process
    (b) An endothermic process
    (c) A neutral process
    (d) A thermostatic process

44. J. B. Sumner isolated first enzyme from Jackbeans as-
    (a) amylase   (b) trypsin
    (c) urease   (d) renin

45. Enzymes are absent in-
    (a) fungi   (b) bacteria
    (c) viruses   (d) algae

46. The enzymes sucrase acts on-
    (a) sucrose only   (b) sucrose and starch
    (c) all disaccharides   (d) any organic monomer

47. One of these vitamins is called erythrocyte maturation factor-
    (a) A   (b) C
    (c) K   (d) B12

48. Saponification involves the hydrolysis of fats and oils by-
    (a) water   (b) washing soda
    (c) stearic acid   (d) caustic soda

49. Photo-synthesis is a/ an-
    (a) exothermic process   (b) endothermic process
    (c) a neutral process   (d) a thermostatic process

50. Which of the following is a physical change ?
    (a) oxidation   (b) reduction
    (c) sublimation   (d) decomposition

51. The process by which an organic compound breaks down into simpler compounds on heating to high temperature is known as-
    (a) Aromatisation   (b) Polymerisation
    (c) Pyrolysis   (d) Reduction

52. The most abundant metal in the earths crust is-
    (a) Zinc
    (b) Copper
    (c) Aluminium
    (d) Iron

53. The gas used to extinguish fire is-
    (a) Neon
    (b) Nitrogen
    (c) Carbon dioxide
    (d) Carbon Monoxide

54. In which of the following activities Silicon Carbide is used ?
    (a) Making cement and glass
    (b) Disinfecting water and ponds
    (c) Making castes for statues
    (d) Cutting very hard substances

55. The two elements that are frequently used for making transistors are-
   (a) Boron and Aluminium
   (b) Silicon and Germenium
   (c) Iridium and Tungsten
   (d) Niobium and Columbium

56. Which of the following gas is not known as green house gas?
   (a) Methane   (b) Carbon dioxide
   (c) Nitrous oxide   (d) CFC

57. The element common to all acids is-
   (a) Oxygen   (b) Hydrogen
   (c) Nitrogen   (d) Sulphur

58. Gobar gas contains mainly-
   (a) Methane   (b) Carbon dioxide
   (c) Butane   (d) Carbon Monoxide

59. The most malleable metal is-
   (a) Silver   (b) Gold
   (c) Aluminium   (d) Sodium

60. Which of the following is used in making smoke bombs ?
   (a) Sulphur   (b) Phosphorus
   (c) Hydrogen   (d) Carbon

61. Caustic Soda is-
   (a) Nacl   (b) Na_2CO_3
   (c) NaOH   (d) $NaHCO_3$

62. Myanmar does not share its international boundary with__?
   (a) Laos   (b) Thailand
   (c) Vietnam   (d) India

63. Who among the following women was the first to be featured on an Indian stemp ?
   (a) Rani Lakshmi Bai   (b) Mirabai
   (c) Indira Gandhi   (d) Razia Sultan

64. The capital of Congo is
   (a) Harare   (b) Lusaka
   (c) Kinshasa   (d) None of the abov

65. National Development Council was set up in
   (a) 1957   (b) 1952
   (c) 1971   (d) 1984

66. The Secretariat of SAARC is located at
   (a) Colombo   (b) Kathmandu
   (c) Male   (d) Dacca

67. In the Constitution of India, Setting up of village panchayats finds mention under
   (a) Article 40   (b) Article 48
   (c) Article 51   (d) None of the Articles

68. Which one of the following refineries refines crude oil obtained from the oilfields of Gujarat ?
   (a) Barauni   (b) Visakhapatnam
   (c) Digboi   (d) Koyali

69. Which one of the following cities lies on the Delhi-Mumbai National Highway?
   (a) Nasik   (b) Jaipur
   (c) Indore   (d) Jhansi

70. Telangana state formation day?
   (a) 4 June   (b) 2 June
   (c) 2 July   (d) 15 July

71. World Hypertension day is observed on which of the following date?
   (a) 17 May   (b) 28 December
   (c) 14 February   (d) 19 June

72. Which state government has launched Zero Budget Natural Farming (ZBNF) project to promote organic farming?
   (a) Punjab   (b) Himachal Pradesh
   (c) West Bengal   (d) Assam

73. The Indian Railways is expected to receive its first high-speed electric locomotive by __________
   (a) December 2018   (b) June 2018
   (c) July 2018   (d) March 2018

74. Kalamandalam Geethanandan of Kerala passed away recently. He was a renowned __________ artist
   (a) Koodiyattam   (b) Ottanthulal
   (c) Theyyam   (d) Kathakali

75. Bihu dance is related to which state?
   (a) Himachal Pradesh   (b) Kerala
   (c) Assam   (d) Andhra Pradesh

RESPONSE SHEET

1. ⓐⓑⓒⓓ	2. ⓐⓑⓒⓓ	3. ⓐⓑⓒⓓ	4. ⓐⓑⓒⓓ	5. ⓐⓑⓒⓓ
6. ⓐⓑⓒⓓ	7. ⓐⓑⓒⓓ	8. ⓐⓑⓒⓓ	9. ⓐⓑⓒⓓ	10. ⓐⓑⓒⓓ
11. ⓐⓑⓒⓓ	12. ⓐⓑⓒⓓ	13. ⓐⓑⓒⓓ	14. ⓐⓑⓒⓓ	15. ⓐⓑⓒⓓ
16. ⓐⓑⓒⓓ	17. ⓐⓑⓒⓓ	18. ⓐⓑⓒⓓ	19. ⓐⓑⓒⓓ	20. ⓐⓑⓒⓓ
21. ⓐⓑⓒⓓ	22. ⓐⓑⓒⓓ	23. ⓐⓑⓒⓓ	24. ⓐⓑⓒⓓ	25. ⓐⓑⓒⓓ
26. ⓐⓑⓒⓓ	27. ⓐⓑⓒⓓ	28. ⓐⓑⓒⓓ	29. ⓐⓑⓒⓓ	30. ⓐⓑⓒⓓ
31. ⓐⓑⓒⓓ	32. ⓐⓑⓒⓓ	33. ⓐⓑⓒⓓ	34. ⓐⓑⓒⓓ	35. ⓐⓑⓒⓓ
36. ⓐⓑⓒⓓ	37. ⓐⓑⓒⓓ	38. ⓐⓑⓒⓓ	39. ⓐⓑⓒⓓ	40. ⓐⓑⓒⓓ
41. ⓐⓑⓒⓓ	42. ⓐⓑⓒⓓ	43. ⓐⓑⓒⓓ	44. ⓐⓑⓒⓓ	45. ⓐⓑⓒⓓ
46. ⓐⓑⓒⓓ	47. ⓐⓑⓒⓓ	48. ⓐⓑⓒⓓ	49. ⓐⓑⓒⓓ	50. ⓐⓑⓒⓓ
51. ⓐⓑⓒⓓ	52. ⓐⓑⓒⓓ	53. ⓐⓑⓒⓓ	54. ⓐⓑⓒⓓ	55. ⓐⓑⓒⓓ
56. ⓐⓑⓒⓓ	57. ⓐⓑⓒⓓ	58. ⓐⓑⓒⓓ	59. ⓐⓑⓒⓓ	60. ⓐⓑⓒⓓ
61. ⓐⓑⓒⓓ	62. ⓐⓑⓒⓓ	63. ⓐⓑⓒⓓ	64. ⓐⓑⓒⓓ	65. ⓐⓑⓒⓓ
66. ⓐⓑⓒⓓ	67. ⓐⓑⓒⓓ	68. ⓐⓑⓒⓓ	69. ⓐⓑⓒⓓ	70. ⓐⓑⓒⓓ
71. ⓐⓑⓒⓓ	72. ⓐⓑⓒⓓ	73. ⓐⓑⓒⓓ	74. ⓐⓑⓒⓓ	75. ⓐⓑⓒⓓ

HINTS & SOLUTIONS

1. (c) All are parts of car.

2. (d) All are planets except sun.

3. (a) 

   $$3 \xrightarrow{+2^3} 11 \xrightarrow{+3^3} 38 \xrightarrow{+4^3} 102 \xrightarrow{+5^3} 227 \xrightarrow{+6^3} 443$$

4. (b) m m̲ l̲ l
   m m̲ l̲ l̲
   m m l̲ l

5. (c) Sister of my brother = My sister
   Father of my sister = My father
   Daughter of my father = My sister

6. (d) 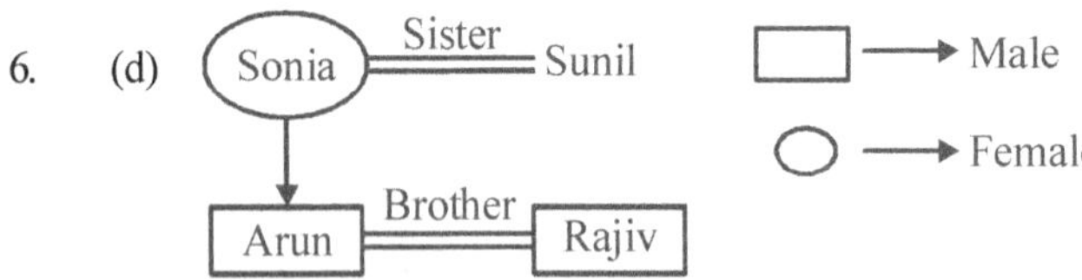

   Therefore, Rajiv is nephew of Sunil.

7. (c) $5, \quad 11, \quad 23, \quad 47, \quad \boxed{\begin{matrix}95\\96\end{matrix}}$

   $5 \times 2 + 1 \quad 11 \times 2 + 1 \quad 23 \times 2 + 1 \quad 47 \times 2 + 1$

8. (d) According to given condition; the correct order is :
   Raju > Vasant > Manohar > Jayant > Dutta
   $\therefore$ Raju is the tallest among them.

9. (a) $\begin{matrix} P & A & L & E \\ +2\downarrow & +2\downarrow & +2\downarrow & +2\downarrow \\ R & C & N & G \end{matrix}$

   Similarly, $\begin{matrix} L & E & A & P \\ +2\downarrow & +2\downarrow & +2\downarrow & +2\downarrow \\ N & G & C & R \end{matrix}$

10. (c) $\begin{matrix} 16 & 15 & 19 & 20 \\ P & O & S & T \\ \downarrow & \downarrow & \downarrow & \downarrow \\ K & L & H & G \\ 16 & 15 & 19 & 20 \end{matrix}$ → In forward direction, when A is taken as 1.

    → In reverse direction, when Z is taken as 1.

    $\therefore \begin{matrix} 14 & 21 & 18 & 19 \\ N & U & R & S \\ \downarrow & \downarrow & \downarrow & \downarrow \\ M & F & I & H \\ 14 & 21 & 18 & 19 \end{matrix}$

11. (a) $\begin{matrix} R & \xleftarrow{+1} & Q & & L \\ \downarrow{+1} & & \uparrow{+1} & & \downarrow{+1} \\ S & & P & & M \\ \downarrow{+1} & & \uparrow{+1} & & \downarrow{+1} \\ T & & O & \xleftarrow{} & N \end{matrix}$

12. (b) $7 \times (10 \div 2) = 35$
    $15 \times (12 \div 2) = 90$
    Similarly, $6 \times (x \div 2) = 12$

    $\Rightarrow \quad 6 \times \dfrac{x}{2} = 12$

    $\Rightarrow \quad 3x = 12$

    $\therefore \quad x = 12 \div 3 = 4$

13. (b) $8 + 2 \div 3 - 4 \times 6$
    $\Rightarrow \quad 8 \div 2 \times 3 \times 4 + 6$
    $\Rightarrow \quad 4 - 12 + 6$
    $\Rightarrow \quad -2$

14. (b) 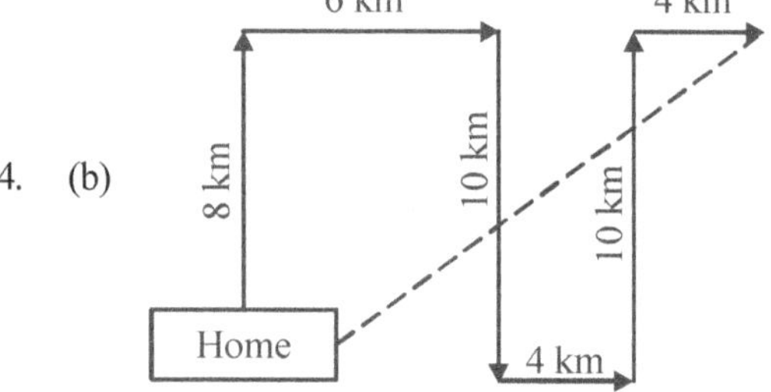

15. (a)

16. (d) Let the side of square = 'x'
    Area of square = x^2

    New length of rectangle = $\dfrac{130}{100} x$

    New Breadth of rectangle = $\dfrac{120}{100} x$

    Hence, Area of so formed rectangle = $\dfrac{130}{100} \times \dfrac{120}{100} \times x^2$

    $= \dfrac{156}{100} x^2$

    Therefore, area of rectangle exceeds the area of square by 56%

17. (a) B's 1 day work = $\dfrac{1}{12}$

    B's 9 day's work = $\dfrac{9}{12} = \dfrac{3}{4}$

    Remaining work = $1 - \dfrac{3}{4} = \dfrac{1}{4}$

    $\therefore$ A can finish this work in $\dfrac{20}{4}$ days = 5 days

18. (b) Let the average of batsman after 11th innings $= A$

$$\frac{\text{Total score made by batsman at the end of 11th innings}}{11} = A$$

$\therefore$ Total score after 11th innings $= 11\,A$

Now, $\dfrac{\text{Total score after 11th innings} + \text{score made in 12th innings}}{12} = A + 2$

$\Rightarrow 11A + 63 = (A + 2) \times 12$

$\Rightarrow 11A - 12A = 24 - 63$

$\Rightarrow A = 39$

12th innings average $= 39 + 2 = 41$

19. (d) In such type of question,

$$\text{Required \% loss} = \frac{(25)^2}{100}\%$$

$$= \frac{625}{100}\% = 6.25\% = 6\frac{1}{4}\%$$

20. (c) Required percentage $= \dfrac{24}{40} \times 100 = 60\%$

21. (c) Required % earned by A

$$= \left\{ 100 \times \frac{(100 - 5)}{100} \times \frac{(100 + 20)}{100} - 100 \right\}\%$$

$$= \left\{ 100 \times \frac{95}{100} \times \frac{120}{100} - 100 \right\}\%$$

$$= (114 - 100)\% = 14\%$$

22. (d) Let MP $= 100$

So, SP $= 100 - 25\%$ of 100

$\qquad = 100 - 25 = 75$

So, Profit percent $= \dfrac{100 - 75}{75} \times 100$

$$= \frac{25}{75} \times 100\% = \frac{1}{3} \times 100 = 33\frac{1}{3}\%$$

23. (a) 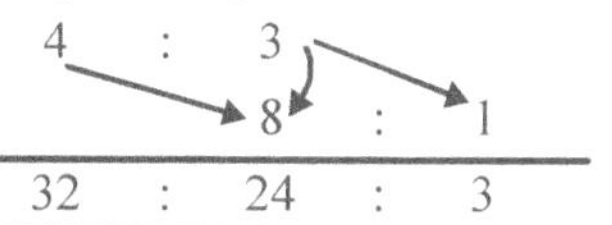

boys : girls   girls : teacher

4 : 3   8 : 1

So, boys : girls : teacher

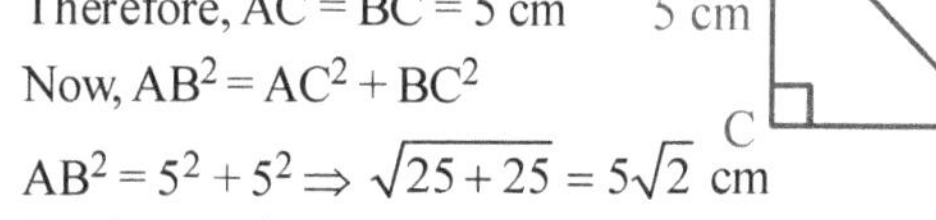

32	:	24	:	3

So, Student : teacher

$\Rightarrow$ (boys + girls) : teacher

$(32 + 24) : 3$

$56 : 3$

24. (c) $\triangle ABC$ is an isocoles triangle.

Therefore, $AC = BC = 5$ cm

Now, $AB^2 = AC^2 + BC^2$

$AB^2 = 5^2 + 5^2 \Rightarrow \sqrt{25 + 25} = 5\sqrt{2}$ cm

25. (d) Let the numbers are x, y.

$x - y = 3 \qquad\qquad \dots(1)$

$x^2 - y^2 = 39$

$\Rightarrow (x - y)(x + y) = 39$

$\Rightarrow x + y = 13 \qquad\qquad \dots(2)$

Adding eqn (1) and (2)

$x + y + x - y = 16$

$\Rightarrow x = 8$

$\therefore y = 5$

Hence, 8 is the larger number.

26.	(b)	27.	(a)	28.	(d)	29.	(c)	30.	(c)
31.	(b)	32.	(c)	33.	(b)	34.	(c)	35.	(c)
36.	(d)	37.	(c)	38.	(b)	39.	(c)	40.	(d)
41.	(c)	42.	(b)	43.	(b)	44.	(c)	45.	(c)
46.	(a)	47.	(d)	48.	(d)	49.	(b)	50.	(c)
51.	(c)	52.	(c)	53.	(c)	54.	(d)	55.	(b)
56.	(c)	57.	(b)	58.	(a)	59.	(b)	60.	(b)
61.	(c)	62.	(c)	63.	(b)	64.	(c)	65.	(b)
66.	(b)	67.	(a)	68.	(d)	69.	(b)	70.	(b)
71.	(a)	72.	(b)	73.	(d)	74.	(b)	75.	(c)

7 PRACTICE SET

Time : 60 Min.　　　　　　　　　　　　　　　**Max. Marks : 75**

1. Four of the following five are alike in a certain way and so form a group. Which is the one that does not belong to that group?
   - (a) Teacher
   - (b) Engineer
   - (c) Architect
   - (d) Doctor

2. Four of the following five are alike in a certain way and hence form a group. Find the one which is different from the other four.
   - (a) Rice
   - (b) Wheat
   - (c) Barley
   - (d) Mustard

3. In a certain code language PRESENTATION is written as ENESTATIPRON. How would INTELLIGENCE be written in that code language ?
   - (a) TETGLLTNENCE
   - (b) LLKKTGTEEBTB
   - (c) LLENLLTNTETG
   - (d) LLTEIGENINCE

DIRECTIONS (Qs. 4) : *Which one set of letters when sequentially placed at the gaps in the given letter series shall complete it ?*

4. ba _ ba _ _ bbaaa _ bbb _ _ aa
   - (a) baabab
   - (b) babbaa
   - (c) baaaab
   - (d) bababa

5. Rakesh ranks 15th from the top and 45th from the bottom in a class. How many students are there in the class?
   - (a) 64
   - (b) 59
   - (c) 54
   - (d) None of these

6. Moni is daughter of Sheela. Sheela is the wife of my wife's brother. How is Moni related to my wife ?
   - (a) Cousin
   - (b) Niece
   - (c) Sister
   - (d) Sister-in-law

7. Ram moves from a point X to 20 metres towards North. Then he moves 40 metres towards West. Then he moves 20 metres North. Then he moves 40 metres towards East and then 10 metres towards right and he reaches to a point Y. Find the distance and direction of Y from X ?
   - (a) 30 metres, North
   - (b) 30 metres, South
   - (c) 40 metres, North
   - (d) 40 metres, South

DIRECTIONS (Qs. 8) : *In questions, find the missing number from the given responses.*

8.

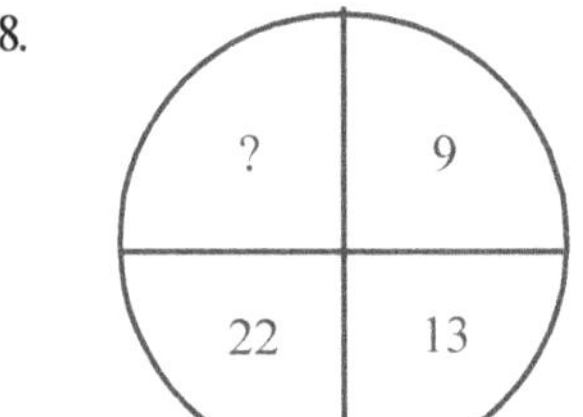

   - (a) 40
   - (b) 38
   - (c) 39
   - (d) 44

9. Nitin's age was equal to square of some number last year and the following year it would be cube of a number. If again Nitin's age has to be equal to the cube of some number, then for how long he will have to wait?
   - (a) 10 years
   - (b) 38 years
   - (c) 39 years
   - (d) 64 years

10. Six persons are sitting in a circle. A is facing B, B is to the right of E and left of C. C is to the left of D. F is to the right of A. Now D exchanges his seat with F and E with B. Who will be sitting to the left of D ?
    - (a) D
    - (b) E
    - (c) A
    - (d) B

11. A bag contains Rs 216 in the form of one rupee, 50 paise and 25 paise coins in the ratio of 2 : 3 : 4. The number of 50 paise coins is :
    - (a) 96
    - (b) 144
    - (c) 114
    - (d) 141

12. A started a business with ₹ 4500 and another person B joined after some period with ₹ 3000. Determine this period after B joined the business if the profit at the end of the year is divided in the ratio 2 : 1
    (a) After 3 months
    (b) After 4 months
    (c) After 6 months
    (d) After $2\frac{1}{2}$ months

13. The L.C.M. of two number is 630 and their H.C.F. is 9. If the sum of numbers is 153, their difference is
    (a) 17
    (b) 23
    (c) 27
    (d) 33

14. If a dividend of ₹ 57,834 is to be divided among Meena, Urmila and Vaishali in the proportion of 3:2:1, find Urmila's share.
    (a) ₹ 19,281
    (b) ₹ 17,350
    (c) ₹ 23,133
    (d) ₹ 19,278

15. For what value of k, will the expression $3x^3 - kx^2 + 4x + 16$ be divisible by $\left(x - \dfrac{k}{2}\right)$?
    (a) 4
    (b) −4
    (c) 2
    (d) 0

16. If the HCF of $x^3 + mx^2 - x + 2m$ and $x^2 + mx - 2$ is a linear polynomial, then what is the value of m?
    (a) 1
    (b) 2
    (c) 3
    (d) 4

17. The average age of a man and his son is 16 years. The ratio of their ages is 15 : 1 respectively. What is the son's age?
    (a) 30 years
    (b) 32 years
    (c) 2 years
    (d) 4 years

18. In a certain way 'Diploma' is related to 'Education'. Which of the following is related to 'Trophy' in a similar way?
    (a) Sports
    (b) Athlete
    (c) Winning
    (d) Prize

19. In a certain code CHEMISTRY is written as NFIDITUSZ. How is BEANSTOCK written in that code?
    (a) CFBOSLDPU
    (b) CFBOSUPDL
    (c) OBFCSUPDL
    (d) OBFCSLDPU

20. By following certain logic 'THEIR' is written as 'TRIHE' and 'SOLDIER' is written 'SROLIED'. How is CUSTOM written in that logic?
    (a) UTSOMC
    (b) CTSUOM
    (c) CUTSOM
    (d) YUSOMC

DIRECTIONS (Qs. 21-22): *In each of the following questions, there are two words / set of letters / numbers to the left of the sign :: which are connected in some way. The same relationship obtains between the third words / set of letters / numbers and one of the four alternatives under it. Find the correct alternative in each question.*

21. Flying : Bird :: Creeping : ?
    (a) Aeroplane
    (b) Snail
    (c) Ground
    (d) Flower

22. Clock : Time :: Thermometer : ?
    (a) Heat
    (b) Radiation
    (c) Energy
    (d) Temperature

DIRECTIONS (Qs. 23): *In each of the following questions a number series is given with one wrong number. Find that wrong number.*

23. 2 3 6 15 45 156.5 630
    (a) 156.5
    (b) 45
    (c) 15
    (d) 6

24. A man pointing to a photograph says, "The lady in the photograph is my nephew's maternal grandmother." How is the lady in the photograph related to the man's sister who has no other sister?
    (a) Cousin
    (b) Sister-in-law
    (c) Mother
    (d) Mother-in-law

25. A is the brother of B. A is the brother of C. To find what is the relation between B and C. What minimum information from the following is necessary?
    (i) Gender of C
    (ii) Gender of B
    (a) Only (i)
    (b) Only (ii)
    (c) Either (i) or (ii)
    (d) both (i) and (ii)

26. One light year is equal to
    (a) 9.46×10^{-15}m
    (b) 9.46×10^{15}m
    (c) 9.46×10^{-13}m
    (d) 9.46×10^{13}m

27. A jet engine works on the principle of conservation of
    (a) linear momentum
    (b) angular momentum
    (c) energy
    (d) mass

28. Which zone of a candle flame is the hottest ?
    (a) Dark innermost zone
    (b) Outermost zone
    (c) Middle luminous zone
    (d) Central zone

29. The surface temperature of the Sun is nearly
    (a) 2000 K
    (b) 4000 K
    (c) 6000 K
    (d) 8000 K

30. SONAR is mostly used by
    (a) Doctors
    (b) Engineers
    (c) Astronauts
    (d) Navigators

31. Which one of the following is used to remove Astigmatism for a human eye?
    (a) Concave lens
    (b) Convex lens
    (c) Cylindrical lens
    (d) Prismatic lens

32. What is the telescope designed to search for earth-size planets in the nearby region of our galaxy, termed as ?
    (a) Hubble telescope
    (b) Kepler telescope

33. Which one of the following substances does not have a melting point?
    (a) Bromine
    (b) Sodium chloride
    (c) Mercury
    (d) Glass

34. Which one of the following metals occurs in nature in free state ?
    (a) Gold
    (b) Sodium
    (c) Aluminium
    (d) Copper

35. Which one of the following noble gases is not found in the atmosphere?
(a) Argon   (b) Krypton
(c) Radon   (d) Xenon

36. Which one of the following elements shows variable equivalent mass?
(a) Zinc   (b) Silver
(c) Calcium   (d) Iron

37. Which one of the following mixtures is homogeneous?
(a) Starch and sugar
(b) Methanol and water
(c) Graphite and charcoal
(d) Calcium carbonate and calcium bicarbonate

38. Which one among the following is not a mixture?
(a) Graphite   (b) Glass
(c) Brass   (d) Steel

39. Which of the following crops would be preferred for sowing in order to enrich the soil with nitrogen ?
(a) Wheat   (b) Mustard
(c) Sunflower   (d) Gram

40. Which part of saffron plant is used to obtain the spice 'saffron' ?
(a) Dry stigma   (b) Leaves
(c) Fruits   (d) Petals

41. In human beings, the digestion of proteins starts in which part of the alimentary canal?
(a) Mouth   (b) Stomach
(c) Doudenum   (d) Ileum

42. The involvement of which one of the following is essential in the control of blood sugar ?
(a) Adrenal   (b) Pancreas
(c) Parathyroid   (d) Spleen

43. Which one of the following is a hereditary disease ?
(a) Cataract   (b) Haemophilia
(c) Pellagra   (d) Osteoporosis

44. In which one of the following animals, is skin a respiratory organ ?
(a) Cockroach   (b) Frog
(c) Shark   (d) Whale

45. Sickle-cell anemia is a disease caused due to the abnormality in
(a) white blood cells
(b) red blood cells
(c) thrombocytes
(d) blood plasma composition

46. Polio disease is caused by
(a) Bacteria   (b) Fungi
(c) Virus   (d) Worm

47. Biodegradable wastes can usually be converted into useful substances with the help of
(a) bacteria   (b) nuclear proteins
(c) radioactive substances (d) viruses

48. Which of the following is biodegradable?
(a) Paper   (b) DDT
(c) Aluminium   (d) Plastic

49. Gas released during Bhopal tragedy was
(a) Sodium isothiocyanate
(b) Ethyl isothiocyanate
(c) Potassium isothiocyanate
(d) Methyl isothiocyanate

50. Which one of the following is responsible for blue baby syndrome?
(a) Fluoride   (b) Nitrate
(c) Arsenic   (d) Lead

51. Which one among the following group of items contain only biodegradable items?
(a) Wood, grass, plastic
(b) Wood, grass, leather
(c) Fruit peels, lime juice, China clay cup
(d) Lime juice, grass, polystyrene cup

52. Food wrappd in newspaper is likely to get contaminated with
(a) lead   (b) aluminium
(c) iron   (d) magnesium

53. Which one among the following industries produces the most biodegradable wastes?
(a) Thermal power plants
(b) Food processing unites
(c) Textile mills
(d) Paper mills

54. The non-biotic pollutant of underground water is
(a) bacteria   (b) algae
(c) arsenic   (d) viruses

55. Sea level is expected to rise because of warmer climate due to the following
(a) oceans expand as they get warmer
(b) glaciers and ice-sheets melt
(c) Both 'a' and 'b'
(d) None of the above

56. The cycling of elements in an ecosystem is called
(a) Chemical cycles   (b) Biogeochemical cycles
(c) Geological cycles   (d) Geochemical cycles

57. In which of the following seas India has building Tsunami warning device?
(a) Arabian Sea   (b) South China Sea
(c) Bay of Bengal   (d) Indian Ocean

58. Which of the following is the India's first indigenously developed vaccine for "Japanese Encephalitis"?
(a) AESVAC   (b) JENVAC
(c) JESVAC   (d) MESVAC

59. When did India make first nuclear weapon explosion ?
(a) 15th May, 1964   (b) 18th May, 1974
(c) 11th May, 1989   (d) 13th May, 1998

60. The instrument used for measuring depth of water table is known as

   (a) Lysimeter (b) Odometer

   (c) Piezometer (d) Evaporimeter

61. "Stevenson Screen" is related to

   (a) Virology

   (b) Remote Sensing

   (c) Agrometeorology

   (d) Biotechnology

62. Name The Chinese supercomputer which is declared is the fastest computer of the world-

   (a) Tianhe-2 (b) Chinhane 1

   (c) Kisova (d) Techo-1

63. In which north east state of India Rongbang dare waterfall is situated?

   (a) Assam (b) Meghalaya

   (c) Manipur (d) Mizoram

64. Kalinga Prize is given in which of the following fields ?

   (a) Arts (b) Medicine

   (c) Creative writing (d) Science

65. Read the Following Railway Headquarters and Identify which is False ?

   (a) South-Central Railway - Secunderabad

   (b) Central railway - Bhopal

   (c) South Railway - Chennai

   (d) North Railway - New Delhi

66. First Indian train was started ?

   (a) From Calcutta to Delhi

   (b) From Mumbai to Thane

   (c) From Mumbai to Surat

   (d) From Mumbai to Madras

67. Which is the longest train in India?

   (a) jansadharan exp

   (b) shivganga express

   (c) duronto

   (d) prayagraj express

68. Jatak stories are written in ancient ...... language.

   (a) Sanskrit

   (b) Brahmi

   (c) Greek

   (d) Pali

69. Who among the following is the Head of Indian Republic ?

   (a) Prime Minister

   (b) President

   (c) Speaker of Lok Sabha

   (d) Vice-President

70. On which of the following dates was the Indian Constitution approved by the Constituent Assembly ?

   (a) November 26, 1949 (b) January 26, 1950

   (c) August 15, 1947 (d) January 30, 1948

71. Vishwanathan Anand is associated with which of the following games ?

   (a) Snooker (b) Billiards

   (c) Chess (d) Ice-Hockey

72. According to some archaeologists, the structure of Lothal indicates to be which of the following ?

   (a) Fort (b) Dockyard

   (c) Public building (d) Great tank

73. Nathu-La is located in Himalayas. What does 'La' mean ?

   (a) Glacier (b) Pass

   (c) Hillock (d) Crevasse

74. Name of India'a first indigenously developed vaccine has received the "pre-qualified" tag by the World Health Organisation

   (a) Rubevac Vaccine

   (b) Norovac Vaccine

   (c) Pneumovac Vaccine

   (d) Rotavac Vaccine

75. As a part of the Republic Day 2018 celebractions, 6 days Bharat Parv event has been organized at which of the given places?

   (a) India Gate

   (b) Red Fort

   (c) Rashtrapati Bhavan

   (d) Qutub Minar

RESPONSE SHEET

1. ⓐⓑⓒⓓ	2. ⓐⓑⓒⓓ	3. ⓐⓑⓒⓓ	4. ⓐⓑⓒⓓ	5. ⓐⓑⓒⓓ
6. ⓐⓑⓒⓓ	7. ⓐⓑⓒⓓ	8. ⓐⓑⓒⓓ	9. ⓐⓑⓒⓓ	10. ⓐⓑⓒⓓ
11. ⓐⓑⓒⓓ	12. ⓐⓑⓒⓓ	13. ⓐⓑⓒⓓ	14. ⓐⓑⓒⓓ	15. ⓐⓑⓒⓓ
16. ⓐⓑⓒⓓ	17. ⓐⓑⓒⓓ	18. ⓐⓑⓒⓓ	19. ⓐⓑⓒⓓ	20. ⓐⓑⓒⓓ
21. ⓐⓑⓒⓓ	22. ⓐⓑⓒⓓ	23. ⓐⓑⓒⓓ	24. ⓐⓑⓒⓓ	25. ⓐⓑⓒⓓ
26. ⓐⓑⓒⓓ	27. ⓐⓑⓒⓓ	28. ⓐⓑⓒⓓ	29. ⓐⓑⓒⓓ	30. ⓐⓑⓒⓓ
31. ⓐⓑⓒⓓ	32. ⓐⓑⓒⓓ	33. ⓐⓑⓒⓓ	34. ⓐⓑⓒⓓ	35. ⓐⓑⓒⓓ
36. ⓐⓑⓒⓓ	37. ⓐⓑⓒⓓ	38. ⓐⓑⓒⓓ	39. ⓐⓑⓒⓓ	40. ⓐⓑⓒⓓ
41. ⓐⓑⓒⓓ	42. ⓐⓑⓒⓓ	43. ⓐⓑⓒⓓ	44. ⓐⓑⓒⓓ	45. ⓐⓑⓒⓓ
46. ⓐⓑⓒⓓ	47. ⓐⓑⓒⓓ	48. ⓐⓑⓒⓓ	49. ⓐⓑⓒⓓ	50. ⓐⓑⓒⓓ
51. ⓐⓑⓒⓓ	52. ⓐⓑⓒⓓ	53. ⓐⓑⓒⓓ	54. ⓐⓑⓒⓓ	55. ⓐⓑⓒⓓ
56. ⓐⓑⓒⓓ	57. ⓐⓑⓒⓓ	58. ⓐⓑⓒⓓ	59. ⓐⓑⓒⓓ	60. ⓐⓑⓒⓓ
61. ⓐⓑⓒⓓ	62. ⓐⓑⓒⓓ	63. ⓐⓑⓒⓓ	64. ⓐⓑⓒⓓ	65. ⓐⓑⓒⓓ
66. ⓐⓑⓒⓓ	67. ⓐⓑⓒⓓ	68. ⓐⓑⓒⓓ	69. ⓐⓑⓒⓓ	70. ⓐⓑⓒⓓ
71. ⓐⓑⓒⓓ	72. ⓐⓑⓒⓓ	73. ⓐⓑⓒⓓ	74. ⓐⓑⓒⓓ	75. ⓐⓑⓒⓓ

HINTS & SOLUTIONS

1. (a) All the rest are exclusive professions while a teacher may, be there in any of these categories.

2. (d) Except 'mustard' each belongs to the same category, viz food grains. Mustard is an oilseed.

3. (d)
$$\frac{PR\ ES\ EN\ TA\ TI\ ON}{1\quad 2\quad 3\quad 4\quad 5\quad 6} \rightarrow \frac{EN\ ES\ TA\ TI\ PR\ ON}{3\quad 2\quad 4\quad 5\quad 1\quad 6}$$

Similarly,

$$\frac{IN\ TE\ LL\ IG\ EN\ CE}{1\quad 2\quad 3\quad 4\quad 5\quad 6} \rightarrow \frac{\textbf{LL TE IG EN IN CE}}{\textbf{3\quad 2\quad 4\quad 5\quad 1\quad 6}}$$

4. (b) ba/ <u>b</u> ba <u>a</u> / <u>b</u> bbaaa/ <u>b</u> bbb <u>a</u> <u>a</u> aa

5. (b) Clearly, no. of students in the class = $14 + 1 + 44 \Rightarrow 59$.

6. (b)

7. (c)

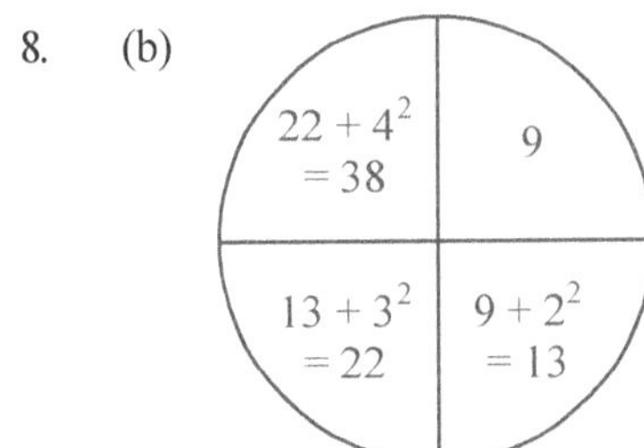

Required distance = XY = AX + AY
$= 20 + 10$
$= 30$ m, North

8. (b)

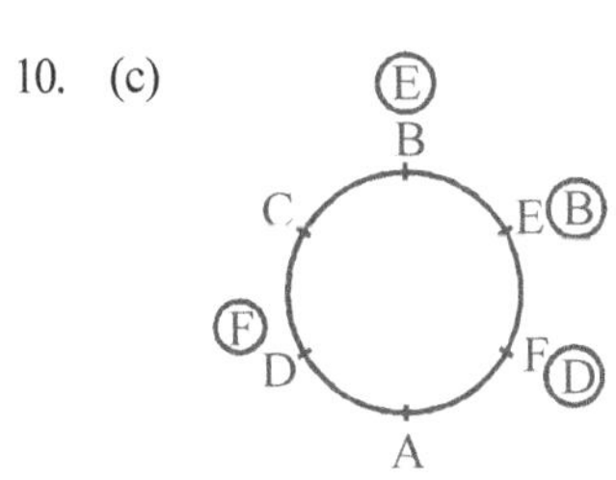

9. (b) Clearly, we have to first find two numbers whose difference is 2 and of which the smaller one is a perfect square and the bigger one a perfect cube.
Such numbers are 25 and 27.
Thus, Nitin is now 26 years old. Since the next perfect cube after 27 is 64,
So required time period = $(64 - 26)$ years = 38 years.

10. (c)

Now, A is to the left of D.

11. (b) Let the no. of one rupee, 50 paise and 25 paise coins be 2x, 3x and 4x respectively.
According to question,

$$₹\left(2x + \frac{3x}{2} + \frac{4x}{4}\right) = Rs.\ 216$$

$$\Rightarrow \frac{8x + 6x + 4x}{4} = 216$$

$$\therefore\ x = 48$$

$\therefore$ Number of 50 paise coins = $48 \times 3 = 144$

12. (a) Let B joined after x months.
Then, $4500 \times 12 : 3000(12 - x) = 2 : 1$
Ratio of their investments

$$= \frac{4500 \times 12}{3000(12 - x)} = \frac{2}{1}$$

$$\Rightarrow x = 3$$

13. (c) Let numbers be x and y.
$\because$ Product of two numbers = their (LCM $\times$ HCF)
$\Rightarrow xy = 630 \times 9$
Also, $x + y = 153$ (given)

since $x - y = = \sqrt{(x + y)^2 - 4xy}$

$$\Rightarrow x - y = \sqrt{(153)^2 - 4(630 \times 9)}$$

$$= \sqrt{23409 - 22680} = \sqrt{729} = 27$$

14. (d) Share of Urmila in dividend = $\left(\frac{2}{6} \times 57834\right)$

$$= ₹\ 19278$$

15. (b) The expression $3x^3 - kx^2 + 4x + 16$ is divisible by $x - \frac{k}{2}$.

Then, $x = \frac{k}{2}$ satisfy the equation

$$\Rightarrow 3\left(\frac{k}{2}\right)^3 - k\left(\frac{k}{2}\right)^2 + 4\left(\frac{k}{2}\right) + 16 = 0$$

$$\Rightarrow \frac{3k^3 - 2k^3 + 16k + 128}{8} = 0$$

$$\Rightarrow k^3 + 16k + 128 = 0$$
$$\Rightarrow (k + 4)(k^2 - 4k + 32) = 0$$
$$\Rightarrow k + 4 = 0$$
$$\Rightarrow k = -4$$

16. (a) Let $f_1(x) = x^3 + mx^2 - x + 2m$
and $f_2(x) = x^2 + mx - 2$
Let $m = 1$
$\therefore\ f_1(x) = x^3 + x^2 - x + 2$
and $f_2(x) = x^2 + x - 2 = (x + 2)(x - 1)$

When $x = 1$,

$f(1) = 1 + 1 - 1 + 2 \neq 0$

When $x = -2$,

$f(-2) = (-2)^3 + (-2)^2 - (-2) + 2 = 0$

Required value of m is 1.

17. (c) Let the age of father and son be 15x years and x years respectively.

Now, according to the question, $\dfrac{15x + x}{2} = 16$

or, $x = \dfrac{16 \times 2}{16} = 2$ years

Hence age of the son = 2 years

18. (a) A successful finish of 'Education' equips one with 'Diploma'. Similary, a successful finish in 'Sports' equips one with 'Trophy'.

19. (c) Reverse the first four letters of the given word. Now, all letters are coded as one place forward as in English alphabet except the middle letter, which remains unchanged.

20. (a) Words are arranged in alphabetical order but from right to left. If becomes UTSOMC.

21. (b) As 'Bird' flies, in the same way, 'snails' creeps.

22. (d) First is an instrument to measure the second.

23. (a) The series is $\times 1.5, \times 2, \times 2.5, \times 3$ and so on.

24. (c) Clearly, the lady is the grandmother of man's sister's son i.e., the mother of the mother of man's sister's son i.e., the mother of man's sister.

So, the lady is man's mother.

25. (d) Without knowing the sex of C, we can't be determined whether B is sister of C or B is brother of C. Similarly without knowing the sex of B we can't be determined whether C is sister of B or C is brother of B. Therefore, both (i) and (ii) are necessary.

26. (b) Distance covered by light in vacuum in 1 year is called light year.

1 ligth year = 9.46×10^{15} m

27. (a)

28. (c) Middle luminous zone of a candle flame is the hottest.

29. (c)

30. (d) astronauts

31. (c) In Astigmatism, eye cannot see objects in two orthogonal directions clearly simultaneously. This abnormality is removed by using cylindrical lens.

32. (a) Hubble telescope is designed to search for earth-size planets in the nearby region of our galaxy.

33. (c) Mercury exists in liquid state hence, it has no melting point.

34. (a) Gold is a stable noble metal and resists the action of the atmosphere and occurs in free state.

35. (c) Radon (Rn) is not found in the atmosphere.

36. (d) Iron shows the variable equivalent mass.

37. (b)

38. (a)

39. (d) Gram would be preferred for sowing in order to enrich the soil with nitrogen. It is because gram is a leguminous crop. The root nodules of leguminous crop contains Rhizobium, a symbiotic bacterium that helps in fixing of nitrogen from atmosphere.

40. (a) Dry stigma of safron plant is used to obtain the spice, Saffron.

41. (b) In human, the digestion of protein starts in the stomach region of alimentary canal where pepsin hydrolyzes proteins into proteases and peptones.

42. (b) Involvement of pancreas is essential in the control of blood sugar. Pancreas produces the hormone insulin which checks the blood sugar level and glucagon which tends to increase the level of blood glucose.

43. (b) Haemophilia is genetic disorder disease in which blood clotting not easily takes place because of recessive X linked chromosome.

44. (b) In Frog, skin is a respiratory organ. Amphibians use their skin as a respiratory surface. Frogs eliminate carbon dioxide 2.5 times as fast through their skin as they do through their lungs. Whale (a fish) obtain 60% of their oxygen through their skin. Humans exchange only 1% of their carbon dioxide through their skin. Constraints of water loss dictate that terrestrial animals must develop more efficient lungs.

45. (b) Sickle cell anemia is an inherited blood disorder that causes chronic anemia, periodic episodes of pain, and other complications. In sickle cell anemia, the red blood cells become rigid and shaped like crescents, or sickles, rather than being flexible and round. This change in shape prevents red blood cells from getting into small blood vessels. As a result, the tissues do not get enough oxygen. Lack of oxygen can cause pain and damage in the arms, legs, and organs (e.g., spleen, kidney, brain).

46. (c) Polio (poliomyelitis) is a highly infectious disease caused by a virus. It invades the nervous system and can cause irreversible paralysis in a matter of hours. Polio can strike at any age, but it mainly affects children under five years old.

47. (a) 48. (a) 49. (d) 50. (b) 51. (b)

52. (a) 53. (b) 54. (c) 55. (c)

56. (b) The cycling of elements is an ecosystem is called Biogeochemical cycles.

57. (b) With an aim of avoiding a repeat of the 2004 catastrophe, India is building Tsunami warning device in the South China Sea, which is likely to operate in the next 10 months.

58. (b) JENVAC is the India's first indigenously developed Japanese Encephalitis vaccine. It has been jointly developed by scientists of National Institute of Virology, Indian Council of Medical Research and Bharat Biotech Ltd.

59. (b) India's first nuclear weapon explosion's assigned code name was 'Pokhran–I' or 'Smiling Buddha'. It took place on 18th May 1974. According to Indian Ministry of External Affairs (MoEA) this test is for peaceful nuclear purposes.

60. (c) A piezometer is a device which measures the pressure of groundwater at a specific point so to measure the water table in ground-water.

61. (c) A Stevenson screen or instrument shelter is a kind of protective enclosure used to shield meteorological instruments against precipitation and direct heat radiation from outer sources. Its purpose is to provide a standardised environment in which to measure temperature, humidity, dew-point and atmospheric pressure by their respective instruments.

62. (a) 63. (b) 64. (d) 65. (b) 66. (b)

67. (c) 68. (d) 69. (b) 70. (a) 71. (c)

72. (b) 73. (b) 74. (d) 75. (b)

<table><tr><td>

8

</td><td>

PRACTICE SET

</td></tr></table>

Time : 60 Min.   **Max. Marks : 75**

DIRECTIONS (Qs. 1 - 2) : *In questions, find the odd word/letters/ number pair from the given alternatives.*

1. (a) Kolkata   (b) Vishakhapatnam
   (c) Bengaluru   (d) Haldia
2. (a) HGFE   (b) PONM
   (c) DCBA   (d) MSTU

DIRECTIONS (Qs. 3-4) : *In questions below, a series is given with one term missing. Choose the correct alternative from the given ones that will complete the series.*

3. 3, 6, 9, 15, 24, 39, 63, ?
   (a) 100   (b) 87
   (c) 102   (d) 99
4. If $A = 1$, $AGE = 13$, then $CAR = ?$
   (a) 19   (b) 20
   (c) 21   (d) 22
5. Govind is 48 years old. He is twice as old as his son Prem is now. How old was Prem seven years before?
   (a) 16   (b) 17
   (c) 13   (d) 18
6. Pointing to a man, a lady said "His mother is the only daughter of my mother". How is the lady related to the man?
   (a) Mother   (b) Daughter
   (c) Sister   (d) Aunt
7. After walking 10 m, Shankar turned left and covered a distance of 6 m, then turned right and covered a distance of 20 m. In the end, he was moving towards the south. From which direction did Shankar start his journey?
   (a) West   (b) North
   (c) South   (d) East
8. If '−' stands for '+', '+' stands for '×', '×' stands for '−' then which one of the following is not correct ?

(a) $22 + 7 - 3 \times 9 = 148$
(b) $33 \times 5 - 10 + 20 = 228$
(c) $7 + 28 - 3 \times 52 = 127$
(d) $44 - 9 + 6 \times 11 = 87$

9.
$$3 \quad \boxed{\begin{matrix} 11 \\ 28 \end{matrix}} \quad 4 \qquad 5 \quad \boxed{\begin{matrix} 22 \\ 57 \end{matrix}} \quad 3 \qquad 6 \quad \boxed{\begin{matrix} 121 \\ ? \end{matrix}} \quad 5$$
$$\quad\quad 5 \quad\quad\quad\quad\quad\quad 20 \quad\quad\quad\quad\quad\quad 25$$

   (a) 176   (b) 115
   (c) 157   (d) 131

10. What is the value of $1.\overline{34} + 4.1\overline{2}$?

   (a) $\dfrac{133}{90}$ (b) $\dfrac{371}{90}$

   (c) $5\dfrac{219}{990}$ (d) $5\dfrac{461}{990}$

11. A sum of money is divided among A, B, C and D in the ratio $3 : 5 : 8 : 9$ respectively. If the share of D is ₹ 1,872 more than the share of A, then what is the total amount of money of B & C together?
   (a) ₹ 4,156   (b) ₹ 4,165
   (c) ₹ 4,056   (d) ₹ 4,068
12. What approximate compound interest can be obtained on an amount of ₹ 3,980 after 2 years at 8 p.c.p.a. ?
   (a) 650   (b) 680
   (c) 600   (d) 662
13. By selling 8 dozen pencils, a shopkeeper gains the selling price of 1 dozen pencils. What is the gain?

   (a) $12\dfrac{1}{2}\%$ (b) $13\dfrac{1}{7}\%$

   (c) $14\dfrac{2}{7}\%$ (d) $87\dfrac{1}{2}\%$

14. The value of k for which the lines $2x + ky + 7 = 0$ and $27x - 18y + 25 = 0$ are perpendicular to each other, is
 (a) $k = -1$　　　　(b) $k = 2$
 (c) $k = 3$　　　　(d) $k = -2$

15. If $x + \dfrac{1}{y} = 1$ and $y + \dfrac{1}{z} = 1$, what is the value of xyz?
 (a) 1　　　　(b) -1
 (c) 0　　　　(d) $\dfrac{1}{2}$

16. An aeroplane flies along the four sides of a square at the speeds of 200, 400, 600 and 800 km/h. Find the average speed of the plane around the field.
 (a) 384 km/h　　　　(b) 370 km/h
 (c) 368 km/h　　　　(d) None of these

17. A, B and C can do a work in 6, 8 and 12 days respectively. Doing that work together they get an amount of Rs. 1350. What is the share of B in that amount?
 (a) ₹ 450　　　　(b) ₹ 168.75
 (c) ₹ 337.50　　　　(d) ₹ 718.75

18. A and B started a business by investing ₹ 35,000 and ₹ 20,000 respectively. B left the business after 5 months and C joined the business with a sum of ₹ 15,000. The profit earned at the end of the year is ₹ 84,125. What is B's share of profit?
 (a) ₹14133　　　　(b) ₹15,000
 (c) ₹13,460　　　　(d) Cannot be determined

19. A hollow cylindrical iron pipe of length 1.4 m has base radius 2.5 cm and thickness of the metal is 1 cm. What is the volume of the iron used in the pipe?
 (a) 2640 cu cm　　　　(b) 2604 cu cm
 (c) 2460 cu cm　　　　(d) None of these

DIRECTIONS (Q. 20): *In each of the following questions a number series is given with one wrong number. Find that wrong number.*

---

20. 36　20　12　8　6　5.5　4.5
 (a) 5.5　　(b) 6　　(c) 12　　(d) 20

21. Find the missing term in the following series.
 240, ... 120, 40, 10, 2
 (a) 480　(b) 240　(c) 220　(d) 120

22. In a certain code BROUGHT is written as SGFVAQN. How is SUPREME written in that code?
 (a) FNFSRTO　　　　(b) RTOSDLD
 (c) DLDSRTO　　　　(d) DLDSTVQ

23. In a certain code 'CLOUD' is written as 'GTRKF'. How is SIGHT written in that code?
 (a) WGJHV　　　　(b) UGHHT
 (c) UHJFW　　　　(d) WFJGV

24. If 'P $ Q' means 'P is brother of Q', 'P # Q' means 'P is mother of Q' and 'P*Q' means 'P is daughter of Q', then who is the father in 'A # B $ C * D'?
 (a) D　　　　(b) B
 (c) C　　　　(d) Data inadequate

25. Pointing to a boy, Meena says, "He is the son of my grandfather's only son." How is the boy's mother related to Meena?
 (a) Mother　　　　(b) Aunt
 (c) Sister　　　　(d) Data inadequate

26. Chemical formula of Water glass is-
 (a) Na_2SiO_3　　　　(b) Al_2O_3
 (c) $NaAlO_2$　　　　(d) $CaSiO_3$

27. The hardest substance available in earth is-
 (a) Platinum　　　　(b) Silicon
 (c) Diamond　　　　(d) Gold

28. Which of the following is the best conductor of electricity ?
 (a) Zinc　　　　(b) Copper
 (c) Gold　　　　(d) Silver

29. The ratio of pure gold in 18 carat gold is-
 (a) 60%　(b) 75%　(c) 80%　(d) 100%

30. Which radioactive pollutant has recently drawn the attention of the public due to its occurance in the building materials ?
 (a) Radium　　　　(b) Radon
 (c) Thorium　　　　(d) Plutonium

31. Bleaching powder is made from-
 (a) Sulphur dioxide and gypsum
 (b) Chlorine and Charcoal
 (c) Soda ash and lime
 (d) Lime and Chlorine

32. Brass is an alloy of-
 (a) Nickel and Copper　　(b) Copper and Silver
 (c) Nickel and Zinc　　(d) Zinc and Copper

33. The element required for Solar energy conversion-
 (a) Beryllium　　　　(b) Silicon
 (c) Tantalum　　　　(d) Ultra pure carbon

34. Monazite is an ore of-
 (a) Sodium　　　　(b) Titanium
 (c) Thorium　　　　(d) Zirconium

35. The gas usually causing explosions in coal mines is-
 (a) Hydrogen　　　　(b) Carbon monoxide
 (c) Air　　　　(d) Methane

36. Which one of the following symptoms of nutritional deficiency disorders is specific to Vitamin C deficiency ?
    - (a) Cracks on lips
    - (b) Spongy bleeding gums
    - (c) Pale conjunctivae
    - (d) Rashes on skin

37. The first Europeans, in modern times, to enter into trade relations with India were the
    - (a) Dutch
    - (b) Portuguese
    - (c) French
    - (d) British

38. The Vedic god Puranadara was the same as
    - (a) Varuna
    - (b) Indra
    - (c) Yama
    - (d) Rudra

39. The decision to form INA (Azad Hind Fauj) Was taken at
    - (a) Tokyo
    - (b) Bangkok
    - (c) Rangoon
    - (d) Calcutta

40. Who was the first Indian to have entered the Indian Civil Service?
    - (a) Satyendra Nath Tagore
    - (b) C.C. Desai
    - (c) S.N. Banerjee
    - (d) Subhash Chandra Bose

41. The Maratha and the Kesari were the newspapers published by Lokmanya Tilak to awaken the people .In which language was the Maratha published ?
    - (a) Marathi
    - (b) Gujarati
    - (c) Hindi
    - (d) English

42. Antacids are found in medicines that cure
    - (a) eyesight
    - (b) stomachache
    - (c) pimpus
    - (d) headache

43. The constituent Assembly set up to prepare a draft on the Constitution of free India was chaired by
    - (a) Dr. Rajendra Prasad
    - (b) Dr. B.R. Ambedkar
    - (c) Jawaharlal Nehru
    - (d) C.Rajagopalachari

44. With which form dance was Mrinalini Sarabhai Associated?
    - (a) Kathak
    - (b) Katahkali
    - (c) Bahartanatyam
    - (d) Kuchipudi

45. The first to implement the concept of planned economy was
    - (a) Jawaharlal Nehru
    - (b) Joseph Stalin
    - (c) Marshal Tito
    - (d) Mao Ze Dong

46. Which spacecraft first landed on the Moon ?
    - (a) Apollo 10
    - (b) Apollo 11
    - (c) Sputnik
    - (d) Apollo 13

47. In India , partyless Democracy was first advocated by
    - (a) Jayprakash Narayan
    - (b) M.N.Roy
    - (c) Vinoda Bhave
    - (d) Mahatama Gandhi

48. The proivision of providing identify cards to voters has been made in
    - (a) the Constitution of India
    - (b) the Representation of the people Act., 1958
    - (c) the Election Laws (Amendment) Act. 1975
    - (d) the criminal and Election Laws (Amendment) Act, 1969

49. Which is the biggest fresh water lake in the world ?
    - (a) Chilka Lake
    - (b) Caspian lake
    - (c) Dal Lake
    - (d) Lake Superior

50. The process of union of two or more molecules of a susbtance to form a large single molecule is called :
    - (a) Fusion
    - (b) Diffusion
    - (c) Polymerisation
    - (d) Synthesis

51. Which one of the following has most corrosive effect ?
    - (a) Air
    - (b) Carbon dioxide
    - (c) Plants
    - (d) Water

52. Who has said," Child is the Father of man" ?
    - (a) Shakespeare
    - (b) Wordsworth
    - (c) Keats
    - (d) Bacon

53. Among the four dynasties listed below, which one minted coins made of lead ?
    - (a) Mauryas
    - (b) Satavahanas
    - (c) Western Kashatrapas
    - (d) Guptas

54. What is the meaning of the term "tour de force '?
    - (a) tour of the armed forces
    - (b) forceful tour
    - (c) a feat of strength
    - (d) None of these

55. By which amendment of the Constitution of India were privy purses and pribileges of princes abolished ?
    - (a) 25th
    - (b) 26th
    - (c) 27th
    - (d) 28th

56. Cow milk is a rich source of-
    - (a) Vitamin A
    - (b) Vitamin B1
    - (c) Vitamin C
    - (d) Vitamin D

57. The element found in the surface of the Moon is-
    - (a) Tin
    - (b) Tungsten
    - (c) Tantalum
    - (d) Titanium

58. The average salinity of sea water is-
    - (a) 2%
    - (b) 3%
    - (c) 2.5%
    - (d) 3.5%

59. The isotope of Uranium capable of sustaining chain reaction is-
    - (a) U235
    - (b) U238
    - (c) U239
    - (d) None of these

60. Radioactive disintegration of Uranium ultimately results in formation of-
    - (a) Radium
    - (b) Thorium
    - (c) Polonium
    - (d) Lead

61. Cotton fibers are made of-
    - (a) cellulose
    - (b) starch
    - (c) proteins
    - (d) fats

62. Which of the following ores does not contain iron?
    (a) Haematite   (b) Magnetite
    (c) Limonite   (d) Cassiterite

63. Which variety of glass is heat resistant?
    (a) Hard glass   (b) Flint glass
    (c) Pyrex glass   (d) Bottle glass

64. Which of the following is used for removing air bubbles from glass during its manufacture ?
    (a) Fledspar   (b) Arsenic oxide
    (c) Potassium Carbonate (d) Soda Ash

65. What are soaps?
    (a) Salts of silicates
    (b) Ester of heavy fatty acids
    (c) Sodium or potassium salts of heavier fatty acids
    (d) Mixture of glycerol and alcohol

66. Which one of the following is the best source of vitamin A?
    (a) Apple   (b) Carrot
    (c) Amla   (d) Raddish

67. Which of the following is not a chemical reaction ?
    (a) Burning of paper
    (b) Digestion of food
    (c) Conversion of water into steam
    (d) Burning of coal

68. Which of the following is a chemical change?
    (a) Rusting of iron   (b) Tempering of iron
    (c) Melting of iron   (d) Bending of iron

69. Photoelectric effect was discovered by-
    (a) Einstein   (b) Hertz
    (c) Bohr   (d) Plank

70. The hydrogenation of the vegetables oils takes place in the presence of finely divided-
    (a) aluminium   (b) charcoal
    (c) silica   (d) nickel

71. Which of the following is not a bleaching agent?
    (a) Sulpher di-oxide   (b) Carbon di-oxide
    (c) Sodium hypochlorite (d) Chlorine

72. The gas usually filled in electric bulb is-
    (a) Hydrogen   (b) Oxygen
    (c) Nitrogen   (d) Carbon di-oxide

73. Who has been conferred with the Badminton Association of India (BAI) Lifetime Achievement Award 2018?
    (a) Prakash Padukone
    (b) Syed Modi
    (c) Dipankar Bhattacharjee
    (d) Arvind Bhat

74. Which among the following stadiums will host the finals of the 2020 ICC World T20 of both the men's and women's?
    (a) Salt Lake Stadium, India
    (b) Melbourne Cricket Ground (MCG), Australia
    (c) Bidvest Wanderers Stadium, South Africa
    (d) Lord's Cricket Ground, United Kingdom

75. What is the India's GDP growth prediction for FY19, according to 2018 Economic Survey of India?
    (a) 6.5 to 7.25%
    (b) 7 to 7.5%
    (c) 6.9 to 7.2%
    (d) 7.5 to 8.0%

RESPONSE SHEET

1. (a) (b) (c) (d)	2. (a) (b) (c) (d)	3. (a) (b) (c) (d)	4. (a) (b) (c) (d)	5. (a) (b) (c) (d)
6. (a) (b) (c) (d)	7. (a) (b) (c) (d)	8. (a) (b) (c) (d)	9. (a) (b) (c) (d)	10. (a) (b) (c) (d)
11. (a) (b) (c) (d)	12. (a) (b) (c) (d)	13. (a) (b) (c) (d)	14. (a) (b) (c) (d)	15. (a) (b) (c) (d)
16. (a) (b) (c) (d)	17. (a) (b) (c) (d)	18. (a) (b) (c) (d)	19. (a) (b) (c) (d)	20. (a) (b) (c) (d)
21. (a) (b) (c) (d)	22. (a) (b) (c) (d)	23. (a) (b) (c) (d)	24. (a) (b) (c) (d)	25. (a) (b) (c) (d)
26. (a) (b) (c) (d)	27. (a) (b) (c) (d)	28. (a) (b) (c) (d)	29. (a) (b) (c) (d)	30. (a) (b) (c) (d)
31. (a) (b) (c) (d)	32. (a) (b) (c) (d)	33. (a) (b) (c) (d)	34. (a) (b) (c) (d)	35. (a) (b) (c) (d)
36. (a) (b) (c) (d)	37. (a) (b) (c) (d)	38. (a) (b) (c) (d)	39. (a) (b) (c) (d)	40. (a) (b) (c) (d)
41. (a) (b) (c) (d)	42. (a) (b) (c) (d)	43. (a) (b) (c) (d)	44. (a) (b) (c) (d)	45. (a) (b) (c) (d)
46. (a) (b) (c) (d)	47. (a) (b) (c) (d)	48. (a) (b) (c) (d)	49. (a) (b) (c) (d)	50. (a) (b) (c) (d)
51. (a) (b) (c) (d)	52. (a) (b) (c) (d)	53. (a) (b) (c) (d)	54. (a) (b) (c) (d)	55. (a) (b) (c) (d)
56. (a) (b) (c) (d)	57. (a) (b) (c) (d)	58. (a) (b) (c) (d)	59. (a) (b) (c) (d)	60. (a) (b) (c) (d)
61. (a) (b) (c) (d)	62. (a) (b) (c) (d)	63. (a) (b) (c) (d)	64. (a) (b) (c) (d)	65. (a) (b) (c) (d)
66. (a) (b) (c) (d)	67. (a) (b) (c) (d)	68. (a) (b) (c) (d)	69. (a) (b) (c) (d)	70. (a) (b) (c) (d)
71. (a) (b) (c) (d)	72. (a) (b) (c) (d)	73. (a) (b) (c) (d)	74. (a) (b) (c) (d)	75. (a) (b) (c) (d)

HINTS & SOLUTIONS

1. (c)

2. (d) $H \xrightarrow{(-1)} G \xrightarrow{(-1)} F \xrightarrow{(-1)} E$

   $P \xrightarrow{(-1)} O \xrightarrow{(-1)} N \xrightarrow{(-1)} M$

   $D \xrightarrow{(-1)} C \xrightarrow{(-1)} B \xrightarrow{(-1)} A$

   $M \xrightarrow{(+6)} S \xrightarrow{(+1)} T \xrightarrow{(+1)} U$

   M S T U is odd word

3. (c) $3 + 3 = 6$

   $6 + 3 = 9$

   $9 + 6 = 15$

   $15 + 9 = 24$

   $24 + 15 = 39$

   $39 + 24 = 63$

   $63 + 39 = 102$

4. (d) As, $A + G + E = 1 + 7 + 5 = 13$

   Similarly, $C + A + R = 3 + 1 + 18 = 22$

5. (b) Govind's age = 48 years

   According to question

   Prem's age = 48/2 = 24 years

   Prem's age seven years before = 24 − 7

   $\qquad\qquad\qquad\qquad = 17$ years.

6. (a)

   Mother

   Mother = Lady

   Man

   (His) mother is the only daughter of (my) mother.

7. (b)

   From the diagram, it is clear that Shankar started his journey from North to South.

8. (c) By options–

   (a) $22 \times 7 + 3 - 9 = 148$

   $\qquad 154 + 3 - 9$

   $\qquad 157 - 9 = 148$ (Correct)

   (b) $33 - 5 + 10 \times 20 = 228$

   $\qquad 33 - 5 + 200$

   $\qquad 200 + 33 - 5$

   $\qquad 233 - 5 = 228$ (Correct)

   (c) $7 \times 28 + 3 - 52 = 127$

   $\qquad 196 + 3 - 52$

   $\qquad 199 - 52 = 147$ (Incorrect)

   (d) $44 + 9 \times 6 - 11 = 87$

   $\qquad 44 + 54 - 11$

   $\qquad 98 - 11 = 87$ (Correct)

9. (a)

   $3 \begin{array}{c} 11 \\ \boxed{\begin{array}{l} 11 + 5 + 4 \times 3 \\ = 16 + 12 = 28 \end{array}} \\ 5 \end{array} 4$ $5 \begin{array}{c} 22 \\ \boxed{\begin{array}{l} 22 + 20 + 5 \times 3 \\ = 42 + 15 = 57 \end{array}} \\ 20 \end{array} 3$ $6 \begin{array}{c} 121 \\ \boxed{\begin{array}{l} 121 + 25 + 6 \times 5 \\ = 146 + 30 = 176 \end{array}} \\ 25 \end{array} 5$

10. (d) $\because 1.\overline{34} = \dfrac{134 - 1}{99} = \dfrac{133}{99}$

    and $4.1\overline{2} = \dfrac{412 - 41}{90} = \dfrac{371}{90}$

    $\therefore 1.\overline{34} + 4.1\overline{2} = \dfrac{133}{99} + \dfrac{371}{90} = \dfrac{1330 + 4081}{990}$

    $= \dfrac{5411}{990} = 5\dfrac{461}{990}$

11. (c) Share of $B + C = \dfrac{1872}{9 - 3} \times (5 + 8) = ₹\ 4056$

12. (d) Equivalent % interest for compound rate of interest of 8% for 2 years

    $= 8 + 8 + \dfrac{8 \times 8}{100} = 16.64\%$

    So, interest = 16.64% of 3980 ≈ 662

13. (c) Let the cost price = ₹ x

    Profit = ₹ x

    Cost price of 8 dozen pencil = ₹ 7x

    Gain per cent = $\dfrac{x}{7x} \times 100$

    $= \dfrac{100}{7} = 14\dfrac{2}{7}\%$

14. (c) $2x + ky + 7 = 0 \Rightarrow ky = -2x - 7 \Rightarrow y = \dfrac{-2}{k}x - \dfrac{7}{k}$

    $27x + 18y + 25 = 0 \Rightarrow 18y = 27x + 25$

    $\Rightarrow y = \dfrac{3}{2}x + \dfrac{25}{18}$

    $\therefore \dfrac{-2}{k} \times \dfrac{3}{2} = 1 \Rightarrow k = 3$

15. (b) Given that, $x + \dfrac{1}{y} = 1$

$$\Rightarrow \qquad xy + 1 = y \qquad \text{...(i)}$$

and $\qquad y + \dfrac{1}{z} = 1 \Rightarrow 1 - \dfrac{1}{z} = y$

$$\Rightarrow \quad \dfrac{z-1}{z} = y \qquad \qquad \text{...(ii)}$$

From eq. (ii),

$$y = \dfrac{z-1}{z}$$

Comparing eqn. (i) with (ii)

$$xy + 1 = \dfrac{z-1}{z}$$

$$\Rightarrow \qquad xyz + z = z - 1$$
$$\Rightarrow \qquad xyz = -1$$

16. (a) Let each side of the square be x km and let the average speed of the plane around the field be y km/h. Then,

$$\dfrac{x}{200} + \dfrac{x}{400} + \dfrac{x}{600} + \dfrac{x}{800} = \dfrac{4x}{y}$$

$$\Rightarrow \dfrac{25x}{2400} = \dfrac{4x}{y} \Rightarrow y = \left(\dfrac{2400 \times 4}{25}\right) = 384.$$

$\therefore$ Average speed = 384 km/h.

17. (a) A's one day's work $= \dfrac{1}{6}$

B's one day's work $= \dfrac{1}{8}$

C's one day's work $= \dfrac{1}{12}$

A's share : B's share : C's share

$$= \dfrac{1}{6} : \dfrac{1}{8} : \dfrac{1}{12}$$

Multiplying each ratio by the L.C.M. of their denominators, the ratios become 4 : 3 : 2

$\therefore$ B's share $= \dfrac{1350 \times 3}{9} = ₹450$

18. (c) Ratio of equivalent capitals of A, B and C for 1 month

$= 35000 \times 12 : 20000 \times 5 : 15000 \times 7$

$= 35 \times 12 : 20 \times 5 : 15 \times 7 = 84 : 20 : 21$

Sum of the ratios $= 84 + 20 + 21 = 125$

$\therefore$ B's share $= ₹\left(\dfrac{20}{125} \times 84125\right) = ₹13460$

19. (a) $\therefore$ Volume of pipe, $V = \pi\left(r_1^2 - r_2^2\right) \times h$

$$= \dfrac{22}{7}[(3.5)^2 - (2.5)^2] \times 140$$

$$= \dfrac{22}{7}(12.25 - 6.25) \times 140$$

$$= 22 \times 6 \times 20 = 2640 \text{ cu cm}$$

20. (a) The series is $-16, -8, -4, -2, -1, 0.5,$ and so on.

21. (b) Ratios of two consecutive terms are 1, 1/2, 1/3, 1/4, and 1/5 respectively.

22. (c) Here the given word is BROUGHT. Reversing the order of the letters, it becomes THGUORB. Now, write each letter one place backward except the middle letter (write middle letter one place forward). It becomes SGFVNQA. Now, reverse the order of the last three letters and it becomes SGFVAQN.

Similarly,

SUPREME $\rightarrow$ EMERPUS $\rightarrow$ DLDSOTR $\rightarrow$ DLDSRTO

23. (a) Here, each letter of the word CLOUD is written as three letters forward and one letter backward alternately. Following this CLOUD becomes FKRTG. After that, reverse the order of the result obtained in the previous operation. Thus, FKRTG becomes GTRKF.

Similarly, SIGHT will change its form as follows:

SIGHT $\rightarrow$ VHJGW $\rightarrow$ WGJHV

24. (a) Clearly, B and C are siblings. While A and D are parents. Now, A is the mother.,Hence, D must be the father.

25. (a) One's grandfather's only son $\Rightarrow$ one's_father. And the son of one's father $\Rightarrow$ One's_brother or oneself. Hence, the mother of the boy is Meena's mother.

26.	(a)	27.	(c)	28.	(d)	29.	(b)	30.	(c)
31.	(d)	32.	(d)	33.	(b)	34.	(c)	35.	(d)
36.	(c)	37.	(b)	38.	(b)	39.	(a)	40.	(c)
41.	(d)	42.	(b)	43.	(a)	44.	(c)	45.	(b)
46.	(b)	47.	(a)	48.	(b)	49.	(d)	50.	(c)
51.	(d)	52.	(b)	53.	(b)	54.	(c)	55.	(b)
56.	(b)	57.	(d)	58.	(d)	59.	(a)	60.	(d)
61.	(a)	62.	(d)	63.	(c)	64.	(b)	65.	(c)
66.	(b)	67.	(c)	68.	(a)	69.	(a)	70.	(d)
71.	(b)	72.	(c)	73.	(a)	74.	(b)	75.	(b)

9 | PRACTICE SET

Time : 60 Min.　　　　　　　　　　　　　　　　　　**Max. Marks : 75**

DIRECTION : Select the related word from given alternatives.

1. hive : bee :: eyrie : ?
   - (a) Pigeon
   - (b) Sparrow
   - (c) Parrot
   - (d) Eagle

DIRECTIONS (Qs. 2-4) : *In questions, find the odd word/letters/ number pair from the given alternatives.*

2.
   - (a) vwqp
   - (b) yxmn
   - (c) gfkl
   - (d) cbrs

3. 24, 35, 20, 31, 16, 27, __, __
   - (a) 9, 9
   - (b) 5, 30
   - (c) 8, 25
   - (d) 12, 23

4. In a language FIFTY is written as CACTY, CAR as POL, TAR as TOL, how can TARIFF be written in that language?
   - (a) TOEFEL
   - (b) TOEFDD
   - (c) TOLADD
   - (d) TOLACC

5. Which one set of letters when sequentially placed at the gaps in the given letter series shall complete it ?

   rtx _ sx _ z _ txy _ _ yz
   - (a) y y r x s
   - (b) y y s x r
   - (c) y y r s x
   - (d) y y x r s

6. A is in the east of B which is in the North of C. If D is in the South of C., then in which direction of A, is D.
   - (a) North – West
   - (b) South
   - (c) East – East
   - (d) South–West

7. Rearrange the given jumbled letters to make a meaningful word.

   Given letters : riytaraplamen
   - (a) Lamination
   - (b) Realignment
   - (c) Parliamentary
   - (d) Replacement

8. Introducing a boy, a girl said, "He is the son of the daughter of the father of my uncle." How is the boy related to the girl?
   - (a) Brother
   - (b) Nephew
   - (c) Uncle
   - (d) Son-in-law

9. In the following figure, the boys who are cricketer and sober are indicated by which number ?

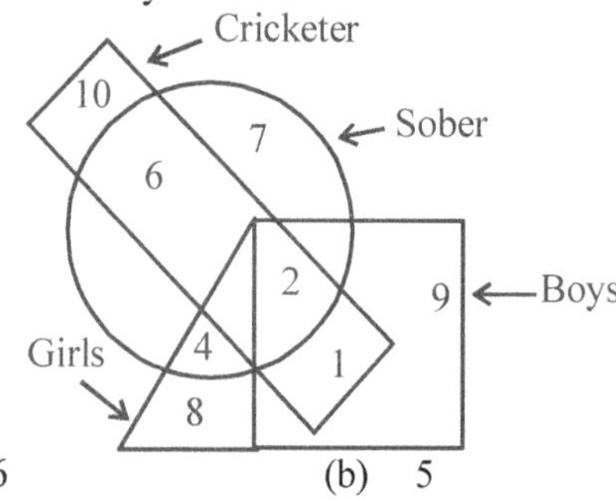

   - (a) 6
   - (b) 5
   - (c) 4
   - (d) 2

10. Some equations are solved on the basis of a certain system. Find the correct answer for the unsolved equation on that basis.

    5 * 6 = 35, 8 * 4 = 28, 6 * 8 = ?
    - (a) 46
    - (b) 34
    - (c) 23
    - (d) 38

DIRECTIONS (Q. 11) : *In following question, select the missing number from the given responses.*

11.

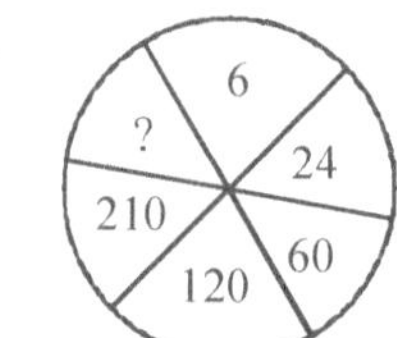

   - (a) 330
   - (b) 336
   - (c) 428
   - (d) 420

12. Six girls are standing in such a way that they form a circle, facing the centre. Subbu is to the left of Pappu, Revathi is between Subbu and Nisha, Aruna is between Pappu and Keertana. Who is to the left of Pappu ?

    (a) Keertana   (b) Nisha
    (c) Aruna   (d) Subbu

13. A three-digit number is divisible by 11 and has its digit in the unit's place equal to 1. The number is 297 more than the number obtained by reversing the digits. What is the number ?
    (a) 121   (b) 231
    (c) 561   (d) 451

14. A trader marked a watch 40% above the cost price and then gave a discount of 10%. He made a net profit of ₹ 468 after paying a tax of 10% on the gross profit. What is the cost price of the watch?
    (a) ₹ 1200   (b) ₹ 1800
    (c) ₹ 2000   (d) ₹ 2340

15. 42 men take 25 days to dig a pond. If the pond would have to be dug in 14 days, then what is the number of men to be employed?
    (a) 67   (b) 75
    (c) 81   (d) 84

16. If the diameter of a wire is decreased by 10%, by how much per cent (approximately) will the length be increased to keep the volume constant?
    (a) 5%   (b) 17%
    (c) 20%   (d) 23%

17. The average age of the family of five members is 24. If the present age of youngest member is 8 yr, then what was the average age of the family at the time of the birth of the youngest member?
    (a) 20 yr   (b) 16 yr
    (c) 12 yr   (d) 18 yr

18. Product of two co-prime numbers is 117. Their L.C.M. should be:
    (a) 1
    (b) 117
    (c) equal to their H.C.F.
    (d) cannot be calculated

19. A candidate appearing for an examination has to secure 35% marks to pass. But he secured only 40 marks and failed by 30 marks. What would be the maximum marks of test ?
    (a) 280   (b) 180
    (c) 200   (d) 150

20. By selling a table for Rs 330, a trader gains 10%. Find the cost price of the table.
    (a) 300   (b) 363
    (c) 297   (d) 270

21. The difference between compound interest and simple interest on a certain amount of money at 5% per annum for 2 years is ₹ 15. Find the sum :
    (a) ₹ 4500   (b) ₹ 7500
    (c) ₹ 5000   (d) ₹ 6000

22. The average age of a lady and her daughter is 28.5. The ratio of their ages is 14 : 5 respectively. What is the daughters age?
    (a) 12 years   (b) 15 years
    (c) 18 years   (d) Cannot be determined

23. The ratio of the length and the breadth of a rectangle is 4 : 3 and the area of the rectangle is 1728 sq cm. What is the ratio of the breadth and the area of the rectangle ?
    (a) 1 : 38   (b) 1 : 24
    (c) 1 : 42   (d) 1 : 48

24. Which one of the numbers is wrong in the series given below ?

12, 18, 27, 90, 270, 945, 3780
    (a) 12   (b) 18
    (c) 945   (d) 27

25. In a certain code 'PENCIL' is written as 'RCTAMJ' then in that code 'BROKEN' is written as
    (a) SPFLIM   (b) SVFLIN
    (c) FVSMGL   (d) None of these

26. On planet Earth, there is no centrifugal force at the
    (a) Equator   (b) Tropic of Cancer
    (c) Tropic of Capricorn (d) Poles

27. The mirror used for the head light of a car is
    (a) spherical concave   (b) plane
    (c) cylindrical   (d) parabolic concave

28. The electric charge is stored in a device called
    (a) Inductor   (b) Capacitor
    (c) Resister   (d) Transformer

29. Magnets attract magnetic substances are iron, nickel, cobalt, etc. They can also repel
    (a) paramagnetic substances
    (b) ferromagnetic substances
    (c) diamagnetic substances
    (d) non-magnetic substances

30. Ohm's law defines
    (a) a resistance
    (b) current only
    (c) voltage only
    (d) both current and voltage

31. Which one of the following is a vector quantity?
    (a) Momentum   (b) Pressure
    (c) Energy   (d) Work

32. The phenomenon of radioactivity was discovered by
    (a) Marie Curie   (b) Pierre Curie
    (c) Henri Becquerel   (d) J.J. Thomson

33. Vinegar is the trade name of
    (a) acetic acid   (b) chloroform
    (c) carbon tetrachloride (d) ethyl alcohol

34. A bee-sting leaves an acid which causes pain and irritation. The injected acid is
    (a) acetic acid   (b) sulphuric acid
    (c) citric acid   (d) methanoic acid

35. Which one among the following is used as a moderator in nuclear reactors?
    (a) Ozone   (b) Heavy hydrogen
    (c) Heavy water   (d) Hydrogen peroxide

36. Which one of the following elements exists in liquid state at room temperature?
    (a) Mercury   (b) Lead
    (c) Sodium   (d) Calcium

37. Which one of the following elements is essential for the construction of nuclear reactors?
    (a) Cobalt
    (b) Nickel
    (c) Zirconium
    (d) Tungsten

38. The most reactive among the halogens is
    (a) Fluorine
    (b) Chlorine
    (c) Bromine
    (d) Iodine

39. The only snake that builds a nest is:
    (a) Chain viper
    (b) King Cobra
    (c) Krait
    (d) Saw-scaled viper

40. Which one of the following is a modified stem?
    (a) Carrot
    (b) Sweet potato
    (c) Coconut
    (d) Potato

41. Which of the following types of light are strongly absorbed by plants?
    (a) Violet and orange
    (b) Blue and red
    (c) Indigo and yellow
    (d) Yellow and violet

42. Which one of the following is an insectivorous plant?
    (a) Passion flower plant
    (b) Pitcher plant
    (c) Night queen
    (d) Flame of the forest

43. A person with 'AB' blood group is sometimes called a universal recipient because of the
    (a) lack of antigen in his blood
    (b) lack of antibodies in his blood
    (c) lack of both antigens and antibodies in his blood
    (d) presence of antibodies in his blood

44. Which one of the following hormones contains iodine?
    (a) Thyroxine
    (b) Testosterone
    (c) Insulin
    (d) Adrenaline

45. Haemophilia is a genetic disorder which leads to
    (a) decrease in haemoglobin level
    (b) rheumatic heart disease
    (c) decrease in WBC
    (d) non-clotting of blood

46. At which stage in its life cycle, does the silk worm yield the fibre of commerce?
    (a) Egg
    (b) Larva
    (c) Pupa
    (d) Imago

47. Global warming is expected to result in
    (a) increase in level of sea
    (b) change in crop pattern
    (c) change in coastline
    (d) All of the above

48. Which one of the following is not a part of India's National Action Plan on Climate Change (NAPCC)?
    (a) National Mission on Sustainable Habitat
    (b) National Water Mission
    (c) National Mission on Pollution Control
    (d) National Mission for Sustainable Agriculture

49. Which one of the following is the most stable ecosystem ?
    (a) Desert
    (b) Mountain
    (c) Ocean
    (d) Forest

50. The Green House effect is mostly caused by
    (a) Carbon dioxide in the atmosphere
    (b) Infra-red Radiation
    (c) Moisture in the atmosphere
    (d) Ozone layer

51. Endangered species are listed in
    (a) Dead Stock Book
    (b) Red Data Book
    (c) Live Stock Book
    (d) None of the above

52. Which one of the following is a part of Geological cycle ?
    (a) Carbon cycle
    (b) Hydrogen cycle
    (c) Hydrological cycle
    (d) Nitrogen cycle

53. The First Navigation Satellite launched by ISRO
    (a) PSLV C 2
    (b) IRNSS-1A
    (c) ISS-1A
    (d) INSAT

54. The Rotavirus vaccine ROTOVAC developed by Indian scientists cures which disease?
    (a) Diarrohea
    (b) Cancer
    (c) Diabetes
    (d) Arthritis

55. India's first DNA Forensic Laboratory is established in which city
    (a) Gurgaon
    (b) Mumbai
    (c) Delhi
    (d) Kanpur

56. What is the approximate height of a geostationary satellite from the surface of the earth?
    (a) 981 km
    (b) 15000 km
    (c) 35000 km
    (d) 55000 km

57. An 'Applet' is a kind of :
    (a) Sweet dish made from apples
    (b) A Java Program
    (c) Marketing Strategy
    (d) The new internet ready computer from Apple

58. Which among the following do/does not belong/belongs to the GSM family of wireless technologies?
    (a) EDGE   (b) LTE
    (c) DSL   (d) Both EDGE and LTE

59. Which one of the following techniques can be used to establish the paternity of a child?
    (a) Protein analysis
    (b) Chromosome counting
    (c) Quantitative analysis of DNA
    (d) DNA finger printing

60. Tides are primarily a result of the -
    (a) Attraction of the moon
    (b) Farrel's Law
    (c) Ocean currents

61. Who shall be the ex-officio Chairman of Council of States?
    (a) The President of India
    (b) The Vice President of India
    (c) The Council of states shall choose a member the council to act as chairman
    (d) The Speaker of the House of People

62. Which of the following systems in independent India goes against the very basis of democracy?
    (a) Caste system
    (b) Economic system
    (c) Party system
    (d) Parliamentary system

63. United Nations Day is observed on
    (a) October 21   (b) October 22
    (c) October 23   (d) October 24

64. World Post Day is observed on
    (a) November 9   (b) November 14
    (c) October 9   (d) October 24

65. Which country has the highest railway line in the world?
    (a) Tanggula   (b) Australia
    (c) India   (d) Japan

66. The world's longest railway platform is in India. In which state is it?
    (a) Madhya Pradesh   (b) Uttar Pradesh
    (c) West Bengal   (d) Punjab

67. Which is the only country to have a fully electrified railway network?
    (a) Japan   (b) China
    (c) India   (d) Switzerland

68. The headquarter of International Olympic Committee is situated at:
    (a) Lausanne, Switzerland
    (b) Geneva, Switzerland
    (c) Zurich, Switzerland
    (d) None of the above

69. Which of the following is NOT a method of voting in the Lok Sabha?
    (a) Voice vote   (b) Division
    (c) Casting vote   (d) Tactial vote

70. What is the ratio of the width of India's National Flag to its length?
    (a) Two to three   (b) One to two
    (c) Three to four   (d) Two to five

71. The first woman to conquer Mount Everest twice is
    (a) Surja Lata Devi   (b) Jyoti Randhawa
    (c) Santosh Yadav   (d) Suma Shirur

72. The drainage pattern developed on folded sedimentary rock is termed as
    (a) Trellis   (b) Dendritic
    (c) Radial   (d) Deranged

73. As a part of the Republic Day 2018 celebrations, 6 days Bharat Parv event has been organized at which of the given places?
    (a) India Gate
    (b) Red Fort
    (c) Rashtrapati Bhavan
    (d) Qutub Minar

74. The 21st edition of India International Seafood Show (IISS) 2018 has been organised in which state of India?
    (a) Tamil Nadu   (b) West Bengal
    (c) Goa   (d) Andhra Pradesh

75. Name the India's first indigenously developed vaccine which has received the "pre-qualified" tag by the World Health Organisation
    (a) Rubevac Vaccine
    (b) Norovac Vaccine
    (c) Pneurmovac vaccine
    (d) Rotavac Vaccine

RESPONSE SHEET

1.	ⓐⓑⓒⓓ	2.	ⓐⓑⓒⓓ	3.	ⓐⓑⓒⓓ	4.	ⓐⓑⓒⓓ	5.	ⓐⓑⓒⓓ
6.	ⓐⓑⓒⓓ	7.	ⓐⓑⓒⓓ	8.	ⓐⓑⓒⓓ	9.	ⓐⓑⓒⓓ	10.	ⓐⓑⓒⓓ
11.	ⓐⓑⓒⓓ	12.	ⓐⓑⓒⓓ	13.	ⓐⓑⓒⓓ	14.	ⓐⓑⓒⓓ	15.	ⓐⓑⓒⓓ
16.	ⓐⓑⓒⓓ	17.	ⓐⓑⓒⓓ	18.	ⓐⓑⓒⓓ	19.	ⓐⓑⓒⓓ	20.	ⓐⓑⓒⓓ
21.	ⓐⓑⓒⓓ	22.	ⓐⓑⓒⓓ	23.	ⓐⓑⓒⓓ	24.	ⓐⓑⓒⓓ	25.	ⓐⓑⓒⓓ
26.	ⓐⓑⓒⓓ	27.	ⓐⓑⓒⓓ	28.	ⓐⓑⓒⓓ	29.	ⓐⓑⓒⓓ	30.	ⓐⓑⓒⓓ
31.	ⓐⓑⓒⓓ	32.	ⓐⓑⓒⓓ	33.	ⓐⓑⓒⓓ	34.	ⓐⓑⓒⓓ	35.	ⓐⓑⓒⓓ
36.	ⓐⓑⓒⓓ	37.	ⓐⓑⓒⓓ	38.	ⓐⓑⓒⓓ	39.	ⓐⓑⓒⓓ	40.	ⓐⓑⓒⓓ
41.	ⓐⓑⓒⓓ	42.	ⓐⓑⓒⓓ	43.	ⓐⓑⓒⓓ	44.	ⓐⓑⓒⓓ	45.	ⓐⓑⓒⓓ
46.	ⓐⓑⓒⓓ	47.	ⓐⓑⓒⓓ	48.	ⓐⓑⓒⓓ	49.	ⓐⓑⓒⓓ	50.	ⓐⓑⓒⓓ
51.	ⓐⓑⓒⓓ	52.	ⓐⓑⓒⓓ	53.	ⓐⓑⓒⓓ	54.	ⓐⓑⓒⓓ	55.	ⓐⓑⓒⓓ
56.	ⓐⓑⓒⓓ	57.	ⓐⓑⓒⓓ	58.	ⓐⓑⓒⓓ	59.	ⓐⓑⓒⓓ	60.	ⓐⓑⓒⓓ
61.	ⓐⓑⓒⓓ	62.	ⓐⓑⓒⓓ	63.	ⓐⓑⓒⓓ	64.	ⓐⓑⓒⓓ	65.	ⓐⓑⓒⓓ
66.	ⓐⓑⓒⓓ	67.	ⓐⓑⓒⓓ	68.	ⓐⓑⓒⓓ	69.	ⓐⓑⓒⓓ	70.	ⓐⓑⓒⓓ
71.	ⓐⓑⓒⓓ	72.	ⓐⓑⓒⓓ	73.	ⓐⓑⓒⓓ	74.	ⓐⓑⓒⓓ	75.	ⓐⓑⓒⓓ

HINTS & SOLUTIONS

1. (d) A hive is a shelter for bees. Whereas, A eyrie is a large nest of an eagle.

2. (a)
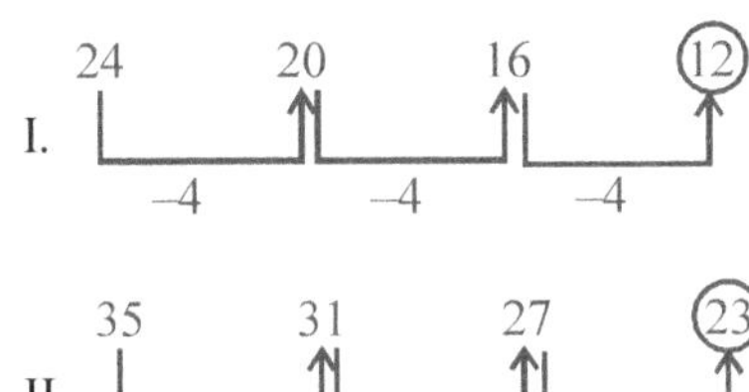

3. (d) There are two numbers series:
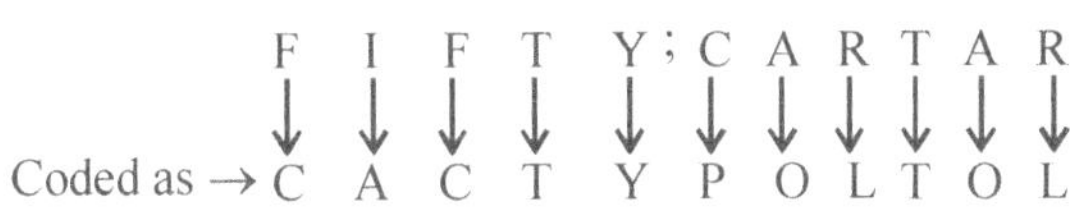

4. (d)

$$
\begin{array}{ccccccccccc}
F & I & F & T & Y & ; & C & A & R & T & A & R \\
\downarrow & \downarrow & \downarrow & \downarrow & \downarrow & & \downarrow & \downarrow & \downarrow & \downarrow & \downarrow & \downarrow
\end{array}
$$
Coded as → C A C T Y   P O L T O L

$$
\begin{array}{cccccc}
T & A & R & I & F & F \\
\downarrow & \downarrow & \downarrow & \downarrow & \downarrow & \downarrow
\end{array}
$$
Coded as T O L A C C

5. (c) rtxy/ sxyz/ rtxy/ sxyz.

6. (b)
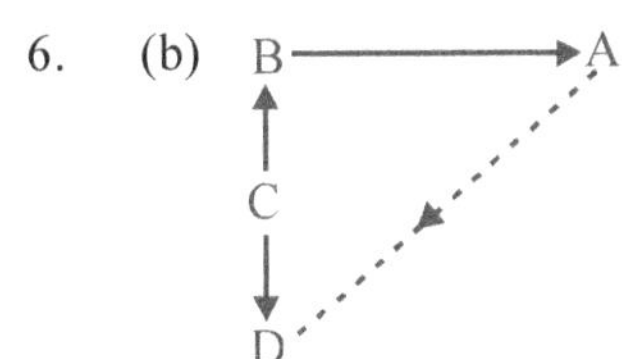

It is clearly shown that, D is in south west of A.

7. (c)

8. (a) The father of the boy's uncle → the grandfather of the boy and daughter of the grandfather → sister of father.

9. (a)

10. (a)

$$
\underline{5 \;\; * \;\; 6/2 \qquad 3\; 5}
$$

$$
\underline{8 \;\; * \;\; 4/2 \qquad 2\; 8}
$$

$$
\underline{6 \;\; * \;\; 8/2 \qquad \boxed{4\; 6}}
$$

11. (b) $1 \times 2 \times 3 = 6$
$2 \times 3 \times 4 = 24$
$3 \times 4 \times 5 = 60$
$4 \times 5 \times 6 = 120$
$5 \times 6 \times 7 = 210$
$6 \times 7 \times 8 = 336$

12. (d)
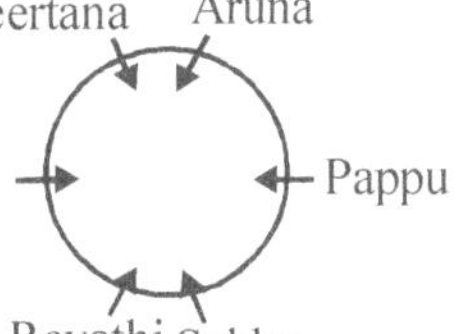

13. (d) On taking option (d).
The reverse digit of 451 is 154.
Now, $154 + 297 = 451$ is equal to the original number.

14. (c) Let the cost price of the watch $= ₹x$
After 40% marked price and 10% discount
$$= x \times \frac{90}{100} \times \frac{140}{100} = \frac{126x}{100}$$

$$\text{Profit} = \frac{126x}{100} - x = \frac{26x}{100}$$

According to question,
Pay 10% tax on profit
$$= \frac{26x}{100} \times \frac{90}{100} = 468$$

$$x = \frac{468 \times 100 \times 100}{26 \times 90} = ₹\, 2000$$

15. (b) Let the number of men be n

Men	Days
$\begin{array}{c}42 \downarrow \\ n\end{array}$	$\begin{array}{c}25 \uparrow \\ 14\end{array}$

$$\therefore \quad \frac{n}{42} = \frac{25}{14} \;\Rightarrow\; n = 75$$

16. (d) Volume of wire $= \pi r^2 h$

New radius of the wire $= \dfrac{r \times 90}{100} = \dfrac{9r}{10}$

Let new length of the wire be L.
$\therefore$ Volume of new wire
$$= \pi \left(\frac{9r}{10}\right)^2 \times L = \frac{81}{100}\pi r^2 L$$

According to question,
$$\pi r^2 h = \frac{81}{100}\pi r^2 L \;\Rightarrow\; L = \frac{100}{81}h$$

$$\text{Increase in length} = \frac{100}{81}h - h = \frac{19}{81}h$$

$$\text{Percent increase} = \frac{19/81h}{h} \times 100\% = 23.46\%$$

$$= 23\% \text{ (approx)}$$

17. (b) Total age of the family of five members $= 24 \times 5 = 120$

Total age of the family of five members before 8 years
$$= 120 - 5 \times 8 = 120 - 40 = 80$$

So, required average age $= \dfrac{80}{5} = 16$ yr.

18. (b) H.C.F of co-prime numbers is 1.

19. (c) Suppose maximum marks $= x$

then $x \times \dfrac{35}{100} = 40 + 30 \Rightarrow x \times \dfrac{35}{100} = 70$

$$\Rightarrow x = \frac{70 \times 100}{35} = 200 \text{ marks}$$

20. (a) S.P. $=$ Rs 330, Gain $= 10\%$

$$\therefore \quad \text{C.P.} = \left(\frac{100}{100 + \text{Gain }\%}\right) \times \text{S.P.}$$

$$= \text{Rs } \frac{100}{100 + 10} \times 330$$

$$= \frac{100}{110} \times 330 = \text{Rs } 300.$$

21. (d) $D = \left(\dfrac{R}{100}\right)^2 \times P$

$$P = D \times \left(\frac{100}{R}\right)^2 = \frac{1500 \times 10000}{25} = ₹\, 6000$$

22. (b) Average age $= 28.5$

$\therefore$ Total age $= 28.5 \times 2 = 57$

$\therefore$ Daughter's age $= \dfrac{5}{19} \times 57 = 15$ years

23. (d) $(4x)(3x) = 1728$

$\Rightarrow x^2 = 144 \therefore x = 12$

$\Rightarrow$ length $= 48$; breadth $= 36$

$\therefore$ Required ratio $= \dfrac{36}{36 \times 48} = 1:48$

24. (d) If 27 is replaced by 36, then the ratios of two consecutive terms are 3/2, 2, 5/2, 3, etc.

25. (d) The first three letters of the word are reversed. Thus PENCIL becomes NEPCIL. Now add 4 to odd-positioned letters and subtract 2 from even-positioned ones. Similarly, BROKEN becomes ORBKEN. Then we do the calculations: $O + 4, R - 2, B + 4, K - 2, E + 4, N - 2$, *i.e.* SPFIIL.

26. (d) There is no centrifugal force at the poles.

27. (d) Parabolic reflectors are used to collect energy from a distant source (for example sound waves or incoming star light) and bring it to a common focal point, thus correcting spherical aberration found in simpler spherical reflectors. Since the principles of reflection are reversible, parabolic reflectors can also be used to project energy of a source at its focus outward in a parallel beam, used in devices such as spotlights and car headlights.

28. (b) Capacitor is a device which stors electric charge.

29. (c) Magnets can repel diamagnetic substances.

30. (a) According to Ohm's law resistance

$$R = \frac{V}{I}; \ 1\,\text{ohm} = \frac{1\,\text{volt}}{1\,\text{ampere}}$$

31. (a) Scalars are quantities that have magnitude only; they are independent of direction. Vectors have both magnitude and direction. Momentum is the product of the mass and velocity of an object $(p = mv)$. Momentum is a vector quantity, since it has a direction as well as a magnitude. The rest of quantities in option pressure, work and energy have magnitude but not direction.

32. (c)

33. (a) Acetic acid is commonly known as vinegar.

34. (d) The acid in bee sting is formic acid which is also known as methanoic acid. However it is not really the acid that causes the pain. Most active ingredients in bee venom is melittin & apamin both of which cause pain & swelling.

35. (c) In nuclear reactor heavy water (D_2O) used to slow down the speed of neutron i.e., act as moderator.

36. (a) Mercury exists in liquid state at room temperature.

37. (c) Zirconium purified metal is primarily used by the nuclear industry to form the outer layer of fuel rods in nuclear reactors. Zirconium's major use is as cladding for nuclear reactors. It is ideal for this use, as it has a limited ability to capture neutrons, strength at elevated temperatures, considerable corrosion resistance, and satisfactory neutron damage resistance.

38. (a) Fluorine is the most reactive among all halogens. However the reactivity deceases from F_2 to I_2 (from top to bottom of group) may be attributed to
(1) Low dissociation enthalpies
(2) High electron affinities

39. (b) King Kobra is the only snake that not only lives in holes but also builds a nest.

40. (d) Potato tuber bears buds in small pits known as eyes. Buds develops to branches. Some of the branches become green, erect & leafy stems that grow horizontally under ground.

41. (b) Photosynthesis occurs between wavelengths of about 400 nm and 750 nm. Red & blue colour wavelength is categories in this wavelength. So, plants absorb these colours. Photosynthesis does not occur in the infra-red or in ultraviolet light.

42. (b) Pitcher plant is an insectivorous plant. It feeds on living creatures including insects and small mammals. These plant attracts the prey with a smell of rotting meat. The victim is dissolved by some chemical enzymes.

43. (b) Person having blood group 'AB' is called universal recepient because the 'AB' blood group has no antibody in the blood plasma. So, the person can accept any type of blood group (i.e. A, B and O)

44. (a) Thyroxine hormone and tri-iodothyronine hormone are secreted by thyroid follicular cells of thyroid gland. The major component of thyroxine hormone is iodine. Deficiency of iodine causes goitre in human.

45. (d) Haemophilia is a sex–linked recessive disorder. Clotting of blood is abnormally delayed that even a simple or small cut will result non stop bleeding in affected individual.

46. (c) Silk worm yield the fibre from pupa stage, which is commercially used to produce clothes.

47. (d) 48. (c)

49. (c) Ocean is the most stable ecosystem.

50. (a) The Green house effect is mostly caused by Carbon dioxide in the atmosphere.

51. (b) Endangered species are listed in Red Data book.

52. (c) Hydrological cycle is a part of Geological cycle.

53. (b) Indian Space Research Organization (ISRO) has successfully launched IRNSS-1A on PSLV C 22 from Satish Dhawan Space Centre, Sriharikota in Andhra Pradesh.

54. (a)

55. (a) Global biotechnology company 'Life Technologies' has launched India's first private DNA forensics laboratory in Gurgaon which is expected to accelerate sampling process thereby reducing the burden on existing forensic laboratories.

56. (c) A geostationary satellite is a satellite whose orbit on the Earth repeats regularly over point on the Earth over time. The orbit of the satellite is known as geosynchronous/geostationary orbit. It has an approximate height of 35000 km from the surface of the Earth.

57. (d)

58. (c) More than 3.8 billion people worldwide used the Global System for Mobile Communications (GSM) family of technologies as of May 2009. GSM is the most widely usesd wireless technology in the world. GSM has strainghtforward, cost-effective migration path to 3G through GPRS, EDGE and UMTS-HSPA, as well as beyond 3G via the HSPA Evolution (HSPA+). LTE and System Architecture Evolution (SAE) initiatives.

59. (d) DNA finger printing technology is the process of establishing the biological paternal relationship between individual and his alleged child on the analysis of sample cells taken from each of them.

60. (a) 61. (b) 62. (a) 63. (d) 64. (c)

65. (a) 66. (c) 67. (d) 68. (a)

69. (d) 70. (a)

71. (c) Santosh Yadav is an Indian mountaineer. She is the first woman in the world to climb Mount Everest twice in less than a year. She first climbed the peak in May 1992 and then did it again in May 1993.

72. (b) A dendritic drainage pattern refers to the pattern formed by the streams, rivers, and lakes in a particular drainage basin. It usually looks like the branching pattern of tree roots and it mainly develops in regions underlain by homogeneous material.

73. (b) 74. (c) 75. (d)

10   PRACTICE SET

Time : 60 Min.   **Max. Marks : 75**

1. Kilowatt- hour is the unit of
   - (a) potential difference
   - (b) electric power
   - (c) electric energy
   - (d) electric potential

2. For which among the following house appliances, magnet is an essential part?
   - (a) Calling bell
   - (b) Fan
   - (c) Washing machine
   - (d) All of the above

3. The working principle of a washing machine is :
   - (a) centrifugation
   - (b) dialysis
   - (c) reverse osmosis
   - (d) diffusion

4. The clouds float in the atmosphere because of their low:
   - (a) temperature
   - (b) velocity
   - (c) pressure
   - (d) density

5. When water is heated from $0°C$ to $10°C$. Its volume:
   - (a) increases
   - (b) decreases
   - (c) does not change
   - (d) first decreases and then increases

6. Optical fibre works on the principle of :
   - (a) total internal reflection
   - (b) refraction
   - (c) scattering
   - (d) interference

7. Which one of the following metals does not form amalgam?
   - (a) Zinc
   - (b) Copper
   - (c) Magnesium
   - (d) Iron

8. Which one of the following polymers is widely used for making bullet proof material?
   - (a) Polyvinyl chloride
   - (b) Polyamides
   - (c) Polyethylene
   - (d) Polycarbonates

9. The characteristic odour of garlic is due to
   - (a) a chloro compound
   - (b) a sulphur compound
   - (c) a fluorine compound
   - (d) acetic acid

10. Acid rain is caused by the pollution of environment by
    - (a) carbon dioxide and nitrogen
    - (b) carbon monoxide and carbon dioxide
    - (c) ozone and carbon dioxide
    - (d) nitrous oxide and sulphur dioxide

11. Which one of the following has the highest fuel value?
    - (a) Hydrogen
    - (b) Charcoal
    - (c) Natural gas
    - (d) Gasoline

12. The wine is prepared by the process of
    - (a) fermentation
    - (b) catalysation
    - (c) conjugation
    - (d) displacement

13. Among the following, which one is not an ape?
    - (a) Gibbon
    - (b) Gorilla
    - (c) Langur
    - (d) Orangutan

14. Which one of the following plants is used for green manuring in India?
    - (a) Wheat
    - (b) Sunnhemp
    - (c) Cotton
    - (d) Rice

15. For which one among the following diseases no vaccine is yet available?
    - (a) Tetanus
    - (b) Malaria
    - (c) Measles
    - (d) Mumps

16. Primary source of vitamin-D for human beings is
    - (a) citrus fruits
    - (b) green vegetables
    - (c) yeast
    - (d) sun

17. Which one of the following is present in chlorophyll which gives a green colour to plant leaves?
    - (a) Calcium
    - (b) Magnesium
    - (c) Iron (d) Manganese

18. The maximum biodiversity is found in
    - (a) Tropical rain forests
    - (b) Temperate forests
    - (c) Coniferous forests
    - (d) Arctic forests

19. Which one of the following is the most important factor responsible for decline of bio-diversity ?
    (a) Genetic assimilation
    (b) Controlling predators
    (c) Destruction of habitat
    (d) Controlling pests

20. Which one of the following is important strategy for the conservation of Biodiversity ?
    (a) Biosphere Reserves (b) Botanical Gardens
    (c) National Parks   (d) Wild Life Sanctuaries

21. Climate change is caused by
    (a) Green house gases
    (b) Depletion of ozone layer
    (c) Pollution
    (d) All the above

22. The concept of carbon credit originated from which one of the following ?
    (a) Kyoto protocol   (b) Earth summit
    (c) Doha round   (d) Montreal Protocol

23. Global Warming is caused due to the emission of
    (a) Nitrogen   (b) Carbon dioxide
    (c) Carbon Mono oxide (d) Hydro carbon

24. Name the place in india where Early Tsunami Warning System have been installed
    (a) Rangachang   (b) Kanyakumari
    (c) Chilka   (d) Mysore

25. Researchers have developed Eco-friendly batteries which can be used in power plants or to store solar energy. These batteries are made up using which material
    (a) Carbon, Tin, Sodium
    (b) Wood, Tin, Carbon
    (c) Wood, Tin and Sodium
    (d) Sodium, carbon, Tin

26. Which among the following is the First cruise missile test fired by India?
    (a) Aakash   (b) Nirbhay
    (c) Agni-3   (d) Aakash-2

27. Cryogenic Engines are used in ______ .
    (a) Atomic Energy   (b) Food Processing
    (c) Oceanography   (d) Space Research

28. The world's highest ground based telescopic observatory is located in :
    (a) Colombia   (b) India
    (c) Nepal   (d) Switzerland

29. The Baikonur Cosmodrome is the world's first and largest operational space launch facility. In which country is it located?
    (a) France   (b) Kazakhstan
    (c) Uzbekistan   (d) Germany

30. The Pilotless target aircraft, fabricated at the Aeronautical Development Establishment, Bengaluru, is:
    (a) Lakshya   (b) Cheetah
    (c) Nishant   (d) Arjun

31. WiMAX is related to which one of the following
    (a) Biotechnology
    (b) Space technology
    (c) Missile technology
    (d) Communication technology

32. One of these trains connects Mumbai and Aurangabad. Name it.
    (a) Sabarmati Express (b) Deviri Express
    (c) Ashram Express   (d) Janata Express

33. Which Railway Zone has introduced Biodiesel for train operations?
    (a) Western Railway
    (b) Central Railways
    (c) South Western Railways
    (d) Southern Railways

34. Where is the Indian Railways Institute of Civil Engineering Institute situated?
    (a) Pune   (b) Chennai
    (c) Nasik   (d) Sikandrabad

35. Which one of the following is not a function of Election Commission?
    (a) Allotment of symbols
    (b) Fixation of election dates
    (c) Maintaining fairness of election
    (d) Selecting the candidates for election

36. If there is a deadlock between Rajya Sabha and Lok Sabha over an ordinary bill, it will be resolved by
    (a) The President
    (b) The Council of Ministers
    (c) The Joint Session of Parliament
    (d) The Supreme Court

37. The national income of a nation is the
    (a) Government's annual revenue
    (b) Sum total of factor incomes
    (c) Surplus of public sector enterprises
    (d) Exports minus imports

38. Prithvi Raj Chauhan was defeated in the Second Battle of Tarain by
    (a) Mahmud Ghazni
    (b) Muhammad Ghori
    (c) Qutbuddin Aibak
    (d) Yalduz

39. Arrange the following in chronological order:
    I.   Dandi March
    II. Simon Commission
    III. Poona Pact
    IV. Gandhi Irwin Pact
    (a) II, I, III, IV   (b) II, I, IV, III
    (c) IV, III, I, II   (d) IV, III, II, I

40. Match correctly the following, deserts and their location by choosing the correct response:

Desert	Location
a. Kalahari	1. South America
b. Atacama	2. Australia
c. Thar	3. Africa
d. Great Victoria	4. Asia

    (a) a-3, b-1, c-4, d-2 (b) a-2, b-3, c-1, d-4
    (c) a-4, b-3, c-2, d-1 (d) a-3, b-2, c-1, d-4

41. The Palk Bay lies between
    (a) Gulf of Kutch and Gulf of Khambhat
    (b) Gulf of Mannar and Bay of Bengal
    (c) Lakshadweep and Maldive Islands
    (d) Andaman and Nicobar Islands

42. Which one of the following rivers originates in Amarkantak?
    (a) Damodar   (b) Mahanadi
    (c) Narmada   (d) Tapi

43. Lakshadweep islands are the product of
    (a) Volcanic activity   (b) Wave action
    (c) Sea floor expansion (d) Reef formation

44. One of the states through which the Tropic of Cancer passes is
    (a) Jammu and Kashmir (b) Himachal Pradesh
    (c) Bihar   (d) Jharkhand

45. Which of the following has the oldest rocks in the country?
    (a) The Himalayas
    (b) The Aravallis
    (c) The Indo-Gangetic plain
    (d) The Shiwaliks

46. In India, how many States share the coastline?
    (a) 7   (b) 8
    (c) 9   (d) 10

47. Which article of the Indian constitution provides for the institution of Panchayti Raj?
    (a) Article 36   (b) Article 39
    (c) Article 40   (d) Article 48

48. When was the Panchayati Raj System introduced in India?
    (a) 1945   (b) 1950
    (c) 1959   (d) 1962

49. In which district of Maharashtra, the Indian Railways will set up a coach factory?
    (a) Mumbai   (b) Thane
    (c) Nagpur   (d) Latur

50. According to the CSO's revised estimates of national income released on January 31, 2018, gross domestic product (GDP) growth rate for 2016-17 is _______ %?
    (a) 7.0%   (b) 7.1%
    (c) 7.2%   (d) 7.5%

DIRECTION (Q. 51) : *In questions below, select the related word/ letters/number from the given alternatives.*

51. STAR : SBUT :: WARD : ?
    (a) XBAW   (b) ESBX
    (c) FAME   (d) DRAW

DIRECTION (Q. 52) : *In questions find the odd word/letters// numbers pair from the given alternatives:*

52. (a) HEAT   (b) MEAT
    (c) MEET   (d) BEAT

DIRECTION (Q 53): *A series is given, with one term missing. Choose the correct alternative from the given ones that will complete the series.*

53. 2, 65, 7, 59, 12, 53, _ , _
    (a) 15, 42   (b) 17, 45
    (c) 17, 47   (d) 18, 48

54. If GOODNESS is coded as HNPCODTR, how can GREATNESS be written in that code?
    (a) HQFZSMFRT   (b) HQFZUFRTM
    (c) HQFZUODTR   (d) HQFZUMFRT

55. Seema walks 30 m North. Then she turns right and walks 30 m then she turns right and walks 55 m. Then she turns left and walks 20 m. Then she again turns left and walks 25m. How many metres away is she from her Original position?
    (a) 45 m   (b) 50 m
    (c) 66 m   (d) 55 m

56. A family consisted of a man, his wife, his three sons, their wives and three children in each son's family. How many members are there in the family?
    (a) 12   (b) 13
    (c) 15   (d) 17

57. If the 5th date of a month is Tuesday, what date will be 3 days after the 3rd Friday in the month?
    (a) 17   (b) 22
    (c) 19   (d) 18

58. 12 year old Rahul is three times as old as his brother Raras. How old will Rahul be when be is twice as old as Paras?
    (a) 14 years   (b) 20 years
    (c) 16 years   (d) 18 years

DIRECTION (59) : *In each of the following questions, select the missing number from the given responses.*

59.

   (a) 6   (b) 7
   (c) 3   (d) 2

60. There are five houses P, Q, R, S and T. P is right of Q and T is left of R and right of P. Q is right of S. Which house is in the middle?
    (a) P   (b) Q
    (c) T   (d) R

61. What is the sum of the digits of the least number which when divided by 52, leaves 33 as remainder, when divided by 78 leaves 59 and when divided by 117, leaves 98 as remainder?
    (a) 17   (b) 18
    (c) 19   (d) 21

62. If 1 is subtracted from the numerator of a fraction it becomes (1/3) and if 5 is added to the denominator the fraction becomes (1/4). Which fraction shall result, if 1 is subtracted from the numerator and 5 is added to the denominator ?

(a) $\dfrac{5}{12}$ (b) $\dfrac{7}{23}$

(c) $\dfrac{1}{8}$ (d) $\dfrac{2}{3}$

63. Prakash, Sunil and Anil started a business jointly investing ₹11 lakhs, ₹ 16.5 lakhs and ₹ 8.25 lakhs respectively. The profit earned by them in the business at the end of three years was ₹ 19.5 lakhs. What will be the 50% of Anil's share in the profit?

(a) ₹4.5 lakhs (b) ₹2.25 lakhs
(c) ₹2.5 lakhs (d) ₹3.75 lakhs

64. If ₹ 8400 is divided among A, B and C in the ratio $\dfrac{1}{5}:\dfrac{1}{6}:\dfrac{1}{10}$, what is the share of A?

(a) ₹3200 (b) ₹3400
(c) ₹3600 (d) ₹3800

65. There are 45 male and 15 female employees in an office. If the mean salary of the 60 employees is ₹ 4800 and the mean salary of the male employees is ₹ 5000, then the mean salary of the female employees is

(a) ₹4200 (b) ₹4500
(c) ₹5600 (d) ₹6000

66. The HCF of $X^4 -1$ and $X^4 -2X^3 -2X^2 - 2X - 3$ is

(a) $(x^2+1)(x-1)$ (b) (x^2+1)
(c) $(x^2+1)(x+1)$ (d) $(x+1)$

67. A cone is inscribed in a hemisphere such that their bases are common. If C is the volume of the cone and H that of the hemisphere, then what is the value of C : H?

(a) $1:2$ (b) $2:3$
(c) $3:4$ (d) $4:5$

68. Which one of the numbers will complete the series ?
8, 13, 10, 15, 12, 17, 14 ... ?
(a) 19 (b) 22
(c) 16 (d) 20

69. Which one number does not belong to the series ?
3, 5, 8, 11, 17, 23
(a) 8 (b) 11
(c) 17 (d) 23

70. In a certain code language the word 'DISPLAY' is written as ' BLQSJDW'. How will the word 'PROJECT' be written in that language?
(a) NUMMCER (b) NUNMCFR
(c) NTNMCFR (d) None of these

71. If CHAIR is coded as FKDLU then RAID is coded as :
(a) ULGD (b) ULKG
(c) ULDG (d) UDLG

72. F is the brother of A. C is the daughter of A. K is the sister of F. G is the brother of C. Who is the uncle of G?
(a) A (b) C
(c) F (d) K

73. A party consisted of a man, his wife, his three sons and their wives and three children in each son's family. How many were there in the party?
(a) 24 (b) 22
(c) 13 (d) 17

74. A and B start walking, from a point, in opposite directions. A covers 3 km and B covers 4 km. Then A turns right and walks 4 km while B turns left and walks 3 km. How far is each from the starting point ?
(a) 5 km (b) 4 km
(c) 10 km (d) 8 km

75. In a row of students, Ramesh is 9th from the left and Suman is 6th from the right. When they both interchange their positions then Ramesh will be 15th from the left. What will be the position of Suman from the right?
(a) 12th (b) 13th
(c) 15th (d) 6th

RESPONSE SHEET

1. ⓐ ⓑ ⓒ ⓓ	2. ⓐ ⓑ ⓒ ⓓ	3. ⓐ ⓑ ⓒ ⓓ	4. ⓐ ⓑ ⓒ ⓓ	5. ⓐ ⓑ ⓒ ⓓ
6. ⓐ ⓑ ⓒ ⓓ	7. ⓐ ⓑ ⓒ ⓓ	8. ⓐ ⓑ ⓒ ⓓ	9. ⓐ ⓑ ⓒ ⓓ	10. ⓐ ⓑ ⓒ ⓓ
11. ⓐ ⓑ ⓒ ⓓ	12. ⓐ ⓑ ⓒ ⓓ	13. ⓐ ⓑ ⓒ ⓓ	14. ⓐ ⓑ ⓒ ⓓ	15. ⓐ ⓑ ⓒ ⓓ
16. ⓐ ⓑ ⓒ ⓓ	17. ⓐ ⓑ ⓒ ⓓ	18. ⓐ ⓑ ⓒ ⓓ	19. ⓐ ⓑ ⓒ ⓓ	20. ⓐ ⓑ ⓒ ⓓ
21. ⓐ ⓑ ⓒ ⓓ	22. ⓐ ⓑ ⓒ ⓓ	23. ⓐ ⓑ ⓒ ⓓ	24. ⓐ ⓑ ⓒ ⓓ	25. ⓐ ⓑ ⓒ ⓓ
26. ⓐ ⓑ ⓒ ⓓ	27. ⓐ ⓑ ⓒ ⓓ	28. ⓐ ⓑ ⓒ ⓓ	29. ⓐ ⓑ ⓒ ⓓ	30. ⓐ ⓑ ⓒ ⓓ
31. ⓐ ⓑ ⓒ ⓓ	32. ⓐ ⓑ ⓒ ⓓ	33. ⓐ ⓑ ⓒ ⓓ	34. ⓐ ⓑ ⓒ ⓓ	35. ⓐ ⓑ ⓒ ⓓ
36. ⓐ ⓑ ⓒ ⓓ	37. ⓐ ⓑ ⓒ ⓓ	38. ⓐ ⓑ ⓒ ⓓ	39. ⓐ ⓑ ⓒ ⓓ	40. ⓐ ⓑ ⓒ ⓓ
41. ⓐ ⓑ ⓒ ⓓ	42. ⓐ ⓑ ⓒ ⓓ	43. ⓐ ⓑ ⓒ ⓓ	44. ⓐ ⓑ ⓒ ⓓ	45. ⓐ ⓑ ⓒ ⓓ
46. ⓐ ⓑ ⓒ ⓓ	47. ⓐ ⓑ ⓒ ⓓ	48. ⓐ ⓑ ⓒ ⓓ	49. ⓐ ⓑ ⓒ ⓓ	50. ⓐ ⓑ ⓒ ⓓ
51. ⓐ ⓑ ⓒ ⓓ	52. ⓐ ⓑ ⓒ ⓓ	53. ⓐ ⓑ ⓒ ⓓ	54. ⓐ ⓑ ⓒ ⓓ	55. ⓐ ⓑ ⓒ ⓓ
56. ⓐ ⓑ ⓒ ⓓ	57. ⓐ ⓑ ⓒ ⓓ	58. ⓐ ⓑ ⓒ ⓓ	59. ⓐ ⓑ ⓒ ⓓ	60. ⓐ ⓑ ⓒ ⓓ
61. ⓐ ⓑ ⓒ ⓓ	62. ⓐ ⓑ ⓒ ⓓ	63. ⓐ ⓑ ⓒ ⓓ	64. ⓐ ⓑ ⓒ ⓓ	65. ⓐ ⓑ ⓒ ⓓ
66. ⓐ ⓑ ⓒ ⓓ	67. ⓐ ⓑ ⓒ ⓓ	68. ⓐ ⓑ ⓒ ⓓ	69. ⓐ ⓑ ⓒ ⓓ	70. ⓐ ⓑ ⓒ ⓓ
71. ⓐ ⓑ ⓒ ⓓ	72. ⓐ ⓑ ⓒ ⓓ	73. ⓐ ⓑ ⓒ ⓓ	74. ⓐ ⓑ ⓒ ⓓ	75. ⓐ ⓑ ⓒ ⓓ

HINTS & SOLUTIONS

1. (c) Kilowatt-hour (kWh) is the unit of electric energy. This unit is generally used by electricity board to measure the electricity consumed in our houses. The board name it as 'unit'.

2. (d) Magnets are usually used in appliances with spinning motors such as a sewing machine or a fan. They are also used in heat induction stoves. There is a magnet under the surface which also serves as a heating element. Wherever the pan makes contact, that's where the plate heats up. In a spinning motor, there are 2 rotating magnets, one regular magnet and one electro-magnet. When electricity travels through the electro-magnet, both magnets will spin because either the south or north poles align and then repel each other. The normal magnet is attached to a shaft which spins a gear which eventually will spin whatever it is attached to.

3. (a) Washing machine works on the principle of centrifugation. Centrifugation is a process that involves the use of the centrifugal force for the separation of mixtures with a centrifuge, used in industry and in laboratory settings. More-dense components of the mixture migrate away from the axis of the centrifuge, while less-dense components of the mixture migrate towards the axis.

4. (d) Because of density. The density of the clouds is less than that of the air. Same phenomena is there behind this, according to which is ship float in a sea.

5. (d) Initially at start of heating from 0°C to 4°C there will be a contraction as a result of which volume decreases. On further heating beyond 4°C to 10°C the molecules gain kinetic energy and start moving more randomly. Thus, intermolecular distance increases as a result of which its volume increases.

6. (a) An optical fibre is a thin, flexible, transparent fibre that acts as a waveguide or "light pipe" to transmit light between the two ends of the fibre. An optical fibre transmits light along its axis, by the process of total internal reflection. When light traveling in a dense medium hits a boundary at an angle larger than the "critical angle" for the boundary, the light will be completely reflected. This effect is used in optical fibres to confine light in the core.

7. (d) Amalgam is an alloy consisting of mercury and any other element.Iron being exceptional in nature not form amalgam with mercury. That's why mercury is stored in vessels made up of iron. Small quantities of an iron amalgam have, however, been formed by immersing sodium amalgam (containing 1 percent sodium) in a clear, saturated solution of ferrous sulphate.While rest three options zinc,copper and magnesium combine with mercury to form there respective amalgam.

8. (d) Polycarbonates are the polymer widely used in making bullet proof material. Bullet proof glass is made by layering a polycarbonate material between pieces of ordinary glass in a process called lamination. A bullet fired will pierce the outside layer of the glass, but the layered polycarbonate glass material is able to absorb the bullet's energy and stop it. Polycarbonate panels are used for covering advertising posters, construction of office buildings for sound proofing and polycarbonate is also used for making bullet proof jackets.

9. (b) Allicin is an oily, yellow liquid, which gives garlic its characteristic odour which is due to the −SO group. It also has a range of medical properties.

10. (d) Acid rain is caused by a chemical reaction that begins when compounds of sulphur dioxide and nitrogen oxide react with molecules in the atmosphere to produce acids.

11. (a) Fuel value can be expressed in terms of calorific value of fuel. The calorific value of a fuel is the amount of heat produced by burning 1 kg of fuel. Hydrogen has the highest calorific value of (141,790 KJ/kg) thus have highest fuel value. Calorific value of charcoal, natural gas and gasoline are (29,600; 43,000; 47,300 kJ/kg) respectively. Natural gas majorly consists of methane.

12. (a)

13. (c) Gibbon, Gorilla and Orangutan are apes, but Langur is not an ape, it is prosimians.

14. (b) Sunnhemp is plant which is used for green manuring in India.

15. (b) Malaria is caused by protozoan infection. No vaccine is yet available for this disease.

16. (d) The body can synthesize vitamin-D itself in presence of sunlight.

17. (b) Chlorophyll is a tetrapyrole ring system that chelate the magnesium ion. The tetrapyrole ring system that chelates this magnesium shows a conjugated double bond. This bond provide the light absorption feature to chlorophyll and gives it green colour.

18. (a) The maximum biodiversity is found in tropical rain forests.

19. (c) Destruction of habitat is the most important factor responsible for decline bio-diversity.

20. (a) Biosphere Reserves is an important strategy for the conservation of biodiversity.

21. (d) All the above factors are responsible for climate change.

22. (a) The concept of carbon credit originated from kyoto protocol.

23. (b) Global warming is caused due to the emission of carbon dioxide.

24. (a) ETWS installed in Rangachang in Andaman and Nicobar Islands to predict Tsunami within three minutes of being triggered.

25. (c)

26. (b) "Nirbhay", First cruise missile of India has a Long-range (1,000-2,000 km) & strikes targets more than 700 km away carrying nuclear warheads.

27. (d) Cryogenic rocket engine is a rocket engine that uses cryogenic fuel or oxidizer, which are gases liquefied and stored at very low temperature.

28. (b) The world's highest ground based telescopic observatory is located at Leh in India.

29. (b)

30. (a)

31. (d)

32. (b) Deviri Express

33. (c)

34. (a) Pune

35. (d) Selecting the candidate of election is the function of the political party

36. (c) The Joint Session of Parliament resolves the deadlock between Lok Sabha and Rajya Sabha over an ordinary bill.

37. (b)

38. (b) 1191 - First Battle of Tarain in which Prithviraj Chauhan defeated Mohd. Ghori. 1192 - Second Battle of Tarain in which Mohd. Ghori defeated Prithviraj Chauhan.

39. (b) Simon Commission (1927) > Dandi March (1930) > Gandhi Irwin Pact (1931) > Poona Pact (1932)

40. (a) Kalahari desert is present in Africa while Atacama Desert is in South America. Thar Desert is in Australia and Great Victoria is in Australia.

41. (b) The Palk strait separates India and Srilanka. It lies between the Gulf of Mannar and the Bay of Bengal.

42. (c) The Narmada river originates from a tank 1057 m high west of Amarkantak plateau in Madhya Pradesh. River Damodar originates from Chhota Nagpur plateau, Mahanadi originates from Bastar plateau and Tapti originates from Satpura hills.

43. (d)   44. (d)   45. (b)

46. (c) 9 states of India shares the coastline.

47. (c) Article 40, of the Indian Constitution provides for the institution of Panchayati Raj

48. (c) In 1959 the Panchayati Raj system was introduced in India.

49. (d)

50. (b)

51. (b) 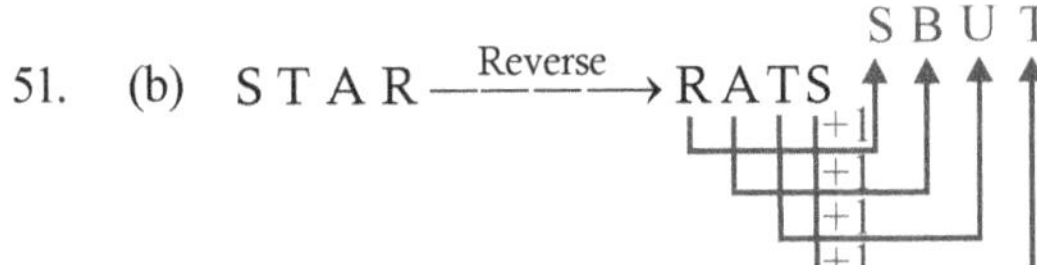

Similarly,

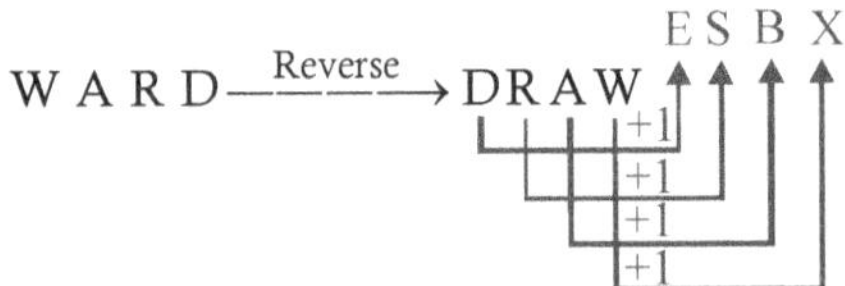

52. (c) In the word MEET, the second and the third letters are the same.

53. (c) 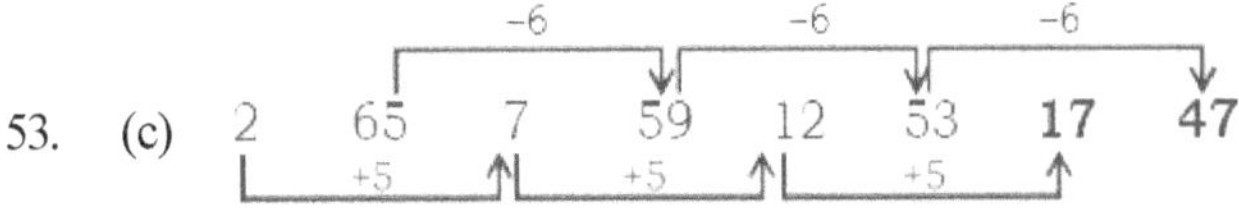

54. (d)
```
G    O    O    D    N    E    S    S
 +1   -1   +1   -1   +1   -1   +1   -1
H    N    P    C    O    D    T    R
```
Similarly,
```
G    R    E    A    T    N    E    S    S
 +1   -1   +1   -1   +1   -1   +1   -1   +1
H    Q    F    Z    U    M    F    R    T
```

55. (b) 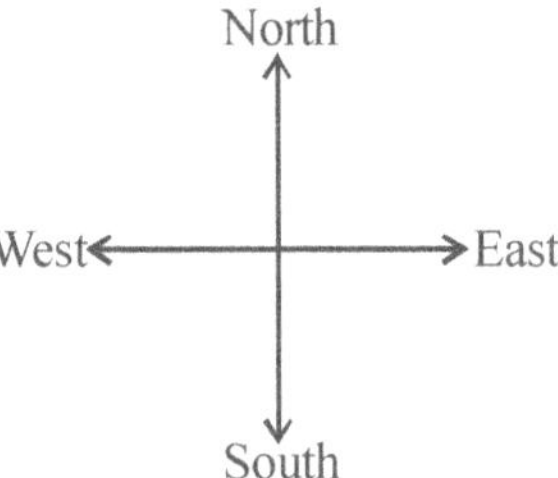

Required distance $= 30\,m + 20\,m = 50\,m$

56. (d) A man + his wife $= 1 + 1 = 2$
His three sons + their wives $= 3 + 3 = 6$
Three children in each one's family $= 3 \times 3 = 9$
Total members $= 2 + 6 + 9 = 17$

57. (d) 5th date of a month is Tuesday
Friday will be on $= 5 + 3$
$= 8^{th}$ of a month
1st Friday is on 1st of a month
2nd Friday is on 8th of a month
3rd Friday will be on 15th of a month
3 days after $15^{th} = 15 + 3 = 18$

58. (c) Rahul's present age $= 12$ yrs,
Paras   ''   '' $= 4$ yrs
Let Rahul be twice as old as Paras after x yrs from now.
Then, $12 + x = 2(4 + x)$
$= 12 + x = 8 + 2x \Rightarrow x = 4$
Hence, Rahul's required age $= 12 + x \Rightarrow 16$ yrs

59. (d) Putting the position of the letters in reverse order
$P = 11$, $S = 8$, $V = 5$ and $Y = 2$.

60. (a)
```
 ↑    ↑    ↑    ↑    ↑
 S    Q    P    T    R
```

61. (a) Here, $52 - 33 = 78 - 59 = 117 - 98 = 19$
Now, $52 = 13 \times 2 \times 2$
$78 = 13 \times 2 \times 3$
$117 = 13 \times 3 \times 3$
$\therefore$ LCM $= 13 \times 2 \times 2 \times 3 \times 3 = 468$
$\therefore$ Required number $= 468 - 19 = 449$
Hence, the sum of digits is 17.

62. (c) Let the numerator and denominator of a fraction are x and y, respectively,
According to question,

$\dfrac{x-1}{y} = \dfrac{1}{3} \Rightarrow 3x - 3 = y \Rightarrow 3x - y = 3 \ldots(i)$

and $\dfrac{x}{y+5} = \dfrac{1}{4} \Rightarrow 4x - y = 5 \qquad \ldots(ii)$

On solving eqs. (i) and (ii), we get

$x = 2$ and $y = 3$

$\therefore$ Required fraction

$= \dfrac{x-1}{y+5} = \dfrac{2-1}{3+5} = \dfrac{1}{8}$

63. (b) Profit will be shared in the ratio of

$11 \times 3 : 16.5 \times 3 : 8.25 \times 3$

$= 11 : 16.5 : 8.25$

$= 44 : 66 : 33$

Anil's share in the profit

$= \dfrac{33}{143} \times 19.5 = 14.5$ lakh

50% of Anil's share = 2.25 lakh

64. (c) Given, $A : B : C = \dfrac{1}{5} : \dfrac{1}{6} : \dfrac{1}{10} = 6 : 5 : 3$

$\therefore$ Share of A

$= \dfrac{6}{6+5+3} \times 8400 = \dfrac{6}{14} \times 8400$

$= ₹\, 3600$

65. (a) Given that,

Number of male employees (M) = 45

Number of female employees (F) = 15

Mean salary of male employee $\left(\overline{x}_M\right)$

$= ₹\, 5000$

Total number of employees = (M + F)

$= 45 + 15 = 60$

Mean salary of employees $\left(\overline{x}_{MF}\right) = ₹\, 4800$

Let mean salary of female employee is $\overline{x}_F$

By formula,

$\overline{x}_{MF} = \dfrac{M\,\overline{x}_M + F\,\overline{x}_F}{(M+F)}$

$\Rightarrow 4800 = \dfrac{45 \times 5000 + 15 \times \overline{x}_F}{60}$

$\Rightarrow 4800 \times 60 - 45 \times 5000 = 15 \times \overline{x}_F$

$\therefore \ \ \overline{x}_F = 4800 \times 4 - 3 \times 5000$

$= 300(16 \times 4 - 50) = 300 \times 14 = 4200.$

66. (c) $x^4 - 1 = (x^2 - 1)(x^2 + 1) = (x - 1)(x + 1)$ $(x^2 + 1)$ Now $x^4 - 2x^3 - 2x^2 - 2x - 3$

Putting $x = -1$ in this equation gives 0, so $(x+1)$ is a factor, divide $x^4 - 2x^3 - 2x^2 - 2x - 3$ by $(x+1)$ gives $x^3 - 3x^2 + x - 3$

Now put $x = 3$, gives 0, so another factor is $(x-3)$, divide $(x-3)$ gives $x^2 + 1$ which cannot be further divided So $x^4 - 2x^3 - 2x^2 - 2x - 3 = (x^2 + 1)(x+1)(x-3)$

Now common factors in both expressions are $(x^2 + 1)(x+1)$ which is the HCF.

67. (a) Volume of cone, $C = \dfrac{1}{3}\pi R^2 H$

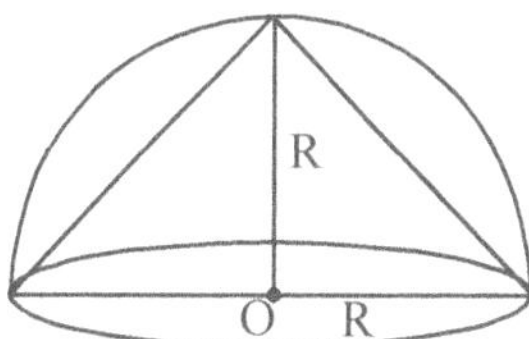

$= \dfrac{1}{3}\pi R^3 \qquad\qquad (\because H = R)$

Volume of hemisphere, $H = \dfrac{2}{3}\pi R^3$

$\therefore \ \ C : H = \dfrac{1}{3}\pi R^3 : \dfrac{2}{3}\pi R^3 = 1 : 2$

68. (a) Second term is greater than first term by 5, while the third term is less than the second term by 3. The same order is repeated.

69. (b) Differences between two consecutive terms are 2, 3, 4, 5 and 6 respectively.

70. (d) The odd-number positioned letters move two letters backward and the even number positioned ones move three letters forward. Thus PROJECT will become NUMMCFR.

71. (d) The word is coded by moving the letters three steps forward

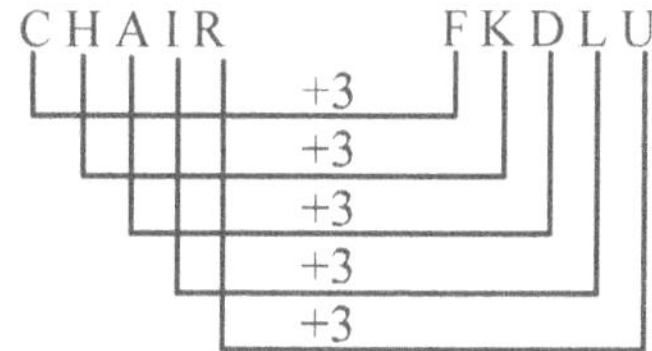

Similarly,

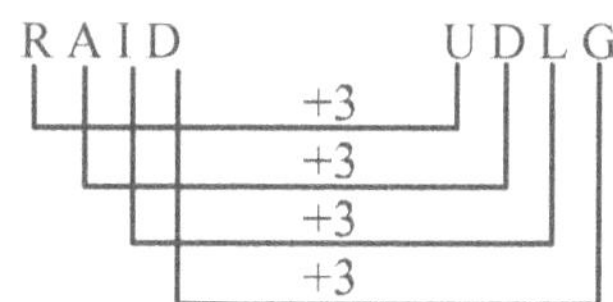

72. (c) G is the brother of C and C is the daughter of A. So, G is son of A. Also, F is the brother of A. So, F is the uncle of G.

73. (d) 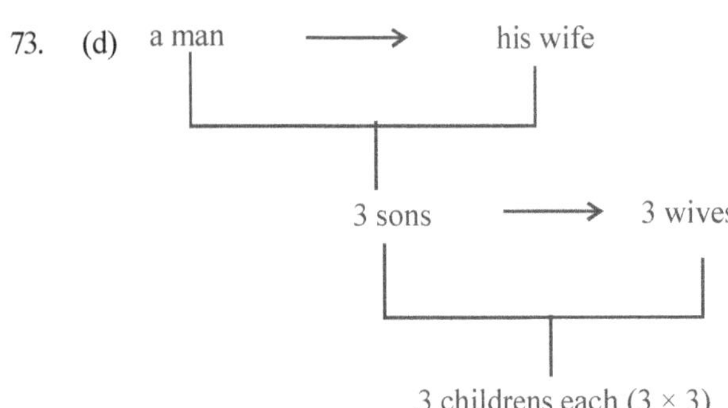

∴ Total No. of people in the party

$= 1 + 1 + 3 + 3 + 3 \times 3$

$= 8 + 9 = 17$

74. (a) Here, O is the starting point.

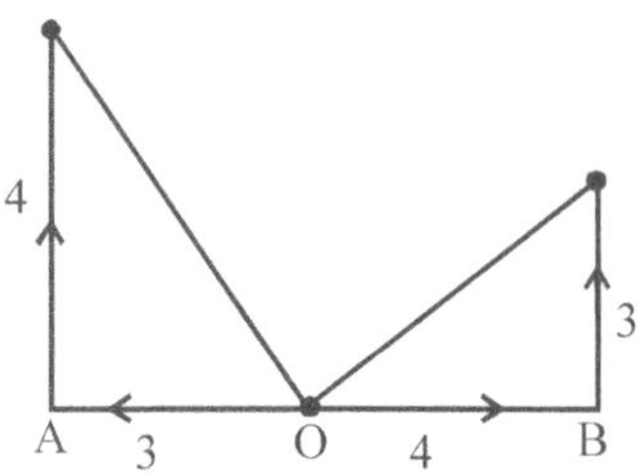

Both A and B are $\sqrt{3^2 + 4^2}$ = 5 km from the starting point.

75. (a) Position of Suman from right

$$= \left[\begin{array}{c} \text{Difference of} \\ \text{Ramesh's position} \end{array} + \begin{array}{c} \text{First position} \\ \text{of Suman} \end{array} \right]$$

$= [(15 - 9) + 6] = 12\text{th}$

11 PRACTICE SET

Time : 60 Min.　　　　　　　　　　　　　　　**Max. Marks : 75**

DIRECTIONS: *In question no. 1 and 2, a series is given, with one term missing. Choose the correct alternative from the given ones that will complete the series.*

1. 7, 14, 23, 34, ?
   (a) 46　　　　　　　(b) 47
   (c) 44　　　　　　　(d) 45
2. AE, FJ, KO, ? UY
   (a) QN　　　　　　　(b) TQ
   (c) NP　　　　　　　(d) PT

DIRECTIONS (Qs. 3-5): *In questions select the related word/ letter/number from the given alternatives.*

3. 3 : 7 : : 15 : ?
   (a) 30　　　　　　　(b) 35
   (c) 45　　　　　　　(d) 49
4. Kalidas : Meghdoot : : Kautilya : ?
   (a) Ramayana　　　　(b) Arthashastra
   (c) Kamayani　　　　(d) Kadambari
5. Water : Ocean : : Sand : ?
   (a) Island　　　　　(b) Waves
   (c) River　　　　　(d) Desert

DIRECTIONS: *Find the odd word/letter/Number pair from the given alternatives.*

6. (a) Engineer　　　　(b) School
   (c) Lawyer　　　　　(d) Doctor
7. A boy introduced a girl as the daughter of the son of the father of his uncle. How is the girl related to the boy ?
   (a) Aunt　　　　　　(b) Grand-daughter
   (c) Niece　　　　　(d) Sister
8. Some equations are solved on the basis of a certain system. Find the correct answer for the unsolved equation on that basis.
   If $7 \times 9 \times 6 \times 5 = 5 \times 7 \times 4 \times 3$,
   then $8 \times 4 \times 14 \times 12 = ?$
   (a) $5 \times 3 \times 7 \times 10$　　　(b) $6 \times 3 \times 9 \times 11$
   (c) $6 \times 2 \times 12 \times 10$　　(d) $6 \times 4 \times 8 \times 9$

9. Deepak is standing facing South. She goes 20 metres ahead and turns right and goes 30 metres. Now she turns left and goes for 40 metres and turns right. In which direction is she headed now ?
   (a) North　　　　　(b) South
   (c) East　　　　　　(d) West
10. In a coded language, MANAGER is written as REGANAM. How will ASSISTANT be written in that code ?
    (a) TNATSISSA　　　(b) TNATISSSA
    (c) TNATSSIA　　　(d) TNATSISAS
11. Identify the diagram that best represents the relationship among the classes given below :
    Doctors, Engineers, Lawyers

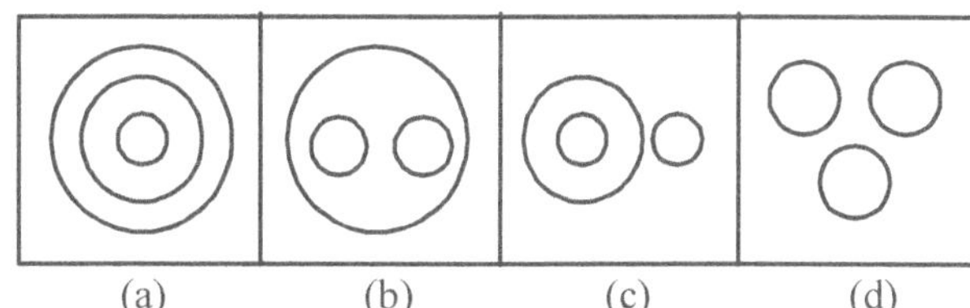

    (a)　　　　(b)　　　　(c)　　　　(d)

12. Find the wrong number in the series :
    28, 33, 31, 36, 34, 29
    (a) 33　　　　　　　(b) 36
    (c) 34　　　　　　　(d) 29
13. Satya's birthday falls on 15th August and Meena's birthday falls on 25th June. If Meena's birthday was on Wednesday, what was the day on Satya's birthday in the same year?
    (a) Friday　　　　　(b) Monday
    (c) Tuesday　　　　(d) Saturday
14. Introducing a girl, a man says, "She is the daughter of the daughter of my wife". How is man related to the girl?
    (a) Maternal uncle　　(b) Son
    (c) Maternal grandfather　(d) Father
15. A railway train 100 metres long is running at the speed of 30 km/hr. In what time does it pass a man standing near a line ?
    (a) 10 seconds　　　(b) 13 seconds
    (c) 12 seconds　　　(d) 15 seconds

16. The length and breadth of a rectangle are 20 m and 15 m respectively. If length is increased by 20% and the breadth by 30%, the percentage increase in its area is
    - (a) 54%
    - (b) 56%
    - (c) 50%
    - (d) 52%

17. The average height of 8 students is 152 cm. Two more students of heights 144 cm and 155 cm join the group. What is the new average height ?
    - (a) 151.5 cm
    - (b) 152.5 cm
    - (c) 151 cm
    - (d) 150.5 cm

18. Aman sells two watches at ₹ 99 each. On one he gets 10% profit and on the other he loses 10%. His net gain or loss percent is
    - (a) loss of 1%
    - (b) no profit no loss
    - (c) profit of 10%
    - (d) loss of 10%

19. If a person lost 8% by selling an article for ₹ 1,035, he bought the article for
    - (a) ₹ 1,135
    - (b) ₹ 1,152
    - (c) ₹ 1,105
    - (d) ₹ 1,125

20. If $2x = 3y = 4z$, find $x : y : z$.
    - (a) 3 : 4 : 6
    - (b) 6 : 4 : 3
    - (c) 4 : 3 : 2
    - (d) 2 : 3 : 4

21. The ratio of the ages of A, B and C is 5 : 8 : 9. If the sum of the ages of A and C is 56 years, the age of B will be
    - (a) 12 years
    - (b) 23 years
    - (c) 21 years
    - (d) 32 years

22. A box contain 280 coins of one rupee, 50 paise and 25 paise. The values of each kind of coin are in the ratio of 8 : 4 : 3. The number of one rupee coins will be
    - (a) 52
    - (b) 81
    - (c) 60
    - (d) 80

23. Rita purchased a car with a marked price of ₹ 2,10,000 at a discount of 5%. If the sales tax charged is 10%, find the amount she has to pay.
    - (a) ₹ 2,19,500
    - (b) ₹ 2,19,000
    - (c) ₹ 2,19,450
    - (d) ₹ 2,20,000

24. A shopkeeper sold an item for ₹ 1,800 at a discount of 10% and gained ₹ 200. Had he not given the discount, his gain would be
    - (a) ₹ 300
    - (b) ₹ 400
    - (c) ₹ 180
    - (d) ₹ 200

25. Raju can do a piece of work in 20 days, while Ram can do it in 30 days. If both of them work at it together, then the number of days in which they will be able to finish the work is
    - (a) 12 days
    - (b) 10 days
    - (c) 50 days
    - (d) 25 days

26. The twin cities are separated by which lake
    - (a) Loktak Lake
    - (b) Chilka Lake
    - (c) Wular Lake
    - (d) Hussain Sagar Lake

27. Name the largest fresh water lake in India?
    - (a) Kolleru Lake
    - (b) Wular Lake
    - (c) Nakhi Lake
    - (d) Dal Lake

28. The brightest planet is _________?
    - (a) Jupiter
    - (b) Mars
    - (c) Venus
    - (d) Mercury

29. What happens to atmospheric pressure with increase in altitude ?
    - (a) It remains constant
    - (b) It decreases
    - (c) It increases
    - (d) It constantly fluctuates

30. What is the approximate length of Konkan Railway?
    - (a) 580 kms
    - (b) 760 kms
    - (c) 940 kms
    - (d) 1050 kms

31. Which Himalayan Peak is also called 'Sagar Matha'?
    - (a) Nanga Parbat
    - (b) Dhaulagiri
    - (c) Mt. Everest
    - (d) Kanchenjunga

32. Select the High Yielding Varieties of seed-crops developed under Green Revolution in India.
    - (a) Rice, Wheat, Pulses, Oil seeds and Sugarcane
    - (b) Maize, Black-gram, Jowar Coffee and Tea
    - (c) Rice, Wheat, Jowar; Bajra and Maize
    - (d) Wheat, Rice, Sugarcane Pulses and Maize

33. Who Among the following rulers fought the fourth Anglo-Mysore war in which he was killed?
    - (a) The Nizam
    - (b) Aurangzeb
    - (c) Tipu Sultan
    - (d) Shivaji

34. Which of the following emperor introduced new land revenue system which initiated the growth of the Mysore silk industry?
    - (a) Narasimha Swamy
    - (b) Daria Daukat Bagh
    - (c) Tipu Sultan
    - (d) None of the above

35. Why are plants grown along river banks?
    - (a) To prevent flood
    - (b) To provide shade
    - (c) To reduce silting and erosion
    - (d) To control pollution

36. Bacteriophages
    - (a) A kind of soil bacteria
    - (b) Bacteria growing in phases
    - (c) Parasitic bacteria infecting man
    - (d) Virus infecting bacteria

37. The process of producing energy in plants is known as
    - (a) Absorption
    - (b) Reduction
    - (c) Photosynthesis
    - (d) Transpiration

38. Fuse wire is made of an alloy of _______.
    - (a) Lead and Copper
    - (b) Tin and Copper
    - (c) Tin and Lead
    - (d) Copper and Silver

39. The 'Abolition of Titles' is a fundamental right classified under:
    - (a) Right against Exploitation
    - (b) Right to Freedom
    - (c) Right to equality
    - (d) Right to freedom of religion

40. Which one of the following is an example for a non-economic good?
    - (a) Doctor's service
    - (b) Teacher's service
    - (c) Mother's service
    - (d) Banker's service

41. During sleep a man's blood pressure
    - (a) increases
    - (b) decreases
    - (c) remains constant
    - (d) fluctuates

42. Who has won maximum filmfare awards as a music director?
    - (a) (a) R. Rahman
    - (b) Laxmikant Pyarelal
    - (c) Pritam
    - (d) S. (d) Burman

43. Instrument for measuring light intensity is called -
    - (a) Lucimeter
    - (b) Cryometer
    - (c) Cyanometer
    - (d) Barometer

44. Nitrogen fixing bacteria found in the root nodules of leguminous plant is:-
    - (a) Saprophytic
    - (b) Parasitic
    - (c) Symbiotic
    - (d) Autotrophic

45. Which one of the following is considered as the drug of last resort for human beings?
    (a) Penicillin   (b) Tetracycline
    (c) Chloramphenicol   (d) Streptomycin
46. Which one of the following is a hereditary disease?
    (a) Cataract   (b) Haemophilia
    (c) Pellagra   (d) Osteoporosis
47. Which of the following reaction is the main cause of energy radiated from Sun?
    (a) Nuclear fission   (b) Nuclear fusion
    (c) Chemical reaction   (d) Diffusion reaction
48. Mendel's principles of inheritance are based on
    (a) Vegetative reproduction
    (b) Asexual reproduction
    (c) Sexual reproduction
    (d) All of the above
49. The operating system called UNIX is typically used for
    (a) Desktop computer   (b) Laptop computer
    (c) Supercomputer   (d) Web server
50. R.N Malhotra committee is associated with
    (a) Sick industries   (b) Tax reforms
    (c) Insurance sector   (d) Banking sector
51. National Renewal Fund was constituted for the purpose of
    (a) Providing pension for retiring employees
    (b) Social security
    (c) Rural reconstruction
    (d) Reconstruction and modernisation of industries
52. The National Deworming Day is celebrated on which date in India?
    (a) February 13   (b) February 10
    (c) February 12   (d) October 2
53. The Fourth Schedule to the Constitution of India deals with :
    (a) Provisions related to the administration of trible areas
    (b) Allocation of seats in the Council of States.
    (c) The Union List, the State List and the Concurrent List
    (d) Recognized language of the Union of India.
54. Who is the head of Municipal Corporation?
    (a) Prime Minister   (b) Sarpanch
    (c) Governor   (d) Mayor
55. Rotational axis of which of the following planet is highly tilted?
    (a) Earth   (b) Uranus
    (c) Neptune   (d) Jupiter
56. How much is the difference of time between any two Consecutive longitudes?
    (a) 10 min   (b) 14 min
    (c) 4 min   (d) 5:30 min
57. Mass of an object is a________.?
    (a) Physical Quantity   (b) Fundamental Quantity
    (c) Scalar Quantituy   (d) All options are correct
58. What is the name of the program initiated by the government which is responsible for water supply in around 500 cities?
    (a) Nirmal Jal Yojana   (b) Amrita Program
    (c) Aradhana Program   (d) Amrut Program
59. What is the present Annual Rate of Interest on Kisan Vikas Patra (KVP)?
    (a) 8.4%   (b) 7.8%
    (c) 7.5%   (d) 7.3%
60. The World Bank headquarters in ________________.
    (a) New York, USA   (b) Paris, France
    (c) Geneva, Switzerland   (d) Washington DC, USA

61. Union Budget 2017 has introduced SANKALP which stands for?
    (a) Skill Acquisition and Knowledge Awareness for Livelihood Promotion Programme
    (b) Skill Acquisition and Knowhow Awareness for Livelihood Promotion Programme
    (c) Skill Acquisition and Knowledge Awareness for Livelihood Promoting Programme
    (d) None of the above
62. Indian Railways will focus on which of the following areas for the coming fiscal, as per the Budget?
    (a) Passenger Safety   (b) Cleanliness
    (c) Women Security   (d) Only a and b
63. Which of the following elements has the lowest melting point?
    (a) Bromine   (b) Zinc
    (c) Lead   (d) Calcium
64. Some roots, called ________, arise from an organ other than the radicle.
    (a) tap roots   (b) stilt roots
    (c) fibrous roots   (d) adventitious roots
65. Spiders belong to which class of animals?
    (a) Arachnids   (b) Aves
    (c) Gastropods   (d) Anthozoa
66. Vitamin A is also known as _____.
    (a) Thiamine   (b) Riboflavin
    (c) Retinol   (d) Calciferol
67. Which one of the following is the name of Nobel Prize winning Indian?
    (a) Vikram Sarabhai   (b) APJ Abdul Kalam
    (c) S. Pancharatnam   (d) (c)V. Raman
68. Organisms that generate energy using light are known as ________.
    (a) Chaemolithotrophs   (b) Oligotrophs
    (c) Bacteria   (d) Photoautotrophs
69. Which among the following is false about natural rubber?
    (a) It is an elastomer
    (b) It is a monomer of cisisoprene
    (c) Natural rubber is a polymer of chloroprene
    (d) It is heated with sulphur compounds to improve its properties
70. Which is the first Hindi newspaper of India?
    (a) Udaan   (b) Azad Vichaar
    (c) Udant Martand   (d) Vichaar Vyakti
71. Who is the author of "The Lowland"?
    (a) Amitav Ghosh   (b) Kiran Desai
    (c) Jhumpa Lahiri   (d) Arvind Adiga
72. The Nagzira Wildlife Sanctuary (NWS) is located in which state?
    (a) Maharashtra   (b) Himachal Pradesh
    (c) Jammu & Kashmir   (d) Nagaland
73. Constitution Day of India is on ________.
    (a) 26th January   (b) 23rd June
    (c) 15th August   (d) 26th November
74. How many layers does Human Skin have?
    (a) 5   (b) 7
    (c) 11   (d) 3
75. Weight of a person at a height of 2R from the centre of the earth, where R is the radius of the earth ________.
    (a) remains same   (b) becomes half
    (c) becomes twice   (d) becomes one fourth

RESPONSE SHEET

1. (a)(b)(c)(d)	2. (a)(b)(c)(d)	3. (a)(b)(c)(d)	4. (a)(b)(c)(d)	5. (a)(b)(c)(d)
6. (a)(b)(c)(d)	7. (a)(b)(c)(d)	8. (a)(b)(c)(d)	9. (a)(b)(c)(d)	10. (a)(b)(c)(d)
11. (a)(b)(c)(d)	12. (a)(b)(c)(d)	13. (a)(b)(c)(d)	14. (a)(b)(c)(d)	15. (a)(b)(c)(d)
16. (a)(b)(c)(d)	17. (a)(b)(c)(d)	18. (a)(b)(c)(d)	19. (a)(b)(c)(d)	20. (a)(b)(c)(d)
21. (a)(b)(c)(d)	22. (a)(b)(c)(d)	23. (a)(b)(c)(d)	24. (a)(b)(c)(d)	25. (a)(b)(c)(d)
26. (a)(b)(c)(d)	27. (a)(b)(c)(d)	28. (a)(b)(c)(d)	29. (a)(b)(c)(d)	30. (a)(b)(c)(d)
31. (a)(b)(c)(d)	32. (a)(b)(c)(d)	33. (a)(b)(c)(d)	34. (a)(b)(c)(d)	35. (a)(b)(c)(d)
36. (a)(b)(c)(d)	37. (a)(b)(c)(d)	38. (a)(b)(c)(d)	39. (a)(b)(c)(d)	40. (a)(b)(c)(d)
41. (a)(b)(c)(d)	42. (a)(b)(c)(d)	43. (a)(b)(c)(d)	44. (a)(b)(c)(d)	45. (a)(b)(c)(d)
46. (a)(b)(c)(d)	47. (a)(b)(c)(d)	48. (a)(b)(c)(d)	49. (a)(b)(c)(d)	50. (a)(b)(c)(d)
51. (a)(b)(c)(d)	52. (a)(b)(c)(d)	53. (a)(b)(c)(d)	54. (a)(b)(c)(d)	55. (a)(b)(c)(d)
56. (a)(b)(c)(d)	57. (a)(b)(c)(d)	58. (a)(b)(c)(d)	59. (a)(b)(c)(d)	60. (a)(b)(c)(d)
61. (a)(b)(c)(d)	62. (a)(b)(c)(d)	63. (a)(b)(c)(d)	64. (a)(b)(c)(d)	65. (a)(b)(c)(d)
66. (a)(b)(c)(d)	67. (a)(b)(c)(d)	68. (a)(b)(c)(d)	69. (a)(b)(c)(d)	70. (a)(b)(c)(d)
71. (a)(b)(c)(d)	72. (a)(b)(c)(d)	73. (a)(b)(c)(d)	74. (a)(b)(c)(d)	75. (a)(b)(c)(d)

HINTS & SOLUTIONS

1. (b) $7 \quad 14 \quad 23 \quad 34 \quad \boxed{47}$

   $+7 \qquad +9 \qquad +11 \qquad +13$

2. (d) $A \xrightarrow{+5} F \xrightarrow{+5} K \xrightarrow{+5} \boxed{P} \xrightarrow{+5} U$

   $E \xrightarrow{+5} J \xrightarrow{+5} O \xrightarrow{+5} \boxed{T} \xrightarrow{+5} Y$

3. (b) $\dfrac{3}{7} = \dfrac{15}{x}$

   $3x = 15 \times 7$

   $x = \dfrac{15 \times 7}{3} = 35$

4. (b) Meghdoot has been written by Kalidas.
   Similarly,
   Arthashastra has been written by kautitya.

5. (d) Ocean is the mass of water
   Similarly,
   Desert is the mass of sand.

6. (c) Except (b) others are connected with a job that needs special skill, while school is an organisation.

7. (c)

   There is no option of cousin sister.

8. (c) $\begin{array}{ccccccc} 7 & \times & 9 & \times & 6 & \times & 5 \\ -2\downarrow & & -2\downarrow & & -2\downarrow & & -2\downarrow \\ 5 & \times & 7 & \times & 4 & \times & 3 \end{array}$

   Similarly

   $\begin{array}{ccccccc} 8 & \times & 4 & \times & 14 & \times & 12 \\ -2\downarrow & & -2\downarrow & & -2\downarrow & & -2\downarrow \\ 6 & \times & 2 & \times & 12 & \times & 10 \end{array}$

9. (d)

10. (a) Reverse order

    ASSISTANT

    Reverse order $\rightarrow$ TNATSISSA

11. (d)

12. (d) $28 + 3 = 31 \ \& \ 36 + 3 = 39$

    $33 + 3 = 36$

    So, wrong no. is 29.

13. (a) The days between both dates 25 June to 15 Aug.
    Total days = 51 days
    So, $51/7 = 49 \ \& \ 2$ days after Wednesday means Friday is correct answer.

14. (c) Man $\equiv$ Wife

    Daughter

    Girl

15. (c) Time taken by train $= \dfrac{100}{30 \times \dfrac{5}{18}} = 12$ seconds

16. (b) Area of rectangle, $A = 20 \text{ m} \times 15 \text{ m} = 300 \text{m}^2$.

    increased area, $A' = \left(20 + \dfrac{20}{100} \times 20\right)\left(15 + \dfrac{30}{100} \times 15\right)$

    $= 24 \times 19.5 = 468 \, \text{m}^2$.

    % increase in area $= \dfrac{468 - 300}{300} \times 100 = 56\%$

17. (a) Total height of 8 students $= 8 \times 152 \text{ cm} = 1216 \text{ cm}$
    Total height of 10 students $= 1216 \text{ cm} + 144 \text{ cm} + 155 \text{ cm} = 1515 \text{ cm}$

    new average $= \dfrac{1515}{10} \text{ cm} = 151.5 \text{cm}$

18. (a) Cost price of watch on which he get 10% Profit,

    $C_1 = 99 \times \dfrac{100}{110} = 90$

    Cost Price of watch on which he losses 10%,

    $C_2 = \dfrac{99 \times 100}{90} = 110$

    Net loss% $\dfrac{(110 + 90) - (99 + 99)}{(110 + 90)} \times 100$

$$= \frac{200-198}{200} \times 100 = 1\%$$

19. (d) Person bought the article for $\frac{1035}{(100-8)} \times 100$

$$= ₹\,1,125$$

20. (b) $2x = 3y = 4z$

$$x = 2z, \; y = \frac{4}{3}z$$

$$x : y : z = 2z : \frac{4}{3}z : z = 6 : 4 : 3$$

21. (d) Let ages of A, B and C are 5x, 8x and 9x respectively.
$5x + 9x = 56$
$x = 4$
Age of B $= 8 \times 4 = 32$ years

22. (d) Ratio of number of coins
$$= 8 : 4 \times 2 : 3 \times 4 = 8 : 8 : 12$$
$$= 2 : 2 : 3$$

Number of one rupee coin $= \dfrac{2}{2+2+3} \times 280 = 80$

23. (c) Selling price of car; S.P. $= 2,10,000 - \dfrac{5}{100} \times 2,10,000$

$$= 1,99,500$$
Sales tax charged is 10%

Total cost for Rita $= 1,99,500 + \dfrac{10}{100} \times 1,99,500$

$$= ₹\,2,19,450$$

24. (b) Let M be the marked price.

$$M - \frac{10}{100} \times M = 1800$$

$$M = \frac{1800}{90} \times 100 = 2000$$

Cost Price, C $= 1800 - 200 = 1600$
If no discount is given
Profit ₹ 2000 − ₹ 1600 = ₹ 400

25. (a) Raju and Ram together can finish the work in

$$\left(\frac{20 \times 30}{20+30}\right) = 12 \text{days}$$

26. (d) The twin cities are separated by the man-made Hussain Sagar lake, which was built during the reign of the Qutb Shahi dynasty in the 16th century.

27. (b) Wular Lake is one of the largest fresh water lakes in Asia. It is sited in Bandipora district in the Indian state of Jammu & Kashmir. The lake basin was formed as a result of tectonic activity and is fed by the Jhelum River.

28. (c) Venus, which can be seen with the unaided eye from Earth, is the brightest planet in our Solar System. Venus was given the nickname evening star and morning star because of its bright, consistent presence.

29. (b) In most circumstances atmospheric pressure is closely approximated by the hydrostatic pressure caused by the mass of air above the measurement point.

30. (b) The Konkan Railway (Railway Symbol:KR)is a railway line which runs along the Konkan coast of India between Mumbai and Mangaluru. It was constructed and is operated by the Konkan Railway Corporation. It runs from Roha in Maharashtra till Thokur in Karnataka for a total distance of 741 km (460 mi), along the west coast of India and Western Ghats.

31. (c) Mount Everest, also known in Nepal as Sagarmatha and in Tibet as Chomolungma, is Earth's highest mountain. It is is Earth's highest mountain. It is located in the Mahalangur mountain range in Nepal. Its peak is 8,848 metres (29,029 ft) above sea level. It is not the furthest summit from the centre of the Earth.

32. (c) Seeds for High Yielding Crops to Improve Farm ProductivityTo feed the growing population and make farming a more sustainable and profitable business, DuPont delivers hybrid seed solutions that increases crop yields in different weather and soil conditions.

33. (c) The Fourth Anglo-Mysore War was a conflict in South India between the Kingdom of Mysore and the British East India Company under the Earl of Mornington. This was the final conflict of the four Anglo-Mysore Wars. The British captured the capital of Mysore. The ruler Tipu Sultan was killed in the battle. Britain took indirect control of Mysore, restoring the Wodeyar Dynasty to the Mysore throne (with a British commissioner to advise him on all issues).

34. (c) Tipu Sultan also known as the Tiger of Mysore and Tipu Sahib, was a ruler of the Kingdom of Mysore. He was the eldest son of Sultan Haidar Ali of Mysore. Tipu introduced a number of administrative innovations during his rule, including his coinage, a new Mauludi lunisolar calendar, and a new land revenue system which initiated the growth of the Mysore silk industry.

35. (c) Plants are grown along river banks to reduce silting and erosion. It is done to prevent excessive soil from getting eroded and getting deposited in the river bed, which then reduces the water carrying capacity of the river.

36. (d) A bacteriophage, also known informally as a phage, is a virus that infects and replicates within a bacterium. The term is derived from "bacteria" and the Greek: φαγεῖν , "to devour" Bacteriophages are composed of proteins that encapsulate a DNA or RNA genome, and may have relatively simple or elaborate structures.

37. (c) The process of producing energy in plants is known as Photosynthesis. Photosynthesis is a process used by plants to convert light energy into chemical energy. Chlorophyll pigment in the plants absorb sunlight which then along with carbon dioxide and water via chemical reaction forms glucose in form of adenosine triphosphate energy molecules.

38. (c) Fuse is made up of the alloy of tin and lead. Since the fuse is placed in the electrical circuit, to tackle an uneven moderation in the circuit and avoid untoward incidents, the metal strip in the fuse has to be of such quality which can break the circuit before any mishap occurs. For their physical properties of breaking when current is excess, tin and lead are used.

39. (c) The Article 18 of Indian constitution stands for abolition of titles under the right to equality. The five articles from Article 14 to 18 fall under the category of equality rights.

40. (c) Non-economic goods are goods or services that are plentiful and free. Air and dirt are considered non-economic goods since they are neither scarce nor valuable. Hence Mother's service is an example of it.

41. (d) Blood pressure has a daily pattern. Blood pressure is normally lower at night while you're sleeping. Your blood pressure starts to rise a few hours before you wake up. Your blood pressure continues to rise during the day, usually peaking in the middle of the afternoon. Then in the late afternoon and evening, your blood pressure begins dropping again.

42. (a) The Filmfare Best Music Album Award is given by the Filmfare magazine as part of its annual Filmfare Awards for Hindi films, to the best composer/arranger of a soundtrack. This category was first presented in 1954. Naushad Ali was the first recipient of this award for his song "Tu Ganga Ki Mauj" from the film Baiju Bawra. A. R. Rahman leads the winners with 10 Best Music Director Filmfare awards, followed by the music director duo of Shankar Jaikishan, who have 9. Laxmikant Pyarelal has the most nominations with 25, followed by Shankar Jaikishan with 20, and R. D. Burman with 17.

43. (a) lucimeter : An instrument for measuring the intensity of light.
Cryometer : A thermometer capable of measuring very low temperature.
Cyanometer: An instrument used for measuring the blueness of the sky.
Barometer: An instrument for measuring atmospheric pressure, used especially in weather forecasting.

44. (c) Nitrogen-fixing bacteria from root nodules of leguminous plants. Symbiosis, any of several living arrangements between members of two different species, including mutualism, commensalism, and parasitism. Both positive (beneficial) and negative (unfavorable to harmful) associations are therefore included, and the members are called symbionts.

45. (c)	46. (b)	47. (b)	48. (c)	49. (a)
50. (c)	51. (d)	52. (b)	53. (b)	54. (d)
55. (b)	56. (c)	57. (d)	58. (d)	59. (d)
60. (d)	61. (a)	62. (d)	63 (a)	64. (d)
65. (a)	66. (c)	67. (d)	68. (d)	69. (b)
70. (c)	71. (c)	72. (a)	73. (d)	74. (d)
75. (d)				

12

PRACTICE SET

Time : 60 Min. **Max. Marks : 75**

1. If $4 \times 2 \times 6 = 1626$, $3 \times 7 \times 4 = 974$, then $5 \times 6 \times 8 = ?$
   (a) 3658
   (b) 2568
   (c) 5664
   (d) 6456

2. Which one set of letters when sequentially placed at the gaps in the given letter series shall complete it?
   a _ b _ c _ a _ bc _ b _ cb
   (a) acbcab
   (b) ccbcca
   (c) ccaccb
   (d) cacabc

DIRECTIONS (Qs. 3 - 5): *In the following questions, a series is given with one term missing. Choose the correct alternative from the given ones that will complete the series.*

3. 15, 23, 31, 39, _?_, 54, 61
   (a) 45
   (b) 47
   (c) 46
   (d) 44

4. 2, 3.5, 5, 6.5, 8, _?_ .
   (a) 9.0
   (b) 9.5
   (c) 10.5
   (d) 11.0

5. 32, 58, 92, 134, _?_ .
   (a) 169
   (b) 184
   (c) 194
   (d) 156

6. If PAINT is coded as 74128 and EXCEL is coded as 93596, how is ACCEPT coded?
   (a) 459578
   (b) 457958
   (c) 459758
   (d) 455978

7. If '+' means '÷', '×' means '+', '–' means '×' and '÷' means '–', then which of the following equations is correct?
   (a) $36 + 6 - 3 \times 2 = 20$
   (b) $36 \times 6 + 3 - 2 < 20$
   (c) $36 \times 6 + 3 \times 2 > 20$
   (d) $36 + 6 \times 3 + 2 = 20$

8. A father is 5 times as old as his son. His son is 6 years old. After how many years, will the father be 4 times as old as his son?
   (a) 2 years
   (b) 5 years
   (c) 6 years
   (d) 4 years

9. Select the missing number from the given responses.

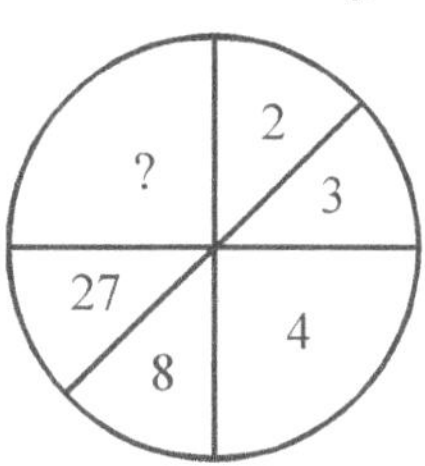

   (a) 56
   (b) 49
   (c) 45
   (d) 64

10. In the given diagram, Circle represents strong men, Square represents short men and Triangle represents military officers. Which region represents military officers who are short but not strong?

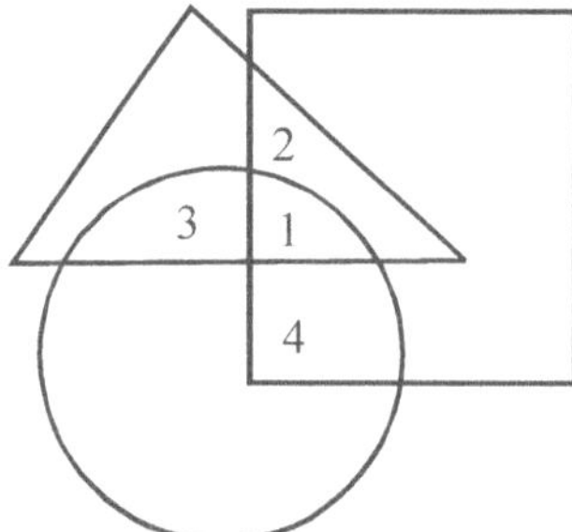

   (a) 2
   (b) 3
   (c) 4
   (d) 1

DIRECTIONS (Qs. 11 - 13) : *Find the odd number/word/number pair from the given alternatives.*

11. (a) Weight
    (b) Eyesight
    (c) Intelligence
    (d) Height

12.   (a)   C. V. Raman   (b)   Amartya Sen
    (c)   Abdul Kalam   (b)   Rabindra Nath Tagore

13. YWUS : QOMK : : ZXVT : ?
    (a)   YWUS   (b)   RPNL
    (c)   RPNM   (d)   XWUT

14. Select the missing number from the given responses.
    1, 3, 7, 15, 31, 63, 127, __?__ .
    (a)   260   (b)   275
    (c)   350   (d)   255

15. A circle is inscribed in an equilateral triangle and a square is inscribed in that circle. The ratio of the areas of the triangle and the square is
    (a) $3\sqrt{3} : 1$ (b) $\sqrt{3} : 4$
    (c) $\sqrt{3} : 8$ (d) $3\sqrt{3} : 2$

16. $\sqrt{\dfrac{9.5 \times 0.085}{0.0017 \times 0.19}}$ equals
    (a)   5   (b)   50
    (c)   500   (d)   0.05

17. The ratio in which a man must mix rice at ₹ 10.20 per kg and ₹ 14.40 per kg so as to make a mixture worth ₹ 12.60 per kg, is
    (a)   3 : 4   (b)   4 : 3
    (c)   2 : 5   (d)   18 : 24

18. If the sum of the length, breadth and height of a rectangular parallelopiped is 24 cm and the length of its diagonal is 15 cm, then its total surface area is
    (a) $351 \, cm^2$ (b) $256 \, cm^2$
    (c) $265 \, cm^2$ (d) $315 \, cm^2$

19. Two successive discounts of 70% and 30% are equivalent to a single discount of
    (a)   89%   (b)   75%
    (c)   79%   (d)   100%

20. A merchant allows a discount of 10% on marked price for the cash payment. To make a profit of 17%, he must mark his goods higher than their cost price by
    (a)   30%   (b)   33%
    (c)   40%   (d)   27%

21. The present ages of two persons are 36 and 50 years respectively, if after n years the ratio of their ages will be 3 : 4, then the value of n is
    (a)   3   (b)   4
    (c)   7   (b)   6

22. Out of 20 boys, 6 are each of 1 m 15 cm height, 8 are of 1 m 10 cm and rest of 1 m 12 cm. The average height of all of them is
    (a)   1 m 12 cm   (b)   1 m 12.1 cm
    (c)   1 m 21.1 cm   (d)   1 m 21 cm

23. Average of first five prime numbers is
    (a)   3.6   (b)   5.3
    (c)   5.6   (d)   5

24. A dishonest grocer sells rice at a profit of 10% and also uses weights which are 20% less than the marked weight. The total gain earned by him will be
    (a)   35%   (b)   37.5%
    (c)   40%   (d)   30.5%

25. A number when reduced by 10% gives 30. The number is
    (a)   35   (b) $33\dfrac{1}{2}$
    (c) $33\dfrac{1}{3}$ (d)   40

26. Which World Heritage Monument has been acclaimed as the "Necropolis of the Mughal dynasty"?
    (a)   Humayun's Tomb
    (b)   Mahabodhi Temple Complex
    (c)   Qutub Minar
    (d)   Red Fort Complex

27. Ozone Day is celebrated on which day?
    (a)   10 September   (b)   12 September
    (c)   14 September   (d)   16 September

28. Which drug is used to cure Osteoporosis?
    (a)   Risedronate   (b)   Tramadol
    (c)   Promethazine   (d)   Levothyroxine

29. Which of the following is present in Nail polish remover?
    (a)   Citric acid   (b)   Acetone
    (c)   Ethylene   (d)   Benzene

30. What is the formula of potassium ion in the noble gas state?
    (a) K^{+} (b) K^{2+}
    (c) K^{2-} (d) K^{-}

31. India's first Lithium-ion Battery unit is set up in which state?
    (a)   Tamilnadu   (b)   Gujarat
    (c)   Himachal Pradesh   (d)   None of these

32. Qatar is the highest per capita emitter of which of the following gases?
    (a)   Carbon Dioxide   (b)   Carbon Monoxide
    (c)   Ammonia   (d)   Hydrogen Sulphide

33. Hyderabad is the Capital City of _____ .
    (a)   Assam/vle   (b)   Chhattisgarh
    (c)   Andhra Pradesh   (d)   Telangana

34. Jahangir was the son of?
    (a)   Babur   (b)   Humayun
    (c)   Akbar   (d)   Shah Jahan

35. Which among the following is false about work?

    (a) If displacement is zero, work is zero

    (b) Work done can be negative

    (c) It is a vector quantity

    (d) Its unit is Joule

36. What is inertia?

    (a) Tendency to resist change in the current state

    (b) Tendency to impart acceleration to a body

    (c) Tendency to bring a body to rest

    (d) Tendency to change its current state

37. Article 356 of the Indian Constitution is about

    (a) Directive Principles of state policy

    (b) Imposition of President's Rule in states

    (c) Hindi as official language

    (d) Special status to Kashmir

38. What is the India's Rank in the 2017 Global Human Capital Index?

    (a) 101st   (b) 102nd

    (c) 103rd   (d) 104th

39. How many states have more than one capital in India?

    (a) 1   (b) 2

    (c) 3   (d) 4

40. Which of the following Harappan towns is divided into three parts?

    (a) Kalibanga   (b) Lothal

    (c) Chanhudaro   (d) Dholavira

41. Which of the following is considered the mainstay of growing population of India?

    (a) Public sector   (b) Business

    (c) Agriculture   (d) Manufacturing

42. Name the author of the book "Pakistan the Gathering Storm".

    (a) Parvez Musharraf   (b) Benazir Bhutto

    (c) Chetan Bhagat   (d) Javier Moro

43. Which world heritage site comprises the tomb of Iltumish?

    (a) Humayun's Tomb

    (b) Mahabodhi Temple Complex

    (c) Qutub Minar

    (d) Red Fort Complex

44. Which drug is used for Pain Relief?

    (a) Risedronate   (b) Tramadol

    (c) Folic Acid   (d) Bupropion

45. Sugarcane is a type of _____.

    (a) creeper   (b) tree

    (c) shrub   (d) grass

46. Who is commonly known as "the Father of Microbiology"?

    (a) Robert Hooke

    (b) Antonie Philips van Leeuwenhoek

    (c) Carl Linnaeus

    (d) Charles Darwin

47. Which of the following is a Synthetic rubber?

    (a) Leoprene   (b) Monoprene

    (c) Neoprene   (d) Isoprene

48. NaCl has _______.

    (a) Non-polar bonds   (b) Polar covalent bonds

    (c) Metallic bonds   (d) Ionic bonds

49. Which of the following is equivalent to 1 Kilobyte?

    (a) 128 Bytes   (b) 256 Bytes

    (c) 512 Bytes   (d) 1024 Bytes

50. For the aquatic organisms, the source of food is

    (a) Phytoplankton   (b) Sea Weed

    (c) Aqua plankton   (d) Zooplankton

51. Haemoglobin has the highest affinity with which of the following?

    (a) SO_2 (b) CO_2

    (c) CO (d) NO_2

52. The Lena river passes through which country?

    (a) China   (b) USA

    (c) Russia   (d) Brazil

53. Mars is the _______ planet from the Sun.

    (a) 2nd   (b) 4th

    (c) 6th   (d) 8th

54. Which city is located on the banks of the river Alaknanda?

    (a) Badrinath   (b) Ayodhya

    (c) Allahabad   (d) Lucknow

55. Kalinga War was fought in the year

    (a) 1604 BC   (b) 261 BC

    (c) 731 AD   (d) 113 AD

56. Who developed the theory of Evolution?

    (a) Charles Darwin   (b) Isaac Newton

    (c) Pranav Mistry   (d) Galileo Galilei

57. Which among the following is not a unit of distance?

    (a) Light year   (b) Longsec

    (c) Astronomical unit   (d) Parsec

58. The apparent weight of a person in a lift which is moving down with uniform acceleration is _______.

    (a) greater than the weight when the person is stationary

    (b) twice the weight when the person is stationary

    (c) less than the weight when the person is stationary

    (d) same as the weight when the person is stationary

59. Prime minister Narendra Modi has launched _____________ mobile application, an integrated platform for government to citizen services.

    (a) Ubern   (b) Upwan

    (c) Umang   (d) Utsah

60. Name the Sri Lankan Prime Minister, who visited India recently?

    (a) Maithripala Sirisena   (b) DM Jayaratne

    (c) Mahinda Rajapaksa   (d) Ranil Wickremesinghe

61. Enerally insects respire through

    (a) Skin   (b) Gill

    (c) Lung   (d) Spiracle

62. Nuclear fission is caused by the impact of

    (a) Proton   (b) Electron

    (c) Neutron   (d) None of these

63. Which of the following types of light are strongly absorbed by plants?

    (a) Violet and orange   (b) Blue and red

    (c) Indigo and yellow   (d) Yellow and violet

64. Which of the following hormone is called emergency hormone?

    (a) Insulin   (b) Adrenaline

    (c) Oestrogen   (d) Oxytocin

65. The standard of living in a country is represented by its

    (a) Poverty Ratio   (b) Per Capita Income

    (c) National Income   (d) Unemployment Rate

66. Which one of the following is generally found in sedimentary rocks?

    (a) Basalt   (b) Silica

    (c) Shale   (d) Magnesium

67. Which of the following elecments has the atomic number greater than that of Phosphorus?

    (a) Aluminium   (b) Silicon

    (c) Chlorine   (d) Magnesium

68. What are the two kinds of Rotatory motion?

    (a) Spin and Vibrational motion

    (b) Spin and Orbital motion

    (c) Spin and Translatory motion

    (d) Spin and Projectile motion

69. Which of the following is known as the "graveyard of RBCs"?

    (a) Spleen   (b) Bone Marrow

    (c) Mitochondria   (d) Small intestine

70. Which of the following organisms are the sole members of Kingdom Monera?

    (a) Bacteria   (b) Virus

    (c) Fungi   (d) Algae

71. Who is the exponent of the theory of economic drain of India during the British rule?

    (a) Dadabhai Naroji   (b) MN Roy

    (c) Jai Prakash Narayan   (d) Ram Manohar Lohiya

72. Who was the surgeon who pioneered antiseptic surgery in 1865?

    (a) Edward Jenner   (b) Joseph Lister

    (c) Henry William   (d) John Sleeman

73. The credit of inventing the television goes to

    (a) Faraday   (b) Baird

    (c) Edison   (d) Marconi

74. The credit of developing the polio vaccine goes to

    (a) Jonas Salk   (b) Alb E. Sabin

    (c) Selman Waksman   (d) None of these

75. Which city is hosting the 2018 Kala Ghoda Arts festival?

    (a) New Delhi   (b) Kochi

    (c) Mumbai   (d) Kolkata

RESPONSE SHEET

1. ⓐⓑⓒⓓ	2. ⓐⓑⓒⓓ	3. ⓐⓑⓒⓓ	4. ⓐⓑⓒⓓ	5. ⓐⓑⓒⓓ
6. ⓐⓑⓒⓓ	7. ⓐⓑⓒⓓ	8. ⓐⓑⓒⓓ	9. ⓐⓑⓒⓓ	10. ⓐⓑⓒⓓ
11. ⓐⓑⓒⓓ	12. ⓐⓑⓒⓓ	13. ⓐⓑⓒⓓ	14. ⓐⓑⓒⓓ	15. ⓐⓑⓒⓓ
16. ⓐⓑⓒⓓ	17. ⓐⓑⓒⓓ	18. ⓐⓑⓒⓓ	19. ⓐⓑⓒⓓ	20. ⓐⓑⓒⓓ
21. ⓐⓑⓒⓓ	22. ⓐⓑⓒⓓ	23. ⓐⓑⓒⓓ	24. ⓐⓑⓒⓓ	25. ⓐⓑⓒⓓ
26. ⓐⓑⓒⓓ	27. ⓐⓑⓒⓓ	28. ⓐⓑⓒⓓ	29. ⓐⓑⓒⓓ	30. ⓐⓑⓒⓓ
31. ⓐⓑⓒⓓ	32. ⓐⓑⓒⓓ	33. ⓐⓑⓒⓓ	34. ⓐⓑⓒⓓ	35. ⓐⓑⓒⓓ
36. ⓐⓑⓒⓓ	37. ⓐⓑⓒⓓ	38. ⓐⓑⓒⓓ	39. ⓐⓑⓒⓓ	40. ⓐⓑⓒⓓ
41. ⓐⓑⓒⓓ	42. ⓐⓑⓒⓓ	43. ⓐⓑⓒⓓ	44. ⓐⓑⓒⓓ	45. ⓐⓑⓒⓓ
46. ⓐⓑⓒⓓ	47. ⓐⓑⓒⓓ	48. ⓐⓑⓒⓓ	49. ⓐⓑⓒⓓ	50. ⓐⓑⓒⓓ
51. ⓐⓑⓒⓓ	52. ⓐⓑⓒⓓ	53. ⓐⓑⓒⓓ	54. ⓐⓑⓒⓓ	55. ⓐⓑⓒⓓ
56. ⓐⓑⓒⓓ	57. ⓐⓑⓒⓓ	58. ⓐⓑⓒⓓ	59. ⓐⓑⓒⓓ	60. ⓐⓑⓒⓓ
61. ⓐⓑⓒⓓ	62. ⓐⓑⓒⓓ	63. ⓐⓑⓒⓓ	64. ⓐⓑⓒⓓ	65. ⓐⓑⓒⓓ
66. ⓐⓑⓒⓓ	67. ⓐⓑⓒⓓ	68. ⓐⓑⓒⓓ	69. ⓐⓑⓒⓓ	70. ⓐⓑⓒⓓ
71. ⓐⓑⓒⓓ	72. ⓐⓑⓒⓓ	73. ⓐⓑⓒⓓ	74. ⓐⓑⓒⓓ	75. ⓐⓑⓒⓓ

HINTS & SOLUTIONS

1. (b) $4 \times 2 \times 6 = 1626 = (4^2)26 = 1626$
   $3 \times 7 \times 4 = 974 \Rightarrow (3^2)74 = 974$
   $\therefore 5 \times 6 \times 8 = (5^2)68 = 2568$

2. (b) $a\,\underline{c}\,b\,/\,\underline{c}\,\,c\,\underline{b}\,/\,a\,\underline{c}\,b\,/\,c\,\underline{c}\,b\,/\,a\,\underline{c}\,b$

3. (b)
   $$15 \quad 23 \quad 31 \quad 39 \quad \boxed{47} \quad 54 \quad 61$$
   $$+8 \quad +8 \quad +8 \quad +8 \quad +7 \quad +7$$

4. (b)
   $$2 \quad 3.5 \quad 5 \quad 6.5 \quad 8 \quad \boxed{9.5}$$
   $$+1.5 \quad +1.5 \quad +1.5 \quad +1.5 \quad +1.5$$

5. (b)
   $$32 \quad 58 \quad 92 \quad 134 \quad \boxed{184}$$
   $$+26 \quad +34 \quad +42 \quad +50$$
   $$+8 \quad +8 \quad +8$$

6. (d)
   $$\begin{array}{ccc} \text{P A I N T} & \text{E X C E L} & \text{A C C E P T} \\ 7\,4\,1\,2\,8 & 9\,3\,5\,9\,6 & 4\,5\,5\,9\,7\,8 \end{array}$$

7. (a) By checking options
   $36 \div 6 \times 3 + 2 = 6 \times 3 + 2 \Rightarrow 20 = 20$

8. (a) Son's age = 6 yrs.
   Father's age = 30 yrs.
   Let 'x' be the yr. after which father will be 4 times as old as his son.
   According to question
   $30 + x = 4(6 + x) = 30 + x = 24 + 4x \Rightarrow 6 = 3x.$
   $x = 2.$
   Hence, require year is 2 yrs.

9. (d) $2^3 = 8; \ 3^3 = 27$
   $\therefore 4^3 = 64$

10. (a) 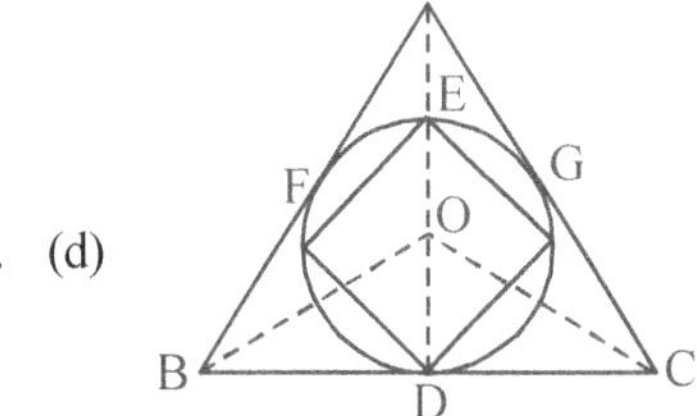

   Hence, darken portion in above diagram represents that there are 2 military officers who are short but not strong.

11. (c) Weight, eyesight and height are medical standards.

12. (c) All others Abdul kalam are/were nobel prize winners.

13. (b)
   $$\begin{array}{cccc|cccc} Y & W & U & S & Q & O & M & K \\ +1\downarrow & +1\downarrow & +1\downarrow & +1\downarrow & +1\downarrow & +1\downarrow & +1\downarrow & +1\downarrow \\ Z & X & V & T & R & P & N & L \end{array}$$

14. (d) 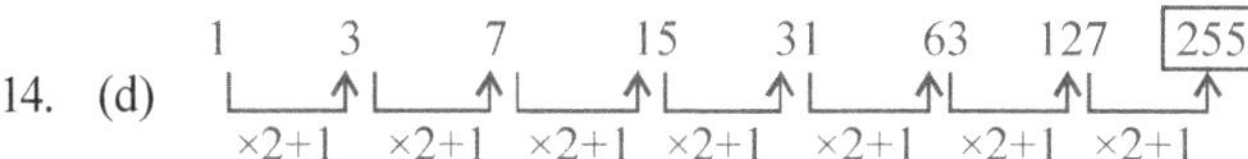

15. (d)

In the given figure ABC is an equilateral Δ of a side with a circle inscribed in it and a square inscribed in the circle.

AD, BO and CO are the angle bisectors of $\angle A$, $\angle B$ and $\angle C$ and O is the centre of the circle.

We know that the angle bisector from the vertex of an equilateral triangle is the perpendicular bisector of the opposite side.

AD is the perpendicular bisector of BC.

$$\Rightarrow BD = \frac{a}{2} \text{ and } \angle DOB = \frac{1}{2}\angle B = \frac{1}{2} \times 60° = 30°$$

Now in ΔBOD

$$\tan 30° = \frac{OD}{BD} = \frac{\text{Radius of circle}}{\dfrac{a}{2}}$$

$$\Rightarrow \text{Radius of circle} = \frac{1}{\sqrt{3}} \times \frac{a}{2} = \frac{a}{2\sqrt{3}}$$

Now in right ΔEDG
$EG^2 + GD^2 = ED^2$ (Pythagoras theorem)

$$2(EG)^2 = 2\,(OD)^2 = \left(\frac{a}{\sqrt{3}}\right)^2 = \frac{a^2}{3}$$

$$\text{Side of the square} = \sqrt{\frac{a^2}{6}} = \frac{a}{\sqrt{6}}$$

Now ar (ΔABC) : ar (ΔEFG)

$$= \frac{\dfrac{\sqrt{3}}{4}a^2}{\dfrac{a}{\sqrt{6}} \times \dfrac{a}{\sqrt{6}}} = \frac{\dfrac{\sqrt{3}}{4}}{\dfrac{1}{6}} = 3\sqrt{3} : 2$$

16. (b) $\sqrt{\dfrac{9.5 \times 0.085}{0.0017 \times 0.19}} = \sqrt{\dfrac{95}{10} \times \dfrac{85}{1000} \times \dfrac{10000}{17} \times \dfrac{100}{19}}$
   $\Rightarrow \sqrt{5 \times 5 \times 100} = 50$

17. (a) By the rule of alligation:
Cost of 1 kg rice of 1st kind   Cost of 1 kg rice of 2nd kind

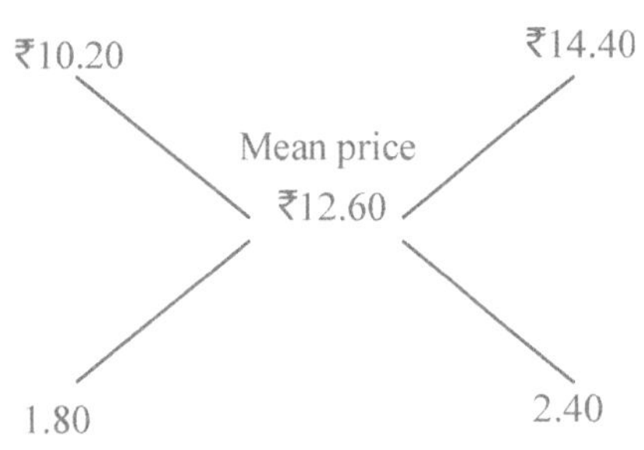

$$\therefore \text{ Required ratio} = 1.80 : 2.40 = 3 : 4.$$

18. (a) Let length $= l$, breadth $= b$, height $= h$.
$l + b + h = 24$ (given) ... (i)
Diagonal of parallellopiped $= 15$ cm
$\sqrt{l^2 + b^2 + h^2} = 15$ or $l^2 + b^2 + h^2 = 225$
Squaring eqn. (i) on both sides
$l^2 + b^2 + h^2 + 2\,lb + 2bh + 2hl = 576$
$2(lb + bh + hl) = 576 - 225 = 351$
$[\because$ Surface area of parallellopiped $= 2(lb + bh + hl)]$

19. (c) Single discount $= x + y + \dfrac{xy}{100}$

$= -70 - 30 + \dfrac{(-70 \times -30)}{100}$

$= -100 + 21 = -79\%$

'–' denotes discount. Hence, single discount equivalent
to 79%

20. (a) Solving this type of question by short cut.

Net profit% $= x + y + \dfrac{xy}{100}$

$17\% = -10 + y + \dfrac{(-10) \times y}{100}$ $[\because$ '–' for dicount]

$27 = y - \dfrac{y}{10} \Rightarrow 27 = \dfrac{10y - y}{10}$

$27 \times 10 = 9y$
$y = 30\%$
Hence, He must mark his goods 30% higher than their
cost price.

21. (d) According to question

$\dfrac{36 + n}{50 + n} = \dfrac{3}{4}$

$36 \times 4 + 4n = 50 \times 3 + 3n$
$4n - 3n = 150 - 144$
$n = 6$

22. (b) Average height $= \dfrac{6 \times (1.15) + 8 \times (1.10) + 6(1.12)}{20}$

$\Rightarrow \dfrac{22.42}{20} = 1.121$ or $1m\ 12.1cm$

23. (c) First five prime numbers are 2, 3, 5, 7, 11

Average $= \dfrac{2 + 3 + 5 + 7 + 11}{5} = \dfrac{28}{5} = 5.6$

24. (b) Let us consider a packet or rice marked 1kg. It's actual
weight is 80% of 1000 gm $= 800$ gm
Let C.P. of each gm be ₹1.
Then, C.P. of this packet $= ₹\ 800$
S.P. of this packet $= 110\%$ of C.P. of 1kg

$= \dfrac{110}{100} \times 1000 = ₹1110$

$\therefore$ Gain % $= \dfrac{(1100 - 800)}{1100} \times 100 = 37.5\%$

25. (c) Let the number is x.
According to question
$x - 10\%$ of $x = 30$

$x - \dfrac{10}{100} x = 30$

$\left(\dfrac{100 - 10}{100}\right) x = 30$

$x = \dfrac{30 \times 100}{90} = 33\dfrac{1}{3}$

Hence, the number is $33\dfrac{1}{3}$

26.	(a)	27.	(d)	28.	(a)	29.	(b)	30.	(a)
31.	(b)	32.	(a)	33.	(d)	34.	(c)	35.	(c)
36.	(a)	37.	(b)	38.	(c)	39.	(c)	40.	(d)
41.	(c)	42.	(b)	43.	(c)	44.	(b)	45.	(d)
46.	(b)	47.	(c)	48.	(d)	49.	(d)	50.	(d)
51.	(c)	52.	(c)	53.	(b)	54.	(a)	55.	(b)
56.	(a)	57.	(b)	58.	(c)	59.	(c)	60.	(d)
61.	(d)	62.	(c)	63.	(b)	64.	(b)	65.	(b)
66.	(b)	67.	(c)	68.	(b)	69.	(a)	70.	(a)
71.	(a)	72.	(b)	73.	(b)	74.	(a)	75.	(c)

PRACTICE SET

Time : 60 Min.   **Max. Marks : 75**

1. Four of the following five are alike in a certain way and so form a group. Which is the one that **does not** belong to that group?
   - (a) 29
   - (b) 85
   - (c) 147
   - (d) 125

2. Four of the following five are alike in a certain way and so form a group. Which is the one that **does not** belong to that group?
   - (a) Crow
   - (b) Vulture
   - (c) Bat
   - (d) Ostrich

3. Four of the following five are alike in a certain way and so form a group. Which is the one that **does not** belong to that group?
   - (a) Food : Hunger
   - (b) Water : Thirst
   - (c) Air : Suffocation
   - (d) Talent : Education

4. In the following number series a **wrong** number is given. Find out the **wrong** number.
   3 10 35 172 885 5346 37471
   - (a) 10
   - (b) 5346
   - (c) 885
   - (d) 35

5. In the following number series a **wrong** number is given. Find out the **wrong** number.
   318 158 76 38 18 8 3
   - (a) 38
   - (b) 18
   - (c) 158
   - (d) 76

DIRECTIONS (QS. 6-8): *In each of these questions a number series is given. Only one number is wrong in each series. You have to find out the wrong number.*

6.   10 15 24 35 54 75 100
   - (a) 35
   - (b) 75
   - (c) 24
   - (d) 15

7.   1 3 4 7 11 18 27 47
   - (a) 27
   - (b) 11
   - (c) 18
   - (d) 7

8.   3 2 3 6 12 37.5 115.5
   - (a) 37.5
   - (b) 12
   - (c) 6
   - (d) 2

9. In a certain code language BEAM is written as 5 % * K and COME is written as $ 7 K %. How is BOMB written in that code?
   - (a) 5 % K5
   - (b) 5 7 K5
   - (c) $ 7 K $
   - (d) 5$ % 5

10. In a certain code PATHOLOGIST is written as PIUBQKSRHFN. How is CONTROVERSY written in that code?
    - (a) SUOPDNXRQDU
    - (b) SUOPDNZTSFW
    - (c) QSMNBPXRQDU
    - (d) QSMNBPZTSFW

11. A is the mother of B. C is the father of B and C has 3 children. On the basis of this information, find out which of the following relations is correct :
    - (a) C has three daughters.
    - (b) C has three sons.
    - (c) B is the son.
    - (d) None of these.

12. Q travels towards East. M travels towards North. S and T travel in opposite directions. T travels towards right of Q. Which of the following is **definitely true**?
    - (a) M and S travel in the opposite directions.
    - (b) S travels towards West.
    - (c) T travels towards North.
    - (d) M and S travel in the same direction.

13. P, Q, R, S and T are sitting around a circular table. *R* is to the right of *P* and is second to the left of *S*. *T* is not between *P* and *S*. Who is second to the left of *R*?

(a) S (b) T

(c) Q (d) Data inadequate

14. Mohan and Suresh study in the same class. Mohan has secured more marks than Suresh in the terminal examination. Suresh's rank is seventh from top among all the students in the class. Which of the following is **definitely true?**

(a) Mohan stood first in the terminal examination.

(b) There is at least one student between Mohan and Suresh in the rank list.

(c) There are at the most five students between Mohan and Suresh in the rank list.

(d) Suresh is five ranks lower than Mohan in the rank list.

15. If '+' means 'minus' '–' means 'multiplied by' ',' means 'plus' and '×' means 'divided by', then

$10 \times 5 , 3 - 2 + 3 = ?$

(a) 5 (b) 21 (c) $\dfrac{53}{3}$ (d) 18

16. How many numbers are there between 300 and 400 in which 7 occurs only once?

(a) 18 (b) 14 (c) 11 (d) 10

17. What is the remainder when 4^{96} is divided by 6?

(a) 0 (b) 2 (c) 3 (d) 4

18. The H.C.F and L.C.M of two numbers are 21 and 4641 respectively. If one of the numbers lies between 200 and 300, then the two numbers are

(a) 273, 357 (b) 273, 361

(c) 273, 359 (d) 273, 363

19. An employer engaged a servant with free boarding and lodging for one year with the condition that the servant will be given ₹ 2500 and a uniform at the end of the year. The servant agreed but served the employer only for 10 months and thus received ₹ 2000 and a uniform. The price of the uniform is:

(a) ₹ 250 (b) ₹ 350 (c) ₹ 400 (d) ₹ 500

20. In a coconut grove, (x + 2) trees yield 60 nuts per year, x trees yield 120 nuts per year and (x – 2) trees yield 180 nuts per year. If the average yield per year per tree be 100, then x is

(a) 3 (b) 4 (c) 5 (d) 6

21. Two-third of one-seventh of a number is 87.5% of 240. What is the number ?

(a) 2670 (b) 2450 (c) 2205 (d) 1470

22. A man sold his book for Rs 891, thereby gaining $\dfrac{1}{10}$ of its cost price. Find his cost price.

(a) ₹ 850 (b) ₹ 810 (c) ₹ 851 (d) ₹ 840

23. On what sum of money lent out at 9% per annum simple interest for 6 years does the simple interest amount to ₹ 810?

(a) ₹ 900 (b) ₹ 1000

(c) ₹ 1200 (d) ₹ 1500

24. If A : B : C = 2 : 3 : 4, then $\dfrac{A}{B} : \dfrac{B}{C} : \dfrac{C}{A}$ is equal to :

(a) 4 : 9 : 16 (b) 8 : 9 : 12

(c) 8 : 9 : 16 (d) 8 : 9 : 24

25. A man walking at the rate of 5 km/h crosses a bridge in 15 minutes. The length of the bridge (in metres) is :

(a) 600 (b) 750

(c) 1000 (d) 1250

26. Public Interest Litigation (PIL) may be linked with

(a) Judicial review (b) Judicial activism

(c) Judicial intervention (d) Judicial sanctity

27. Tripitakas are sacred books of ________.

(a) Sikhs (b) Jews

(c) Buddhists (d) Muslims

28. Energy is stored in liver and muscles in the form of-

(a) carbohydrate (b) fat

(c) protein (d) glycogen

29. The phenomenon of radioactivity was discovered byjsfM;

(a) Marie Curie (b) Pierre Curie

(c) Henri Becquerel (d) J.J Thomson

30. The scientist who first discovered that the Earth revolves round the Sun was-

(a) Newton (b) Dalton

(c) Copernicus (d) Einstein

31. Which country was a part of the Axis Powers during World War 2?

(a) Yugoslavia (b) Poland

(c) Belgium (d) Hungary

32. Chapchar Kut is a festival celebrated in the State of

(a) Arunachal Pradesh (b) Assam

(c) Mizoram (d) Sikkim

33. Which of the following Acts introduced communal electorate in India?

(a) Indian Council Act, 1861

(b) Indian Council Act, 1892

(c) Indian Council Act, 1909

(d) Government of India Act, 1919

34. Which one of the following is not an example of eukaryotic organism?

(a) Yeast (b) Bacteria

(c) Plant (d) Human being

35. Commonest mammal is
    - (a) Elephant
    - (b) Lion
    - (c) Man (Homo sapiens)
    - (d) Panther
36. The following is an amplifying device:
    - (a) a transformer
    - (b) a transistor
    - (c) a diode
    - (d) a resistor
37. As per the latest data, which among the following states/ union territories of India makes maximum revenue by legal gambling and accounts for 95 percent of all legal gambling in the country?
    - (a) Sikkim
    - (b) Manipur
    - (c) Goa
    - (d) Nagaland
38. Green manure is obtained from
    - (a) Fresh animal excreta
    - (b) Decomposing green legume plants
    - (c) Domestic vegetable waste
    - (d) Oil seed husk cakes
39. In which of the following States, is the Child Sex Ratio the lowest in India?
    - (a) Punjab
    - (b) Haryana
    - (c) Chhattisgarh
    - (d) Bihar
40. Sharda Act fixed the minimum age of marriage of girls and boys respectively as-
    - (a) 12 and 16
    - (b) 14 and 18
    - (c) 15 and 21
    - (d) 16 and 24
41. Heat given to a body which raises its temperature by $1°C$ is known as -
    - (a) water equivalent
    - (b) thermal capacity
    - (c) specific heat
    - (d) temperature gradient
42. Bimbisara was the king of which dynasty?
    - (a) Haryanka
    - (b) Maurya
    - (c) Shunga
    - (d) Nanda
43. Light waves projected on oil surface show seven colours due to the phenomenon of
    - (a) polarisation
    - (b) refraction
    - (c) reflection
    - (d) interference
44. Who discovered bacteria?
    - (a) Fleming
    - (b) Lamble
    - (c) Temin
    - (d) Leeuwenhoek
45. The Government has renamed MNREGA scheme and the name associated with the scheme is that of
    - (a) Rajeev Gandhi
    - (b) Indira Gandhi
    - (c) Mahatama Gandhi
    - (d) Jawaharlal Nehru
46. Who among the following was associated with the formulation of the basic ideas of the Mahayana Buddhism ?
    - (a) Nagarjuna
    - (b) Kashyapa Matanga
    - (c) Menander
    - (d) Kanishka
47. The world's first hybrid electric tram powered by hydrogen fuel cells has started running its operation in _______________.
    - (a) Japan
    - (b) USA
    - (c) Russia
    - (d) China
48. Which of the following country will host the next United Nations (UN) global wildlife conference in 2020?
    - (a) Malaysia
    - (b) Indonesia
    - (c) Russia
    - (d) India
49. Prime Minister Narendra Modi dedicated the Bidar - Kalaburagi New Railway Line to the Nation by unveiling a plaque at Bidar Railway Station, in __________.
    - (a) Kerala
    - (b) Assam
    - (c) Tripura
    - (d) Karnataka
50. Name the country which is building the world's biggest floating solar power plant.
    - (a) Canada
    - (b) Russia
    - (c) India
    - (d) China
51. Study of earthquakes is known as
    - (a) Ecology
    - (b) Seismology
    - (c) Numismatics
    - (d) None of these
52. Ecology deals with
    - (a) Birds
    - (b) Cell formation
    - (c) Relation between Organisms and their environment
    - (d) Tissues
53. Who among the following evolved the concept of relationship between mass and energy?
    - (a) Einstein
    - (b) Planck
    - (c) Dalton
    - (d) Rutherford
54. In which one of the following places is the Shompen tribe found?
    - (a) Nilgiri Hills
    - (b) Nicobar Islands
    - (c) Spiti Valley
    - (d) Lakshadweep Islands
55. The Pangolakha Wildlife Sanctuary (PWS) is located in which state?
    - (a) Mizoram
    - (b) Arunachal predash
    - (c) Sikkim
    - (d) Goa
56. Which of the following is an example of conjugated protein?
    - (a) Albumin
    - (b) Globulin
    - (c) Glutelin
    - (d) Glycoprotein
57. Name the country that will host the 2023 World Cup.
    - (a) England
    - (b) South Africa
    - (c) Australia
    - (d) India
58. The device used to change the speed of an electric fan is—
    - (a) Amplifier
    - (b) Regulator
    - (c) Switch
    - (d) Rectifier

59. Which scripture was called his 'mother' by Gandhiji ?

   (a) Ramayana   (b) The New Testament

   (c) Bhagwat Gita   (d) The Holy Quran

60. On which of the following rivers is the Tehri Hydropower Complex located ?

   (a) Alaknanda   (b) Mandakini

   (c) Dhauli Ganga   (d) Bhagirathi

61. Nobel Prize winning Indian Amartya Sen is known for his work in which area ?

   (a) Physics

   (b) Environmental Protection

   (c) Chemistry

   (d) Economics

62. Which acid is present in the stomach of humans?

   (a) sulphuric acid   (b) hydrochloric acid

   (c) nitric acid   (d) citric acid

63. Transpiration in plants is a process of—

   (a) Food production   (b) Respiration

   (c) Water loss   (d) None of the above

64. Which of the following is a skin disease ?

   (a) Rickets   (b) Osteomalacia

   (c) Anaemia   (d) Pellagra

65. Name the tiny pores present on the surface of leaves in plants.

   (a) Pits   (b) Stomata

   (c) Trichomes   (d) Hydathodes

66. Cylindrical lens is used by a person suffering from

   (a) astigmatism   (b) myopia

   (c) hypermetropia   (d) None of these

67. The mass of water vapour per unit volume of air is known as

   (a) relative humidity   (b) specific humidity

   (c) absolute humidity   (d) variable humidity

68. Who is internationally recognised as a father of the modern digital computer?

   (a) George Stibitz   (b) Clifford Berry

   (c) Nikolay Brusentsov   (d) None of these

69. The member of Shivaji's Ashta Pradhan who looks after foreign affairs was

   (a) Peshwa   (b) Sachiv

   (c) Pandit Rao   (d) Sumant

70. Which one of the following is a warm ocean current ?

   (a) Labrador current   (b) Kuroshio current

   (c) Peru current   (d) Benguela current

71. Which one of the following is responsible for the stimulating effect of tea?

   (a) Tannin   (b) Steroid

   (c) Alkaloid   (d) Flavonoid

72. Which one of the following non-metals is not a poor conductor of electricity ?

   (a) Sulphur   (b) Selenium

   (c) Bromine   (d) Phosphorus

73. Mid-Day Meal Scheme was started in year :

   (a) 1995   (b) 1996

   (c) 1997   (d) 1998

74. The book is written by "Narendra Modi: The Making of a Legend"?

   (a) Sanjay Tripathi   (b) Bindeshwar Pathak

   (c) Aditya Sen   (d) Mohan Verma

75. The main thinking part of the brain is

   (a) midbrain   (b) hypothalamus

   (c) forebrain   (d) hindbrain

RESPONSE SHEET

1. (a)(b)(c)(d)	2. (a)(b)(c)(d)	3. (a)(b)(c)(d)	4. (a)(b)(c)(d)	5. (a)(b)(c)(d)
6. (a)(b)(c)(d)	7. (a)(b)(c)(d)	8. (a)(b)(c)(d)	9. (a)(b)(c)(d)	10. (a)(b)(c)(d)
11. (a)(b)(c)(d)	12. (a)(b)(c)(d)	13. (a)(b)(c)(d)	14. (a)(b)(c)(d)	15. (a)(b)(c)(d)
16. (a)(b)(c)(d)	17. (a)(b)(c)(d)	18. (a)(b)(c)(d)	19. (a)(b)(c)(d)	20. (a)(b)(c)(d)
21. (a)(b)(c)(d)	22. (a)(b)(c)(d)	23. (a)(b)(c)(d)	24. (a)(b)(c)(d)	25. (a)(b)(c)(d)
26. (a)(b)(c)(d)	27. (a)(b)(c)(d)	28. (a)(b)(c)(d)	29. (a)(b)(c)(d)	30. (a)(b)(c)(d)
31. (a)(b)(c)(d)	32. (a)(b)(c)(d)	33. (a)(b)(c)(d)	34. (a)(b)(c)(d)	35. (a)(b)(c)(d)
36. (a)(b)(c)(d)	37. (a)(b)(c)(d)	38. (a)(b)(c)(d)	39. (a)(b)(c)(d)	40. (a)(b)(c)(d)
41. (a)(b)(c)(d)	42. (a)(b)(c)(d)	43. (a)(b)(c)(d)	44. (a)(b)(c)(d)	45. (a)(b)(c)(d)
46. (a)(b)(c)(d)	47. (a)(b)(c)(d)	48. (a)(b)(c)(d)	49. (a)(b)(c)(d)	50. (a)(b)(c)(d)
51. (a)(b)(c)(d)	52. (a)(b)(c)(d)	53. (a)(b)(c)(d)	54. (a)(b)(c)(d)	55. (a)(b)(c)(d)
56. (a)(b)(c)(d)	57. (a)(b)(c)(d)	58. (a)(b)(c)(d)	59. (a)(b)(c)(d)	60. (a)(b)(c)(d)
61. (a)(b)(c)(d)	62. (a)(b)(c)(d)	63. (a)(b)(c)(d)	64. (a)(b)(c)(d)	65. (a)(b)(c)(d)
66. (a)(b)(c)(d)	67. (a)(b)(c)(d)	68. (a)(b)(c)(d)	69. (a)(b)(c)(d)	70. (a)(b)(c)(d)
71. (a)(b)(c)(d)	72. (a)(b)(c)(d)	73. (a)(b)(c)(d)	74. (a)(b)(c)(d)	75. (a)(b)(c)(d)

HINTS & SOLUTIONS

1. **(c)** All other numbers are in the form of $n^2 + 4$ where n is a natural number.

2. **(c)** Except it others are birds whereas bat is a mammal

3. **(d)** Lack of first one causes second one.

4. **(d)** Series is $\times 2 + 2^2, \times 3 + 3^2, \times 4 + 4^2, ...$

5. **(d)** The series is $\div 2 - 1$ in each term.

6. **(a)** The series is $+5, +9, +13, +17$ .... The difference in successive nos. $9 - 5 = 13 - 9 = 17 - 13 = ... = 4$. Hence, 35 is wrong. It should be 37.

7. **(a)** The sum of the first two nos. is the third no. Hence, 27 is wrong. It should be 29.

8. **(b)** The series is $\times 0.5 + 0.5, \times 1 + 1, \times 1.5 + 1.5$ .... Hence, 12 is wrong. It should be 14.

9. **(b)** Here, $B \Rightarrow 5, E \Rightarrow \%, A \Rightarrow *,$
   $M \Rightarrow K, C \Rightarrow \$, O \Rightarrow 7$
   Therefore, $BOMB \Rightarrow 57K5$

10. **(a)**

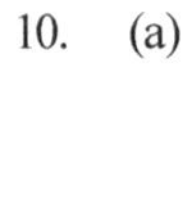

Five letters of the word PATHOLOGIST are reversed first and then coded as one place forward. Similarly, the last five letters of the word are reversed then coded as one place backward. Middle letter is coded as one place backward.

Hence, CONTROVERSY will be written as SUOPDNXRQDU.

11. **(d)**

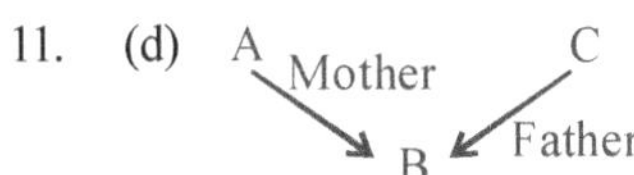

$\because$ C has three children but we can't say that he has three daughters or three sons.

So, options (a) and (b) are incorrect.

Also, we don't know that B is a boy or girl.

So, option (c) is also incorrect.

12. **(d)** We have been given that Q travels towards East and M travels towards North. Now, T travels towards right of Q implies that T travels towards South. Hence, S travels towards North (because S and T travel in opposite directions). Therefore, it is definitely true that M and S travel in the same direction i.e., North.

13. **(c)**

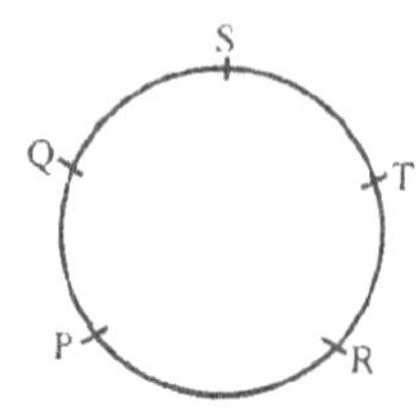

Q is second to the left of R.

14. **(c)**

15. **(a)**

$+ \Rightarrow -$	$- \Rightarrow \times$
$\div \Rightarrow +$	$\times \Rightarrow \div$

$10 \times 5 \div 3 - 2 + 3 = ?$
or, $? = 10 \div 5 + 3 \times 2 - 3$
or, $? = 2 + 6 - 3 = 5$

16. **(a)** The required numbers are 307, 317, 327, 337, 347, 357, 367, 370, 371, 372, 373, 374, 375, 376, 378, 379, 387, 397. Hence there are 18 numbers.

17. **(d)** Let us divide the different powers of 4 by 6 and find the remainder.
   So remainder for $4^1 = 4, 4^2 = 4, 4^3 = 4, 4^4 = 4, 4^5 = 4, 4^6 = 4$ and so on.
   Hence remainder for any power of 4 will be 4 only.

18. **(a)** Product of the numbers
   $= \text{HCF} \times \text{LCM} = 21 \times 4641$
   $= 21 \times 3 \times 7 \times 13 \times 17$
   $= 3 \times 7 \times 3 \times 7 \times 13 \times 17$
   $\therefore$ The required numbers can be
   $3 \times 7 \times 13$ and $3 \times 7 \times 17 = 273$ and 357

19. **(d)** 12 months wages $= ₹2500 + $ Uniform; and
   10 months wages $= ₹2000 + $ Uniform
   $\Rightarrow$ 2 months wages $= ₹500$
   12 months wages $= ₹3000.$
   $\therefore$ cost of the uniform $= ₹500.$

20. **(b)** $\dfrac{(x+2) \times 60 + x \times 120 + (x-2) \times 180}{(x+2) + x + (x-2)} = 100$
   $\Rightarrow \dfrac{360x - 240}{3x} = 100$
   $\Rightarrow 60x = 240 \Rightarrow x = 4$

21. **(c)** Let number be x then,
   $\dfrac{2}{3} \times \dfrac{1}{7} \times x = \dfrac{240 \times 87.5}{100}$
   or $\dfrac{2x}{21} = 87.5 \times 2.4$
   or $x = 2205$

22.   (b) Let C. P. = ₹ x then profit = S.P. – C. P.

$$\Rightarrow \frac{1}{10} \times x = 891 - x \Rightarrow \frac{11x}{10} = 891$$

$$\Rightarrow x = \frac{891 \times 10}{11} = ₹\ 810$$

23.   (d) $S.I. = \dfrac{P \times R \times T}{100}$

$$\Rightarrow P = \frac{810 \times 100}{9 \times 6} = ₹1500$$

24.   (d) Let A = 2x, B = 3x and C = 4x. Then,

$$\frac{A}{B} = \frac{2x}{3x} = \frac{2}{3},\ \frac{B}{C} = \frac{3x}{4x} = \frac{3}{4}\ \text{and}\ \frac{C}{A} = \frac{4x}{2x} = \frac{2}{1}$$

$$\Rightarrow \frac{A}{B} : \frac{B}{C} : \frac{C}{A} = \frac{2}{3} : \frac{3}{4} : \frac{2}{1} = 8 : 9 : 24.$$

25.   (d) $\text{Speed} = \left(5 \times \dfrac{5}{18}\right) \text{m/sec} = \dfrac{25}{18}\ \text{m/sec}.$

Distance covered in 15 minutes

$$= \left(\frac{25}{18} \times 15 \times 60\right) m = 1250\ m.$$

26.	(b)	27.	(c)	28.	(d)	29.	(c)	30.	(c)
31.	(d)	32.	(c)	33.	(c)	34.	(b)	35.	(c)
36.	(b)	37.	(c)	38.	(b)	39.	(b)	40.	(b)
41.	(b)	42.	(a)	43.	(d)	44.	(d)	45.	(c)
46.	(a)	47.	(d)	48.	(d)	49.	(d)	50.	(d)
51.	(b)	52.	(c)	53.	(a)	54.	(b)	55.	(c)
56.	(d)	57.	(d)	58.	(b)	59.	(c)	60.	(d)
61.	(d)	62.	(b)	63.	(c)	64.	(d)	65.	(b)
66.	(a)	67.	(c)	68.	(a)	69.	(d)	70.	(b)
71.	(c)	72.	(b)	73.	(a)	74.	(b)	75.	(c)

PRACTICE SET

Time : 60 Min. | **Max. Marks : 75**

1. Four of the following five are alike in a certain way and so form a group. Which is the one that does not belong to that group?
   - (a) Teacher
   - (b) Engineer
   - (c) Architect
   - (d) Doctor

2. Four of the following five are alike in a certain way and hence form a group. Which one of the following does not belong to that group?
   - (a) 126
   - (b) 122
   - (c) 65
   - (d) 50

3. Four of the following five are alike in a certain way and hence form a group. Which one of the following is different from the group?
   - (a) 226
   - (b) 290
   - (c) 360
   - (d) 170

DIRECTIONS (Qs. 4-6): *In each of the following number series, a wrong number is given. Find out that number.*

4. 2   8   32   148   765   4626   32431
   - (a) 765
   - (b) 148
   - (c) 8
   - (d) 32

5. 2   3   11   38   102   229   443
   - (a) 11
   - (b) 229
   - (c) 120
   - (d) 38

6. 5   10   17   27   37   50   65
   - (a) 10
   - (b) 17
   - (c) 27
   - (d) 37

7. Which sequence of letters when placed at the blanks one after another will complete the given letter series ?
   ba _ b _ aab _ a _ b
   - (a) abaa
   - (b) abba
   - (c) baab
   - (d) babb

8. Which sequence of letters when placed at the blanks one after another will complete the given letter series ?
   c _ bba _ cab _ ac _ ab _ ac
   - (a) abcbc
   - (b) acbcb
   - (c) babcc
   - (d) bcacb

9. In a certain code language NATIONALISM is written as OINTANMSAIL. How is DEPARTMENTS written in that code?
   - (a) RADEPTSTMNE
   - (b) RADPETSTMNE
   - (c) RADPESTMTNE
   - (d) RADPETSTNME

10. In a certain code language OUTCOME is written as OQWWEQOE. How is REFRACT written in that code?
    - (a) RTGITCET
    - (b) RTGTICET
    - (c) RTGITECT
    - (c) RTGICTET

11. A is the brother of B. A is the brother of C. To find what is the relation between B and C. What minimum information from the following is necessary?
    - (i) Gender of C
    - (ii) Gender of B
    - (a) Only (i)
    - (b) Only (ii)
    - (c) Either (i) or (ii)
    - (d) both (i) and (ii)

12. Of the five villages P, Q, R, S and T situated close to each other, P is to west of Q, R is to the south of P, T is to the north of Q, and S is to the east of T. Then, R is in which direction with respect to S?
    - (a) North-West
    - (b) South-East
    - (c) South-West
    - (d) Data Inadequate

13. M is to the East of D, F is to the South of D and K is to the West of F. M is in which direction with respect to K?
    - (a) South-West
    - (b) North-West
    - (c) North-East
    - (d) South-East

14. If the positions of the first and the fifth digits of the number 83721569 are interchanged, similarly, the positions of the second and the sixth digits are interchanged, and so on, which of the following will be the third from the right end after the rearrangement?

(a)　6　　　　　　　　　(b)　3

(c)　2　　　　　　　　　(d)　7

15.　If $> = \div$, $\vee = \times$, $< = +$, $\wedge = -$, $+ = <$, $\times = =$, $- = >$

(a)　$6 > 2 > 3 \wedge 8 \vee 4 + 13$

(b)　$6 \wedge 2 < 3 > 8 < 4 - 13$

(c)　$6 \vee 2 < 3 \wedge 8 > 4 \times 13$

(d)　$6 > 2 \vee 3 < 8 \wedge 4 + 13$

16.　The numbers 1 to 29 are written side by side as follows
12345678910 11............................28 29

　　If the number is divided by 9, then what is the remainder?

(a)　3　　　　　　　　　(b)　1

(c)　0　　　　　　　　　(d)　None of these

17.　The digit in the unit's place of the number represented by $(7^{95} - 3^{58})$ is:

(a)　0　　　　　　　　　(b)　4

(c)　6　　　　　　　　　(d)　7

18.　The L.C.M. of two number is 630 and their H.C.F. is 9. If the sum of numbers is 153, their difference is

(a)　17　　　　　　　　(b)　23

(c)　27　　　　　　　　(d)　33

19.　Tanya's grandfather was 8 times older to her 16 years ago. He would be 3 times of her age 8 years from now. Eight years ago, what was the ratio of Tanya's age to that of her grandfather?

(a)　$1:2$　　　　　　　(b)　$1:5$

(c)　$3:8$　　　　　　　(d)　None of these

20.　30 pens and 75 pencils were purchased for Rs 510. If the average price of a pencil was Rs 2.00, find the average price of a pen.

(a)　₹10　　　　　　　(b)　₹11

(c)　₹12　　　　　　　(d)　cannot be determined

21.　The sum of two numbers is $\dfrac{28}{25}$ of the first number. The second number is what percent of the first?

(a)　12%　　　　　　　(b)　14%

(c)　16%　　　　　　　(d)　18%

22.　If the cost price is 96% of the selling price, then what is the profit percent?

(a)　4.5%　　　　　　　(b)　4.2%

(c)　4%　　　　　　　　(d)　3.8%

23.　What annual instalment will discharge a debt of ₹4,200 due in 5 years at 10% simple interest?

(a)　₹500 per year　　　(b)　₹600 per year

(c)　₹700 per year　　　(d)　₹800 per year

24.　The income of A and B are in the ratio 3 : 2 and expenses are in the ratio 5 : 3. If both save ₹200, what is the income of A?

(a)　₹1000　　　　　　(b)　₹1200

(c)　₹1500　　　　　　(d)　₹1800

25.　A cyclist covers a distance of 750 m in 2 min 30 sec. What is the speed in km/h of the cyclist ?

(a)　18 km/h　　　　　(b)　15 km/h

(c)　20 km/h　　　　　(d)　None of these

26.　By the late 19th century, India was one of the producers and exporters of

(a)　cotton yarn and wheat　(b)　sugar and rice

(c)　sugar and alcohol　　　(d)　iron and steel

27.　'Breakbone fever' most commonly known as?

(a)　Typhoid　　　　　(b)　Rhinitis

(c)　Yellow fever　　　　(d)　Dengue

28.　Bagases, a by-product of sugar manufacturing industry , is used for the production of

(a)　Glass　　　　　　(b)　Paper

(c)　Rubber　　　　　(d)　Cement

29.　The Greek ambassador sent to Chandragupta Mauryan's court was

(a)　Kautilya　　　　　(b)　Seleucus Nicator

(c)　Megasthenes　　　(d)　Faxian

30.　Which one of the following is a wild life sanctuary?

(a)　Jaldapara　　　　　(b)　Grumara

(c)　Jim Corbett　　　　(d)　All of these

31.　13th Vice President of India, M Venkaiah Naidu hails from-

(a)　Andhra Pradesh　　(b)　New Delhi

(c)　Tamilnadu　　　　(d)　Kerala

32.　The term of the Lok Sabha

(a)　cannot be extended under any circumstances

(b)　can be extended by six month at a time

(c)　can be extended by one year at a time during the proclamation of emergency

(d)　can be extended for two years at a time during the proclamation of emergency

33.　The League of Nations was formed at the end of

(a)　World War I　　　　(b)　World War II

(c)　Gulf War I　　　　(d)　Gulf War II

34.　Haemophilia is a genetic disorder which lead to

(a)　decrease in haemoglobin level

(b)　rheumatic heart disease

(c)　decrease in WBC

(d)　non-clotting of blood

35.　In the pressure cooker, cooking is faster because the increase in vapour pressure

(a)　increase the specific heat

(b)　decreases the specific heat

(c)　decreases the boiling point

(d)　increases the boiling point

36. The living content of cell is called protoplasm. It is composed of-
    (a) Cytoplasm only
    (b) Cytoplasm and nucleoplasm
    (c) Nucleoplasm only
    (d) Cytoplasm, nucleoplasm and other organelles

37. Which one of the following types of glass can cut off ultraviolet rays ?
    (a) Soda glass   (b) Pyrex glass
    (c) Jena glass   (d) Crookes glass

38. Which of the following hormone is called emergency hormone?
    (a) Insulin   (b) Adrenaline
    (c) Oestrogen   (d) Oxytocin

39. Which one of the following types of coal contains a higher percentage of carbon than the rest?
    (a) Bituminous coal   (b) Lignite
    (c) Peat   (d) Anthracite

40. India has signed how much amount of loan agreement with World Bank (WB) for UP Tourism Project?
    (a) $75 million   (b) $54 million
    (c) $33 million   (d) $40 million

41. Which union minister has launched Livestock Disease Forewarning (LDF) Mobile App?
    (a) Rajnath Singh   (b) Narendra Modi
    (b) Narendra Singh Tomar (d) Radha Mohan Singh

42. Kidney stones are mainly formed by which of the following compound
    (a) Sodium chloride   (b) Silicates
    (c) Calcium bicarbonate   (d) Calcium oxalate

43. Which of the following techniques can be used to establish the paternity of a child?
    (a) Protein analysis
    (b) Chromosome counting
    (c) Quantitative analysis of DNA
    (d) DNA finger printing

44. Which of the following vitamin combines with avidin contained in egg-white forming a compound that cannot be absorbed by the intestine and is therefore, excreted
    (a) vitamin B_2 (b) vitamin B_3
    (c) vitamin B_7 (d) vitamin A

45. Which state government has launched a free household power connection scheme 'Prakash hai to vikas hai' for the poor in the state?
    (a) Punjab   (b) Uttar Pradesh
    (c) Haryana   (d) Rajasthan

46. Which city has become the first Indian city to get its own logo?
    (a) Pune   (b) Patna
    (c) Kochi   (d) Bengaluru

47. Where is the Central Rice Research institute located?
    (a) Kanpur   (b) Bengaluru
    (c) Coimbatore   (d) Cuttack

48. The National Gandhi Museum (NGM) is located in which city?
    (a) Chandigarh   (b) Ahmedabad
    (c) New Delhi   (d) Gandhinagar

49. The acid contained in vinegar is
    (a) Acetic acid   (b) Ascorbic acid
    (c) Citric acid   (d) Tartaric acid

50. The anti-malarial drug quinine is made from a plant. The plant iseysfj;
    (a) Neem   (b) Eucalyptus
    (c) Cinnamon   (d) Cinchona

51. Amniocentesis is a technique used
    (a) to determine the sex of foetus
    (b) to test of amino acid
    (c) to test brain
    (d) None of the above

52. An object is in static equilibrium when it is ________.
    (a) at rest
    (b) moving in a circular path
    (c) moving with uniform velocity
    (d) accelerating at high speed

53. Blood Circulation was discovered by
    (a) Mary Anderson   (b) Virginia Apgar
    (c) William Harvey   (d) Robert Feulgen

54. Which of the following programmes meet the credit needs of poor women?
    (a) Mahila Samriddhi Yojna
    (b) Rashtriya Mahila Kosh
    (c) Indira Mahila Yojna
    (d) Mahila Samakhya Programme

55. Who will be the brand ambassador of the India's global food fair 2017?
    (a) Priyanka Chopra   (b) Sanjeev Kapoor
    (c) Ranveer Singh   (d) Amitabh Bachchan

56. Who has been awarded the 63rd Dadasaheb Phalke Award?
    (a) Dilip Kumar   (b) Manoj Kumar
    (c) Pran   (d) Shashi Kapoor

57. The Nawabganj Bird Sanctuary is located
    (a) Kerala   (b) Uttar Pradesh
    (c) Tripura   (d) Tamilnadu

58. Which among the following has the world's largest reserves of uranium?
    (a) Australia   (b) Canada
    (c) Russia   (d) USA

59. When heated from $0°$ to $10°C$ volume of a given mass of water will :
    (a) Increase gradually
    (b) Decrease gradually
    (c) Increase and after will decrease
    (d) Decrease and after will increase

60. A person standing on a railway platform listens to the whistles of arriving and departing trains. The whistle heard is.
    (a) the same in both cases in all respects
    (b) of higher intensity when train arrives
    (c) of higher pitch when train arrives
    (d) of higher pitch when train departs

61. Pencillin is extracted from -
    (a) yeast   (b) algae
    (c) fungus   (d) lichen

62. The Modi script was employed in the documents of the
    (a) Wodeyars   (b) Zamorins
    (c) Hoysalas   (d) Marathas

63. In which of the following states maximum iron ore is found?
    (a) $FeCO_3$ (b) $Fe2O_3$
    (c) $Fe3O_4$ (d) FeS_2

64. "BHIM" mobile app has been launched by Union Government to make digital payments easier. What does "BHIM" stands for?
    (a) Build interface for money
    (b) Built-up interface for money
    (c) Bi-aural interface for money
    (d) Bharat interface for money

65. What is the India's rank in the 2017 Global Innovation Index (GII)?
    (a) 60th   (b) 75th
    (c) 68th   (d) 97th

66. A larger force on a rotating body results in larger ______.?
    (a) Mass   (b) Torque
    (c) Axis of rotation   (d) Centre of mass

67. While catching a ball, a player pulls down his hands to lower the -
    (a) force/cy   (b) momentum
    (c) impulse   (d) catching time

68. What is the name of vessel that delivers the nutrient rich blood from the stomach and small intenstine to the liver?
    (a) left hepatic artery   (b) Hepatic vein
    (c) Right hepatic artery   (d) Hepatic portal vein

69. Instrument used for measuring specific gravity is called ______.
    (a) Bathymeter   (b) Cryometer
    (c) Areometer   (d) Cymometer

70. Structural unemployment arise due to :
    (a) deflationary conditions
    (b) heavy industry bias
    (c) shortage of raw materials
    (d) inadequate productive capacity

71. In which session of Congress the demand "Poorna Swaraj" was accepted as the aim of the Congress?
    (a) Calcutta   (b) Madras
    (c) Nagpur   (d) Lahore

72. All noble gases are-
    (a) Colourless
    (b) Odourless
    (c) Colourless and Odourless
    (d) Light blue

73. Which of the following is not a compound of calcium?
    (a) Gypsum   (b) Marble
    (c) Chalk   (d) Molybdenum

74. Elements that show the properties of both metals and non-metals are called-
    (a) Allotropes   (b) Metalloids
    (c) Alloys   (d) Colloids

75. "Yellow Cake" an item of smuggling across border is-
    (a) a crude form of cocaine
    (b) a crude form of heroin
    (c) unrefined gold
    (d) uranium oxide

RESPONSE SHEET

1. ⓐⓑⓒⓓ	2. ⓐⓑⓒⓓ	3. ⓐⓑⓒⓓ	4. ⓐⓑⓒⓓ	5. ⓐⓑⓒⓓ
6. ⓐⓑⓒⓓ	7. ⓐⓑⓒⓓ	8. ⓐⓑⓒⓓ	9. ⓐⓑⓒⓓ	10. ⓐⓑⓒⓓ
11. ⓐⓑⓒⓓ	12. ⓐⓑⓒⓓ	13. ⓐⓑⓒⓓ	14. ⓐⓑⓒⓓ	15. ⓐⓑⓒⓓ
16. ⓐⓑⓒⓓ	17. ⓐⓑⓒⓓ	18. ⓐⓑⓒⓓ	19. ⓐⓑⓒⓓ	20. ⓐⓑⓒⓓ
21. ⓐⓑⓒⓓ	22. ⓐⓑⓒⓓ	23. ⓐⓑⓒⓓ	24. ⓐⓑⓒⓓ	25. ⓐⓑⓒⓓ
26. ⓐⓑⓒⓓ	27. ⓐⓑⓒⓓ	28. ⓐⓑⓒⓓ	29. ⓐⓑⓒⓓ	30. ⓐⓑⓒⓓ
31. ⓐⓑⓒⓓ	32. ⓐⓑⓒⓓ	33. ⓐⓑⓒⓓ	34. ⓐⓑⓒⓓ	35. ⓐⓑⓒⓓ
36. ⓐⓑⓒⓓ	37. ⓐⓑⓒⓓ	38. ⓐⓑⓒⓓ	39. ⓐⓑⓒⓓ	40. ⓐⓑⓒⓓ
41. ⓐⓑⓒⓓ	42. ⓐⓑⓒⓓ	43. ⓐⓑⓒⓓ	44. ⓐⓑⓒⓓ	45. ⓐⓑⓒⓓ
46. ⓐⓑⓒⓓ	47. ⓐⓑⓒⓓ	48. ⓐⓑⓒⓓ	49. ⓐⓑⓒⓓ	50. ⓐⓑⓒⓓ
51. ⓐⓑⓒⓓ	52. ⓐⓑⓒⓓ	53. ⓐⓑⓒⓓ	54. ⓐⓑⓒⓓ	55. ⓐⓑⓒⓓ
56. ⓐⓑⓒⓓ	57. ⓐⓑⓒⓓ	58. ⓐⓑⓒⓓ	59. ⓐⓑⓒⓓ	60. ⓐⓑⓒⓓ
61. ⓐⓑⓒⓓ	62. ⓐⓑⓒⓓ	63. ⓐⓑⓒⓓ	64. ⓐⓑⓒⓓ	65. ⓐⓑⓒⓓ
66. ⓐⓑⓒⓓ	67. ⓐⓑⓒⓓ	68. ⓐⓑⓒⓓ	69. ⓐⓑⓒⓓ	70. ⓐⓑⓒⓓ
71. ⓐⓑⓒⓓ	72. ⓐⓑⓒⓓ	73. ⓐⓑⓒⓓ	74. ⓐⓑⓒⓓ	75. ⓐⓑⓒⓓ

HINTS & SOLUTIONS

1. (a) All the rest are exclusive professions while a teacher may, be there in any of these categories.

2. (a) The rest are based on the expression $x^2 + 1$. But $126 = 11^2 + 5$.

3. (c) After a close look you will get that except 360 each number is one more than square of a natural number, i.e., $226 = 15^2 + 1$; $290 = 17^2 + 1$; $170 = 13^2 + 1$; $122 = 11^2 + 1$

4. (d) The series is $\times 2 + 2^2, \times 3 + 3^2, \times 4 + 4^2, \times 5 + 5^2$ ..... Hence, 32 is wrong. It should be 33.

5. (b) The series is $+ 1^3, + 2^3, + 3^3, + 4^3$ ..... Hence, 229 is wrong. It should be 227.

6. (c) The series is $+ 5, + 7, + 9, + 11, ...$

7. (b) ba$\underline{ab}$/$\underline{ba}$ab/ba$\underline{ab}$

8. (b) ca$\underline{bb}$ac/cab$\underline{ba}$c/$\underline{ca}$bbac.

9. (b) Divide the word into two groups of five letters each. The first five letters are in group I and the last five letters are in group II. Now, for its coding the middle letters remain unchanged. While the letters in each group change their position as $1 \to 3, 2 \to 5, 3 \to 4, 4 \to 2$ and $5 \to 1$.

10. (a) The first letter is coded as two letters: the first remains unchanged and the second two letters forward as in English alphabet. The second, fourth, fifth and sixth letters are coded as two letters forward while the third letter is coded as three letters forward as in English alphabet. The last letter remains unchanged.

11. (d) Without knowing the sex of C, we can't be determined whether B is sister of C or B is brother of C. Similarly without knowing the sex of B we can't be determined whether C is sister of B or C is brother of B. Therefore, both (i) and (ii) are necessary.

12. (c) 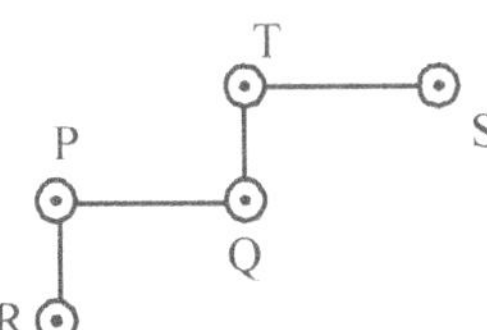

Hence, R is to the South-West with respect to S.

13. (c) 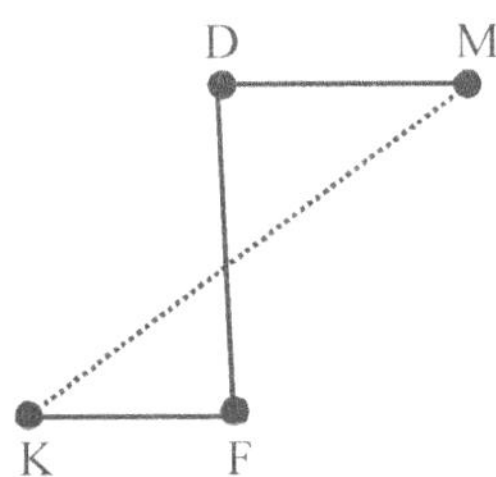

M is to the North-East of K.

14. (b) New arrangement of numbers is as follows: 15698372 Hence, third number from right end is 3.

15. (c)

16. (a) Sum of the digits of the 'super' number
$= 1 + 2 + 3 + ... + 29$

$= \dfrac{29}{2}.\{2 \times 1 + (29 - 1).1\}$

$= \dfrac{29}{2}.(2 + 28) = \dfrac{29 \times 30}{2} = 29 \times 15 = 435$

Thus $x = 7, y = 6$

17. (b) Unit digit in 7^4 is 1. So, unit digit in 7^{92} is 1.
$\therefore$ Unit digit in 7^{95} is 3.
Unit digit in 3^4 is 1.
$\therefore$ Unit digit in 3^{56} is 1.
$\therefore$ Unit digit in 3^{58} is 9.
$\therefore$ Unit digit in $(7^{95} - 3^{58}) = (13 - 9) = 4.$

18. (c) Let numbers be x and y.
$\because$ Product of two numbers = their (LCM × HCF)
$\Rightarrow xy = 630 \times 9$
Also, $x + y = 153$ (given)
since $x - y = \sqrt{(x + y)^2 - 4xy}$

$\Rightarrow x - y = \sqrt{(153)^2 - 4(630 \times 9)}$

$= \sqrt{23409 - 22680} = \sqrt{729} = 27$

19. (d) 16 years ago, let $T = x$ years and $G = 8x$ years.
After 8 years from now, $T = (x + 16 + 8)$ years and $G = (8x + 16 + 8)$ years.
$\therefore$ $8x + 24 = 3(x + 24) \Rightarrow 5x = 48$

8 years ago, $\dfrac{T}{G} = \dfrac{x + 8}{8x + 8} = \dfrac{\dfrac{48}{5} + 8}{8 \times \dfrac{48}{5} + 8} = \dfrac{88}{424} = \dfrac{11}{53}$

20. (c) Since average price of a pencil = Rs 2
$\therefore$ Price of 75 pencils = Rs 150
and Price of 30 pens = Rs $(510 - 150)$ = Rs 360

$\therefore$ Average price of a pen $= \dfrac{360}{30} = $ Rs 12

21. (a) Let the numbers be x and y. Then,

$x + y = \dfrac{28}{25}x \Rightarrow y = \dfrac{28}{25}x - x \Rightarrow y = \dfrac{3}{25}x$

$\Rightarrow \dfrac{y}{x} = \left(\dfrac{3}{25} \times 100\right)\% = 12\%.$

22. (b) Let S.P. $= ₹\,100$. Then, C.P. $= ₹\,96$; Profit $= ₹\,4$.

$\therefore$ Profit $\% = \left(\dfrac{4}{96} \times 100\right)\% = \dfrac{25}{6}\% = 4.17\%. \approx 4.2\%$

23. (c) Shortcut method :
If borrowed amount be ₹ M and it is to be paid in equal instalments, then

$$M = na + \frac{ra}{100 \times Y} \times \frac{n(n-1)}{2}$$

where Y = no. of instalments per annum
a = annual instalment
Here, M = 4200, y = 1, r = 10, n = 5, a = ?

$$4200 = 5a + \frac{10a}{100} \times \frac{5(5-1)}{2}$$

$$\Rightarrow 4200 = a[5+1] \Rightarrow 6a = 4200$$

$$\Rightarrow a = ₹\,700$$

24. (b) Let income of A = ₹ 3x, income of B = ₹ 2x
and expenditure of A = ₹ 5y,
expenditure of B = ₹ 3y
Now, saving = income – expenditure
$\therefore 3x - 5y = 2x - 3y = 200$
$\Rightarrow x = 2y$ and $y = 200$

$\therefore x = 400$

$\therefore$ A's income = ₹ 1200

25. (a) Speed $= \left(\dfrac{750}{150}\right)$ m / sec = 5 m / sec

$$= \left(5 \times \frac{18}{5}\right) \text{km / hr} = 18 \text{ km / hr.}$$

26. (a)	27. (d)	28. (b)	29. (c)	30. (d)
31. (a)	32. (c)	33. (a)	34. (d)	35. (d)
36. (d)	37. (d)	38. (b)	39. (d)	40. (d)
41. (d)	42. (d)	43. (d)	44. (c)	45. (b)
46. (d)	47. (d)	48. (c)	49. (a)	50. (d)
51. (a)	52. (a)	53. (c)	54. (b)	55. (b)
56. (b)	57. (b)	58. (a)	59. (d)	60. (c)
61. (c)	62. (d)	63. (b)	64. (d)	65. (a)
66. (b)	67. (c)	68. (d)	69. (c)	70. (d)
71. (d)	72. (c)	73. (d)	74. (b)	75. (d)

INSTRUCTIONS

1. This practice set consists of 75 questions will be of objective type with multiple choices.

2. Practice set have MCQs from Mathematics, General Intelligence & Reasoning, General Science and General Awareness on Current Affairs.

3. Duration of practice set is 60 minutes.

Time : 60 Min.   **Max. Marks : 75**

1. Four of the following five are alike in a certain way and hence form a group. Find the one which is different from the other four.
   (a) Rice   (b) Wheat
   (c) Barley   (d) Mustard

2. Four of the following five are alike in a certain way and hence from a group. Find the one which is different from the other four.
   (a) Arrow   (b) Sword
   (c) Knife   (d) Axe

3. Four of the following five are alike in a certain way and so form a group. Which is the one that **does not** belong to the group?
   (a) 169   (b) 179   (c) 135   (d) 149

DIRECTIONS (Qs. 4-7): *In each as the following number series a wrong number is given. Find out that number.*

4. 108 54 36 18 9 6 4
   (a) 54   (b) 36   (c) 18   (d) 9

5. 2 3 5 8 14 23 41 69
   (a) 5   (b) 8   (c) 69   (d) 41

6. 0 1 9 36 99 225 441
   (a) 9   (b) 36   (c) 99   (d) 225

7. 3 7.5 15 37.5 75 167.5 375
   (a) 167.5   (b) 75   (c) 37.5   (d) 15

8. If B is coded as 8, F is coded as 6, Q is coded as 4, D is coded as 7, T is coded as 2, M is coded as 3, and K is coded as 5, then what is the coded form of QKTBFM?
   (a) 452683   (b) 472683
   (c) 452783   (d) None of these

9. In a certain code language BORN is written as APQON and LACK is written as KBBLK. How will the word GRID be written in that code language?
   (a) FQHCD   (b) FSHED
   (c) HSJED   (d) FSHCD

10. Pointing to a photograph, a lady tells Pramod, "I am the only daughter of this lady and her son is your maternal uncle," How is the speaker related to Pramod's father?
    (a) Sister-in-law
    (b) Wife
    (c) Neither (a) nor (b)
    (d) Aunt

11. Alok walked 30 metres towards east and took a right turn and walked 40 metres. He again took a right turn and walked 50 metres. Towards which direction is he from his starting point?
    (a) South   (b) West
    (c) South-West   (d) South-East

12. Ruchi's house is to the right of Vani's house at a distance of 20 metres in the same row facing North. Shabana's house is in the North- East direction of Vani's house at a distance of 25 metres. Determine that Ruchi's house is in which direction with respect of Shabana's house.
    (a) North-East   (b) East
    (c) South   (d) West

13. In a queue, Vijay is fourteenth from the front and Jack is seventeenth from the end, while Mary is in between Vijay and Jack. If Vijay be ahead of Jack and there be 48 persons in the queue, how many persons are there between Vijay and Mary?
    (a) 8   (b) 7   (c) 6   (d) 5

14. Which one of the following is correct?
    6 * 4 * 9 * 15
    (a) ×, = , −   (b) ×, −, =
    (c) =, ×, −   (d) −, ×, =

15. There is one number which is formed by writing one digit 6 times (e.g. 111111, 444444 etc.). Such a number is always divisible by:
    (a) 7 and 11   (b) 11 and 13
    (c) 7, 11 and 13   (d) None of these

16. Find the unit's digit in the product $(2467)^{153} \times (341)^{72}$.
 (a) 6   (b) 7   (c) 8   (d) 9

17. Which is the least number that must be subtracted from 1856, so that the remainder when divided by 7, 12 and 16 will leave the same remainder 4?
 (a) 137   (b) 1361   (c) 140   (d) 172

18. If $\dfrac{1}{x} = \dfrac{1}{y} + \dfrac{1}{z}$, then z equals :
 (a) $\dfrac{xy}{(x-y)}$ (b) $x-y$ (c) $\dfrac{xy}{(y-x)}$ (d) $\dfrac{(x-y)}{(xy)}$

19. If $(x-3)(2x+1)=0$, then the possible values of $2x+1$ are :
 (a) 0 only   (b) 0 and 3   (c) $-\dfrac{1}{2}$ and 3   (d) 0 and 7

20. A batsman in his 12th innings makes a score of 65 and thereby increases his average by 2 runs. What is his average after the 12th innings if he had never been 'not out'?
 (a) 42   (b) 43   (c) 44   (d) 45

21. If 10 % of an electricity bill is deducted, ₹ 45 is still to be paid. How much was the bill?
 (a) ₹ 50   (b) ₹ 60   (c) ₹ 55   (d) None of these

22. If the manufacturer gains 10%, the wholesale dealer 15% and the retailer 25%, then find the cost of production of a table, the retail price of which is ₹ 1265?
 (a) ₹ 800   (b) ₹ 1000   (c) ₹ 900   (d) ₹ 600

23. Simple interest on a certain sum is 16 over 25 of the sum. Find the rate per cent and time, if both are equal.
 (a) 8% and 8 years   (b) 6% and 6 years
 (c) 10% and 10 years   (d) 12 % and 12 years

24. The fourth proportional to 5, 8, 15 is:
 (a) 18   (b) 24   (c) 19   (d) 20

25. If a man walks to his office at 5/4 of his usual rate, he reaches office 30 minutes early than usual. What is his usual time to reach office.
 (a) 2 hr   (b) $2\dfrac{1}{2}$ hr   (c) 1 hr 50 min   (d) 2 hr 15 min

26. The Megaliths of South India are mainly associated with
 (a) Mesolithic age   (b) Neolithic age
 (c) Chalcolithic age   (d) Iron age

27. Which one of the following dynasties built the Khajuraho temple?
 (a) Chandellas   (b) Chauhans
 (c) Paramaras   (d) Tomars

28. With whose permission did the English set up their first factory in Surat?
 (a) Akbar   (b) Jahangir
 (c) Shahjahan   (d) Aurangzeb

29. Which one of the following stars is nearest to the Earth?
 (a) Polaris   (b) Alpha Centauri
 (c) Sun   (d) Sirius

30. The 'Chilka lake region' lies in between the deltas of:
 (a) Ganga and Mahanadi
 (b) Godavari and Krishna
 (c) Mahanadi and Godavari
 (d) Krishna and Cauvery

31. Total schedules in Indian Constitution are:
 (a) 22   (b) 10   (c) 16   (d) 12

32. Which article of the constitution of India deals with the 'Right to constitutional remedies'?
 (a) Article 19   (b) Article 14
 (c) Article 21   (d) Article 32

33. Madhubani; a style of folk paintings, is popular in which of the following states in India?
 (a) Uttar Pradesh   (b) Rajasthan
 (c) Madhya Pradesh   (d) Bihar

34. Who is the author of "An Uncertain Glory: India and its Contradictions"?
 (a) Amatya Sen & Michael Bush
 (b) Amartya Sen & Satya Paul
 (c) Amartya Sen & Jean Dreze
 (d) Amartya Sen & Zeenat Shaukat
 (e) Amartya Sen & Salman Rushdie

35. Who is the author of the book India 2020?
 (a) Nibal Singh   (b) R.K. Narayan
 (c) Sidney Shelton   (d) Dr. A.P.J.Abdul Kalam
 (e) None of these

36. Where is the extreme north of India a railway station?
 (a) Guwahati   (b) Pathancoat
 (c) Amritsar   (d) Jammutavi

37. Where is the headquarters of Central Railway situated?
 (a) Mumbai (V.T)   (b) Mumbai (Church Gate)
 (c) Gwalior   (d) Gorakhpur

38. When did Indian railway nationalize?
 (a) 1949   (b) 1951   (c) 1950   (d) 1952

39. The Sun's energy is produced by
 (a) Nuclear fission   (b) Burning of gases
 (c) Nuclear fusion   (d) None of these

40. The cells used in mobile phone are
 (a) Dry Cells
 (b) Lithium Ion cells
 (c) Nickel Candmium Cells
 (d) Mercury Cells

41. Which type of mirror is used in rear view mirrors of vehicles?
 (a) Concave mirror   (b) Convex Mirror
 (c) Plane Mirror   (d) Plano Concave Lens

42. Which of the following acid is found in apple ?
 (a) Hydrochloric acid   (b) Acetic acid
 (c) Oxalic acid   (d) Malic acid

43. The branch of clinical study related to hearing , taste and smell is
 (a) Otalaryngology   (b) Ophthalmology
 (c) Dermatology   (d) Osteology

44. Freon Gas is used in
 (a) Air-conditioners   (b) Refrigerators
 (c) Television   (d) Nuclear reactors

45. The method of Radio-carbon dating is used to find the age of
 (a) Fossils   (b) Stars
 (c) Skeletons   (d) Trees

46. Which element causes 'Itai-itai disease' ?
 (a) Sulphates   (b) Cadmium
 (c) Chromium   (d) Mercury

47. Which of the following is not a mosquito borne disease?
    (a) Dengue (b) Malaria
    (c) Sleeping sickness (d) Filariasis
48. Insulin for Diabets is invented by
    (a) Edward Jenner (b) Alexander Fleming
    (c) E.F. Banting (d) Hoffman
49. Which of the following colours has got the maximum refractive index for glass ?
    (a) Blue (b) Green
    (c) Red (d) Indigo
50. For digestion of fat, bile is needed. This is secreted by the-
    (a) stomach (b) pituitary gland
    (c) pancreas (d) liver
51. Excessive secretion from the pituitary gland in children results in-
    (a) increased height (b) retarded growth
    (c) weakening of bones (d) None of the above
52. Weight of an object put in a satellite orbiting in space around the earth is-
    (a) the same as on the earth
    (b) slightly more then that on the earth
    (c) less then that on the earth
    (d) reduced to zero
53. Which of the following food articles contain only one of the five constituents of diet, viz., fasts, carbohydrates, proteins, mineral salts and vitamins ?
    (a) Bread (b) Mongo (c) Milk (d) Sugar
54. Which of the following in the human body is popularly called the Adams Apple?
    (a) Adrenal (b) Liver
    (c) Thyroid (d) Thymus
55. Which one of the following substances is obtained by the fractionation of human blood ?
    (a) Antivenom serum (b) Gamma globulin
    (c) Polio vaccine (d) Diphtheria antitoxin
56. Of the blood groups A, B, AB and O, which one is transfused into a person whose blood group is A ?
    (a) Group A only (b) Group B only
    (c) Group A and O (d) Group AB only
57. The three abundant elements in the earths crust are aluminium, oxygen and silicon. The correct order of their abundance is-
    (a) oxygen, aluminium, silicon
    (b) aluminium, silicon, oxygen
    (c) oxygen, silicon, aluminium
    (d) silicon, oxygen, aluminium
58. Penicillin is widely used as-
    (a) an antiseptic (b) a disinfectant
    (c) an antibiotic (d) an insecticide
59. Which of the following vitamins is stored in the liver ?
    (a) Vitamin A (b) Vitamin C
    (c) Vitamin E (d) Vitamin K
60. The theory of inheritance of acquired characters was propounded by-
    (a) Charles Darwin (b) Gregor Mendel
    (c) J. B. Lamarck (d) Weismann
61. Which one of the following is not allied to Geophysical Sciences ?
    (a) Hydrology (b) Meteorology
    (c) Palaeontology (d) Seismology
62. Brain of a normal human adult weighs about-
    (a) 1 lb (b) 2 lb (c) 3 lb (d) 4 lb
63. Photophobia is-
    (a) a disease caused by too much sunlight
    (b) abnormal intolerance of light
    (c) the adjustment of the eye for light
    (d) the ability to perceive light
64. Which one of the following elements is least likely to be found in commercial fertilisers ?
    (a) Nitrogen (b) Phosphorus
    (c) Potassium (d) Silicon
65. At what temperature are the temperature on Celsius and Fahrenheit scales equal?
    (a) 273° Celsius (b) –273° Celsius
    c) –40° Celsius d) 40° Celsius
66. At what temperature a body0 will not radiate any heat energy?
    (a) 0° C (b) 273° C
    (c) 100° C (d) –273° C
67. ________ is called as 'Father of Genetics'.
    (a) Charles Darwin
    (b) Hugo de Vries
    (c) Gregor Johann Mendel
    (d) Jean Baptiste Lamarck
68. The ozone layer protects us from
    (a) Ultra violet rays (b) Radio waves
    (c) Visual radiation (d) Infrared radiation
69. The I.C Chip used in a computer is made up of________.
    (a) Silicon (b) Chromium
    (c) Gold (d) Lead
70. Typhoid fever is caused by ________.
    (a) Salmonella (b) Clostridium
    (c) Leptospira (d) Xanthomonas
71. Nichrome wire is used in an electric heater because __________.
    (a) It has high resistance
    (b) It has high melting point
    (c) It can resist a current upto approx 5 amperes
    (d) For all of the above reasons
72. Automatic wrist watches get energy from
    (a) twist in spring (b) liquid crystal
    (c) kinetic energy (d) movement of our hands
73. What was the theme of the World Wetlands Day 2018?
    (a) Wetlands For Our Future: Sustainable Livelihoods
    (b) Wetlands for Disaster Risk Reduction
    (c) Wetlands for a Sustainable Urban Future
    (d) Wetlands and Agriculture: Partners for Growth
74. The 2nd edition of Nobel Prize Series India 2018 has been inaugurated in which Indian state?
    (A) Goa (B) Maharashtra (C) Karnataka (D) Haryana
75. The Indira Gandhi National Centre for the Arts (IGNCA) is located in which city?
    (a) Mumbai (b) New Delhi
    (c) Varanasi (d) Gurgaon

RESPONSE SHEET

1. ⓐ ⓑ ⓒ ⓓ	2. ⓐ ⓑ ⓒ ⓓ	3. ⓐ ⓑ ⓒ ⓓ	4. ⓐ ⓑ ⓒ ⓓ	5. ⓐ ⓑ ⓒ ⓓ
6. ⓐ ⓑ ⓒ ⓓ	7. ⓐ ⓑ ⓒ ⓓ	8. ⓐ ⓑ ⓒ ⓓ	9. ⓐ ⓑ ⓒ ⓓ	10. ⓐ ⓑ ⓒ ⓓ
11. ⓐ ⓑ ⓒ ⓓ	12. ⓐ ⓑ ⓒ ⓓ	13. ⓐ ⓑ ⓒ ⓓ	14. ⓐ ⓑ ⓒ ⓓ	15. ⓐ ⓑ ⓒ ⓓ
16. ⓐ ⓑ ⓒ ⓓ	17. ⓐ ⓑ ⓒ ⓓ	18. ⓐ ⓑ ⓒ ⓓ	19. ⓐ ⓑ ⓒ ⓓ	20. ⓐ ⓑ ⓒ ⓓ
21. ⓐ ⓑ ⓒ ⓓ	22. ⓐ ⓑ ⓒ ⓓ	23. ⓐ ⓑ ⓒ ⓓ	24. ⓐ ⓑ ⓒ ⓓ	25. ⓐ ⓑ ⓒ ⓓ
26. ⓐ ⓑ ⓒ ⓓ	27. ⓐ ⓑ ⓒ ⓓ	28. ⓐ ⓑ ⓒ ⓓ	29. ⓐ ⓑ ⓒ ⓓ	30. ⓐ ⓑ ⓒ ⓓ
31. ⓐ ⓑ ⓒ ⓓ	32. ⓐ ⓑ ⓒ ⓓ	33. ⓐ ⓑ ⓒ ⓓ	34. ⓐ ⓑ ⓒ ⓓ	35. ⓐ ⓑ ⓒ ⓓ
36. ⓐ ⓑ ⓒ ⓓ	37. ⓐ ⓑ ⓒ ⓓ	38. ⓐ ⓑ ⓒ ⓓ	39. ⓐ ⓑ ⓒ ⓓ	40. ⓐ ⓑ ⓒ ⓓ
41. ⓐ ⓑ ⓒ ⓓ	42. ⓐ ⓑ ⓒ ⓓ	43. ⓐ ⓑ ⓒ ⓓ	44. ⓐ ⓑ ⓒ ⓓ	45. ⓐ ⓑ ⓒ ⓓ
46. ⓐ ⓑ ⓒ ⓓ	47. ⓐ ⓑ ⓒ ⓓ	48. ⓐ ⓑ ⓒ ⓓ	49. ⓐ ⓑ ⓒ ⓓ	50. ⓐ ⓑ ⓒ ⓓ
51. ⓐ ⓑ ⓒ ⓓ	52. ⓐ ⓑ ⓒ ⓓ	53. ⓐ ⓑ ⓒ ⓓ	54. ⓐ ⓑ ⓒ ⓓ	55. ⓐ ⓑ ⓒ ⓓ
56. ⓐ ⓑ ⓒ ⓓ	57. ⓐ ⓑ ⓒ ⓓ	58. ⓐ ⓑ ⓒ ⓓ	59. ⓐ ⓑ ⓒ ⓓ	60. ⓐ ⓑ ⓒ ⓓ
61. ⓐ ⓑ ⓒ ⓓ	62. ⓐ ⓑ ⓒ ⓓ	63. ⓐ ⓑ ⓒ ⓓ	64. ⓐ ⓑ ⓒ ⓓ	65. ⓐ ⓑ ⓒ ⓓ
66. ⓐ ⓑ ⓒ ⓓ	67. ⓐ ⓑ ⓒ ⓓ	68. ⓐ ⓑ ⓒ ⓓ	69. ⓐ ⓑ ⓒ ⓓ	70. ⓐ ⓑ ⓒ ⓓ
71. ⓐ ⓑ ⓒ ⓓ	72. ⓐ ⓑ ⓒ ⓓ	73. ⓐ ⓑ ⓒ ⓓ	74. ⓐ ⓑ ⓒ ⓓ	75. ⓐ ⓑ ⓒ ⓓ

HINTS & SOLUTIONS

1. **(d)** Except 'mustard' each belongs to the same category, viz food grains. Mustard is an oilseed.

2. **(a)** All others are held in the hand and not shot out.

3. **(a)** The rest are not squares of a number.

4. **(d)** The series is $\div 2, \div 1.5$ alternately.

5. **(c)** The series is an alternate series, having
$S_1 = 2\ 5\ 14\ 41 : \times 3 - 1$ in each term
$S_2 = 3\ 8\ 23\ 69 : \times 3 - 1$ in each term

6. **(c)** The differences are $1 - 0 = 1 = 1^3 ; 9 - 1 = 8$
$= 2^3; 36 - 9 = 27 = 3^3; 99 - 36 = 63 \neq 4^3,$
but $100 - 36 = 64 = 4^3; 225 - 100 = 125 = 5^3;$
$441 - 225 = 216 = 6^3$

7. **(a)** The series is $\times 2.5, \times 2$ alternately.

8. **(d)** Q K T B F M = 4 5 2 8 6 3

9. **(b)**
B   O   R   N
$-1\ +1\ -1\ +1$
A   P   Q   O   N
L   A   C   K
$-1\ +1\ -1\ +1$
K   B   B   L   K

Similarly,
G   R   I   D
$-1\ +1\ -1\ +1$
F   S   H   E   D

10. **(b)** Clearly, the speaker's brother is Pramod's maternal uncle. So, the speaker is Pramod's mother or his father's wife.

11. **(c)**

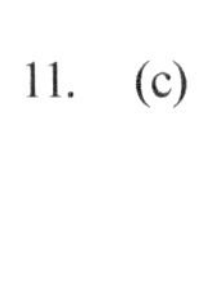

12. **(c)**

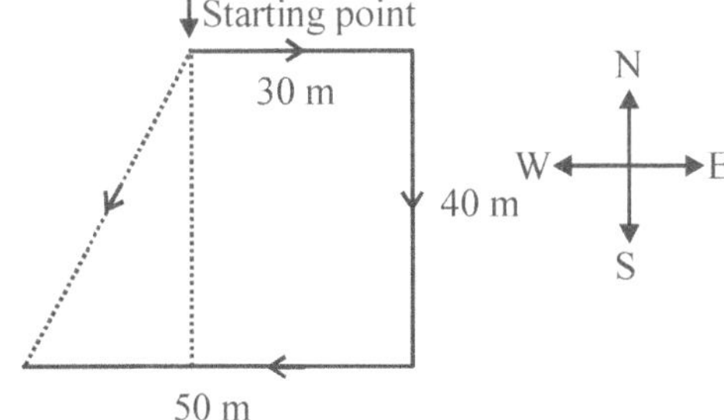

13. **(b)** Number of persons between Vijay and Jack
$= 48 - (14 + 17) = 17$
Now, Mary lies in middle of these 17 persons i.e., at the eighth position.
So, number of persons between Vijay and Mary = 7.

14. **(b)** $6 \times 4 - 9 = 15$

15. **(c)** Since 111111 is divisible by each one of 7, 11 and 13, so each one of given type of numbers is divisible by each one of 7, 11, and 13. as we may write, $222222 = 2 \times 111111, 333333 = 3 \times 111111$, etc.

16. **(b)** Clearly, unit's digit in the given product = unit's digit in $7^{153} \times 1^{72}$.
Now, 7^4 gives unit digit 1.
$\therefore 7^{153}$ gives unit digit $(1 \times 7) = 7$. Also 1^{72} gives unit digit 1.
Hence, unit's digit in the product $= (7 \times 1) = 7$.

17. **(d)** Suppose least no. be x
$1856 - x = n(\text{LCM of } 7,12,16) + 4$
or $1856 - x = n(336) + 4$
we should take n = 5 so that n(336) is nearest to 1856 and n (336) < 1856
$1856 - x = 1680 + 4 = 1684$
$x = 1856 - 1684 = 172$

18. **(c)** $\dfrac{1}{x} = \dfrac{1}{y} + \dfrac{1}{z}$

or $\dfrac{1}{z} = \dfrac{1}{x} - \dfrac{1}{y} = \dfrac{y - x}{xy}$ or $z = \dfrac{xy}{(y - x)}$

19. **(d)** $(x - 3)(2x + 1) = 0$
$\Rightarrow (x - 3) = 0$ or $(2x + 1) = 0$
when $x - 3 = 0$ then $x = 3$

when $2x + 1 = 0$ then $x = -\dfrac{1}{2}$

If $x = 3$, then $(2x + 1) = 7$
and $2x + 1 = 0$

when $x = -\dfrac{1}{2}$

Possible value of $(2x + 1)$ are 0 and 7.

20. **(b)** Let 'x' be the average score after 12 th innings
$\Rightarrow 12x = 11 \times (x - 2) + 65$
$\therefore x = 43$

21. **(a)** Let the bill be ₹ x. Then 90% of x = 45
$\Rightarrow x = \dfrac{45 \times 100}{90} = ₹ 50$

22. **(a)** Let the cost of production of the table be ₹ x. Then, 125% of 115% of 110% of x = 1265
$\Rightarrow \dfrac{125}{100} \times \dfrac{115}{100} \times \dfrac{110}{100} \times x = 1265$
$\Rightarrow \dfrac{253}{160} x = 1265 \Rightarrow x = \left(\dfrac{1265 \times 160}{253}\right) = ₹ 800$

23. (a) $\dfrac{16}{25}P = \dfrac{P \times R \times R}{100}$

$\Rightarrow R^2 = \dfrac{1600}{25} \Rightarrow R = \dfrac{40}{5} = 8\%$

Also, time = 8 years

24. (b) Let the fourth proportional to 5, 8, 15 be x.

Then, $5 : 8 :: 15 : x \Rightarrow 5x = (8 \times 15) \Rightarrow x = \dfrac{(8 \times 15)}{5} = 24$.

25. (b) usual time $\times \left(\dfrac{4}{5} - 1\right) = \dfrac{-30}{60}$

$\Rightarrow$ usual time $= \dfrac{1}{2} \times 5 = 2\dfrac{1}{2}$ hr

26. (d)

27. (a) Khajuraho is a village in the Indian state of Madhya Pradesh, located in Chhatarpur District, about 385 miles southeast of Delhi, the capital city of India. The Khajuraho group of monuments has been listed as a UNESCO World Heritage site. Khajuraho temples were constructed between 950 and 1050 AD. During the reign of Chandel Empire.

28. (b) James-I William Hawkins was sent to the court of Jahangir and Jahangir provided the farman which allowed East India Co. to set up a factory at Surat in 1613.

29. (c) Sun is the star nearest to the earth. It is 150 million kilometer away from earth. Sun has temperatures of over 15 million °C.

30. (c)

31. (d)

32. (d) Article 32 of the constitution of India deals with the 'Right to constitutional Remedies'

33. (d)

34. (b) Rosetta is a robotic spacecraft built and launched by the European Space Agency to perform a detailed study of comet 67P/Churyumov-Gerasimenko. It is part of the ESA Horizon 2000 cornerstone missions and is the first mission designed to both orbit and land on a comet.

35. (a) India observes 23rd December, the birthday of Chaudry Charan Singh, as Kisan Diwas (Farmers Day) every year. Charan Singh was the fifth Prime Minister of India. He served country as Prime Minister from 28 July 1979 until 14 January 1980.

36. (d) Jammutavi

37. (a) Mumbai (V.T)

38. (c) 1950

39.	(c)	40.	(b)	41.	(b)	42.	(d)	43.	(a)
44.	(b)	45.	(a)	46.	(b)	47.	(c)	48.	(c)
49.	(c)	50.	(d)	51.	(a)	52.	(d)	53.	(d)
54.	(c)	55.	(b)	56.	(c)	57.	(d)	58.	(c)
59.	(a)	60.	(c)	61.	(c)	62.	(c)	63.	(b)
64.	(d)	65.	(c)	66.	(d)	67.	(c)	68.	(a)
69.	(a)	70.	(a)	71.	(d)	72.	(a)	73.	(c)
74.	(a)	75.	(b)						

Time : 60 Min.   **Max. Marks : 75**

1. Three of the following four are alike in a certain way and so form a group. Which is the one that **does not** belong to the group'?
   - (a) Listen
   - (b) Feel
   - (c) Think
   - (d) Sing

2. Three of the following four are alike in a certain way and so form a group. Which is the one that **does not** belong to that group?
   - (a) Jowar
   - (b) Wheat
   - (c) Mustard
   - (d) Bajra

3. Three of the following four are alike in a certain way and so form a group. Which is the one that **does not** belong to that group?
   - (a) Volume
   - (b) Size
   - (c) Large
   - (d) Shape

DIRECTIONS (Qs. 4-6): *In each of the following questions, a number series is given in which one number is wrong. You have to find out that number and have to follow the new series which will be started by that number. By following this, which will be the third number of the new series?*

4. 1   2   6   33   148   765   4626
   - (a) 46
   - (b) 124
   - (c) 18
   - (d) 72

5. 2   9   5   36   125   648   3861
   - (a) 12
   - (b) 11
   - (c) 75
   - (d) None of these

6. 3   4   12   45   190   1005   6066
   - (a) 98
   - (b) 96
   - (c) 384
   - (d) 386

7. Which sequence of letters when placed at the blanks one after another will complete the given letter series ?
   abca _ bcaab _ ca _ bbc _ a
   - (a) ccaa
   - (b) bbaa
   - (c) abac
   - (d) abba

8. What will be the next term in : BDF, CFI, DHL, ?
   - (a) CJM
   - (b) EIM
   - (c) EJO
   - (d) EMI

9. In a certain code language STREAMLING is written as CGTVUHOJMN. How will the word PERIODICAL be written in that language?
   - (a) PJSFQMNBJE
   - (b) QKTGRMBDJE
   - (c) QKTGRMCEKF
   - (d) PJSFQMBDJE

10. If 'green' is called `white', 'white' is called `yellow', 'yellow' is called `red', 'red' is called `orange', then which of the following represents the colour of sunflower?
    - (a) red
    - (b) yellow
    - (c) brown
    - (d) indigo

11. Anil, introducing a girl in a party, said, she is the wife of the grandson of my mother. How is Anil related to the girl?
    - (a) Father
    - (b) Grandfather
    - (c) Husband
    - (d) Father-in-law

12. Y is to the East of X, which is to the North of Z. If P is to the South of Z, then P is in which direction with respect to Y?
    - (a) North
    - (b) South
    - (c) South-East
    - (d) None of these

13. One afternoon, Manisha and Madhuri were talking to each other face to face in Bhopal on M.G. Roa(d) If Manisha's shadow was exactly to the left of Madhuri, which direction was Manisha facing?
    - (a) North
    - (b) South
    - (c) East
    - (d) Data inadequate

14. In a line of boys, Ganesh is 12th from the left and Rajan is 15th from the right. They interchange their positions. Now, Rajan is 20th from the right. What is the total no. of boys in the class?
    - (a) 30
    - (b) 29
    - (c) 32
    - (d) 31

15. In the following question you have to identify the correct response from the given premises stated according to the following symbols.
If '+' means '÷', '−' means '×', '÷' means '+' and '×' means '−', then $63 \times 24 + 8 \div 4 + 2 - 3 = ?$
(a) 54 (b) 66
(c) 186 (d) 48

16. The unit's digit in the product $(7^{71} \times 6^{59} \times 3^{65})$ is:
(a) 1 (b) 2
(c) 4 (d) 6

17. Which digits should come in place of * and $ if the number 62684*$ is divisible by both 8 and 5?
(a) 4, 0 (b) 0, 4
(c) 0, 0 (d) 4, 4

18. The LCM of two numbers is 280 and their ratio is 7 : 8. The two numbers are :
(a) 70, 80 (b) 54, 68
(c) 35, 40 (d) 28, 36

19. In a two-digit number, if it is known that its unit's digit exceeds its ten's digit by 2 and that the product of the given number and the sum of its digits is equal to 144, then the number is:
(a) 24 (b) 26
(c) 42 (d) 46

20. The average age of A and B is 20 years. If C were to replace A, the average would be 19 and if C were to replace B, the averge would be 21. What are the age of A, B and C?
(a) 22, 18, 20 (b) 20, 20, 18
(c) 18, 22, 20 (d) None of these

21. Chunilal invests 65% in machinery, 20% in raw material and still has ₹ 1,305 cash with him. Find his total investment.
(a) ₹ 6,500 (b) ₹ 7,225
(c) ₹ 8,500 (d) None of these

22. A man buys 50 pencils for Rs 100 and sells 45 pencils for ₹ 90. Find his gain or loss %.
(a) 20% (b) 35%
(c) 25% (d) No gain or loss

23. What annual instalment will discharge a debt of ₹ 4,200 due in 5 years at 10% simple interest?
(a) ₹ 500 per year (b) ₹ 600 per year
(c) ₹ 700 per year (d) ₹ 800 per year

24. There are 240 doctors and nurses at a hospital. If the ratio of doctors to nurses is 5 : 7, then the nurses at the hospital are
(a) 20 (b) 60
(c) 100 (d) 140

25. Cars C_1 and C_2 travel to a place at a speed of 30 and 45 km/h respectively. If car C_2 takes $2\frac{1}{2}$ hours less time than C_1 for the journey, the distance of the place is
(a) 300 km (b) 400 km
(c) 350 km (d) 225 km

26. Which pollutant in water causes 'Blue baby syndrome' ?
(a) Sulphates (b) Fluoride
(c) Nitrates (d) Benzene

27. Which of the following acid is found in 'Grapes' ?
(a) Hydrochloric acid (b) Acetic acid
(c) Oxalic acid (d) Citric acid

28. Which of the following acid is found in vinegar ?
(a) Hydrochloric acid (b) Acetic acid
(c) Oxalic acid (d) Citric acid

29. The filament of an electric bulb is made of
(a) tungsten (b) nichrome
(c) graphite (d) iron

30. Soda water contains
(a) carbonic acid (b) sulphuric acid
(c) carbon dioxide (d) nitrous acid

31. Diamond is an allotropic form of
(a) germanium (b) carbon
(c) silicon (d) sulphur

32. Gastric Juice is
(a) Acidic (b) Neutral
(c) Alkaline (d) None of these

33. How many pairs of heart exist in Earthworm ?
(a) Two pairs (b) Three pairs
(c) One pair (d) Four pairs

34. What is laughing gas?
(a) Nitrous Oxide (b) Carbon monoxide
(c) Sulphur dioxide (d) Hydrogen peroxide

35. Which of the following is in liquid form at room temperature?
(a) Lithium (b) Sodium
(c) Francium (d) Cerium

36. What is increasing order of the wave lengths of the following colours- 1. Orange 2. Indigo 3. Yellow 4. Violet
(a) 1, 2, 3, 4 (b) 3, 4, 1, 2
(c) 4, 3, 2, 1 (d) 4, 2, 3, 1

37. Atoms are composed of-
(a) Electrons only (b) Protons only
(c) Electrons and Protons (d) Electrons and Nuclei

38. Paper is manufactured by-
(a) Wood and resin
(b) Wood, Sodium and Bleaching powder
(c) Wood and bleaching powder
(d) Wood, Calcium, hydrogen sulphate and resin

39. Which synthetic fibre is known as artificial silk ?
(a) Cotton (b) Rayon
(c) Terylene (d) Nylon

40. Deep blue colour is imparted to glass by the presence of-
(a) Iron oxide (b) Cupric oxide
(c) Nickel oxide (d) Cobalt oxide

41. The gas predominantly responsible for global warning is
(a) Carbon dioxide (b) Carbon monoxide
(c) Nitrous oxide (d) Nitrogen peroxide

42. Which of the following plants is a source of biodiesel ?
(a) Neem (b) Cotton
(c) Eucalyptus (d) Jatropha

43. Dental caries are due to
(a) Viral infection (b) Contaminated water
(c) Bacterial infection (d) Hereditary causes

44. The speed of light with the rise in the temperature of the medium
    - (a) Increases
    - (b) Decreases
    - (c) Remains unaltered
    - (d) Drops sharply
45. Stem cuttings are commonly used for re-growing
    - (a) Cotton
    - (b) Banana
    - (c) Jute
    - (d) Sugar Cane
46. Most soluble in water is-
    - (a) Camphor
    - (b) Sugar
    - (c) Sulphur
    - (d) Common Salt
47. Washing soda is the common name for
    - (a) Calcium carbonate
    - (b) Calcium bicarbonate
    - (c) Sodium carbonate
    - (d) Sodium bicarbonate
48. Palak leaves are rich source of
    - (a) Vitamin A
    - (b) Iron
    - (c) Carotene
    - (d) Vitamin E
49. Persons with which blood group are called universal donors
    - (a) AB
    - (b) A
    - (c) O
    - (d) B
50. Vaccines are substances that confer immunity against______.
    - (a) All kind of diseases
    - (b) Communicable diseases
    - (c) Specific diseases
    - (d) Non communicable diseases
51. Which one of the following terms is not related to Budhhism ?
    - (a) Sangha
    - (b) Mahayana
    - (c) Ashvamedha
    - (d) Nirvana
52. The Dandi March was undertaken by Gandhji to
    - (a) Break the salt Law
    - (b) Resolve the dispute among the Gujarat mill workers
    - (c) Press the demand for Purna Swaraj
    - (d) Oppose the Round Table Conference
53. Who among the following Governor-Generals of India was called the "Maker of Modern India"?
    - (a) Lord Elgin
    - (b) Lord Dalhousie
    - (c) Lord Mayo
    - (d) Lord Ripon
54. The alloy of steel used in making automobile parts and utensils is
    - (a) Stainless steel
    - (b) Nickel steel
    - (c) Tungsten Steel
    - (d) Chromium Steel
55. Who among the following is regarded as the "father of Russian Revolution"?
    - (a) Kerensky
    - (b) Trotsky
    - (c) Karl Marx
    - (d) Lenin
56. The American Declaration of Independence was written by
    - (a) George Washington
    - (b) Thomas Jefferson
    - (c) James Madison
    - (d) John Adams
57. Who among the following leaders is known for her work in the field of the empowerment of women ?
    - (a) Sheik Hasina
    - (b) Benazir Bhutto
    - (c) Mary Rabinson
    - (d) Chandrika Kumaratunga
58. In India,In which one of the following areas are the tropical evergreen forests found ?
    - (a) The Eastern Ghats
    - (b) The Western Ghats
    - (c) The western Himalaya
    - (d) The Central Himalaya
59. Amnesty international is
    - (a) a human rights group
    - (b) a UN agency to fight global terrorism
    - (c) A refugee camp in Croatia
    - (d) a wing of the World Bank
60. Which one of the following dynasties was ruling at the time of Alexander's Invasion?
    - (a) The Nanda dynasty
    - (b) The Maurya dynasty
    - (c) The Sunga dynasty
    - (d) The Kanva dynasty
61. Who was the first woman Chief Minister of Independent India ?
    - (a) jayalalitha
    - (b) Padmaja Naidu
    - (c) Sucheta kriplani
    - (d) Vijayalakshmi pandit
62. The Hozagiri Dance belongs to which States ?
    - (a) Mizoram
    - (b) Nagaland
    - (c) Sikkim
    - (d) Tripura
63. How many schedules are there in the Indian constitution ?
    - (a) 11
    - (b) 12
    - (c) 13
    - (d) 14
64. Cooking gas supplied in cylinder by gas agaencies is
    - (a) liquid
    - (b) gaseous
    - (c) solid
    - (d) a solution
65. Ornithology is the study of
    - (a) Snakes
    - (b) Ornaments
    - (c) Precious gems
    - (d) Birds
66. One litre of water is equivalent to how many kilograms?
    - (a) 1.5 kg
    - (b) 1 kg
    - (c) 1.25 kg
    - (d) 90 kg
67. Who is called the 'Nightingale of India'?
    - (a) Mother teresa
    - (b) Vijayalakshmi Pandit
    - (c) Indira Gandhi
    - (d) Sarojini Naidu
68. Who appoints the Judges of International Court of Justice?
    - (a) general Assembly only
    - (b) Security Council only
    - (c) Secretary - General of the UN
    - (d) General Assembly and Security Council
69. Bully is a term associated with
    - (a) Polo
    - (b) Football
    - (c) Hockey
    - (d) Billiards
70. India's first garbage fest 'Kachra Mahotsav 2018' has organized by which state?
    - (a) Madhya Pradesh
    - (b) Chhattisgarh
    - (c) Assam
    - (d) Punjab
71. Which country's team has won the 5th edition of Blind Cricket World Cup 2018?
    - (a) Nepal
    - (b) Bangladesh
    - (c) Sri Lanka
    - (d) India
72. Which country is hosting the 10th Global Forum for Food & Agriculture (GFFA-2018)?
    - (a) France
    - (b) Germany
    - (c) India
    - (d) China
73. Who is the author of the book "The Heartfulness Way"?
    - (a) Nandan Banerjee
    - (b) Chetan Bhagat
    - (c) Sushant Gupta
    - (d) Kamlesh Patel
74. Which of the following vitamins is helpful for coagulation of blood ?
    - (a) C
    - (b) D
    - (c) E
    - (d) K
75. For purifying drinking water, alum is used-
    - (a) for coagulation of mud particles
    - (b) to kill bacteria
    - (c) to remove salts
    - (d) to remove gases

RESPONSE SHEET

1. ⓐⓑⓒⓓ	2. ⓐⓑⓒⓓ	3. ⓐⓑⓒⓓ	4. ⓐⓑⓒⓓ	5. ⓐⓑⓒⓓ
6. ⓐⓑⓒⓓ	7. ⓐⓑⓒⓓ	8. ⓐⓑⓒⓓ	9. ⓐⓑⓒⓓ	10. ⓐⓑⓒⓓ
11. ⓐⓑⓒⓓ	12. ⓐⓑⓒⓓ	13. ⓐⓑⓒⓓ	14. ⓐⓑⓒⓓ	15. ⓐⓑⓒⓓ
16. ⓐⓑⓒⓓ	17. ⓐⓑⓒⓓ	18. ⓐⓑⓒⓓ	19. ⓐⓑⓒⓓ	20. ⓐⓑⓒⓓ
21. ⓐⓑⓒⓓ	22. ⓐⓑⓒⓓ	23. ⓐⓑⓒⓓ	24. ⓐⓑⓒⓓ	25. ⓐⓑⓒⓓ
26. ⓐⓑⓒⓓ	27. ⓐⓑⓒⓓ	28. ⓐⓑⓒⓓ	29. ⓐⓑⓒⓓ	30. ⓐⓑⓒⓓ
31. ⓐⓑⓒⓓ	32. ⓐⓑⓒⓓ	33. ⓐⓑⓒⓓ	34. ⓐⓑⓒⓓ	35. ⓐⓑⓒⓓ
36. ⓐⓑⓒⓓ	37. ⓐⓑⓒⓓ	38. ⓐⓑⓒⓓ	39. ⓐⓑⓒⓓ	40. ⓐⓑⓒⓓ
41. ⓐⓑⓒⓓ	42. ⓐⓑⓒⓓ	43. ⓐⓑⓒⓓ	44. ⓐⓑⓒⓓ	45. ⓐⓑⓒⓓ
46. ⓐⓑⓒⓓ	47. ⓐⓑⓒⓓ	48. ⓐⓑⓒⓓ	49. ⓐⓑⓒⓓ	50. ⓐⓑⓒⓓ
51. ⓐⓑⓒⓓ	52. ⓐⓑⓒⓓ	53. ⓐⓑⓒⓓ	54. ⓐⓑⓒⓓ	55. ⓐⓑⓒⓓ
56. ⓐⓑⓒⓓ	57. ⓐⓑⓒⓓ	58. ⓐⓑⓒⓓ	59. ⓐⓑⓒⓓ	60. ⓐⓑⓒⓓ
61. ⓐⓑⓒⓓ	62. ⓐⓑⓒⓓ	63. ⓐⓑⓒⓓ	64. ⓐⓑⓒⓓ	65. ⓐⓑⓒⓓ
66. ⓐⓑⓒⓓ	67. ⓐⓑⓒⓓ	68. ⓐⓑⓒⓓ	69. ⓐⓑⓒⓓ	70. ⓐⓑⓒⓓ
71. ⓐⓑⓒⓓ	72. ⓐⓑⓒⓓ	73. ⓐⓑⓒⓓ	74. ⓐⓑⓒⓓ	75. ⓐⓑⓒⓓ

HINTS & SOLUTIONS

1. (d) All others are the features of sense organes.

2. (c) Mustard is an oilseed while the rest are foodgrains.

3. (c) 'Large' is an adjective whereas others are noun.

4. (c) The series is $\times 1 + 1^2$, $\times 2 + 2^2$, $\times 3 + 3^2$, $\times 4 + 4^2$....

5. (d) The series is $\times 1 + 7$, $\times 2 - 11$, $\times 3 + 15$....

6. (d) The series is $\times 1 + 1^2$, $\times 2 + 2^2$, $\times 3 + 3^2$, $\times 4 + 4^2$....

7. (c) The series is abc/a<u>a</u>bc/aab<u>b</u>c/a<u>a</u>bbc<u>c</u>/a.

8. (c) Clearly, the first, second and third letters of each term are respectively moved one, two and three steps forward to obtain the corresponding letters of the next term. So, the next term is EJO.

9. (b) Split the word STREAMLING into two groups consisting of equal letters. You get STREA and MLING. Now, reverse both the groups. You get AERTS and GNILM. Now, write each letter of first group two places forward. You get CGTVU. Write each letter of second group one place forward. You get HOJMN. Now, join both the groups without changing the order of letters. You get CGTVUHOJMN.

    Similarly, PERIODICAL is coded as

    PERIODICAL → OIREPLACID → QKTGRMBDJE

10. (a) The colour of sunflower is yellow and yellow is called 'red'. Hence sunflower is red.

11. (d) Clearly, the grandson of Anil's mother is son of Anil and wife of Anil's son is daughter in-law of Anil. Thus, Anil is the father-in-law of the girl.

12. (d)

13. (a) In the afternoon the sun is in the west. Hence the shadow is in the east. Now, east is to the left of Madhuri. So, Madhuri is facing south. Therefore, Manisha, who is face to face with Madhuri, is facing north.

14. (d) Total students
    = [First position of Ganesh + Second position of Rajan]
    $\quad$ – 1
    = [12 + 20] – 1 = 31

15. (b)

$+ \Rightarrow \div$	$- \Rightarrow \times$
$\div \Rightarrow +$	$\times \Rightarrow -$

    $63 \times 24 + 8 \div 4 + 2 - 3 = ?$

    or, $? = 63 - 24 \div 8 + 4 \div 2 \times 3$

    or, $? = 63 - 3 + 2 \times 3$

    or, $? = 66$

16. (c) Unit digit in 7^4 is 1.

    Unit digit in 7^{68} is 1.

    $\therefore$ Unit digit in $7^{71} = 1 \times 7^3 = 3$

    Again, every power of 6 will give unit digit 6.

    $\therefore$ Unit digit in 6^{59} is 6.

    Unit digit in 3^4 is 1.

    $\therefore$ Unit digit in 3^{64} is 1. Unit digit in 3^{65} is 3.

    $\therefore$ Unit digit in $(7^{71} \times 6^{59} \times 3^{65})$

    = Unit digit in $(3 \times 6 \times 3) = 4$.

17. (a) Since the given number is divisible by 5, so 0 or 5 must come in place of \$. But, a number ending with 5 is never divisible by 8. So, 0 will replace \$.

    Now, the number formed by the last three digits is 4*0, which becomes divisible by 8, if * is replaced by 4.

    Hence, digits in place of * and \$ are 4 and 0 respectively.

18. (c) Let the numbers be 7x and 8x.

    $\Rightarrow$ Their HCF = x

    Now, LCM × HCF = Product of Numbers

    i.e. $280 \times x = 56 x^2$

    or $x = 5$

    Hence, the numbers are 35 and 40.

19. (a) Let the ten digit be x. Then, unit's digit = x + 2

    Number = 10x + (x + 2) = 11x + 2;

    Sum of digits = x + (x + 2) = 2x + 2

    $\therefore (11x + 2)(2x + 2) = 144 \Rightarrow 22x^2 + 26x - 140 = 0$

    $\Rightarrow (11x + 35)(x - 2) = 0 \Rightarrow x = 2$

    Hence, required number = 24.

20. (a) Given $A + B = 40 \quad$ ...(i)

    $\qquad C + B = 38 \quad$ ... (ii)

    $\qquad A + C = 42 \quad$ ...(iii)

    (i) + (ii) + (iii) $\Rightarrow A + B + C = 60 \qquad$ ...(iv)

    from (i) and (iv), we get

    C = 20 years

    $\therefore$ B = 18 years and A = 22 years

21. (d) Let he had originally ₹ x. Then

    65% of x + 20% of x + 1305 = x

    0.65x + 0.2 x + 1305 = x

    $\Rightarrow 0.15 x = 1305 \Rightarrow x = ₹ 8700$

    $\therefore$ His total investment = 65% of 8700 + 20% of 8700

    = 85% of 8700 = ₹ 7395

22. (d) C. P. for 50 pencils $= ₹\, 100$

$\therefore$ C. P. for 45 pencils $= \dfrac{100}{50} \times 45 = ₹\, 90$

$=$ S.P. of 45 pencils

$\therefore$ No gain , no loss

23. (c) Shortcut method :

If borrowed amount be $₹\, M$ and it is to be paid in equal instalments, then

$$M = na + \dfrac{ra}{100 \times Y} \times \dfrac{n(n-1)}{2}$$

where $Y = $ no. of instalments per annum

$a = $ annual instalment

Here, $M = 4200, y = 1, r = 10, n = 5, a = ?$

$$4200 = 5a + \dfrac{10a}{100} \times \dfrac{5(5-1)}{2}$$

$\Rightarrow 4200 = a[5+1] \Rightarrow 6a = 4200$

$\Rightarrow a = ₹\, 700$

24. (d) Number of nurses $= \dfrac{7}{12} \times 240 = 140$

25. (d) Let C_1 takes t hrs. Then,

$\because$ Distance is same.

$\therefore\ 30t = 45\left(t - \dfrac{5}{2}\right)$

$\Rightarrow t = \dfrac{15}{2}$ hrs

$\therefore$ Distance $= 30 \times \dfrac{15}{2} = 225$ km

26. (c)	27. (d)	28. (b)	29. (a)	30. (c)
31. (b)	32. (c)	33. (d)	34. (a)	35. (c)
36. (d)	37. (d)	38. (d)	39. (b)	40. (d)
41. (a)	42. (d)	43. (c)	44. (c)	45. (d)
46. (b)	47. (c)	48. (b)	49. (c)	50. (c)
51. (c)	52. (a)	53. (b)	54. (a)	55. (d)
56. (b)	57. (c)	58. (b)	59. (a)	60. (a)
61. (c)	62. (d)	63. (b)	64. (a)	65. (d)
66. (d)	67. (d)	68. (d)	69. (c)	70. (b)
71. (d)	72. (b)	73. (d)	74. (d)	75. (a)

Time : 60 Min. | **Max. Marks : 75**

1. Three of the following four are alike in a certain way and so form a group. Which is the one that **does not** belong to that group?
   - (a) 72
   - (b) 42
   - (c) 152
   - (d) 110

2. Three of the following four are alike in a certain way and so form a group. Which is the one that **does not** belong to that group?
   - (a) Guava
   - (b) Orange
   - (c) Apple
   - (d) Lichi

3. Three of the following four are alike in a certain way and so from a group. Which is the one that **does not** belong to that group?
   - (a) Aluminium
   - (b) Copper
   - (c) Mercury
   - (d) Iron

DIRECTIONS (Qs. 4-5): *In each of the following questions, a number series is given in which one number is wrong. You have to find out that number and have to follow the new series which will be started by that number. By following this, which will be the third number of the new series?*

4. 6   10.5   23   59.5   183   644   2580
   - (a) 183.5
   - (b) 182.5
   - (c) 183
   - (d) 182

5. 2 7   19   43   99   209   431
   - (a) 181
   - (b) 183
   - (c) 87
   - (d) 85

DIRECTION (Q.6): *In each of the following questions a number series is given with one wrong number. Find that wrong number.*

6. 2   3   6   15   45   156.5   630
   - (a) 156.5
   - (b) 45
   - (c) 15
   - (d) 6

7. Which sequence of letters when placed at the blanks one after another will complete the given letter series ?

   b _ b _ bb _ bbb _ bb _ b
   - (a) bbbbba
   - (b) bbaabb
   - (c) ababab
   - (d) aabaab

8. What is the next number in this sequence ?
   1, 3, 8, 19, 42, 89, ?
   - (a) 108
   - (b) 184
   - (c) 167
   - (d) 97

9. In a certain code language GEOPHYSICS is written as IOPDHZRJBT. How is ALTIMETER written in that code'?
   - (a) NHULBFSDQT
   - (b) NIUKBFSDQT
   - (c) NHUKCFSDQT
   - (d) None of these

10. In a certain code BROUGHT is written as SGFVAQN. How is SUPREME written in that code?
    - (a) FNFSRTO
    - (b) RTOSDLD
    - (c) DLDSRTO
    - (d) DLDSTVQ

11. Deepak said to Nitin, "That boy playing with the football is the younger of the two brothers of the daughter of my father's wife." How is the boy playing football related to Deepak?
    - (a) Son
    - (b) Brother
    - (c) Causin
    - (d) Nephew

12. A and B start walking, from a point, in opposite directions. A covers 3 km and B covers 4 km. Then A turns right and walks 4 km while B turns left and walks 3 km. How far is each from the starting point ?
    - (a) 5 km
    - (b) 4 km
    - (c) 10 km
    - (d) 8 km

13. Anuj started walking positioning his back towards the sun. After sometime, he turned left, then turned right and then towards the left again. In which direction is he going now?
    - (a) North or South
    - (b) East or West
    - (c) North or West
    - (d) South or West

14. Sarita is on 11th place from upwards in a group of 45 girls. If we start counting from downwards, what will be her place?
    (a) 36th   (b) 34th
    (c) 35th   (d) Can not be determined
15. Find out the correct answer for the unsolved equation on the basis of the given equations.
    If $6 * 5 = 91$, $8 * 7 = 169$, $10 * 7 = 211$, then $11 * 10 = ?$
    (a) 331   (b) 993
    (c) 678   (d) 845
16. A number is successively divided by 5,6,8; leaving remainders 3, 4, 7 respectively. What will be the remainders if the order of divisors be reversed?
    (a) 7,4,3   (b) 5,3,4
    (c) 2,5,4   (d) 1,5,4
17. The least number which must be subtracted from 6709 to make it exactly divisible by 9 is:
    (a) 2   (b) 3
    (c) 4   (d) 5
18. Find the greatest number that will divide 148, 246 and 623 leaving remainders 4, 6 and 11 respectively.
    (a) 11   (b) 12
    (c) 13   (d) 14
19. Rajan got married 8 years ago. His present age is $\frac{6}{5}$ times his age at the time of his marriage. Rajan's sister was 10 years younger to him at the time of his marriage. The age of Rajan's sister is:
    (a) 32 years   (b) 36 years
    (c) 38 years   (d) 40 years
20. A cricketer whose bowling average is 12.4 runs per wicket takes 5 wickets for 26 runs and thereby decreases his average by 0.4. The number of wickets taken by him till the last match was:
    (a) 64   (b) 72
    (c) 80   (d) 85
21. An Inspector rejects 0.08% of the metres as defective. How many metres will he examine to reject 2 metres?
    (a) 200 m   (b) 250 m
    (c) 250 m   (d) 3000 m
22. A dealer sold a mixer for ₹ 420 at a loss of 12.5%. At what price should he have sold it to gain 12.5%.
    (a) ₹ 620   (b) ₹ 540
    (c) ₹ 650   (d) ₹ 750
23. What will be the ratio of simple interest earned by certain amount at the same rate of interest for 6 years and that for 9 years?
    (a) 1 : 3   (b) 1 : 4
    (c) 2 : 3   (d) Data inadequate
24. If $0.75 : x :: 5 : 8$, then x is equal to:
    (a) 1.12   (b) 1.20
    (c) 1.25   (d) 1.30
25. If a man walks to his office at 3/4 of his usual rate, he reaches office 1/3 of an hour later than usual. What is his usual time to reach office.
    (a) $\frac{1}{2}$ hr   (b) 1 hr
    (c) $\frac{3}{4}$ hr   (d) None of these

26. Micro organism include?
    (a) Bacteria & virus
    (b) Bacteria, virus, microalgae and fungi
    (c) Bacteria, virus, microalgae, fungi and protozoa
    (d) All animals & plants
27. Bacteria cannot survive in a highly salted picked because?
    (a) Bacteria get plasmolysed and are consequently killed
    (b) Salt inhibits reproduction
    (c) The pickel does not contain nutrient necessary for bacteria to survive
    (d) Bacteria do not get enough light for photosynthisis
28. Ampere is the unit of:
    (a) Current electricity   (b) Magnetic field
    (c) Electric charge   (d) Resistence
29. Oxidation is defined as?
    (a) Loss of electrons   (b) Gain of electrons
    (c) Accept protons   (d) Donate protons
30. Citric acid is obtained from?
    (a) Apples   (b) Lemon
    (c) Grapes   (d) Tomato
31. A rolling plan refers to a plan which?
    (a) Does not change its targets every year
    (b) Changes its allocations every year
    (c) Changes its allocations and targets every year
    (d) Changes only its targets every year
32. When the terminal velocity is reached, the acceleration of a body moving through a viscous medium is?
    (a) Zero   (b) Positive
    (c) Negative   (d) None of these
33. The most suitable unit for expressing nuclear radious is
    (a) Micron   (b) Nano meter
    (c) Fermi   (d) Angstrom
34. Decibel is the unit of
    (a) Speed of light   (b) Intensity of sound
    (c) Intensity of heat   (d) None of these
35. Tidal range is quite high?
    (a) In equatorial regions of ocean
    (b) In shallow continental shelves
    (c) In narrow estuaries
    (d) Benzuela current
36. A substance which changes readily into vapour without heating is called ?
    (a) efflorescent   (b) synthetic
    (c) volatile   (d) effervescent
37. Amino acids (proteins) are present in the cell walls of ?
    (a) Gymnosperms   (b) Mosses
    (c) Angiosperms   (d) Bacteria
38. Which of the following rays are the most penetrating ?
    (a) Beta rays   (b) Alpha rays
    (c) Gamma rays   (d) X-rays
39. Bt Cotton is ?
    (a) Cloned plant   (b) Transgenic plant
    (c) Hybrid plant   (d) Mutated plant
40. The type of glass used in making lenses and prisms is ?
    (a) soft glass   (b) pyrex glass
    (c) jena glass   (d) flint glass
41. Food can be preserved when pH of the medium is
    (a) acidic   (b) basic
    (c) neutral   (d) none of these

42. Glass is made of the mixture of
    (a) Quartz and mica   (b) Sand and salt
    (c) Sand and silicates   (d) None of these
43. In an atomic nucleus, neutrons and protons are held together by
    (a) Gravitational forces   (b) Exchange forces
    (c) Coulombic forces   (d) Magnetic forces
44. One fathom is equal to ?
    (a) 6 meters   (b) 6 feet
    (c) 60 feet   (d) 60 meters
45. The gases used in different types of welding would include
    (a) Oxygen and Hydrogen
    (b) Oxygen, Hydrogen, Acetylene and Nitrogen
    (c) Oxygen, Acetylene and Argon
    (d) Oxygen and Acetylene
46. There are rings around which of the following?
    (a) Saturn   (b) Mars
    (c) Jupiter   (d) Uranus
47. Earth quake waves travel fastest in
    (a) Soil   (b) Molten rock
    (c) Water   (d) Flexible rock
48. The removal of top soil by water or wind is called
    (a) Soil wash   (b) Soil erosion
    (c) Soil creep   (d) Silting of soil
49. The gas predominantly responsible for global warning is
    (a) Carbon dioxide   (b) Carbon monoxide
    (c) Nitrous oxide   (d) Nitrogen peroxide
50. The wonder pigment chlorophyll is present in
    (a) Mitochondria   (b) Centrosomes
    (c) Quantosomes   (d) Lysosomes
51. Freezing point of Water
    (a) $0°$ F   (b) $32°$F
    (c) $4°$ F   (d) $4°$ F
52. The Panda belongs to the same family as that of
    (a) Bear   (b) Cat
    (c) Dog   (d) Rabbit
53. Which out of the following organs dies not eliminate waste products from the body ?
    (a) Large intestine   (b) Liver
    (c) Kidney   (d) Skin
54. The volume of which of the following materials decreases when it is heated from $0°C$ to $5°C$?
    (a) Air   (b) Copper
    (c) Water   (d) Mercury
55. If the length of the pendulum is increased by four times, then its period of oscillation will become
    (a) Half   (b) Twice
    (c) Four times   (d) eight times
56. The Ministry of Railways has recently launched which app for freight managers?
    (a) SFOORTI app   (b) SKOORTI app
    (c) SNOORTI app   (d) SMOORTI app
57. Who has won the 2018 Kolkata Open International Invitation Snooker Championship?
    (a) Aditya Mehta   (b) Brijesh Damani
    (c) Alfie Burden   (d) Laxman Rawat
58. The government of India has imposed restriction on use of national flag madeup of which of these materials ahead of Republic Day celebration?
    (a) Plastic   (b) Nylon Fabric
    (c) Cotton   (d) Paper
59. What is the new foreign direct investment (FDI) limit allowed by the Union government in single-brand retail trading and construction development?
    (a) 74%   (b) 49%
    (c) 100%   (d) 26%
60. Which of the following is used in pencils?
    (a) Graphite   (b) Silicon
    (c) Charcoal   (d) Phosphorous
61. Deficiency of iron leads to
    (a) Anorexia   (b) Anaemia
    (c) Polycythemia   (d) Leucopenia
62. Pollination by birds is called
    (a) Autogamy   (b) Ornithophily
    (c) Entomophily   (d) Anemophily
63. The earliest language of the Aryans was
    (a) Sanskrit   (b) Prakrit
    (c) Pali   (d) Persian
64. Lingaraja temple at Bhubaneswar is built, in
    (a) Nagara style   (b) Vesara style
    (c) Dravidian style   (d) Rock - cut
65. Young Bengal Movement was started by
    (a) Alexander Duft   (b) H.V. Derozio
    (c) Jonathan Duncan   (d) Swami Vivekanand
66. Which one of the following types of coal contains a higher percentage of carbon than the rest?
    (a) Bituminous coal   (b) Lignite
    (c) Peat   (d) Anthracite
67. In India, how many States share the coastline?
    (a) 7   (b) 8
    (c) 9   (d) 10
68. Who was the President of the Constituent Assembly?
    (a) Rajendra Prasad   (b) B. R. Ambedkar
    (c) K. M. Munshi   (d) G. V. Mavlankar
69. The decision to conduct Panchayat Elections is taken by which of the following?
    (a) The Central Government
    (b) The State Government
    (c) The District Judge
    (d) The election Commission
70. Which of the following social network had launched emergency alert system which could be useful in natural disasters or other emergencies?
    (a) Orkut   (b) Facebook
    (c) Twitter   (d) Skype
71. Dhanwantari award is conferred to the field :
    (a) Medical Science   (b) Sports
    (c) Indian Philosophy   (d) Agriculture
72. Who is the author of the book 'Harry Potter' and the 'Half-Blood Prince'?
    (a) Mark Twain   (b) J. K. Rowling
    (c) William Shakespeare   (d) Jules Verne
73. Which country is the winner of Davis Cup- 2014?
    (a) Serbia   (b) USA
    (c) Switzerland   (d) Russia
74. At which of the following place Diesel Component Works is established ?
    (a) Jamshedpur   (b) Patiala
    (c) Perambur   (d) Warangal
75. ______ Zone is the largest in Indian Railways ?
    (a) Central Railway   (b) Northern Railway
    (c) Eastern Railway   (d) Western Railway

RESPONSE SHEET

1. ⓐⓑⓒⓓ	2. ⓐⓑⓒⓓ	3. ⓐⓑⓒⓓ	4. ⓐⓑⓒⓓ	5. ⓐⓑⓒⓓ
6. ⓐⓑⓒⓓ	7. ⓐⓑⓒⓓ	8. ⓐⓑⓒⓓ	9. ⓐⓑⓒⓓ	10. ⓐⓑⓒⓓ
11. ⓐⓑⓒⓓ	12. ⓐⓑⓒⓓ	13. ⓐⓑⓒⓓ	14. ⓐⓑⓒⓓ	15. ⓐⓑⓒⓓ
16. ⓐⓑⓒⓓ	17. ⓐⓑⓒⓓ	18. ⓐⓑⓒⓓ	19. ⓐⓑⓒⓓ	20. ⓐⓑⓒⓓ
21. ⓐⓑⓒⓓ	22. ⓐⓑⓒⓓ	23. ⓐⓑⓒⓓ	24. ⓐⓑⓒⓓ	25. ⓐⓑⓒⓓ
26. ⓐⓑⓒⓓ	27. ⓐⓑⓒⓓ	28. ⓐⓑⓒⓓ	29. ⓐⓑⓒⓓ	30. ⓐⓑⓒⓓ
31. ⓐⓑⓒⓓ	32. ⓐⓑⓒⓓ	33. ⓐⓑⓒⓓ	34. ⓐⓑⓒⓓ	35. ⓐⓑⓒⓓ
36. ⓐⓑⓒⓓ	37. ⓐⓑⓒⓓ	38. ⓐⓑⓒⓓ	39. ⓐⓑⓒⓓ	40. ⓐⓑⓒⓓ
41. ⓐⓑⓒⓓ	42. ⓐⓑⓒⓓ	43. ⓐⓑⓒⓓ	44. ⓐⓑⓒⓓ	45. ⓐⓑⓒⓓ
46. ⓐⓑⓒⓓ	47. ⓐⓑⓒⓓ	48. ⓐⓑⓒⓓ	49. ⓐⓑⓒⓓ	50. ⓐⓑⓒⓓ
51. ⓐⓑⓒⓓ	52. ⓐⓑⓒⓓ	53. ⓐⓑⓒⓓ	54. ⓐⓑⓒⓓ	55. ⓐⓑⓒⓓ
56. ⓐⓑⓒⓓ	57. ⓐⓑⓒⓓ	58. ⓐⓑⓒⓓ	59. ⓐⓑⓒⓓ	60. ⓐⓑⓒⓓ
61. ⓐⓑⓒⓓ	62. ⓐⓑⓒⓓ	63. ⓐⓑⓒⓓ	64. ⓐⓑⓒⓓ	65. ⓐⓑⓒⓓ
66. ⓐⓑⓒⓓ	67. ⓐⓑⓒⓓ	68. ⓐⓑⓒⓓ	69. ⓐⓑⓒⓓ	70. ⓐⓑⓒⓓ
71. ⓐⓑⓒⓓ	72. ⓐⓑⓒⓓ	73. ⓐⓑⓒⓓ	74. ⓐⓑⓒⓓ	75. ⓐⓑⓒⓓ

HINTS & SOLUTIONS

1. (c) $72 = 9^2 - 9$
$42 = 7^2 - 7$
$152 = 12^2 + 8$
$110 = 11^2 - 11$
$156 = 13^2 - 13$
Except 152, others show the trend $x^2 - x$.

2. (d) Lichi has only one seed inside whereas others have many seeds.

3. (c) All others are found in solid state while mercury is found in liquid state.

4. (a) The series is $\times 1.5 + 1.5, \times 2 + 2, \times 2.5 + 2.5, \times 3 + 3 \ldots$

5. (b) The series is $\times 2 + 3, \times 2 + 5, \times 2 + 7, \times 2 + 9 \ldots$

6. (a) The series is $\times 1.5, \times 2, \times 2.5, \times 3$ and so on.

7. (c) The series is b<u>ab</u>b/bb<u>ab</u>/bbb<u>a</u>/bb<u>bb</u>.
Thus, in each sequence, 'a' moves one step forward and 'b' takes its place and finally in the fourth sequence, it is eliminated.

8. (b) Each of the numbers is doubled and 1, 2, 3, 4, 5, 6 is added in turn, so $89 \times 2 + 6 = 184$.

9. (d) Divide the word into two halves. Now, reverse the order of the letters of the first half and replace odd positioned letters with one letter forward and even positioned letter with one letter backward as in English alphabet.

   For the second half letters, the odd-positioned letters are coded as one letter forward and even-positioned letters are coded as one letter backward'as in English alphabet.

10. (c) Here the given word is BROUGHT. Reversing the order of the letters, it becomes THGUORB. Now, write each letter one place backward except the middle letter (write middle letter one place forward). It becomes SGFVNQA.
Now, reverse the order of the last three letters and it becomes SGFVAQN.
Similarly,
SUPREME $\rightarrow$ EMERPUS $\rightarrow$ DLDSOTR $\rightarrow$ DLDSRTO

11. (b) Father's wife — Mother; Mother's daughter — Sister; Sister's younger brother — His brother. So, the boy is Deepak's brother.

12. (a) Here, O is the starting point.

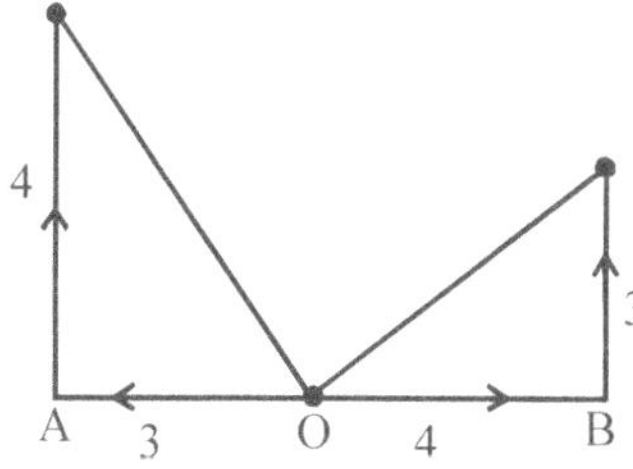

Both A and B are $\sqrt{3^2 + 4^2}$ = 5 km from the starting point.

13. (a) Clearly, there are two possible movements of Anuj as shown below:

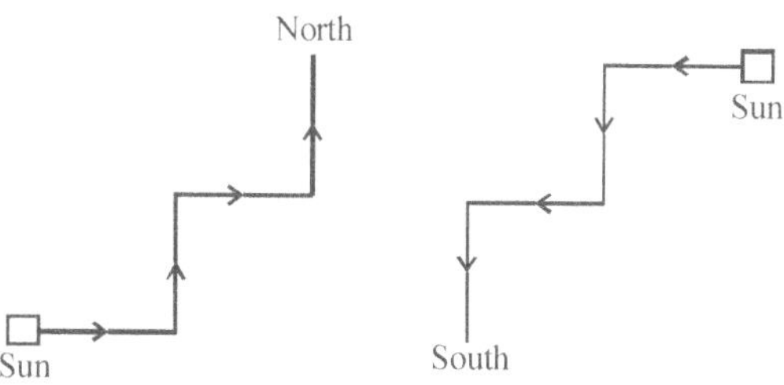

14. (c) Sarita's place from downwards
$$= \left[\begin{array}{c} \text{Total} \\ \text{girls} \end{array} - \begin{array}{c} \text{Sarita's place} \\ \text{from upwards} \end{array} \right] + 1 = [45 - 11] + 1 = 35\text{th}$$

15. (a) $6 \times 5 = 30, 30 \times 3 + 1 = 91, 8 \times 7 = 56, 56 \times 3 + 1 = 169, 10 \times 7 = 70, 70 \times 3 + 1 = 211$
Similarly $11 \times 10 = 110, 110 \times 3 + 1 = 331$

16. (d) Complete remainder $= d_1 d_2 r_3 + d_1 r_2 + r_1$
$= 5 \times 6 \times 7 + 5 \times 4 + 3 = 233$.
Dividing 233, by reversing the divisors i.e. by 8, 6, 5; respective remainders are 1, 5, 4.

17. (c) On dividing 6709 by 9, we get remainder $= 4$.
$\therefore$ Required number to be subtracted $= 4$.

18. (b) Required number
$= $ H.C.F of $(148 - 4), (246 - 6)$ and $(623 - 11)$
$= $ H.C.F of 144, 240 and 612 $= 12$

19. (c) Let Rajan's present age be x years. Then, his age at the time of marriage $= (x - 8)$ years.

   $$\therefore \quad x = \frac{6}{5}(x - 8) \Rightarrow 5x = 6x - 48 \Rightarrow x = 48.$$

   Rajan's sister's age at the time of his marriage
   $= (x - 8) - 10 = (x - 18) = 30$ years.
   $\therefore$ Rajan's sister's present age $= (30 + 8)$ years
   $= 38$ years.

20. (d) Let the number of wickets taken till the last match be x. Then,

   $$\frac{12.4x + 26}{x + 5} = 12 \Rightarrow 12.4x + 26 = 12x + 60$$

   $$\Rightarrow 0.4x = 34 \Rightarrow x = \frac{34}{0.4} = \frac{340}{4} = 85.$$

21. (c) Let the inspector examined x metres, then 0.08% of $x = 2$

   $$\Rightarrow \frac{x \times 0.08}{100} = 2 \text{ or } x = \frac{200}{0.08} = 2500 \text{ metres}$$

22. (b) $(100 - \text{loss}) : S_1 :: (100 + \text{gain}) : S_2$
$\therefore (100 - 12.5) : 420 :: (100 + 12.5) : S_2$
$87.5 : 420 :: 112.5 : S_2$
$\Rightarrow 87.5 \times S_2 = 420 \times 112.5$
$$\Rightarrow S_2 = \frac{420 \times 1125}{875} = 540$$

23. (c) Let the principal be P and rate of interest be R%.

$$\therefore \text{ Required ratio} = \left[\frac{\left(\dfrac{P \times R \times 6}{100}\right)}{\left(\dfrac{P \times R \times 9}{100}\right)}\right] = \frac{6PR}{9PR} = \frac{6}{9} = 2:3.$$

24. (b) $(x \times 5) = (0.75 \times 8) \Rightarrow x = \dfrac{6}{5} = 1.20.$

25. (b) If new speed is $\dfrac{a}{b}$ of original speed, then

$$\text{usual time} \times \left(\frac{b}{a} - 1\right) = \text{change in time}$$

$$\therefore \text{ usual time} \times \left(\frac{4}{3} - 1\right) = \frac{1}{3}$$

$$\Rightarrow \text{usual time} = \frac{1}{3} \times 3 = 1 \text{ hr}$$

26. (c) 27. (a) 28. (a) 29. (a) 30. (b) 31. (c)

32. (a) 33. (c) 34. (b) 35. (d) 36. (c) 37. (d)
38. (c) 39. (b) 40. (d) 41. (a) 42. (c) 43. (b)
44. (b) 45. (d) 46. (a) 47. (c) 48. (b) 49. (a)
50. (c) 51. (b) 52. (a) 53. (a) 54. (c) 55. (b)
56. (a) 57. (a) 58. (a) 59. (c) 60. (a) 61. (b)
62. (b) 63. (a) 64. (a)

65. (b) Young Bengal Movement was started by H.V. Derozio.
66. (d) Anthracite is a dense, shiny coal that has a high carbon content. Very little volatile matter is present in it. It gives a clean flame while burning.
67. (c) 9 states of India shares the coastline.
68. (a)
69. (b) The decision to conduct Panchayat elections is taken by the State Government.
70. (c) Twitter launched a system for emergency alerts which can help spread critical information when other lines of communications are down. The alerts could be useful in natural disasters or other emergencies when traditional channel may be overloaded or unavailable.
71. (a) 72. (a)
73. (c) Switzerland defeated France by 3-1 to win Davis Cup- 2014.
74. (b) 75. (c)

PRACTICE SET

Time : 60 Min.　　　　　　　　　　　　　　　　　　　　　　　　**Max. Marks : 75**

1. Three of the following four are alike in a certain way and so form a group. Which is the one that **does not** belong to that group?
   (a) 143　　　　　　(b) 63
   (c) 257　　　　　　(d) 15

2. Three of the following four are alike in a certain way and so form a group. Which is the one that does not belong to that group?
   (a) May　　　　　　(b) December
   (c) July　　　　　　(d) January

3. Three of the following four are alike in a certain way and so form a group. Which his the one that **does not** belong to that group?
   (a) Jackal　　　　　(b) Cheetah
   (c) Tiger　　　　　　(d) Dog

DIRECTIONS (Qs. 4-6): *In each of the following questions a number series is given with one wrong number. Find that wrong number.*

4. 36　20　12　8　6　5.5　4.5
   (a) 5.5　　(b) 6　　(c) 12　　(d) 20

5. 1　3　9　31　128　651　3913
   (a) 651　　(b) 128　　(c) 31　　(d) 9

6. 2　3　10　40　172　885　5346
   (a) 3　　(b) 855　　(c) 40　　(d) 172

7. Which is the number that comes next in this sequence ?
   5, 16, 51, 158, ...
   (a) 1452　(b) 483　　(c) 481　　(d) 1454

8. Which one of the numbers will complete the series ?
   8, 13, 10, 15, 12, 17, 14 ... ?
   (a) 19　　(b) 22　　(c) 16　　(d) 20

9. In a certain code 'CLOUD' is written as 'GTRKF'. How is SIGHT written in that code?

   (a) WGJHV　　　　　(b) UGHHT
   (c) UHJFW　　　　　(d) WFJGV

10. In a certain code CHAIR is written as # * • ÷ % and HIDE is written as * ÷ + $. How is DEAR written in that code?
    (a) $ + • % 2　　　　　(b) + $ ÷ %
    (c) $ + % ÷ 4　　　　(d) None of these

11. Introducing Rajesh, Neha said, "His brother's father is the only son of my grand father". How Neha is related to Rajesh?
    (a) Sister　　　　　(b) Daughter
    (c) Mother　　　　　(d) Niece

12. If South-east becomes North, North-east becomes West and so on, what will West become?
    (a) North-east　　　(b) North-west
    (c) South-east　　　(d) South-west

13. P, Q, R and S are playing a game of carrom. P, R and S, Q are partners. S is to the right of R who is facing west. Then, Q is facing
    (a) North　　　　　(b) South
    (c) East　　　　　　(d) West

14. Rakesh is on 9th position from upwards and on 38th position from downwards in a class. How many students are in class?
    (a) 47　　(b) 45　　(c) 46　　(d) 48

15. If L stands for +, M stands for –, N stands for ×, P stands for ÷, then 14 N 10 L 42 P 2 M 8 = ?
    (a) 153　　　　　　(b) 216
    (c) 248　　　　　　(d) 251

16. A boy multiplied a certain number x by 13. He found that the resulting product consisted of all nines entirely. Find the smallest value of x.
    (a) 76913　　　　　(b) 76933
    (c) 76923　　　　　(d) 75933

17. When 7^{84} is divided by 342, what is the remainder?

    (a) 0   (b) 1

    (c) 49   (d) 341

18. Three wheels can complete respectively 60, 36, 24 revolutions per minute. There is a red spot on each wheel that touches the ground at time zero. After how much time, all these spots will simultaneously touch the ground again?

    (a) 5/2 seconds   (b) 5/3 seconds

    (c) 5 seconds   (d) 7.5 seconds

19. If a number is decreased by 4 and divided by 6, the result is 8. What would be the result if 2 is subtracted from the number and then it is divided by 5?

    (a) $9\frac{2}{3}$ (b) 10   (c) $10\frac{1}{5}$ (d) $11\frac{1}{5}$

20. The average age of P and Q is 20 years. If R were to replace P, the average would be 19 and if R were to replace Q, the average would be 21. What are the age of P, Q and R ?

    (a) 22, 18, 20   (b) 20, 16, 22

    (c) 26, 20, 22   (d) 28, 16, 22

21. If 90% of A = 30% of B and B = $2x$% of A, then the value of x.

    (a) 450   (b) 400

    (c) 220   (d) 250

22. A fruitseller sells 8 oranges at a cost price of 9. The profit per cent is

    (a) $12\frac{1}{2}$ (b) $11\frac{1}{9}$ (c) $5\frac{15}{17}$ (d) $8\frac{2}{3}$

23. A certain amount earns simple interest of ₹ 1750 after 7 years Had the interest been 2% more, how much more interest would it have earned?

    (a) ₹ 35   (b) ₹ 245

    (c) ₹ 350   (d) Cannot be determined

24. A sum of money is to be divided among A, B and C in the ratio 2 : 3 : 7. If the total share of A and B together is ₹ 1,500 less than C, What is A's share in it?

    (a) ₹ 1,000   (b) ₹ 1,500

    (c) ₹ 2,000   (d) Data insufficient

25. An aeroplane flies along the four sides of a square at the speeds of 200, 400, 600 and 800 km/h. Find the average speed of the plane around the field.

    (a) 384 km/h   (b) 370 km/h

    (c) 368 km/h   (d) None of these

26. Usually the North Pole of a magnetic needle is painted _______.

    (a) red   (b) blue

    (c) black   (d) green

27. Which of the following is NOT an element of weather?

    (a) Humidity   (b) Temperature

    (c) Soil   (d) Rain

28. Red worms grind their food with the help of _______.

    (a) gizzard   (b) stomach

    (c) teeth   (d) tentacles

29. Which of the following is in liquid form at room temperature?

    (a) Lithium   (b) Sodium

    (c) Francium   (d) Cerium

30. Water vapours present in the atmosphere is called

    (a) humidity   (b) precipitation

    (c) climate   (d) rain fall

31. The water fit for drinking is called _______.

    (a) rain water   (b) potable water

    (c) river water   (d) ground water

32. Birds are adapted to fly because of ___________.

    (a) streamlined body   (b) light bones

    (c) feathers and wings   (d) all of these

33. Heavy water is

    (a) deuterium oxide   (b) PH7

    (c) rain water   (d) tritium oxide

34. Sodium metal is kept under

    (a) petrol   (b) alcohol

    (c) water   (d) kerosene

35. Oceans and seas cover _______ of the earth.

    (a) one third   (b) two third

    (c) half   (d) three fourth

36. Standard (SI) unit of length is _____.

    (a) centimetre   (b) metre

    (c) inches   (d) foot

37. Which of the following is a physical change?

    (a) Rusting of Iron   (b) Heating of Iron

    (c) Burning of Wood   (d) Ripening of a fruit.

38. Formation of gas bubbles is _________.

    (a) a physical change   (b) a physical property

    (c) a chemical change   (d) a chemical property

39. Motion of wheel of a car is an example of _________.

    (a) circular motion   (b) translatory motion

    (c) rectilinear motion   (d) curvilinear motion

40. Turning milk into curd is a

    (a) physical change   (b) physical property

    (c) chemical change   (d) chemical property

41. Which one of the following in NOT a predator?

    (a) Eagle   (b) Bear

    (c) Antelope   (d) Lion

42. Sea animals like dolphins and whales breathe through _______.

    (a) nose   (b) blow holes

    (c) gills   (d) fins

43. Who among the following invented the small pox vaccine?

    (a) Robert Koch   (b) Edward Jenner

    (c) Robert Hooke   (d) Louis Pasteur

44. Which of the following is not an isotope of hydrogen?

    (a) Tritium   (b) Deuterium

    (c) Protium   (d) Yttrium

45. Heavy water is

    (a) deuterium oxide   (b) PH7

    (c) rain water   (d) tritium oxide

46. Hemoglobin is an important component of

    (a) RBC   (b) WBC

    (c) Platletes   (d) CytopLASM

47. At what temperature are the temperature on Celsius and Fahrenheit scales equal?
    (a) 273° Celsius   (b) –273° Celsius
    (c) –40° Celsius   (d) 40° Celsius
48. Which one of the following is a water soluble vitamin?
    (a) Vitamin A   (b) Vitamin C
    (c) Vitamin D   (d) Vitamin K
49. Fire in the diesel engine is produces by which of the following?
    (a) Compression   (b) Spark plug
    (c) Friction   (d) Self starter
50. The stone formed in human kidney consist mostly of
    (a) calcium oxalate   (b) sodium oxalate
    (c) sodium acetate   (d) calcium
51. Galvanometer can be converted into a voltmeter by using
    (a) Low resistance in series (b) High resistance in series
    (c) Low resistance in parallel(d) High resistance in parallel
52. Which among the following is the best conductor of electricity?
    (a) Gold   (b) Lead
    (c) Silver   (d) Copper
53. Select the one which is not a mixture
    (a) Air   (b) Gasoline
    (c) LPG   (d) Distilled water
54. At what temperature a body will not radiate any heat energy?
    (a) 0° C   (b) 273° C
    (c) 100° C   (d) -273° C
55. Silk is produced by
    (a) Egg of silkworm   (b) Pupa of silkworm
    (c) Larva of silkworm   (d) Insect itself
56. PH of blood remains constant due to
    (a) blood pressure   (b) buffer action
    (c) perspiration   (d) respiration
57. The part of the brain in control of voluntary muscles is
    (a) cerebellum   (b) medulla oblongata
    (c) pons   (d) cerebrum
58. Colour vision is made possible by the cells in the retina called
    (a) rods   (b) cones
    (c) fovea   (d) blind spot
59. The hormone that contains iodine is
    (a) Prolactin   (b) Vasopressin
    (c) Thyroxine   (d) Adrenalin
60. Name the 2018 theme country for the 42nd Kolkata Book Fair?
    (a) Australia   (b) Brazil
    (c) Italy   (d) France
61. he Sports Minister launched the three-stroke Khelo India logo recently in New Delhi at the Nehru Stadium. The logo has been designed by _________
    (a) Omnicon Group   (b) Ogilvy India
    (c) Publicis Group   (d) Interpublic Group
62. World Champion Saksham Yadav who died recently belonged to which sports?
    (a) Mixed Martial Arts   (b) Boxing
    (c) Powerlifting   (d) Wrestling

63. The concept of 'Gotra' become established in which period?
    (a) Rig Vedic age   (b) Later Vedic age
    (c) Pre Mauryan Period   (d) Mauryan period
64. Sultan of Delhi who is reputed to have built the biggest network of canals in India was:
    (a) Iltutmish   (b) Ghiyasuddin Tughlaq
    (c) Firoz Shah Tughlaq   (d) Sikandar Lodi
65. Vasco da Gama discovered the sea-route to India in which one of the following years ?
    (a) A.D. 1498   (b) A.D. 1492
    (c) A.D. 1494   (d) A.D. 1453
66. Who was the propounder of the Drain Theory in India ?
    (a) R.C. Dutta   (b) Henry Cotton
    (c) S.N. Banerjee   (d) Dadabai Naoroji
67. The earth's rotation does not cause
    (a) deflection of ocean currents
    (b) phases of the moon
    (c) tides
    (d) difference in time between two meridians
68. Where is the Nanda Devi peak located ?
    (a) Himachal Pradesh   (b) Uttarakhand
    (c) Sikkim   (d) Nepal
69. The Gulf of Mannar is situated along the coast of
    (a) Tamil Nadu   (b) Kerala
    (c) Karnataka   (d) Andhra Pradesh
70. The 73rd Amendment of the Indian Constitution deals with
    (a) Panchayati Raj
    (b) Compulsory Primary Education
    (c) Nagar Palikas
    (d) Minimum Age of Marriage
71. Panchayati Raj in India is laid down under:
    (a) Fundamental Rights
    (b) Directive Principle of state
    (c) Fundamental Duties
    (d) Election Commission Act Policy
72. The term mixed economy denoted existence of both
    (a) rural and urban sectors
    (b) private and public sector
    (c) heavy and small industry
    (d) developed and underdeveloped sectors.
73. Which of the following countries has imposed ban on Skype, WhatsApp and Viber recently?
    (a) China   (b) Pakistan
    (c) Sri Lanka   (d) France
74. Which of the following books was written by Gandhiji ?
    (a) Discovery of India (b) My Experience with Truth
    (c) India wins Freedom (d) Freedom at Midnight
75. After Kolkata, which city in India started a metro railway?
    (a) New Delhi   (b) Mumbai
    (c) Bengaluru   (d) Hyderabad

RESPONSE SHEET

1. ⓐⓑⓒⓓ	2. ⓐⓑⓒⓓ	3. ⓐⓑⓒⓓ	4. ⓐⓑⓒⓓ	5. ⓐⓑⓒⓓ
6. ⓐⓑⓒⓓ	7. ⓐⓑⓒⓓ	8. ⓐⓑⓒⓓ	9. ⓐⓑⓒⓓ	10. ⓐⓑⓒⓓ
11. ⓐⓑⓒⓓ	12. ⓐⓑⓒⓓ	13. ⓐⓑⓒⓓ	14. ⓐⓑⓒⓓ	15. ⓐⓑⓒⓓ
16. ⓐⓑⓒⓓ	17. ⓐⓑⓒⓓ	18. ⓐⓑⓒⓓ	19. ⓐⓑⓒⓓ	20. ⓐⓑⓒⓓ
21. ⓐⓑⓒⓓ	22. ⓐⓑⓒⓓ	23. ⓐⓑⓒⓓ	24. ⓐⓑⓒⓓ	25. ⓐⓑⓒⓓ
26. ⓐⓑⓒⓓ	27. ⓐⓑⓒⓓ	28. ⓐⓑⓒⓓ	29. ⓐⓑⓒⓓ	30. ⓐⓑⓒⓓ
31. ⓐⓑⓒⓓ	32. ⓐⓑⓒⓓ	33. ⓐⓑⓒⓓ	34. ⓐⓑⓒⓓ	35. ⓐⓑⓒⓓ
36. ⓐⓑⓒⓓ	37. ⓐⓑⓒⓓ	38. ⓐⓑⓒⓓ	39. ⓐⓑⓒⓓ	40. ⓐⓑⓒⓓ
41. ⓐⓑⓒⓓ	42. ⓐⓑⓒⓓ	43. ⓐⓑⓒⓓ	44. ⓐⓑⓒⓓ	45. ⓐⓑⓒⓓ
46. ⓐⓑⓒⓓ	47. ⓐⓑⓒⓓ	48. ⓐⓑⓒⓓ	49. ⓐⓑⓒⓓ	50. ⓐⓑⓒⓓ
51. ⓐⓑⓒⓓ	52. ⓐⓑⓒⓓ	53. ⓐⓑⓒⓓ	54. ⓐⓑⓒⓓ	55. ⓐⓑⓒⓓ
56. ⓐⓑⓒⓓ	57. ⓐⓑⓒⓓ	58. ⓐⓑⓒⓓ	59. ⓐⓑⓒⓓ	60. ⓐⓑⓒⓓ
61. ⓐⓑⓒⓓ	62. ⓐⓑⓒⓓ	63. ⓐⓑⓒⓓ	64. ⓐⓑⓒⓓ	65. ⓐⓑⓒⓓ
66. ⓐⓑⓒⓓ	67. ⓐⓑⓒⓓ	68. ⓐⓑⓒⓓ	69. ⓐⓑⓒⓓ	70. ⓐⓑⓒⓓ
71. ⓐⓑⓒⓓ	72. ⓐⓑⓒⓓ	73. ⓐⓑⓒⓓ	74. ⓐⓑⓒⓓ	75. ⓐⓑⓒⓓ

HINTS & SOLUTIONS

1. (c) The given numbers can be written as follows:
   $143 = 12^2 - 1$; $63 = 8^2 - 1$; $195 = 14^2 - 1$;
   $15 = 4^2 - 1$
   But, $257 = 16^2 + 1$
   Obviously, except 257, others can be written in the form $x^2 - 1$.

2. (a) Except it others are either followed or preceded by a month of 31 days.

3. (d) Others are wild animals.

4. (a) The series is $-16, -8, -4, -2, -1, 0.5$, and so on.

5. (b) The series is $\times 1 + 2, \times 2 + 3, \times 3 + 4$, and so on.

6. (c) The series is $\times 1 + 1^2, \times 2 + 2^2, \times 3 + 3^2$ and so on.

7. (c) $16 = 5 \times 3 + 1$, $51 = 16 \times 3 + 3$,
   $158 = 51 \times 3 + 5$
   $\therefore$ Next term $= 158 \times 3 + 7 = 481$

8. (a) Second term is greater than first term by 5, while the third term is less than the second term by 3. The same order is repeated.

9. (a) Here, each letter of the word CLOUD is written as three letters forward and one letter backward alternately. Following this CLOUD becomes FKRTG. After that, reverse the order of the result obtained in the previous operation. Thus, FKRTG becomes GTRKF.

   Similarly, SIGHT will change its form as follows:

   SIGHT $\rightarrow$ VHJGW $\rightarrow$ WGJHV

10. (d)

Letter:	#	*	•	÷	%	+	$
Code:	C	H	A	I	R	D	E

    Therefore, code for DEAR = + $ • %

11. (a) Father of Rajesh's brother is the father of Rajesh. Rajesh's father is the only son of Neha's grandfather. Hence, Rajesh's father is Neha's father. So, Neha is the sister of Rajesh.

12. (c) Here, each direction moves $90° + 45° = 135°$

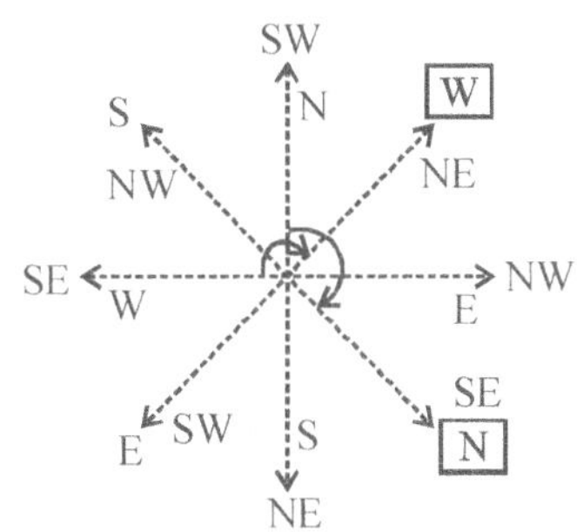

13. (a) Here, R faces towards West. S is to the right of R. So, S is facing towards South. Thus, Q who is the partner of S, will face towards North.

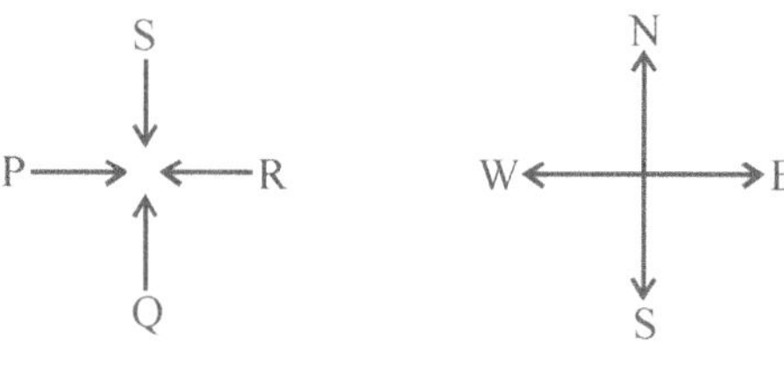

14. (c) Total students
    $=$ [Rakesh's position from upwards + Rakesh's position from downwards] -1
    $= [9 + 38] - 1 = 46$

15. (a) Using the proper signs, we get
    Given expression $= 14 \times 10 + 42 \div 2 - 8$
    $= 140 + 21 - 8$
    $= 153$

16. (c) By actual division, we find that 999999 is exactly divisible by 13. The quotient 76923 is the required number.

17. (b) $7^{84}/342 = (7^3)^{28}/(7^3 - 1)$
    $$= ((7^3)^{28} - 1 + 1)/(7^3 - 1)$$
    $$= ((7^3)^{28} - 1)/(7^3 - 1) + 1/(7^3 - 1)$$
    $((7^3)^{28} - 1) / (7^3 - 1)$ is always divisible as it is in the form of $(x^n - y^n)/(x - y)$, hence the remainder is 1.

18. (c) A makes 1 rev. per sec
    B makes $\dfrac{6}{10}$ rev per sec
    C makes $\dfrac{4}{10}$ rev. per sec

    In other words A, B and C take $1, \dfrac{5}{3} \& \dfrac{5}{2}$ seconds to complete one revolution.

    L.C.M of $1, \dfrac{5}{3} \& \dfrac{5}{2} = \dfrac{\text{L.C.M. of } 1,5,5}{\text{H.C.F. of } 1,3,2} = 5$

    Hence, after every 5 seconds the red spots on all the three wheels touch the ground

19. (b) Let the number be x. Then,
    $$\frac{x - 4}{6} = 8 \Rightarrow x - 4 = 48 \Rightarrow x = 52$$
    $$\therefore \frac{x - 2}{5} = \frac{52 - 2}{5} = \frac{50}{5} = 10.$$

20. (a) Let the ages of P, Q and R are a, b, c
    $\Rightarrow$ $a + b = 40$, $b + c = 38$ and $c + a = 42$
    $\Rightarrow$ $a + b + c = \dfrac{40 + 38 + 42}{2} = 60$
    $\Rightarrow$ $a = 22$, $b = 18$ and $c = 20$

21. (d) $\dfrac{A \times 90}{100} = \dfrac{B \times 30}{100}$

$\Rightarrow \quad 3A = B$

$\Rightarrow \quad 3A = A \times \dfrac{2x}{100}$

$\Rightarrow \quad x = 150$

22. (a) Let C.P. of one orange = Re 1

Then C.P. of 8 oranges = ₹ 8

S.P of 8 oranges = ₹ 9

$\therefore$ Gain % $= \dfrac{9-8}{8} \times 100 = \dfrac{100}{8} = 12\dfrac{1}{2}\%$

23. (d) We need to know the S.I., principal and time to find the rate. Since the principal is not given, so data is inadequate.

24. (b) Let A's share = ₹ 2x, B's share = ₹ 3x and C's share = ₹ 7x

Now, $7x - (2x + 3x) = 1500 \Rightarrow x = 750$

$\therefore$ A's share = ₹ 2x = ₹ 1500

25. (a) Let each side of the square be x km and let the average speed of the plane around the field be y km/h. Then,

$\dfrac{x}{200} + \dfrac{x}{400} + \dfrac{x}{600} + \dfrac{x}{800} = \dfrac{4x}{y}$

$\Rightarrow \dfrac{25x}{2400} = \dfrac{4x}{y} \Rightarrow y = \left(\dfrac{2400 \times 4}{25}\right) = 384.$

$\therefore$ Average speed = 384 km/h.

26.	(a)	27.	(c)	28.	(a)	29.	(c)	30.	(a)
31.	(b)	32.	(d)	33.	(a)	34.	(d)	35.	(b)
36.	(b)	37.	(b)	38.	(c)	39.	(d)	40.	(c)
41.	(c)	42.	(b)	43.	(b)	44.	(d)	45.	(a)
46.	(a)	47.	(c)	48.	(b)	49.	(a)	50.	(a)
51.	(b)	52.	(c)	53.	(d)	54.	(d)	55.	(c)
56.	(b)	57.	(d)	58.	(b)	59.	(c)	60.	(d)
61.	(b)	62.	(c)	63.	(b)				

64. (c) Firoz Shah Tughlaq built and repaired a large number of canals.

65. (a) Vasco da Gama reached Calicut in India on May 27, 1498.

66. (d) Dadabhai Naoroji was the propounder of the 'Drain Theory' in India.

67. (d)

68. (b) Nanda Devi Peak (7817 m) is situated in Uttarakhand.

69. (a) The Gulf of Mannar is a shallow bay situated between south eastern tip of India and Sri Lanka draining into the gulf. It has 3600 species of flora and fauna.

70. (a) The 73rd Amendment of the Indian constitution deals with Panchayati Raj

71. (b) Panchayati Raj in India is laid down under Directive Principles of state.

72. (b) The term mixed economy denotes the existence of both private and public sectors.

73. (c)

74. (b)   75. (a)

19

PRACTICE SET

Time : 60 Min.　　　　　　　　　　　　　　　　　　　　　**Max. Marks : 75**

---

1. Three of the following four are alike in a certain way and so form a group. Which is the that does not belong to that group?
   (a) Cheese　　　　　(b) Butter
   (c) Milk　　　　　　(d) Curd

2. Three of the following four are alike in a certain way and so form a group. Which is the one that does not belong to that group?
   (a) 131　　　　　　(b) 151
   (c) 181　　　　　　(d) 161

3. Three of the following four are alike in a certain way and so form a group. Which is the one that does not belong to that group?
   (a) Anxiety　　　　(b) Anger
   (c) Feeling　　　　(d) Joy

DIRECTIONS (QS. 4-6): *In the following number series, a wrong number is given. Find out that wrong number.*

4. 5　8　16　26　50　98　194
   (a) 8　　(b) 26　　(c) 50　　(d) 16

5. 2　11　38　197　1172　8227　65806
   (a) 11　　(b) 38　　(c) 197　　(d) 1172

6. 16　19　21　30　46　71　107
   (a) 19　　(b) 21　　(c) 30　　(d) 46

DIRECTION: *Find the missing term in following series*

7. 3, 15, 4, 16, 5, 17, 6, ?, 7
   (a) 12　　(b) 18　　(c) 15　　(d) 13

8. Find the missing term in the following series.
   240, ... 120, 40, 10, 2
   (a) 480　　(b) 240　　(c) 220　　(d) 120

9. In a code language "1357" means "We are very happy", "2639" means "They are extremely lucky", and "794" means "Happy and lucky". Which digit in that code language stands for "very"?
   (a) 1　　　　　　(b) 5
   (c) 7　　　　　　(d) Data inadequate

10. In a certain code language 'CREATIVE' is written as 'BDSBFUJS'. How is 'TRIANGLE' written in that code?
    (a) BSHSFHKM　　　(b) BHSSMHHF
    (c) BSSHFMKH　　　(d) BHSSFKHM

11. A man said to a woman, "Your brother's only sister is my mother." What is the relation of the woman with the maternal grandmother of that man?
    (a) Mother　　　　(b) Sister
    (c) Niece　　　　　(d) Daughter

12. If A is to the south of B and C is to the east of B, in what direction is A with respect to C?
    (a) North-east　　(b) North- west
    (c) South-east　　(d) South-west

13. One morning after sunrise, Gopal was facing a pole. The shadow of the pole fell exactly to his right. Which direction was he facing?
    (a) South　　　　(b) East
    (c) West　　　　　(d) Data inadequate

14. In a row of boys Akash is fifth from the left and Nikhil is eleventh from the right. If Akash is twenty-fifth from the right then how many boys are there between Akash and Nikhil?
    (a) 14　　(b) 13　　(c) 15　　(d) 12

15. If '20 – 10' means 200, '8 ÷ 4' means 12, '6 × 2' means 4 and '12 + 3' means 4, then
    $100 - 10 \times 1000 \div 1000 + 100 \times 10 = ?$
    (a) 1090　　(b) 0　　(c) 1900　　(d) 20

16. If x959y is divisible by 44 and y > 5, then what are values of the digit x and y?
    (a) x=7, y=6　　　　(b) x=4, y=8
    (c) x=6, y=7　　　　(d) None of these

17. What least number must be subtracted from 427398 so that the remaining number is divisible by 15?
    (a) 3　　(b) 6　　(c) 11　　(d) 16

18. Find the greatest number that will divide 55, 127 and 175, so as to leave the same remainder in each case.
    (a) 11   (b) 16
    (c) 18   (d) 24

19. Two numbers are such that if the first be added to 5 times the second, their sum becomes 52, and if the second be added to 8 times the first, their sum becomes 65. The two numbers are:
    (a) 9, 7   (b) 3, 7   (c) 7, 9   (d) 7, 3

20. The average weight of 45 students in a class is 52 kg. 5 of them whose average weight is 48 kg leave the class and other 5 students whose average weight is 54 kg join the class. What is the new average weight (in kg) of the class ?

    (a) 52.6   (b) $52\frac{2}{3}$

    (c) $52\frac{1}{3}$ (d) None of these

21. A store raised the price of an item by exactly 10 per cent. Which of the following could not be the resulting price of the item ?
    (a) ₹ 5.50   (b) ₹ 7.60
    (c) ₹ 11.00   (d) ₹ 12.10

22. A man buys milk at Rs 6 per litre and adds one third of water to it and sells mixture at Rs 7.20 per litre. The gain is
    (a) 40%   (b) 80%   (c) 60%   (d) 25%

23. A sum was put at simple interest at a certain rate for 4 years Had it been put at 2% higher rate, it would have fetched ₹ 56 more. Find the sum.
    (a) ₹ 500   (b) ₹ 600
    (c) ₹ 700   (d) ₹ 800

24. Zinc and copper are melted together in the ratio 9 : 11. What is the weight of melted mixture, if 28.8 kg of zinc has been consumed in it?
    (a) 58 kg   (b) 60 kg   (c) 64 kg   (d) 70 kg

25. Walking $\frac{6}{5}$ of his usual speed, a person takes 10 min less to reach his office. His usual time taken to reach the office is
    (a) 50 min   (b) 55 min
    (c) 60 min   (d) None of these

26. In normal adult human, what is the rate of heartbeat per minute?
    (a) 72-80   (b) 70-75
    (c) 80-97   (d) 82-87

27. Ethanol containing 5% spirit is known as
    (a) rectified spirit   (b) absolute alcohol
    (c) dilute alcohol   (d) power alcohol

28. Radioisotopes which are used in medical diagnosis are known as
    (a) tracers   (b) silver bullets
    (c) markers   (d) dyes

29. Sodium stearate is a salt and is used
    (a) in gunpoweder   (b) in paint
    (c) to make soap   (d) to make fertilizer

30. Evaporation from water surfaces exposed to air is not dependent of the
    (a) velocity of the wind   (b) humidity
    (c) temperature   (d) depth of the water

31. A device used to measure the amount of moisture in the atmosphere is called
    (a) hydrometer   (b) hygrometer
    (c) anemometer   (d) barometer

32. Polio vaccine invented by ?
    (a) Linus Pauling   (b) Jonas Salk
    (c) Melvin Calvin   (d) Selman Waksman

33. Earth quake waves travel fastest in
    (a) Soil   (b) Molten rock
    (c) Water   (d) Flexible rock

34. The average weight of the human brain is
    (a) 1,500 grams   (b) 1,200 grams
    (c) 1,400 grams   (d) 1,300 grams

35. Which of the following plants is not capable of manufacturing own food?
    (a) Algae   (b) Mushroom
    (c) Carrot   (d) Cabbage

36. An astronomical unit of distance is
    (a) a kilomitere
    (b) light year
    (c) the average distance from the earth to the sun
    (d) none of the above

37. The sun continuously produces an enormous amount of energy. This is due to
    (a) nuclear fission   (b) nuclear fusion
    (c) chemical combustion   (d) boiling

38. The unit of power in SI is
    (a) Joule   (b) Newton
    (c) Joule/ Sec   (d) Erg/ Sec

39. Where does the CG of a rubber ring lie?
    (a) on the outer surface
    (b) in the inner surface
    (c) at the centre of the ring
    (d) none of the above

40. Who discovered that the free fall acceleration is the same for any object at a given place?
    (a) Newton   (b) Pascal
    (c) Archimedes   (d) Galileo

41. A stationary elevated object has
    (a) Kinetic energy
    (b) potential energy
    (c) momentum
    (d) both potential and kinetic energy

42. On applying a constant force to a mass, it moves with a uniform
    (a) velocity   (b) momentum
    (c) acceleration   (d) angular velocity

43. A pressure gauge for fluids is called
    (a) a hydrometer   (b) a manometer
    (c) a lactometer   (d) an anemometer

44. The aneroid barometer uses
    (a) mercury   (b) distilled water
    (c) alcohol   (d) does not use any liquid

45. The instrument used to measure atmospheric pressure is
    (a) Pyrometer   (b) Eudiometer
    (c) Barometer   (d) Hydrometer

46. Typhoid is caused by
    (a) Salmonella typhi   (b) Pseudomonas sp.
    (c) Staphylococcus   (d) Bacillus

47. A gas used as a disinfectant in drinking water is
    (a) Hydrogen   (b) Oxygen
    (c) Fluorine   (d) Chlorine

48. What is the average lifespan of a red blood cell ?
    (a) 100 - 200 days   (b) 100 - 120 days
    (c) 160 - 180 days   (d) 150 - 200 days
49. The most abundant organic molecule on the surface of the Earth is
    (a) chitin   (b) DNA
    (c) hemoglobin   (d) cellulose
50. Which of the following acids is used in a car battery?
    (a) hydrochloric acid   (b) sulphuric acid
    (c) nitric acid   (d) carbonic acid
51. The function of heavy water in a nuclear reactor is to
    (a) Slow down the speed of neutrons
    (b) Increase the speed of neutrons
    (c) Cool down the reactor
    (d) Stop the nuclear reaction
52. The larva of the housefly is called
    (a) maggot   (b) caterpillar
    (c) grub   (d) wriggler
53. Which one of the following is used to induce artificial rain?
    (a) Ammonium chloride
    (b) Calcium carbonate
    (c) Silver Iodide
    (d) Potassium Nitrate
54. Seawater freezes at
    (a) the same temperature as fresh water.
    (b) at a slightly higher temperature than fresh water
    (c) at a slightly lower temperature than fresh water.
    (d) seawater does not freeze.
55. What is the mixture of potassium nitrate, powdered charcoal and sulphur called?
    (a) glass   (b) gun powder
    (c) cement   (d) paint
56. Which one among the following waves bats use to detect the obstacles in thier flying path ?
    (a) infrared waves   (b) electromagnetic waves
    (c) ultrasonic waves   (d) radio waves
57. Leaves of which of the following plants are not used for the rearing of silkworms ?
    (a) Mulberry   (b) Castor
    (c) Oak   (d) Teak
58. The purity of milk is determined by
    (a) hydrometer   (b) lactometer
    (c) stalagmometer   (d) hygrometer
59. What was the theme of the 26th New Delhi World Book Fair being organised at Pragati Maidan?
    (a) Towards 100 years of Indian Cinema
    (b) Environment and Climate Change
    (c) Suryodaya: Emerging voices from North East India
    (d) Indigenous Voices: Mapping India's Folk & Tribal Literature
60. Name the Indian entity which has partnered with Chinese gaming company AGTech to launch new mobile gaming platform?
    (a) Freecharge   (b) Mobikwik
    (c) JioMoney   (d) Paytm
61. The Asia's longest bi-directional Zojila Pass Tunnel has been approved for construction in which state of India by the Union Cabinet?
    (a) Jammu and Kashmir   (b) Himachal Pradesh
    (c) Uttarakhand   (d) Punjab
62. The UNESCO has recently included the "bird language", prevalent in which country, in its list of Intangible Cultural Heritage citing it as an endangered part of world heritage?
    (a) Turkey   (b) Egypt
    (c) Lebanon   (d) Yemen
63. The polity of the Indus Valley people was
    (a) Oligarchy (Merchants)
    (b) Secular federalism
    (c) Theocratic federalism
    (d) Theocratic unitary
64. Between whom was the Battle of Chausa fought?
    (a) Bahadur Shah of Gujarat and Humayun
    (b) Humayun and Sher Khan
    (c) Akbar and Rana Pratap
    (d) Jehangir and Rana Amar Singh
65. Who founded the Fort William College at Calcutta?
    (a) Lord Cornwallis   (b) Lord Ellenborough
    (c) Lord Macaulay   (d) Lord Wellesley
66. The freedom fighter who died in Jail due to hunger strike was
    (a) Ram Prasad Bismil   (b) Bipin Chandra Pal
    (c) Jatin Das   (d) R. Das
67. The difference in the duration of day and night increases as one moves from
    (a) west to east
    (b) east and west of the prime meridian
    (c) poles to equator
    (d) equator to poles
68. The state with the largest area under waste land is
    (a) Gujarat   (b) Madhya Pradesh
    (c) Jammu and Kashmir   (d) Rajasthan
69. Which area in India gets the summer monsoon first?
    (a) The Himalayas   (b) The Eastern Ghats
    (c) The Western Ghats   (d) The Indo-Gangetic plains
70. Under which article the president of India can be removed by the process of impeachment
    (a) Article 79   (b) Article 76
    (c) Article 57   (d) Article 61
71. The vacancy of the office of the President of India must be filled up within
    (a) 90 days
    (b) 6 months
    (c) one year
    (d) within the period decided by the Parliament
72. Three-tier system of Panchayati Raj consists of
    (a) Gram Panchayat, Panchayat Samiti, Block Samiti
    (b) Gram Panchayat, Block Samiti, Zila Parishad
    (c) Gram Panchayat, Panchayat Samiti, Zila Parishad
    (d) None of these
73. Government of India plans to launch which Mobile Scheme under which one member of every rural household can get free mobile device
    (a) Gramin Bharat   (b) Bharat Mobile
    (c) Gramin Mobile   (d) Connect
74. The highest dam of India is
    (a) Mettur   (b) Rihand
    (c) Tehri   (d) Bhakra
75. Mumbai has the world's busiest suburban railway network. Name it.
    (a) Western Line   (b) Harbour Line
    (c) Central Line   (d) Eastern Line

RESPONSE SHEET

1. a b c d	2. a b c d	3. a b c d	4. a b c d	5. a b c d
6. a b c d	7. a b c d	8. a b c d	9. a b c d	10. a b c d
11. a b c d	12. a b c d	13. a b c d	14. a b c d	15. a b c d
16. a b c d	17. a b c d	18. a b c d	19. a b c d	20. a b c d
21. a b c d	22. a b c d	23. a b c d	24. a b c d	25. a b c d
26. a b c d	27. a b c d	28. a b c d	29. a b c d	30. a b c d
31. a b c d	32. a b c d	33. a b c d	34. a b c d	35. a b c d
36. a b c d	37. a b c d	38. a b c d	39. a b c d	40. a b c d
41. a b c d	42. a b c d	43. a b c d	44. a b c d	45. a b c d
46. a b c d	47. a b c d	48. a b c d	49. a b c d	50. a b c d
51. a b c d	52. a b c d	53. a b c d	54. a b c d	55. a b c d
56. a b c d	57. a b c d	58. a b c d	59. a b c d	60. a b c d
61. a b c d	62. a b c d	63. a b c d	64. a b c d	65. a b c d
66. a b c d	67. a b c d	68. a b c d	69. a b c d	70. a b c d
71. a b c d	72. a b c d	73. a b c d	74. a b c d	75. a b c d

HINTS & SOLUTIONS

1. (c) Others are the products made from 'milk.
2. (d) The digit-sums are as follows:
    $131 \to 1 + 3 + 1 = 5$
    $151 \to 1 + 5 + 1 = 7$
    $181 \to 1 + 8 + 1 = 10 \to 1 + 0 = 1$
    $171 \to 1 + 7 + 1 = 9$
    $161 \to 1 + 6 + 1 = 8$
    Only 161 has its digit-sum even.
3. (c) All others are specific feelings.
4. (d) The series is $\times 2 - 2$
5. (d) The series $\times 3 + 5, \times 4 - 6, \times 5 + 7, \times 6 - 8....$
6. (a) The series is $+ 1^2, + 2^2, + 3^2, + 4^2,...$
7. (b) There are two alternate series.
    1st series : 3, 4, 5, 6, 7 .... and so on.
    2nd series : 15, 16, 17,18, 19 .... and so on.
8. (b) Ratios of two consecutive terms are 1, 1/2, 1/3, 1/4, and 1/5 respectively.
9. (d)
10. (d) C R E A T I V E
    When the letters in both the halves are reversed, we get

A	E	R	C	E	V	I	T
+1↓	−1↓	+1↓	−1↓	+1↓	−1↓	+1↓	−1↓
B	D	S	B	F	U	J	S

    Next, the letters have been written as one place forward and one place backward alternately.

    Similarly, TRIANGLE is coded as follows:

    T R I A N G L E

A	I	R	T	E	L	G	N
+1↓	−1↓	+1↓	−1↓	+1↓	−1↓	+1↓	−1↓
B	H	S	S	F	K	H	M

    Hence, code for TRIANGLE is BHSSFKHM
11. (d) The only sister of the brother of the woman will be the woman herself and she is the mother of that man. Thus, the woman is the daughter of the maternal grandmother of that man.
12. (d) Clearly, comparing the direction of A w.r.t. C in the second diagram with that in the first diagram, A will be south-west of (c)

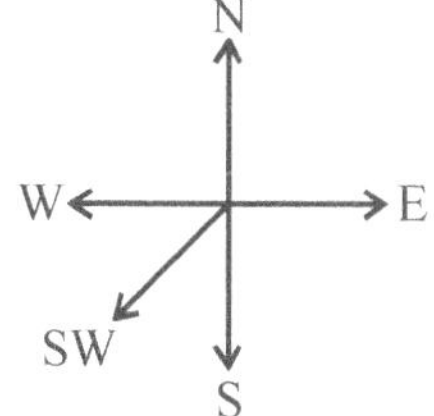
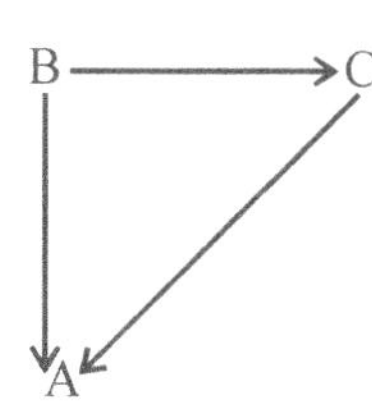

13. (a) The Sun rises in the east. So, in morning, the shadow falls towards the west. Now, shadow of pole falls to the right of Gopal. Therefore, Gopal's right side is the west. So, he is facing South.
14. (b) There are (25 – 11– 1 =) 13 boys between Akash and Nikhil.
15. (b) Since, $20 \times 10 = 200$, therefore, – means $\times$
    $8 + 4 = 12$, therefore, $\div$ means $+$.
    $6 - 2 = 4$, therefore, $\times$ means $-$.
    and $12 \div 3 = 4$, therefore, $+$ means $\div$.
    Now, given expression
    $= 100 \times 10 - 1000 + 1000 \div 100 - 10$
    $= 100 0 - 1000 + 10 - 10 = 0$
16. (a)
17. (a) On dividing 427398 by 15, we get remainder $= 3$.
    ∴ Required number to be subtracted $= 3$.
18. (d) Required number $=$ H.(c)F of $(127 - 55)$, $(175 - 127)$ and $(175 - 55)$
    $=$ HCF of 72, 48 and $120 = 24$
19. (c) Let the numebrs be x & y
    then $x + 5y = 52$ and $8x + y = 65$
    $\Rightarrow x = 7, y = 9$
20. (b) Total weight of 45 students
    $= 45 \times 52 = 2340 \, kg$
    Total weight of 5 students who leave
    $= 5 \times 48 = 240 \, kg$
    Total weight of 5 students who join
    $= 5 \times 54 = 270 \, kg$
    Therefore, new total weight of 45 students
    $= 2340 - 240 + 270 = 2370$
    $\Rightarrow$ New average weight $= \dfrac{2370}{45} = 52\dfrac{2}{3} kg$
21. (b) $5 + 10\% = 5.50$
    $10 + 10\% = 11$
    $11 + 10\% = 12.10$
22. (b) (c) P. of one litre $= ` 6$
    After adding water to it
    One has to pay Rs 7.20 for $\dfrac{2}{3}$ litre of milk.
    So S.P. of $\dfrac{2}{3}$ litre of milk $=$ Rs 7.20
    $\Rightarrow$ S.P. of 1 litre of milk $=$ Rs $\dfrac{7.20 \times 3}{2} = ₹ 10.80$
    ∵ S.P. $>$ C.P.
    Hence gain $= \dfrac{10.80 - 6}{6} \times 100 = \dfrac{4.80}{6} \times 100$
    $= 0.80 \times 100 = 80\%$

23. (c) Difference in S.I. $= \dfrac{P \times T}{100}(R_1 - R_2)$

$$\Rightarrow 56 = \dfrac{P \times 4 \times 2}{100} \quad (Q\ R_1 - R_2 = 2)$$

$$\Rightarrow P = \dfrac{56 \times 100}{4 \times 2} = ₹\,700$$

24. (c) For 9 kg zinc, mixture melted $= (9 + 11)$ kg.
For 28.8 kg zinc, mixture melted

$$= \left(\dfrac{20}{9} \times 28.8\right) \text{kg} = 64 \text{ kg.}$$

25. (c) Usual time $= \dfrac{-10}{\left(\dfrac{5}{6} - 1\right)} = 60$ min

26.	(a)	27.	(a)	28.	(a)	29.	(c)	30.	(d)
31.	(b)	32.	(b)	33.	(c)	34.	(c)	35.	(b)
36.	(b)	37.	(b)	38.	(b)	39.	(c)	40.	(d)
41.	(b)	42.	(c)	43.	(b)	44.	(d)	45.	(c)
46.	(a)	47.	(d)	48.	(b)	49.	(d)	50.	(b)
51.	(a)	52.	(a)	53.	(c)	54.	(c)	55.	(b)

56.	(c)	57.	(d)	58.	(b)	59.	(b)	60.	(d)
61.	(a)	62.	(a)	63.	(a)				

64. (b) The Battle of Chausa was fought between Mughal rular Humaun and Sher Khan in 1539. In this battle Sher Khan defeated Humayun and became India's emperor.

65. (d) Lord Wellesley founded Fort William College at Calcutt(a)

66. (c) Jatindra Nath Das (27 October 1904 - 13 September 1929), also known as Jatin Das, was an Indian freedom fighter and revolutionary. He died in Lahore jail after a continuous hunger strike for 63 days demanding equality for Indian prisoners and undertrials.

67. (d) 68. (c) 69. (c)

70. (d) Under Article 61, the president of India can be removed by the process of impeachment.

71. (b) The vacancy of the office of the President of India must be filled up within 6 months

72. (d) Three-tier system of Panchayati Raj consists of Gram Panchayat, Panchayat Samiti and Zila Parisha(d)

73. (b)

74. (c) Tehri dum is the highest dam in India is on Bhagirathi river in Tehri, Uttarakhand.

75. (c)

PRACTICE SET

Time : 60 Min.   **Max. Marks : 75**

1. Four of the following five words are alike in a certain way and so form a group. Which is the one that **does not** belong to that group?
   - (a) Three
   - (b) Four
   - (c) Five
   - (d) Six

2. Four of the following five are alike in a certain way and so form a group. Which is the one that does not belong to that group?
   - (a) Anxiety
   - (b) Worry
   - (c) Inhibition
   - (d) Curiosity

3. Four of the following five are alike in a certain way and so form a group. Which is the one that does not belong to that group?
   - (a) Touch : Skin
   - (b) Tongue : Taste
   - (c) Hear : Ears
   - (d) See : Eye

DIRECTIONS (Qs. 4-6): *In each of these questions a number series is given in each series only one number is wrong. Find out the wrong number.*

4. 7 9 16 25 41 68 107 173
   - (a) 107
   - (b) 16
   - (c) 41
   - (d) 68

5. 4 2 3.5 7.5 26.25 118.125
   - (a) 118.125
   - (b) 26.25
   - (c) 3.5
   - (d) 2

6. 16 4 2 1.5 1.75 1.875
   - (a) 1.875
   - (b) 1.75
   - (c) 1.5
   - (d) 2

7. Complete the following series :
   6.25, 9, 12.25, 16, 20.25, 25, 30.25, ?
   - (a) 36
   - (b) 32
   - (c) 28.25
   - (d) 40.25

8. Which sequence of letters when placed at the blanks one after another will complete the given letter series ?
   – aba – cabc – dcba – bab – a
   - (a) abdca
   - (b) bcadc
   - (c) abcdd
   - (d) cbdaa

9. If DELHI is coded as 73541 and CALCUTTA as 82589662, how can CALICUT be coded?
   - (a) 5279431
   - (b) 5978213
   - (c) 8251896
   - (d) 8543691

10. If REASON is coded as 5 and BELIEVED as 7, what is the code number for GOVERNMENT?
    - (a) 6
    - (b) 8
    - (c) 9
    - (d) 10

11. In a joint family, there are father, mother, 3 married sons and one unmarried daughter. Of the sons, two have 2 daughters each and one has a son. How many females members are there in the family?
    - (a) 2
    - (b) 3
    - (c) 6
    - (d) 9

12. 'X' started walking straight towards South. He walked a distance of 5 metres and then took a left turn and walked a distance of 3 metres. Then he took a right turn and walked a distance of 5 metres again. 'X' is facing which direction now?
    - (a) North-East
    - (b) South
    - (c) North
    - (d) South-West

13. A rat runs 20' towards east and turns to right, runs 10' and turns to right, runs 9' and again turns to left, runs 5' and then to left, runs 12' and finally turns to left and runs 6'. Now, which direction is the rat facing?
    - (a) East
    - (b) West
    - (c) North
    - (d) South

14. Abhay gave an application for a new ration card to the clerk on Monday afternoon. Next day was a holiday. So the clerk cleared the papers on the next working day on resumption of duty. The senior clerk checked it on the same day but forwarded it to the head clerk on next day. The head clerk decided to dispose the case on the subsequent day. On which of the following days was the case put up to the head clerk by the senior clerk?
   (a) Wednesday   (b) Thursday
   (c) Friday   (d) Saturday

15. If '÷' means '+' ; '–' means '×' ; '+' means '÷' and '×' means '–' then $20 \div 12 \times 4 + 8 - 6 = ?$
   (a) 8   (b) 29
   (c) 32   (d) 26

16. $55^3 + 17^3 - 72^3$ is divisible by
   (a) both 3 and 13   (b) both 7 and 17
   (c) both 3 and 17   (d) both 7 and 13

17. At a college football game, 4/5 of the seats in the lower deck of the stadium were sold. If 1/4 of all the seating in the stadium is located in the lower deck, and if 2/3 of all the seats in the stadium were sold, then what fraction of the unsold seats in the stadium was in the lower deck ?
   (a) 3/20   (b) 1/6
   (c) 1/5   (d) 1/3

18. In a school there are 391 boys and 323 girls. These are to be divided into the largest possible equal classes, so that there are equal number of boys and girls in each class. How many classes are possible?
   (a) 32   (b) 37
   (c) 42   (d) 49

19. The sum of a rational number and its reciprocal is $\dfrac{13}{6}$, find the number.
   (a) $\dfrac{2}{3}$ or $\dfrac{3}{2}$ (b) $\dfrac{3}{4}$ or $\dfrac{4}{3}$
   (c) $\dfrac{2}{5}$ or $\dfrac{5}{2}$ (d) None of these

20. The captain of a cricket team of 11 players is 25 years old and the wicket-keeper is 3 years older. If the age of these two players are replaced by that of another two players, the average of the cricket team drops by 2 years. Find the average age of these two players.
   (a) 15 years   (b) 15.5 years
   (c) 17 years   (d) 16.5 years

21. The length of a rectangular plot is increased by 25%. To keep its area unchanged, the width of the plot should be :
   (a) kept unchanged   (b) increased by 25%
   (c) increased by 20% (d) reduced by 20%

22. A dishonest fruit seller professes to sell his goods at the cost price but weighs 800 grams for a kg weight. Find his gain percent.
   (a) 100%   (b) 150%
   (c) 50%   (d) 200%

23. In how many minimum number of complete years, the interest on ₹ 212.50 P at 3% per annum will be in exact number of rupees?
   (a) 6   (b) 8
   (c) 9   (d) 7

24. Given that 24 carat gold is pure gold, 18 carat gold is $\dfrac{3}{4}$ gold and 20 carat gold is $\dfrac{5}{6}$ gold, the ratio of the pure gold in 18 carat gold to the pure gold in 20 carat gold is :
   (a) 3 : 8   (b) 9 : 10
   (c) 15 : 24   (d) 8 : 5

25. A person can swim in still water at 4 km/h. If the speed of water is 2 km/h, how many hours will the man take to swim back against the current for 6 km.
   (a) 3   (b) 4
   (c) $4\dfrac{1}{2}$ (d) Insufficient data

26. Which of the following ran the first train from Bori Bunder to Thane in 1853?
   (a) Bombay Baroda Railway
   (b) The Scindia Railway
   (c) Central India Railway
   (d) Great Indian Peninsula Railway

27. The Maitree Express connects India with which of the following countries?
   (a) Myanmar   (b) Pakistan
   (c) Bangladesh   (d) Nepal

28. After the Kalinga war, Ashoka :
   (a) restored all the kingdoms he had conquered
   (b) abandoned the policy of physical conquests in favour of cultural conquests.
   (c) renounced his kingdom and became a sadhu
   (d) followed the policy of physical occupation more rigorously

29. Sangam literature is :
   (a) Pali literature dealing with the history of the Buddhist Samghas
   (b) Classical Sanskrit literature patronised by the Guptas
   (c) Sanskrit works of Puranic nature dealing with the sanctity of the place where there is confluence of rivers in Prayaga
   (d) Early Tamil literature attributed to the first three centuries of the Christian Era

30. Which one among the following newspapers was published first?
   (a) The Madras Mail
   (b) The Indian Social Reformer
   (c) The Bengal Gazette
   (d) The Times of India

31. Tinkathia System in Champaran meant
   (a) Cultivation of Indigo on the 3/20 area of land.
   (b) Cultivation of Indigo on the 3/19 area of land.
   (c) Cultivation of Indigo on the 3/18 area of land.
   (d) None of the above

32. Which part of India receives rain when the summer monsoon recedes ?
   (a) Coastal Odisha   (b) Malabar Coast
   (c) North East India (d) Tamil Nadu Coast

33. By Which name/names is our country mentioned in the constitution?
    (a) India and Bharat
    (b) India and Hindustan
    (c) Bharat Only
    (d) India, Bharat and Hindustan
34. The Prime Minister of India is the head of the
    (a) State Government
    (b) Central Government
    (c) Both the State and Central Government
    (d) None of them
35. Economic liberalisation in India started with
    (a) Sustantial changes in Industrial licensing policy
    (b) the convertibility of Indian rupee
    (c) doing away with procedural formalties for foreign direct investment
    (d) Significant reduction in tax rates
36. Name the place in india where Early Tsunami Warning System have been installed
    (a) Rangachang   (b) Kanyakumari
    (c) Chilka   (d) Mysore
37. Who is the author of the book "A Secular Agenda"?
    (a) Mahatma Gandhi   (b) Graham Greene
    (c) Arun Shourie   (d) Dushyant Sharma
38. Who has authored the recently released book - "India and the Global Financial Crisis"?
    (a) Y. V. Reddy   (b) Shankar Acharya
    (c) Rakesh Mohan   (d) C. Rangarajan
39. The power of a lens is measured in :
    (a) diopters   (b) aeon
    (c) lumen   (d) candela
40. Which one of the following types of Laser is used in Laser Printers?
    (a) Semiconductor laser (b) Excimer Laser
    (c) Dye Laser   (d) Gas Laser
41. Albert Einstein was awarded Nobel Prize for his path-breaking research and formulation of the:
    (a) Theory of Relavitity
    (b) Laws of Photo-Electric Effect
    (c) Principle of Wave-Particle Duality
    (d) Theory of Critical Opalescence
42. The instrument that measures arterial blood pressure is known as :
    (a) Pyknometer   (b) Hypsometer
    (c) Sphygmoscope   (d) Sphygmomanometer
43. L.P.G. is a hydrocarbon consisting of a mixture of :
    (a) Methane and Butane
    (b) Propane and Butane
    (c) Ethane and Propane
    (d) Ethane and Butane
44. Gammaxene, D.D.T. and Bleaching powder are important compounds of :
    (a) Chlorine   (b) Nitrogen
    (C) Sulphur   (d) Phosphorus
45. 'Amalgam' is a term used for an alloy of a metal with :
    (a) Copper   (b) Mercury
    (c) Lead   (d) Aluminium

46. The nutritional supplements Spirulina, Chorella and the Vitamin-C supplement, Dunaliella are actually :
    (a) Algae   (b) Lichens
    (c) Probiotics   (d) Bryophytes
47. What did "x" mean in "x-rays"?
    (a) Cross   (b) Mark
    (c) Star   (d) Unknown
48. When we put 2-3 drops of iodine solution on a food item containing starch, its colour turn
    (a) Green black   (b) Brown black
    (c) Blue black   (d) Black
49. Which of the following solution is used to test presence of protein in food item?
    (a) Iodine   (b) Copper sulphate
    (c) Sodium chloride   (d) None of the above
50. The following is needed for the growth and repair of our body.
    (a) Fats   (b) Carbohydrates
    (c) Proteins   (d) Vitamins
51. Which of the following is a source of iodine for our body?
    (a) Spinach   (b) Banana
    (c) Egg   (d) Fish
52. The broad, green part of the leaf is called
    (a) Petiole   (b) lamina or blade
    (c) Midrib   (d) Vein
53. The innermost part of a flower is called
    (a) Pistil   (b) Sepals
    (c) Stamens   (d) Petals
54. The lowermost and swollen part of the pistil is called
    (a) Stigma   (b) Style
    (c) Ovary   (d) None of the above
55. There is a joint between the upper jaw and the rest of the head which is a
    (a) Ball and socket joint (b) Pivotal joint
    (c) Hinge joint   (d) Fixed joints
56. The material which do not allow passage of electric current through it is known as
    (a) Conductor   (b) Insulator
    (c) Semiconductor   (d) Superconductor
57. In fertilizers, NPK stands for
    (a) Nitrogen, Phosphorus, Potassium
    (b) Nitrogen, Phosphorus, Krypton
    (c) Sodium, Phosphate, Potassium
    (d) Neon, Potassium, Calcium
58. Which bacterium promotes the formation of curd?
    (a) Lactobacillus   (b) Actinobacillus
    (c) Bacterionema   (d) Chlorobiales
59. "Rust of wheat" disease is caused by
    (a) Virus   (b) Fungi
    (c) Bacteria   (d) None of the above
60. 4R principle consist of
    (a) Reduce - Reuse - Recycle - Recover
    (b) Refuse - Reuse - Recycle - Recover
    (c) Reduce - Reuse - Recycle - Remix
    (d) Reduce - Reuse - Recycle - Reproduce
61. The large area of protected land for conservation of wild life, plant and animal resources and traditional life of the tribals living in the area is known as
    (a) Sanctuary   (b) National Park
    (c) Biosphere reserve   (d) All of the above

62. Pressure is calculated as
    (a) Force/Area (b) Force x Area
    (c) Force / Volume (d) Force x Volume
63. The average salinity of sea water is
    (a) 3% (b) 3.5%
    (c) 2.5% (d) 2%
64. Heavy water is
    (a) deuterium oxide (b) PH7
    (c) rain water (d) tritium oxide
65. Carbon, diamond and graphite are together called
    (a) allotropes (b) isomers
    (c) isomorphs (d) isotopes
66. The wavelength of X-rays is of the order of
    (a) 10 micron (b) 1 angstrom
    (c) 1 cm (d) 1 m
67. What is the wavelength of visible spectrum?
    (a) 8500 - 9800 angstrom (b) 7800 - 8000 angstrom
    (c) 3900 - 7600 angstrom (d) 1300 - 3000 angstrom
68. Nuclear fission is caused by the impact of
    (a) neutron (b) proton
    (c) deuteron (d) electron
69. The lifespan of Red Blood Cells is __________ days.
    (a) 60 (b) 120
    (c) 180 (d) 240
70. Which of the following is true for "Sound"?
    (a) Sound cannot travel through a vacuum
    (b) Sound cannot travel through gases
    (c) Sound cannot travel through liquids
    (d) Sound cannot travel through solids
71. When white light is passed through a prism, it splits into __________ colours.
    (a) 5 (b) 6
    (c) 7 (d) 8
72. 1 nanometer = ?
    (a) 10^{-3} meter (b) 10^{-6} meter
    (c) 10^{-9} meter (d) 10^{-12} meter
73. In the Union Budget 2018, the Central Government has allocated Rs 48,000 crore for which scheme to encourage farmers for solar farming?
    (a) KUSUM scheme (b) KUTSUB scheme
    (c) KUSUN scheme (d) KUTUB scheme
74. The book "Exam Warriors" has been authored by which union minister?
    (a) Piyush Goyal (b) Maneka Gandhi
    (c) Prakash Javadekar (d) Narendra Modi
75. In the Union Budget 2018, the Union government has announced to build a tunnel through the Sela Pass. The Sela pass is located in which state?
    (a) Sikkim (b) Arunachal Pradesh
    (c) Manipur (d) Himachal Pradesh

RESPONSE SHEET

1. ⓐⓑⓒⓓ	2. ⓐⓑⓒⓓ	3. ⓐⓑⓒⓓ	4. ⓐⓑⓒⓓ	5. ⓐⓑⓒⓓ
6. ⓐⓑⓒⓓ	7. ⓐⓑⓒⓓ	8. ⓐⓑⓒⓓ	9. ⓐⓑⓒⓓ	10. ⓐⓑⓒⓓ
11. ⓐⓑⓒⓓ	12. ⓐⓑⓒⓓ	13. ⓐⓑⓒⓓ	14. ⓐⓑⓒⓓ	15. ⓐⓑⓒⓓ
16. ⓐⓑⓒⓓ	17. ⓐⓑⓒⓓ	18. ⓐⓑⓒⓓ	19. ⓐⓑⓒⓓ	20. ⓐⓑⓒⓓ
21. ⓐⓑⓒⓓ	22. ⓐⓑⓒⓓ	23. ⓐⓑⓒⓓ	24. ⓐⓑⓒⓓ	25. ⓐⓑⓒⓓ
26. ⓐⓑⓒⓓ	27. ⓐⓑⓒⓓ	28. ⓐⓑⓒⓓ	29. ⓐⓑⓒⓓ	30. ⓐⓑⓒⓓ
31. ⓐⓑⓒⓓ	32. ⓐⓑⓒⓓ	33. ⓐⓑⓒⓓ	34. ⓐⓑⓒⓓ	35. ⓐⓑⓒⓓ
36. ⓐⓑⓒⓓ	37. ⓐⓑⓒⓓ	38. ⓐⓑⓒⓓ	39. ⓐⓑⓒⓓ	40. ⓐⓑⓒⓓ
41. ⓐⓑⓒⓓ	42. ⓐⓑⓒⓓ	43. ⓐⓑⓒⓓ	44. ⓐⓑⓒⓓ	45. ⓐⓑⓒⓓ
46. ⓐⓑⓒⓓ	47. ⓐⓑⓒⓓ	48. ⓐⓑⓒⓓ	49. ⓐⓑⓒⓓ	50. ⓐⓑⓒⓓ
51. ⓐⓑⓒⓓ	52. ⓐⓑⓒⓓ	53. ⓐⓑⓒⓓ	54. ⓐⓑⓒⓓ	55. ⓐⓑⓒⓓ
56. ⓐⓑⓒⓓ	57. ⓐⓑⓒⓓ	58. ⓐⓑⓒⓓ	59. ⓐⓑⓒⓓ	60. ⓐⓑⓒⓓ
61. ⓐⓑⓒⓓ	62. ⓐⓑⓒⓓ	63. ⓐⓑⓒⓓ	64. ⓐⓑⓒⓓ	65. ⓐⓑⓒⓓ
66. ⓐⓑⓒⓓ	67. ⓐⓑⓒⓓ	68. ⓐⓑⓒⓓ	69. ⓐⓑⓒⓓ	70. ⓐⓑⓒⓓ
71. ⓐⓑⓒⓓ	72. ⓐⓑⓒⓓ	73. ⓐⓑⓒⓓ	74. ⓐⓑⓒⓓ	75. ⓐⓑⓒⓓ

HINTS & SOLUTIONS

1. (d) All others have two vowels.

2. (d) All others are negative.

3. (b) Others represent sensation and respective organs. Here the order is reversed.

4. (d) The series is $7 + 9 = 16$; $16 + 9 = 25$;
$25 + 16 = 41; 41 + 25 = 66; 66 + 41 = 107...$

5. (c) The series is $\times 0.5$, $\times 1.5$, $\times 2.5$, $\times 3.5$,...

6. (b) The series is $\times 0.25$, $\times 0.5$, $\times 0.75$, $\times 1$,...

7. (a) There are two alternate series
Series I- 6.25, 12.25, 20.25, 30.25 (sequence is +6, +8, +10)
Series II- 9, 16, 25, 36, (sequence is +7, +9, +11)

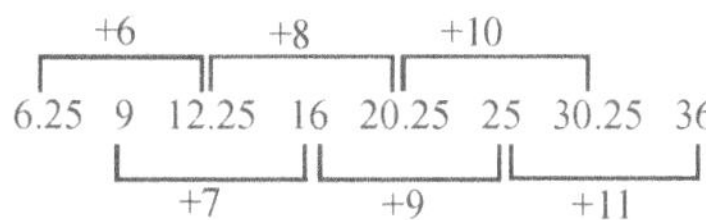

8. (a) The series formed is :
a a b a b c a b c d d c b a c b a b a a
in which the letters equi–distant from the beginning and end are the same.

9. (c) The alphabets are coded as follows:

D	E	L	H	I	C	A	U	T
7	3	5	4	1	8	2	9	6

So, in CALICUT, C is coded as 8, A as 2, L as 5, I as 1, U as 9 and T as 6. Thus, the code for CALICUT is 8251896.

10. (c) Code for the given word = (Number of letters in the word) –1.
So, code for GOVERNMENT = 10 – 1 = 9.

11. (d) The female members are:-
(i) mother
(ii) Wives of 3 married sons
(iii) unmarried daughter
(iv) 2 daughter of each of two sons
∴ Total No of females
$= 1 + 3 + 1 + 2 \times 2 = 9$

12. (b) 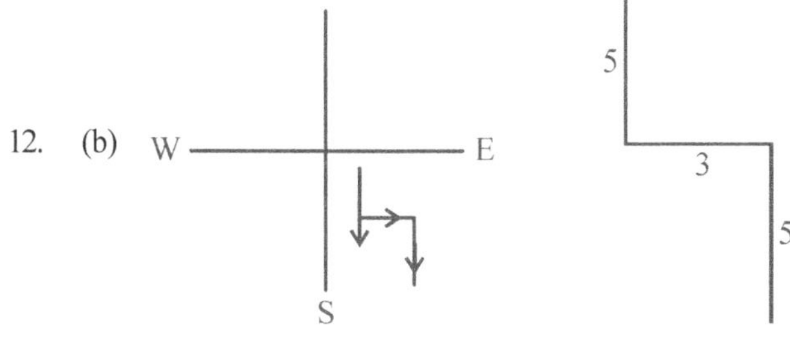

13. (c) The movements of rat are as shown in figure. Clearly, it is finally walking in the direction FG i.e. North.

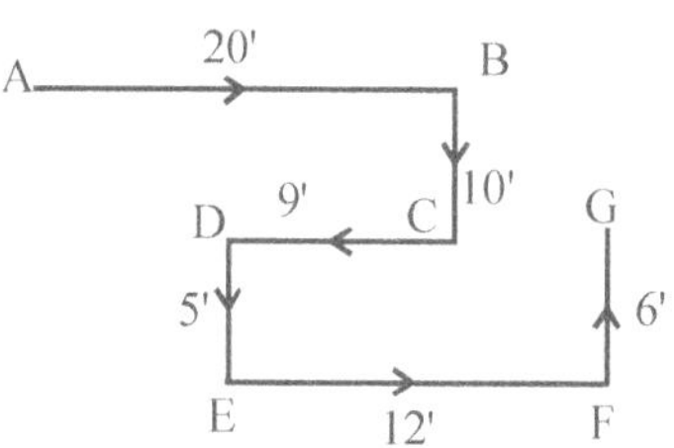

14. (b) (i) Submitted application form : Monday
(ii) Holiday : Tuesday
(iii) Clearance from clerk : Wednesday
(iv) Clearance from senior clerk : Wednesday
(v) Submitted to the head clerk : Thursday

15. (b) $20 + 12 - 4 \div 8 \times 6 = 29$

16. (c) $55^3 + 17^3 - 72^3 = (55)^3 + (17)^3 - (55 + 17)^3$
$= 55^3 + 17^3 - \{(55)^3 + (17)^3 - 3 \times 55 \times 17 \times 72\}$
$= -3 \times 55 \times 17 \times 72$

17. (a) Let total number of seats in the stadium be p; number of seats in the lower deck be x and number of seats in upper deck be y.
∴ $p = x + y$, $x = p/4$, $y = 3p/4$
Now in the lower deck, 4x/5 seats were sold and x/5 seats were unsold.
No. of total seats sold in the stadium = 2p/3.
No. of unsold seats in the lower deck = x/5 = p/20
No. of unsold seats in the stadium = p/3
∴ Required fraction $= \dfrac{p/20}{p/3} = \dfrac{3}{20}$

18. (c) The number of boys and girls in each class is the H.C.F. of 391 and 323 which is 17.
Number of classes $= \dfrac{391}{17} + \dfrac{323}{17} = 23 + 19 = 42$

19. (a) Let the number be x.
Then, $x + \dfrac{1}{x} = \dfrac{13}{6} \Rightarrow \dfrac{x^2 + 1}{x} = \dfrac{13}{6} \Rightarrow 6x^2 - 13x + 6 = 0$
$\Rightarrow 6x^2 - 9x - 4x + 6 = 0 \Rightarrow (3x - 2)(2x - 3) = 0$
$\Rightarrow x = \dfrac{2}{3}$ or $x = \dfrac{3}{2}$.
Hence, the required number is $\dfrac{2}{3}$ or $\dfrac{3}{2}$.

20. (b) Let average of team = x years
Then, $25 + 28 + S_9 = 11x$ ...(i)

where S_9 is the sum of ages of remaining players

Also, $Np + S_9 = 11(x - 2)$, ... (ii)

where Np is the sum of ages of new players

$(i) - (ii) \Rightarrow 53 - Np = 22$

$$\Rightarrow Np = 31$$

$\therefore$ Average age of new two players $= \dfrac{31}{2} = 15.5$ years

21. (d) Let the original length and breadth be both 10 cm each.

Then original area $= 100$ cm^2

New length $= 10 \times 1.25 = 12.5$ cm

Let new breadth be x. Then, $12.5x = 100$

$$\Rightarrow x = \dfrac{100}{12.5} = 8\text{cm}$$

Hence, % reduction in breadth

$$= \dfrac{2}{10} \times 100 = 20\%$$

22. (a) He gives 800 grams but charges the price of 1000 grams (1 kg)

$\Rightarrow$ on every 800 grams, he gains $(1000 - 800)$ grams i.e. 200 grams.

$$\therefore \text{ His gain \%} = \dfrac{200}{800} \times 100 = 25\%$$

Short cut : Gain % $= \dfrac{\text{error}}{\text{true weight} - \text{error}}$

$$= \dfrac{200}{(1000 - 200)} \times 100 = 25\%$$

23. (b) Interest for one year $= ₹\, 212.50 \times \dfrac{3}{100} \times 1 = ₹\, \dfrac{51}{8}$

Thus in 8 years, the interest is ₹ 51.

24. (b) 18 carat gold

$$= \dfrac{3}{4} \text{ pure gold} = \dfrac{3}{4} \times 24 = 18 \text{ carat gold}$$

$$20 \text{ carat gold} = \dfrac{5}{6} \text{ pure gold} = \dfrac{5}{6} \times 24 = 20 \text{ carot gold}$$

Required ratio $= 18 : 20 = 9 : 10$

25. (a) Man's speed in upstream $= 4 - 2 = 2$ km/h.

$$\therefore \text{ Required time } = \dfrac{6}{2} = 3 \text{ hours}$$

26. (d) 27. (c) 28. (b) 29. (d)

30. (c) Bengal Gazette was published by James Augustus Hikkey in 1780.

31. (a) Tinkathia system in Champaran meant cultivation of Indigo on the 3/20 area of land. According to the Tinkathia system, farmers were allowed to take only one-third of the indigo produced by themselves while two-thirds had to be given to the British planters.

32. (d)

33. (a) Our country is mentioned in the constitution by the name of India and Bharat

34. (b) The Prime Minister of India is the head of the Central Government.

35. (d) GDP is defined as the value of all final goods and services produced in an economy in a year.

36. (a) Raga Todi which was invented by Mian Tansen is sung early in the morning.

37. (b) To commemorate the birth anniversary of Maulana Abdul Kalam Azad, National Education Day is observed on November 11.

38.	(d)	39.	(a)	40.	(a)	41.	(b)	42.	(c)
43.	(b)	44.	(a)	45.	(b)	46.	(a)	47.	(d)
48.	(c)	49.	(b)	50.	(c)	51.	(d)	52.	(b)
53.	(a)	54.	(c)	55.	(d)	56.	(b)	57.	(a)
58.	(a)	59.	(b)	60.	(a)	61.	(c)	62.	(a)
63.	(b)	64.	(a)	65.	(a)	66.	(b)	67.	(c)
68.	(a)	69.	(b)	70.	(a)	71.	(b)	72.	(c)
73.	(a)	74.	(d)	75.	(b)				